THE SOVIET UNION

FINLAND

OLAND
CZECHOSLOVAKIA
HUNGARY
ROMANIA
UG.
BULGARIA
LB.
GREECE
TURKEY
LEBANON
SYRIA
ISRAEL
JORDAN
IRAQ
IRAN
KUWAIT
QATAR
UNITED ARAB
EMIRATES
OMAN
SAUDI ARABIA
IBYA
EGYPT
HAD
SUDAN
NORTH YEMEN
SOUTH YEMEN
DJIBOUTI
ENTRAL
FRICAN
EP.
ETHIOPIA
UGANDA
SOMALIA
ZAIRE
KENYA
RWANDA
BURUNDI
TANZANIA
NGOLA
ZAMBIA
MALAWI
MOZAMBIQUE
MADAGASCAR
ZIMBABWE
OTSWANA
SWAZILAND
LESOTHO
SOUTH AFRICA

AFGHANISTAN
PAKISTAN
NEPAL
BHUTAN
INDIA
BANGLADESH
MYANMAR
SRI LANKA

MONGOLIA

CHINA

NORTH
KOREA
SOUTH
JAPAN

TAIWAN

LAOS
THAILAND
CAMBODIA
VIETNAM
PHILIPPINES

MALAYSIA
SINGAPORE
INDONESIA

PAPUA NEW GUINEA

AUSTRALIA

NEW ZEALAND

Conflict and Compromise

An Introduction to Politics

Herbert R. Winter
Rhode Island College

Thomas J. Bellows
The University of Texas at San Antonio

HarperCollins*Publishers*

In Memoriam

Sadly, I must report the sudden death of Dr. Herbert R. Winter on June 17, 1991. Herb was a close friend and valued colleague. Like many of his fellow political scientists, I have benefited over the years from his insight, his wisdom, and his humanity. Herb has touched our lives in innumerable ways. He will be sorely missed by his family, his many friends, and his colleagues.

—Thomas J. Bellows

Sponsoring Editor: Lauren Silverman
Development Editor: Carol Einhorn
Project Editor: Claire M. Caterer
Design Supervisor: Peter Noa
Cover Design: A Good Thing, Inc.
Photo Research: Mira Schachne
Production: Jeffrey Taub
Compositor: ComCom Division of Haddon Craftsmen, Inc.
Printer and Binder: R. R. Donnelley & Sons Company
Cover Printer: The Lehigh Press, Inc.

Conflict and Compromise

Library of Congress Cataloging-in-Publication Data

Winter, Herbert R., 1928–
    Conflict and compromise: an introduction to politics / Herbet R.
    Winter, Thomas J. Bellows.
        p.   cm.
    Includes bibliographical references and index.
    ISBN 0-673-38807-7
    1. Political science.   I. Bellows, Thomas J., 1935–   .
    II. Title.
    JA71.W468   1992
    320—dc20   90-21498
                                                   CIP

91 92 93 94   9 8 7 6 5 4 3 2 1

Brief Contents

Detailed Contents

Preface

Conflict and Compromise: An Introduction to Politics is written for students who are taking their first course in political science and who intend to major in the field, as well as for those who are majoring in another discipline but wish to obtain a basic understanding of the subject matter of political science. The book surveys the major areas of the political process and relates the parts of the political system to each other. The topics follow in a logical order, progressing from the basics of political analysis to an examination of the input and output processes and concluding with a discussion of political change in the Third World and international relations. Examples and case studies come from different polities throughout the world.

Part One describes the foundation of political science: the scope of the discipline, its approaches and concepts, as well as major political theories and ideologies. Part Two examines the input activities, the forces that, in democracies, form the major popular participatory part of the political process. Included in this section are the formation of political attitudes, the roles of interest groups and political parties, as well as political participation as reflected in elections and representation. Part Three is devoted to an examination of the output agencies that make, administer, and enforce policy. This includes the legislative system, the executive branch, and the judiciary. Part Four deals with political change and international relations. Our discussion of political change emphasizes the processes of political development in the Third World. This is followed by an examination of politics among countries, international law and organization, as well as regional integration.

Important terms appear in boldface print when first mentioned in the text and can be found in the glossary at the end of the text. The glossary provides students with a handy reference in the course of their reading.

Our framework of analysis is based on the assumption that politics can be viewed as an assembly or combination of mutually interacting units that affect each other and form a complex whole such as the political order in a given country. By emphasizing how the different parts of the political system interact and affect each other, we can make some sense out of the seeming confusion of modern politics.

The political systems of the 170-odd countries of our time share certain similar characteristics such as the following: All countries are influenced by their particular political heritages, which range from the lengthy evolution of democracy in Britain to the authoritarian tradition of Russian society. Polities adhere to an ideology of one kind or another, be it liberal democracy, democratic socialism, developmental socialism, communism, or fascism. All countries seek to develop processes for the political socialization of the young and the old, although these procedures differ from society to society and range from uttering the pledge of allegiance to totalitarian brainwashing.

Democracies have viable input agencies for articulation and aggregation in the form of interest groups and political parties. These serve as instruments for popular participation, expression of public opinion, and the selection of candidates for public office. In contrast, some of the Communist countries still have basically one-party systems and interest groups that follow the course set by the party leadership. Most of the developing countries still have little in terms of interest groups or viable political parties. However, as the economic systems of these countries become more developed, these societies will become more pluralistic, giving rise to the formation of autonomous interest groups and political parties.

All countries have means for selecting their legislative, executive, and judicial officials. This selection procedure is constitutionalized in the democracies—for example, officials are elected or appointed according to established law. In contrast, in many other countries change still occurs by violence, and gross nepotism may be exercised in the appointment of government officials.

All countries have institutions for rule making, rule application, and rule adjudication in the forms of a legislature, an executive, and a judiciary. These agencies are more viable in some countries than in others. For example, the United States has a viable tripartite national government. In contrast, the executive branch dominates the governmental process in many of the developing countries. In these societies legislatures and judiciaries have not yet developed to a state of equality with the executive.

All political systems are subject to change. Political change can take one of two forms: (1) It can be evolutionary and relatively peaceful through the use of the ballot, or (2) change can be brought about by revolutionary means using the gun to alter the political system. The latter approach is usually more drastic and far-reaching (as, for example, during the Russian Revolution of 1917) than evolutionary change.

Our approach permits us to use political features common to all societies as convenient starting points for analysis and discussion. It provides an orderly framework for the comparative examination of political phenomena and is, perhaps, the most logical way to analyze a variety of political systems. The examples we use for illustrative purposes are drawn from many countries; however, we have made it a point to include in all the chapters dealing with input and output agencies examples from democracies, Communist countries (the number of which is declining rather rapidly), and developing societies.

Some of our examples are drawn from the realm of micropolitics and others from macropolitics. Micropolitics focuses on the individual rather than political groups or institutions, whereas macropolitics focuses on groups, institutions, and societies. Micropolitics and macropolitics complement each other. Consequently, this book discusses the various ways in which people organize to make political decisions or to influence the decision makers. We also examine political organizations, as well as individual attitudes and behavior.

No introductory textbook can include detailed discussion of all aspects of a discipline; therefore, we emphasize those aspects that we consider to be of greatest importance for students taking the first course in political science and hope that this textbook will give a better understanding of politics and the institutions and processes it entails. Furthermore, we hope that it will kindle in the reader a continuing interest in politics and political analysis. In writing the book, one of our principal objectives has been to give the reader a basis for participating more effectively in the political process.

ACKNOWLEDGMENTS

A number of people have been helpful in producing this textbook. We are grateful to those of our students who, by way of their comments, helped us to sharpen our own ideas. We appreciate the constructive criticism of professors Alan Isaak, Western Michigan University; David Schmitt, Northeastern University; and Jonathan Webster, Walla Walla Community College, who critiqued our original draft. Their comments were very constructive. Colleagues Francis Leazes, Victor Profughi, Carey Rickabaugh, and Eugene Matteodo provided fitting suggestions and support at crucial times.

We would like to thank various members of the HarperCollins staff, especially Lauren Silverman, Claire M. Caterer, Carol Einhorn, and Karen Bednarski, for their assistance.

Last but not least, our wives, Ursula and Marilyn, deserve recognition for their encouragement, help, and patience (a rare commodity in the high-tech age), all of which have contributed to the timely completion of this book.

Herbert R. Winter
Thomas J. Bellows

PART ONE

Foundations and Fundamentals

Chapter 1

The Nature and Scope of Political Science

Citizens of the United States of America enjoy a number of blessings, but, like people in other countries, we are also confronted by a number of issues and problems. To mention a few of the more important ones, they include the plight of the homeless, the high rate of crime, the need to provide better care for the elderly, the trade deficit, the rapidly increasing national deficit, the specter of political terrorism, worldwide pollution, and the nightmare created by nuclear weapons. We are divided on major moral, social, and civic questions: What should be our national **government**'s policy regarding abortion? Should some or all controlled substances be legalized? Should the government establish a national youth corps?

The above are issues, problems, and questions in the public realm, the sum total of all political input and output activities. **Inputs** are the actions pursued by interest groups, political parties, public opinion, and those decisions of foreign governments that have an impact on our country. **Outputs** are the activities, decisions, and regulations of governmental agencies. Inputs and outputs interact in the political arena and produce the subject matters that the mass media bring daily to our attention.

Past generations also have had their share of crises and problems, but people often tend to feel that present-day public problems are more severe than those of the past. Modern politics, on a larger scale, is involving more people and more questions than ever before. Governmental activities have expanded considerably in most countries.[1] This expansion has brought the government closer to the people, while at the same time making it more complex and difficult to understand. (The term "government" refers to the legally established political leadership and administrative hierarchy of a country, state, or local community. Governments exercise executive, legislative, and judicial functions.) More public services are available, but, concurrently, governments encroach increasingly on the day-to-day affairs of their citizens.

We are better informed politically and more attentive than our ancestors; however, one may ask whether the increase in available information and the growth of governmental activities have made us more active political participants. One standard indicator used to examine political participation is that of voter turnout on election day. By and large, voter turnout has remained fairly constant in the developed countries or has even declined slightly during the last two decades. It is still too early to ascertain trends of this type in the developing countries.

Rather than a general increase in the standard types of political participation, the past three decades have shown a pattern of "flash" activities and movements centering around specific issues. We have witnessed a rising concern about arms control, pollution, natural resource depletion, and conservation. The composite picture of political behavior shows an additional phenomenon. Rising interest in the public issues of the day has been accompanied by a specific concern about priorities set by governments and the corresponding allocation of resources.

---

[1]For detailed information on the growth of the public sector, see Charles L. Taylor and David Jodice, *World Handbook of Political and Social Indicators,* 3rd ed. (New Haven, Conn.: Yale University Press, 1983).

I'm terribly sorry, sir, but in the process of cutting out programs for the poor we inadvertently cut out a program for the rich

Drawing by Dana Fradon; © 1979 The New Yorker Magazine, Inc.

Many of the demonstrations staged by students, members of minority groups, and others in this country have had to do with governmental priorities because these priorities concern individual and group welfare. People demand greater input in the public policy-making process.

Governmental decisions made in Washington have a bearing on whether an American will have to fight in the Middle East or some other part of the world, whether his or her taxes will be increased, and whether a large percentage of his or her tax money will be used for furthering the arms race or for improving medical services, housing, public transportation, and conservation needs.

Demonstrations protesting governmental policies are common outside the industrialized countries of the West. In many of the developing countries demonstrations are a frequent occurrence, as people who do not have a voice in public office attempt to make their wants known.

These criticisms indicate a growing civic awareness in segments of the population here and abroad. This book addresses itself to these interests and concerns by placing them into an analytic framework, that of political science.

WHAT IS POLITICAL SCIENCE?

Political science is a discipline within the social sciences. It is akin to anthropology, economics, geography, sociology, social psychology, and history. In general, the study of social science is concerned with the nature of human behavior, past and present. Each of the social science disciplines examines a particular aspect of human behavior—but all these parts are closely related to each other, thus creating the possibility for broad interdisciplinary studies. One famous study of this type is Almond and Verba's *The Civic Culture,* an examination of the political aspirations, beliefs, and participatory phenomena of the people in Italy, Mexico, the United States, the United Kingdom, and West Germany.[2]

Political science deals basically with those aspects of human behavior labeled "political." It is the study of political behavior, institutions, and processes in the public realm. This covers a wide area, as indicated by the number of subdisciplines that have appeared in the field, especially in recent years. For all practical purposes, however, most political science undergraduate programs in this country feature courses grouped into the following subdisciplines. They are American politics and political behavior, comparative politics, international relations, political theory, public administration, public law, public policy, and state and local politics. The following is a brief explanation of the content of these areas:

1. *American politics and political behavior* focuses on politics in the United States. It involves the study of input agencies and forces (interest groups, political parties, and public opinion), the election process, as well as the activities of the output agencies (Congress, the presidency, and the Supreme Court).

2. *Comparative politics* denotes, by and large, the comparative study of several political systems, such as the major democratic and communist countries, or countries within a block, such as the comparative study of democratic societies, the communist countries, or the developing nation-states.

3. *International relations* is the study of transnational politics. It has two major related components: international politics (the study of relations between countries) and international and regional organizations and international law.

4. *Political theory* serves as a kind of underpinning for all political science study. It deals with major concepts, ideas, and values. Throughout the ages major political theorists have asked the question, What constitutes a good government and how can it be established? Political theory speculates about "what ought to be" rather than "what is."

5. **Public administration** deals with the administration and enforcement of public policies at all levels of government with some focus on the bureaucracy, its organization, and personnel.

6. **Public law** is the subdiscipline that focuses on the judicial process and, particularly, on the making and the enforcement of laws in the public realm.

7. *Public policy* embraces all the laws, regulations, and rules made by the output agencies (i. e., legislature, executive, and judiciary) of a polity. It constitutes the total authoritative output of a political system.

---

[2]Gabriel A. Almond and Sidney Verba, *The Civic Culture* (Boston: Little, Brown, 1965). See also the follow-up anthology by the same authors, *The Civic Culture Revisited* (Boston: Little, Brown, 1980).

8. *State and local government,* as the title implies, deals with the political activities and agencies closest to home, namely, those on the local and state level.[3]

These eight subdisciplines relate closely to each other. The basic concepts and principles underlying political science analysis, as discussed subsequently in this text, relate to all of them. Having examined briefly the major components of political science, we now turn our attention to the development of the discipline.

The Discipline of Political Science

The study of and the writing about political phenomena dates back to Plato and Aristotle. The systematic development of the academic discipline called political science is, however, of much more recent vintage. Here in the United States political science courses were taught first by such European-trained scholars as Francis Lieber and John W. Burgess in the mid-nineteenth century and graduate training in political science did not appear until the late nineteenth century.[4]

Since then political science has experienced a steady growth in this country. Particular political and military happenings have stimulated the rapid growth of particular subdisciplines in the field. For example, the study of international relations gained substantial momentum shortly after World War II, while the rise of the multitude of new countries in Africa, Asia, and other areas stimulated the growth of area studies within a comparative framework.

Among the approximately 2,000 colleges and universities in the United States, 760 had separate political science departments in 1988, with 121 of these offering a Ph.D. program in the field.[5]

The United States has more trained political scientists than the rest of the world put together. Gabriel A. Almond reported in 1967 that "nine out of every ten political scientists in the world today are American, and probably two out of every three political scientists who ever lived are alive and practicing today."[6] Since Almond conducted his research, the nine out of ten ratio has dropped to perhaps seven out of ten.

What do political scientists do? How successful are they in pursuing their aims? Most political scientists teach about politics at colleges and universities. Their teaching and research concerns politics in the public realm. Very little has yet been

---

[3]For a more detailed discussion of the subareas see Ronald J. Stupak et al., *Understanding Political Science: The Arena of Power* (Port Washington, N.Y.: Alfred, 1977) and Ada W. Finifter, ed., *Political Science: The State of the Discipline* (Washington, D.C.: The American Political Science Association, 1983).

[4]Albert Somit and Joseph Tannenhaus, *The Development of American Political Science: From Burgess to Behavioralism* (New York: Irvington Publishers, 1982), p. 7.

[5]From data compiled by the American Political Science Association.

[6]Gabriel A. Almond, "Political Theory and Political Science," in Ithiel Pool, ed., *Contemporary Political Science: Toward Empirical Theory* (New York: McGraw-Hill, 1967), p. 3.

written by political scientists about politics in the world of business, social organizations, religious organizations, or organized crime.[7] The importance of one of these categories to political scientists was stated some time ago by Hans Morgenthau:

> The curriculum of political science must take theoretical notice of the actual development of private governments in the form of giant corporations and labor unions. These organizations exercise power within their organizational limits, in their relations to each other, and in their relations to the state. The state in turn exercises power in regard to them. These power relations constitute a new field for theoretical understanding.[8]

A similar reasoning could be applied to the political importance of the other categories too. The fact is, however, that most political scientists have assumed, and still assume, that political science should deal with politics in the public realm.

What are the legitimate tasks of those who teach political science? What are the merits of studying political science? Most of us, presumably, would agree with Dwight Waldo, who speaks of teaching citizenship as the first pursuit of the political science teacher.[9] We are talking about teaching citizenship in the sense of providing data, facts, and methods of analysis pertaining to political processes and systems in the hope that students will become interested in politics and become more intelligent observers of, and participants in, the political arena. Although political scientists do not have ready-made answers to all political issues and problems, they can—and should—educate students in citizenship.

A second task of those who teach political science is to provide preprofessional and professional training, such as preparing young people for public service. Each year thousands of college graduates take jobs with the federal, state, and local governments. Many of these are political science majors whose academic training has given them a suitable academic and preprofessional background for their future careers.

A third task, according to Waldo, is to train students for political science research. The last function is more applicable to graduate instruction than to undergraduate. Now we shall turn our attention to the substance of political science.

THE FOCUS OF POLITICAL SCIENCE: POLITICS

Political science, we have said, deals with human political behavior. In short, it deals with politics. Thus, there is no need to define political science further; rather,

---

[7]One of the most informative books on organized crime in the United States has been written by a former police officer and a journalist. See Ralph Salerno and John S. Tompkins, *The Crime Confederation* (Garden City, N.Y.: Doubleday, 1969).

[8]Hans J. Morgenthau, "Power as a Political Concept," in Roland Young, ed., *Approaches to the Study of Politics* (Evanston, Ill.: Northwestern University Press, 1958), p. 77.

[9]Dwight Waldo, "Values in the Political Science Curriculum," in ibid., p. 110.

we should define and discuss politics. What is politics? What are its features and ingredients? The word "politics" stems from **polis,** the Greek word for city-state. Athens was a *polis* at the time of Plato and Aristotle. Aristotle, in his discussion of human associations, stated that the "most sovereign and inclusive association is the *polis,* as it is called, or the political association."[10] The variety of meanings that the term "politics" has in the minds of people can be illustrated by the following responses that were given by students in the introduction to political science course at Rhode Island College (1985–1988) when asked to register their association with the word "politics":

abuses	diplomacy
arguments	distortion of facts
Bill of Rights	double talk
bureaucracy	elections
campaigns	embezzlement
capital punishment	empty promises
civil rights	equal rights
communism	exploitation
competence	foreign affairs
compromise	fraud
conflict	freedom of choice
Congress	freedom of speech
connections	government
conservatism	greed
conspiracies	homeless people
Contras	hush money
control	ideology
controversy	imperialism
corruption	incompetence
cover-up	indictment
debates	inefficiency
decision making	influence
democracy	influence peddling
demonstrations	issues

---

[10]Ernest Barker, ed. and trans., *The Politics of Aristotle* (New York: Oxford University Press, 1962), p. 1.

laws	power
lies	prejudice
lobbying	prestige
manipulation	promises
media coverage	propaganda
money	red tape
name calling	right to vote
officials	struggle for power
organizations	taxes
organized crime	trust
patronage	truth
people	unions
political parties	war
political terrorism	White House
politicians	

You will notice that these association responses present a broad spectrum of value judgments including negative words (corruption, fraud, double talk, greed), issue-oriented labels (capital punishment, civil rights, homeless people), and a number of institution- or process-related responses (bureaucracy, elections, diplomacy). We have found that the number of cynical or negative responses has declined during the past two decades.

A search through political science textbooks confounds the student with a number of definitions, stating that politics is the process of making governmental policies, the making of decisions by public means, the authoritative allocation of values, the quest for power, and so forth. The ethical scope of political activities has been expressed candidly by Peter Merkl in the following words: "At its best, politics is a noble quest for a good order and justice; at its worst, a selfish grab for power, glory and riches."[11]

To most political scientists the word "politics" denotes all the activities and processes that take place in the public realm, some overt and others of a more covert nature. Our discussion in the following chapters will be limited to the public scope of politics.

Quincy Wright, in his classic study of international relations, defines international politics as "the art of influencing, manipulating, or controlling major groups in the world so as to advance the purposes of some against the opposition of others."[12] This definition could be applied readily to domestic as well as international politics.

---

[11]Peter H. Merkl, *Political Continuity and Change* (New York: Harper & Row, 1967), p. 13.

[12]Quincy Wright, *The Study of International Relations* (New York: Appleton-Century-Croft, 1955), p. 130.

A sizable number of American political scientists adhere to a definition attributed to David Easton: Politics is the authoritative allocation of values.[13] However, the definition attributed to Easton ignores the competition and struggle that occur before an allocation of values can set in. We suggest that **politics can be defined as a struggle between actors pursuing conflicting desires on issues that may result in an authoritative allocation of values.** Political science involves the systematic analysis and study of politics in the public realm.

The Range of Politics

Political activities may be considered *legitimate* or *nonlegitimate.* Legitimate activities are sanctioned by law and custom. Examples of legitimate political functions would be the act of voting on election day, the passage of a statute by a legislative body, or a demonstration permitted by the authorities. However, politics goes beyond the legitimate area: A demonstration held despite the authorities' refusal to grant permission is a political act, although this type of politics might lead to turmoil and fighting in the streets. A coup d'état is a political act, although it might involve military force. A revolution clearly has political overtones. The Prussian General Karl von Clausewitz extended the range even further by stating: "War is simply a continuation of political intercourse, with the addition of other means. . . . War is not a mere act of policy, the political object is the goal, war is the means."[14]

Although political scientists deal primarily with politics within the public realm, politics is *not* limited to the public realm. As stated by Robert Dahl, the political arena transcends the public realm. He defines a political system as "any persistent pattern of human relationships that involves, to a significant extent, control, influence, power, or authority."[15] Dahl's definition implies that politics is not limited to the public realm, but includes conflict-of-interest situations and struggles for power, as well as policy-making activities in business firms, civic groups, religious organizations, crime syndicates, college organizations, families, and other groups—entities that are not of a public political and governmental nature.

College students demonstrating against an undesirable policy set by their institution's administration engage in politics. Members of a minority group rioting to protest miserable living conditions pursue politics. Politics can be found in the armed forces, be it over promotions or budget allocations. Politics is found in

---

[13]This definition is a loose paraphrase of statements made by David Easton. At no place does he give the above definition verbatim. See David Easton, "An Approach to the Analysis of Political Systems," *World Politics,* 9 (1957), pp. 383–400; *A Framework for Political Analysis* (Englewood Cliffs, N.J.: Prentice-Hall, 1965), p. 47ff.; and *The Political System: An Inquiry into the State of Political Science,* 2nd ed. (New York: Alfred A. Knopf, 1971), p. 129ff.

[14]Quoted in Frederick A. Hartmann, *The Relations of Nations,* 6th ed. (New York: Macmillan, 1983), p. 171.

[15]Robert A. Dahl, *Modern Political Analysis,* 4th ed. (Englewood Cliffs, N.J.: Prentice-Hall, 1984), p. 10.

business, where promotion to executive position may involve a great deal of maneuvering behind the scenes. The world of academe involves considerable politics.

There is also an enormous amount of politics in organized crime, politics that has to do with the maintenance of hierarchical order, promotions within the syndicate, discussions about the ends to be pursued and the methods to be employed, and debate about the division of territory among the families. There is also politics in the sense that in some communities the activities of crime syndicates are tightly interlocked with those of the established authorities.

The smallest group subject to politics is the family. The pursuit of desires and issues in the family often has political overtones in that father and mother pursue differing or at times contradictory aims and compete for the children's support for their stand. The playing of favorites serves as an enticement or as a payoff. Children, at times, try to play the parents against each other. These examples, we hope, serve to illustrate that the phenomenon labeled "politics" is an unavoidable fact of human life and that everybody is involved in it in one fashion or another.

The Language of Politics

One other item merits discussion before we turn to a consideration of the importance of politics. The metallurgist speaking on iron or lead, the ornithologist talking about bluebirds or goldfinches, the artist discussing the techniques of Rubens or Van Dyck can speak more objectively about his or her subject than the political scientist discussing democracy or communism. This is because these two labels refer to something of an amorphous quality, in contrast to the known entities of iron, lead, bluebirds, goldfinches, or the paintings of Rubens and Van Dyck. Many terms used to describe political phenomena have, at best, ambiguous meanings. This language complexity obviously is not unique to political science vocabulary, but presents a problem in other social science disciplines too.

While social scientists attempt to define their terminology with some precision, society at large often uses political labels very loosely. What do we mean by the terms **democracy**, **communism**, **fascism**, or **socialism**? What is a **liberal**; what are the characteristics of a **conservative**? Which societies are **democratic**, which **authoritarian**, and which **totalitarian**?

We shall discuss the ideological terms in some detail in Chapter 3, "Political Theories and Ideologies." For our present purposes we would like to point out that even within the United States, people's conceptions of what constitutes democracy, socialism, communism, or fascism differ considerably. One's own political perspective will have a bearing on how one applies the labels. The language used during the demonstrations in the United States in the late 1960s serves as an interesting illustration. People strongly opposed to the demonstrations were quite likely to label the demonstrators "communists," whereas some of the demonstrators who were taken into custody by the police would accuse the police (and other officials) of being "fascists" or "fascist pigs." Obviously, the labels, in their true meanings, do not apply to either of the groups.

Much confusion arises about the use of such terms as "liberal" and "conservative." People sharing the political philosophy of Senator Jesse Helms of North

Carolina, a conservative, will view those who are less conservative as being "liberal." In turn, supporters of a liberal such as Senator Ted Kennedy of Massachusetts will look upon those who are less liberal as being "conservative." The point is that the terms "liberal" and "conservative" are used not so much in reference to ideologies, but in a relative way, describing a person's political philosophy relative to one's own. This brings to mind the old saying that "where you stand depends on where you sit."

In discussions on matters of international politics, basic terms such as "country," "nation," and "state," although unfortunately used as synonyms by many writers and political spokespeople in this country, are *not* the same, and a great deal of unrest and military conflict has occurred because of this. There have been numerous occasions during the past two centuries where national groups, in their pursuit of self-determination, have tried to split away from the multinational country they were part of. Some of these efforts were successful, others were suppressed by brute force. On the other hand, leaders of various countries have tried, by using military force, to annex areas adjacent to their country because they were populated with people of their own nationality. The term "state" is applied these days more correctly to subunits of a country (i.e., the 50 states of the United States of America) than to a country at large.

Some countries come close to being a nation because of their highly homogeneous population (Denmark, Norway, and Sweden, for example), others are multinational (the Soviet Union and Yugoslavia are good examples), whereas in other instances several countries constitute a nation (such as North and South Korea). Finally, some nations have no country-type home at all, but are distributed over several countries, such as the Armenians, the Kurds, or the Jewish people prior to the establishment of the country of Israel.

Political vocabulary has more meaning if the user clarifies the use of a term and what is meant by it. One important service political scientists can render is to help to define political vocabulary more clearly.

The Importance of Politics

Politics surrounds everyone. A modern citizen is unlikely to play, either by choice or by fate, the isolated role of Robinson Crusoe. People are, by necessity, either actors or subjects in the web of politics. Their roles will be of a given type in the societal authority structure; for example, one might be a leader, an active participant, a passive subject, or play a role somewhere in between. What importance does a certain role or position have? Politics, if used wisely, can enhance human freedom and well-being. Although we cannot achieve all our desires, we can, through political pursuit, exercise more choice and achieve some of our aspirations to render our lives more secure and master a greater degree of our own fates.

How much influence do individuals have in effecting change in regard to national and global issues? The political role that an individual can play in a society depends upon the authority structure of a given society. The average citizen living under a dictatorship enjoys very little freedom in contrast to the person living in a democratic society. Note, for example, the impact which Rosa Parks, the black woman who refused to sit in the back of a bus in Montgomery, Alabama, had on activating the civil rights movement in this country.

Freedom of action, in the above context, involves such matters as freedom of speech, assembly, press, religion, travel (both within and beyond one's country), and social and economic advancement and opportunity. All these freedoms are relative in the sense that there is no country where there prevails complete freedom and none where there exists no degree of freedom at all. A society's authority structure, however, has a considerable bearing on the degree of freedom that prevails.

Politics affects people's lives in many ways. One important example would be the allocation of scarce resources by government. This presumes that the resources people regard as important are never sufficient, whether we are talking about clean air, clean water, or money. This does not mean that government determines or influences all aspects of our lives. If it did, we would be living in a completely totalitarian society, as depicted in George Orwell's *Nineteen Eighty-Four.* Where government is involved, however, it usually is making a decision (a choice between alternatives) about how a resource shall be allocated. One situation that occurs regularly concerns appropriations for education. We may have to raise taxes or spend less on defense, highways, welfare measures, and so forth, if we are going to allocate more for schools.

Once people have gone beyond an idyllic **state of nature**—where popula-

New politics in the Soviet Union: Muscovites scan an official election poster depicting Boris Yeltsin and Yevgeny Brakov, who competed for a seat in the national parliament in the March 26, 1989, election.

tions are small, people are assumed always to be rational, and there are few, if any, conflicts—people are either forcibly organized or organize themselves into a society with rules and obligations. At this point some members of the society believe that certain objectives (for example, defense, security, or a transportation network) or values (such as respect for human life) can be achieved only by rules or laws that bind everyone. If many people are allowed legally to participate in deciding procedures, objectives, policies, and values, we have some form of what is commonly called *democracy*. If few have the right to participate, we have some type of authoritarian or totalitarian system. The institution that promulgates and enforces such laws is government, and government in one aspect or another is a subject in which all political scientists are interested. Disagreements, competing points of views, or conflicts that are appealed to government for response are called *political conflicts*. The age we live in is much more **politicized** than those of previous generations because many more conflicts involve government and therefore are political. There are several reasons for this:

1. Today there are approximately 170 legally independent countries in the world. When the United States declared its independence in 1776, there were approximately 40 countries, whereas in 1945 the number stood at 70. Thus, the number of independent countries has more than doubled during the last 40 years. The main reason for this increase is the dissolution of the colonial empires. Most of the people who have achieved independence from colonial rule since 1945 live in Africa, Asia, and the Middle East. With independence they have progressively come to acquire a sense of common political identity. Their governments are stimulating a sense of nationalism that they hope will ultimately transcend tribal and regional loyalties. Thus, the world has become increasingly politicized because nowadays more people are self-consciously organized in countries than ever before.

2. Related to the first point is the fact that on occasion more people are participating in the political system. Now, after several decades of independence, many of the developing world's peoples have become involved in influencing government policy or political leaders. One can point to such countries as Ghana, India, Indonesia, Jordan, Nigeria, and Syria, where substantial elements of the population have been active in the political process since independence. In much of the developing world and even in most communist countries, there are more or less regularly scheduled elections; however, in a majority of these political systems few if any opposition candidates are permitted. One purpose of single-party elections in these countries is to manipulate political awareness and create support for the government. In contrast, the United States serves as an example where enfranchising segments of the population has led to a meaningful increase in political participation due to the passage of the Nineteenth, Twenty-Third, and Twenty-Sixth Amendments to the United States Constitution. The Nineteenth Amendment, ratified in 1920, granted suffrage to women. The Twenty-Third Amendment, ratified in 1961, gave voters in the District of Columbia the right to vote for president and vice president of the United States. The Twenty-Sixth Amendment, ratified in 1971, gave citizens 18 years and older the vote in federal, state, and local elections. More people are participating in the political process in the contemporary world, whether mobilized by authoritarian governments or voluntarily, as in the democratic societies.

3. We also have become more politicized in the last 100 years as citizens have turned increasingly to government to solve problems previously considered outside the jurisdiction of government. Formerly, most governments throughout the world were responsible principally for defense, internal security, and maintaining some form of transportation—communication network. Today governments often are held responsible not only for inflation and deflation, but also for the price of gasoline and sugar, for encouraging industrialization to provide jobs, for establishing minimum wages and working conditions, and for implementing retirement systems such as social security. The list could go on for several pages. The notion of what are government responsibilities has expanded considerably within the last 100 years. As groups support certain issues, such as gun registration or increasing the minimum wage, other groups oppose them. It is inevitable that political competition and disagreement expand as more issues are being pursued by various groups or individuals. The cumulative impact leads to increased politicization.

The more complex, specialized, and interdependent the economic and social systems become within a country and the more economic, political, and national security policies are influenced by international forces outside the country, the more governments must respond on behalf of the political community. Governments are expected to deal with multiplying problems, national and international. The balancing and accommodating of numerous demands and pressures and the choice among alternatives are often decisions only governments can make and enforce. Even in this age of specialization and division of labor, governments should not be expected "to do everything" and solve all problems; however, the role of political institutions is critical. The linchpin status of government today results in increased politicization.

4. Another reason for increased politicization is that we have experienced a communications revolution in this century. Radio increased political participation and awareness in the United States and abroad. Television has brought a new dimension to observing events and has replaced radio as the prime source of political information in the more advanced countries, though political participation did not itself increase. Television is nowadays the principal source of news for many people throughout the world. Greater in-depth understanding does not necessarily occur, but awareness of the politically newsworthy and dramatic events of the moment is increased. Riots, wars, and impeachment proceedings are filmed live or shown within hours of the event. This often takes the form of a superficial dramatization of politics and may actually draw attention away from a reasoned and studied understanding of major political problems.

In sum, the world of today is more politicized than ever before, and politics is an important element of our life.

THE SCIENTIFIC CONTENT OF POLITICAL INQUIRY

How scientific a *science* can political science be? No single school or mood in political science provides the exclusive answer to the question. For, as Gaetano Salvemini has stated so succinctly:

Scientific research is a series of successive approaches to the truth, comparable to an exploration in an unknown land. Each explorer checks and adds to the findings of his predecessors, and facilitates for his successors the attainment of the goal they all have in common. This is why history and the social sciences, more than any of the physical sciences, need an atmosphere of free competition between different schools of thought, in which all hypotheses and all proconceptions [sic] can be pitted one against the other. If liberty is suppressed in favor of a single school, it is the death warrant of our studies. . . . If they do not demand free competition not only for themselves but for their rivals as well, the historian and the social scientist, more than any scholars, accept both moral and intellectual degradation.[16]

Political science is not a science in the sense of the so-called hard sciences, such as biology, chemistry, or physics. These hard sciences deal with phenomena that can be examined in controlled experiments in a laboratory setting, while, in political science, it is just not possible to examine a voter, a political candidate, or an office holder in the same fashion. For that matter, some people believe that political science is not a science at all, but an art.

The great physicist Albert Einstein was asked once by a colleague why mankind has been able to unlock the secrets of the atom but has been unable to devise the political means necessary to keep the atom from destroying civilization. Einstein replied, "This is simple, politics is more difficult than physics."

When studying human behavior, it is impossible to achieve true critical distance. A political scientist's findings are by nature more subjective and open to dispute than those of the natural scientist. The complexity of political phenomena and the influence of values make it impossible for the political scientist to be as objective as a colleague in the natural sciences. This does not mean, however, that political science inquiry is not scientific. Science starts with empiricism, the observation and verification of facts, and the formulation of generalizations and propositions. Scientific inquiry calls for adding new knowledge to what is known already. The perennial debate over the scientific nature of any or all of the social sciences has been influenced all too often by the commonly held notion that the term "science" should be reserved for those disciplines that show constant progress in obvious ways and use standard research techniques to achieve this progress.

We should take note, however, of Abraham Kaplan:

> Each science—and indeed, each inquiry—finds some techniques appropriate and others inappropriate and even impossible. The microscope is of very limited use to astronomy (for the present, at least), while the biologist cannot learn much about terrestrial life with the telescope. But to note this difference is not to say that these two sciences have different methods.[17]

In his famous essay, *The Structure of Scientific Revolutions*, Thomas S. Kuhn defines science as "research firmly based upon one or more past scientific achieve-

---

[16]Gaetano Salvemini, *Historians and Scientists* (Cambridge, Mass.: Harvard University Press, 1939), pp. 112–113.

[17]Abraham Kaplan, *The Conduct of Inquiry: Methodology for Behavioral Science* (San Francisco: Chandler Publishing, 1964), p. 31.

ments that some particular scientific community acknowledges for a time as supplying the foundation for its further practice."[18] According to Kuhn, science has not been quite the logical process that many scientists have claimed it to be. Rather, he maintains that the history of science consists of a number of drastic changes, or revolutions, by which the theories of a given time, called *paradigms* by Kuhn, are rendered obsolete by new discoveries. These lead to the shaping of new paradigms which, again, will become obsolete at some later date. According to Kuhn, the history of science is a continuous process, consisting of a chain of paradigms.[19]

Political science is self-conscious about the need to be as "scientific" as possible. It strives to be scientific in its methods, in the ways facts are collected, examined, and organized. The rigorous survey research that occurs in the United States is an example and outgrowth of this scientific research. Countrywide surveys by the Gallup and Harris polls or the Michigan Survey Research Center interview 1,200 to 1,600 adults. These surveys describe American political opinion or vote intention of more than 100 million adults within a maximum of 2 or 3 percent margin of error.[20]

As we will see in the following chapters, political science is making progress in identifying and explaining political relationships. Moreover, new theories have been developed and older ones have been reexamined in new settings. New horizons have been opened for research. Political science has grown to become a more exact and more scientific discipline of scholarly pursuit. One other sign of its growing importance can be seen in the fact that in the past three decades the presidents of this country, as well as state executives, have increasingly sought the advice of selected political scientists.

Having examined the nature and scope of political science, we now turn our attention to the approaches or methods used by political scientists to study political phenomena and the key concepts involved.

SUMMARY

Political science is the study of politics in the public realm, the area in which governmental decisions are made that may be binding on all of us. Living, as we do, in organized societies, it is impossible for us to keep ourselves completely removed from the political arena. Therefore, it is of some importance for us to have some understanding about the political process in our society. Because the world becomes increasingly interdependent, we should have some knowledge about politics in the other countries, too.

People are the actors in the political arena. Because human beings are less

---

[18]Thomas S. Kuhn, *The Structure of Scientific Revolutions* (Chicago: The University of Chicago Press, 1962), p. 10.

[19]Ibid., pp. 1–90.

[20]For more detailed discussions of the scientific nature of political science, see Alan C. Isaak, *Scope and Methods of Political Science: An Introduction to the Methodology of Political Inquiry*, 4th ed. (Chicago: The Dorsey Press, 1985), Chapters 1–5.

"How're you doing, Professor?"

Allen Johnson, *Providence Journal.*

predictable than physical elements, political scientists find it more difficult to make as accurate predictions as their colleagues in the physical sciences. Forecasting political developments involves often a multitude of variables. Nevertheless, substantial progress has been made in recent decades by political scientists in increasing their accuracy of determining the desires of people on given issues and how people are likely to vote in elections.

RECOMMENDED READINGS

Blondel, Jean. *The Discipline of Political Science.* London: Butterworths, 1981. A leading British political scientist examines the progress in political science since WWII and counters the scepticism raised by its critics.

Dahl, Robert A. *Modern Political Analysis,* 4th ed. Englewood Cliffs, N.J.: Prentice-Hall, 1984. This is an excellent analysis of the foundations of the political process, written by one of this country's top political scientists.

Finifter, Ada W., ed. *Political Science: The State of the Discipline.* Washington, D.C.: The American Political Science Association, 1983. A collection of informative essays presented by senior U.S. political scientists which explains recent developments in their areas of speciality.

Lipset, Seymour Martin. *Political Man: The Social Basis of Politics,* expanded and updated ed. Baltimore, Md.: The John Hopkins University Press, 1981. This is a superb analysis of the social foundations of politics.

Lipson, Leslie. *The Great Issues of Politics,* 8th ed. Englewood Cliffs, N.J.: Prentice-Hall, 1989. This work is a thorough discussion of some of the fundamental issues in politics and their meaning in the context of history and philosophy.

Ricci, David M. *The Tragedy of Political Science: Politics, Scholarship, and Democracy.* New Haven, Conn.: Yale University Press, 1984. The author presents a critical examination of political science with emphasis on its major shortcomings.

Somit, Albert, and Joseph Tannenhaus. *The Development of American Political Science: From Burgess to Behavioralism,* enlarged ed. New York: Irvington, 1982. This work is the most detailed discussion of the development of political science in the United States.

Stupak, Ronald J., et al. *Understanding Political Science: The Arena of Power.* Sherman Oaks, Calif.: Alfred Publishing Co., 1978. This collection of articles presents a thorough discussion of the major subareas in political science and the important questions raised in each of them.

Weisberg, Herbert F., ed. *Political Science: The Science of Politics.* New York: Agathon Press, 1986. The articles in this anthology focus on the scientific aspects of the study of political behavior and institutions.

Wiegele, Thomas C. *Biopolitics: Search for a More Human Political Science.* Boulder, Colo.: Westview Press, 1979. This is an informative biopolitical study of political behavior.

Chapter 2

Political Science: Approaches and Concepts

The study of politics in the late nineteenth century was heavily legalistic, as illustrated by the title of one of the major works of that era, John Burgess's *Political Science and Comparative Constitutional Law* (1890). Many American political scientists then had received at least some of their graduate training at European universities and were influenced by the legalistic training in these schools, but during the late nineteenth century some political scientists in this country already had begun to shift away from constitutionalism and legal inquiry, moving toward a study of governmental institutions and organizations and how they actually worked. This can be seen, for example, in Woodrow Wilson's *Congressional Government: A Study in American Politics* (1885). Political scientists use various methods to conduct their inquiries. Modern political science is shaped by different methodological approaches and considerable debate over the appropriateness of each.

THE STUDY OF POLITICS

A new mood or spirit entered political science in the 1920s. Some political scientists began to supplement their library research with interview and survey fieldwork, adding to the historical, legalistic, and constitutional approaches employed by the traditionalists. The new movement soon to become known as behavioralism, aimed at making political science a more scientific discipline, one that studied politics as it operated in the real world.

Behavioralism initially focused on the beliefs and activities of individuals. Emphasis on individual and group behavior led the behavioralist to study eventually the leadership role of a president or the performances of members of Congress and judges and how they carry out their responsibilities, instead of focusing on institutions such as the Constitution, the executive, the Congress, or the judiciary. While the traditionalist's concern was largely with institutions, the behavioralist stressed individuals rather than large political units.

The behavioralists acquired many of the research tools used in anthropology, economics, mathematics, psychology, and sociology. They advocate a quantitative empiricism and extensive use of statistical methods. Election statistics, public opinion surveys, and legislative role calls were recorded in tables, graphs, and charts. The less statistically inclined described some of this as number crunching because often little analysis or explanation accompanied the data.

The behavioral approach seeks to achieve a greater accuracy in identifying and explaining regularities of politics that apply to many political systems; for example, what conditions will lead to instability and insurgency. Science in the term "political science" is stressed. Some early behavioralists even believed that we could begin to predict or foretell political events, on the assumption that politics was an orderly system governed by universal, discoverable laws. Most political scientists now believe that after careful analysis we can perceive trends and probabilities. However, we cannot predict because we cannot identify and examine every condition or circumstance that will influence future political events.

The most successful areas of inquiry for the behavioralist are studies of voting behavior and investigations of beliefs and attitudes held by individuals and how these influenced political behavior. Table 2.1 is one example of measuring people's attitudes. Six thousand people were surveyed in four countries. All four were surveyed in 1959 and the former West Germany again in 1978. The individuals surveyed were asked, ''Generally speaking, what are the things about this country that you are most proud of?'' This table indicates that Americans and the British took considerable pride in their political system in 1959 and Mexican nationals took modest pride. The Germans showed little pride in their political system in 1959, but such pride increased markedly by 1978. Only through political surveys by the behavioralists have we become aware of different national attitudes and begun to look for the political significance of these differences. In addition to providing an example of behavioralism, Table 2.1 suggests the following: Democracy can more easily survive challenges if there is substantial pride and satisfaction with the political system. Widespread alienation, distrust, or disinterest with politics may prove to be an additional danger if the country is subjected to severe economic, social, or international stress.

Table 2.1   ASPECTS OF COUNTRY IN WHICH RESPONDENTS REPORT PRIDE, BY COUNTRY

Respondent is most proud of:	1959				1978
	U.S. (%)	U.K. (%)	Mexico (%)	(Former) West Germany (%)	(Former) West Germany (%)
Governmental, political institutions	85	46	30	7	31
Social legislation	13	18	2	6	18
Position in international affairs	5	11	3	5	9
Economic system	23	10	24	33	40
Characteristics of people	7	18	15	36	25
Spiritual virtues and religion	3	1	8	3	6
Contributions to arts and sciences	4	13	10	23	23
Physical attributes of country	5	10	22	17	14
Nothing, don't know	13	21	16	18	10
Total Percentage[a]	158	148	130	148	176
Total Number of Respondents	(970)	(963)	(1,007)	(955)	(2,030)

[a]Percentages exceed 100 because of multiple responses.

Sources: David P. Conradt, ''Changing German Political Culture,'' in Gabriel A. Almond and Sidney Verba, eds., The Civic Culture Revisited (Boston: Little, Brown, 1980), p. 230; and Gabriel A. Almond and Sidney Verba, The Civic Culture (Boston: Little, Brown, 1965), p. 64.

During the past decade behavioralism has become an integral part of the political science discipline, and many members of the profession now rely on a combination of methods of inquiry derived from the traditional and behavioral schools. This new postbehavioral synthesis is not concerned exclusively with individuals; it also is concerned with the functioning and impact of political institutions and influence of relevant geographic, economic, historical, legal, and cultural factors. This combining of various approaches has been influenced increasingly by the political and social crises of our time and the awareness that so many factors influence political events.

This text is designed to use the most appropriate approaches for the beginning student in his or her study of politics. We believe that a basic familiarity with political science principles will enable the student to better understand contemporary political issues and to analyze and contribute toward the making of government decisions by voting, working in a political campaign, or perhaps becoming a government official. A democracy such as ours requires informed and interested citizens who can take part in the political process.

We believe that the most appropriate approach to political science for the beginning student is political systems analysis. This orientation stresses that politics inevitably involves interaction, cooperation, and conflict.

THE POLITICAL SYSTEMS APPROACH

We use the concept of the political system as an approach to recognizing and understanding patterns and relationships and to organize what is often a large, unorganized mass of political information. It is a way to organize your information, whether from a book, a lecture, a newspaper, or television, and to understand the real world in a more coherent way.

We study political systems and not just government. Government is the center of the political system, but many other parts are involved. The political systems approach does two things: It enables us to perceive what is important and to organize our information. It also alerts us to the interrelationships between obviously political phenomena—for example, political parties, the chief executive, civil service commission—and other phenomena in society that are sometimes politically important—such as the family, educational, or economic systems.

Any system, whether we are discussing the political system, the heating system in a house, or the individual's physiological system, has five characteristics:

1. The system is made up of many parts.
2. Some parts are more important than others.
3. The parts interact.
4. To varying degrees the parts are interdependent.
5. The system has boundaries.

A major difference between the heating system of a house and the political system is that in the former the boundaries are tangible and readily observable. The parts of the heating system (thermostat, furnace, wiring, ducts) are apparent to the eye, and it is obvious where the physical boundaries are. This is not true with the political system; its boundaries are abstract and must be identified and explained by the political scientist. You are not participating in the political system if you have a date or go to a football game. You are in the political system if you attend a political rally, write a letter to a government official, vote, study and discuss politics in this class, or participate in a demonstration.

In any system some parts are more important than others, and some parts interact more than others. Changes in one part may or may not affect other parts or processes in the system. If you have your appendix removed, there is little apparent change in your physiological system. If you lose a kidney the consequences are serious; without a heart, the body will not function. There are similar variations in the political system. Political parties and elections are very important in the American political system. The military may be the most important institution to study in some political systems in Africa, Asia, Latin America, and the Middle East, where there are many military governments. The concept of political system will not itself explain particular events. The first step, however, is to organize data information within a general framework, in this case, the political system. Figure 2.1 helps you visualize what we are discussing.

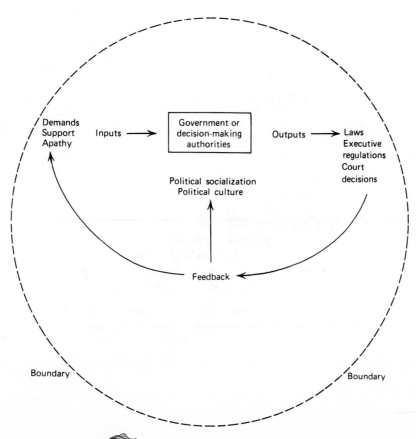

Figure 2.1 Political system.

The Importance of Government

Government is the center of any political system. It is the legally established political leadership and administrative hierarchy of a national or local community. Government successfully upholds a claim to the exclusive regulation of the legal use of physical force in making and enforcing political policies. It is the most inclusive institution in society. No other organization (fraternity, sorority, trade union, church) in national society includes everyone in the country; government does. Government in all of its parts (executive, legislative, and judicial branches) can be described as the decision-making authority that has conversion as a principal function. Conversion modifies, rejects, or takes only part of the inputs that add to or lead to outputs.

Government sometimes allows other groups to use physical force, but only in a restricted manner. A parent may discipline a child physically, but this must be limited. Too much physical force becomes child abuse, and child abuse is against the law. Generally, when physical force is used by someone other than government officials it is done illegally. In a political system run under law, government officials also must obey the law or are subject to being charged with a crime. Even a police officer can legally use physical force only in certain circumstances. Most violence that actually occurs in society is outside the law, or what is generally described as crime. If crime and violence become too widespread, government effectiveness rapidly diminishes. When groups initiate political violence in an effort to establish a different government, or change drastically the existing political system, then there is an insurgency or a revolution.

The use of force should be the ultimate government sanction. Generally, the less physical force required, the more effective government is and the more it is popularly accepted. The arbitrary and unpredictable use of force characterizes **totalitarian** governments, which seek to terrorize and thus more easily control their subjects. A totalitarian government seeks to control all aspects of a person's existence, restructure society brutally, and export revolution. A government such as the U.S. government uses physical force in limited ways, but it is used. In order that a government does not have to spend excessive money on internal security, 90 to 95 percent of the population should—out of commitment, understanding, self-interest, or habit—obey the law. If a police officer had to be on duty 24 hours a day to enforce stoplights, for example, too many government resources (taxes, appropriations, personnel) would have to be committed. Fortunately, most drivers obey traffic signals.

The most common uses of force by the U.S. government are arrest and incarceration. As shown in Table 2.2, the numbers are substantial.

A recent survey by the Office of Justice Statistics studied locally administered jails (city and county).[1] These jails are usually facilities holding people awaiting trial or sentenced to short terms of a year or less. Long-term prisoners are soon moved to state or federal prisons. In the one-year period ending June 30, 1988, 9.7 million people were put into a jail cell at the local level. During the same year, approximately 9.6 million people were released from jail. Not all people arrested

---

[1]Associated Press, *Express-News* (San Antonio), February 5, 1990, p. 2A.

Table 2.2   **PERSONS ARRESTED OR INCARCERATED IN THE UNITED STATES**

	1975	1980	1985	1987
Arrested	8,051,000	12,042,000	11,249,000	10,796,000
Incarcerated (state and federal prisons)	240,593	315,974	481,393	557,256

Source: U.S. Bureau of the Census, *Statistical Abstract of the United States; 1989,* 109th ed. (Washington, D.C.: Author, 1989), pp. 173 and 183. The arrest figures are supplied by the FBI and based on data from 10,000 reporting agencies. Thus, arrests by nonreporting agencies, covering 18 percent of the population, are not included.

remain in jail for extended periods of time. The average time in a local jail in 1988 was three days, and 39 percent of inmates spent one day or less behind bars.

Another example of the role of government and the uncommon but ultimate use of physical coercion by democratic governments is *eminent domain.* In the United States, eminent domain, or the acquiring of private property for public use after the payment of fair compensation, is usually accomplished without a court trial or resort to force. There are exceptions, such as the hypothetical individual who is required to sell his or her property for an interstate highway interchange. The person may believe the price the government offers for the property is too low; therefore, a jury trial becomes necessary to determine the price. On a few tragic occasions, government force is used. The following example also involves the question of whether or not "justice" was actually served.

> Consider the 1964 case of a Los Angeles resident named Steven Anthony who refused to vacate his home which had been condemned by Los Angeles County under the laws of eminent domain. The land was to be turned over to a private group for the construction of the Hollywood Motion Picture and Television Museum. For ten weeks Anthony barricaded himself in his home, holding off with a shotgun the deputies who sought to evict him. Finally, two plainclothes policemen gained access by posing as sympathizers. Anthony was arrested and jailed. The next day the house was demolished by court order. The judge labeled this previously unknown man "an anarchist, a rabble rouser, and a publicity seeker" and sentenced him to a year in jail for battery and resisting arrest. . . . All plans for building the museum have been abandoned due to dissension among the ranks of the Hollywood promoters. The property is currently being used as a parking lot.[2]

Many governments today do *not* spend most of their time extracting taxes and restraining or limiting behavior. This was the case, though, through most of recorded history.

Today a majority of governments are more proactive. Democratic governments especially are active in promoting and protecting civil rights, political equality, and equality of opportunity. Governments, even in authoritarian systems, direct some of their outputs toward providing public goods which all or some citizens can use.

---

[2]Susan Love Brown et al., *The Incredible Bread Machine* (San Diego, Calif.: World Research, 1974), pp. 2–3. The original story appeared in the *Los Angeles Times* (April 4, 1965).

Examples include public education, public housing, highways, mass transit, medical assistance, retirement programs, job training programs, and so forth. Most governments are more delivery oriented in **society** today and are expected to do more in this century than in previous centuries.

Inputs

Government is the center of the political system, but many other activities and institutions are included as part of the system.

The **input** side of Figure 2-1 includes claims or demands, support, and apathy. *Demands* refer to actions people want government to undertake or reject. The method that peacefully involves the largest number of people is that of competitive elections where most of the adult population is eligible to vote. Voters make few specific policy choices, but they do select candidates who have committed themselves on specific issues. Demonstrations, petitions, and donations of time and money are also means of making input.

Interest groups and political parties, discussed in more detail in Chapters 5 and 6, are important means of making claims. For example, the National Rifle Association (NRA) actively and successfully opposes gun-control legislation. In a democratic political system, the opportunities are greater for groups to organize autonomously without the control of government. Individuals also can make claims or present demands by writing letters, meeting a government official, running for office, and, of course, through the electoral ballot.

Providing input—bringing the fate of the underprivileged to the attention of the policy makers.

Within a government there are many complex and sometimes obscure decisions made that generate scant public input. This is part of the conversion process. Such decisions might include the choice of one type of fighter plane over another or U.S. loans to Algeria. Only a small number of people are involved. Government officials talk to one another and make a decision, and there is little popular interest or awareness about an issue at the time. The decision to increase economic and military assistance and the number of advisors to South Vietnam to 20,000 by the end of 1963 did not reflect popular demands. David Easton calls these "within-puts," occurring within the black box called government.[3]

An absence of popular inputs, and too many withinputs, can be detrimental to a viable political system. An illustration of this is Soviet leader Mikhail Gorbachev's policies of *glasnost* and *perestroika*—the gradual liberalizing and restructuring of society. It is moving too slowly. Soviet reformers believe, though, they must have more popular input and participation and, hence, enthusiasm if the country's stunted economic growth is to be reversed.

Supports are given to the political system as a whole and to that part of the system referred to as the "regime." **Regime** is the overall constitutional process or political rules of the game, "those arrangements that regulate the way in which the demands put into the system are settled and the way in which decisions are put into effect."[4] Supports generally evolve over decades or even centuries. One can be loyal to the system and regime without necessarily being in agreement with the political party in office. You may have voted against the president or the member of Congress representing you, but still be loyal to the existing political arrangement, which in the case of the United States is a constitutional representative government.

A common phenomenon is **support-inputs** given to a particular government or even a major opposition group by an interested foreign power. In many countries in Africa, Asia, Latin America, and the Middle East, international inputs and support are crucial if a group of leaders is to continue in power or be replaced. In Afghanistan, the current Communist government would not have survived for more than a decade without massive Soviet support, including 110,000 Soviet soldiers. Similarly, it is unlikely the Salvadoran government could survive without substantial American aid, though American military advisors number less than 100.

The Philippines represents the complexity of international support-inputs. The late President Ferdinand Marcos declared martial law in 1972, two years before the end of his second presidential term. Competitive politics came to an end in the islands. Corruption and poverty, as well as a communist rebellion, grew during the Marcos years, and long-standing political freedom almost disappeared. Underpinning the special U.S./Filipino relationship are two major U.S. military facilities, Clark Air Force Base and Subic Naval Base. By 1985 public doubts grew both inside

---

[3]David Easton, *A Framework for Political Analysis* (Englewood Cliffs, N.J.: Prentice-Hall, 1965), p. 114. David Easton is a political scientist who has written extensively on political systems.

[4]David Easton, "An Approach to the Analysis of Political Systems," *World Politics*, 9:1 (1957), p. 392.

and outside the U.S. government about misuse of public funds, including U.S. assistance, and the deteriorating political situation. President Reagan's close confidant, Senator Paul Laxalt (Republican/Nevada), was sent to the Philippines in October 1985 to convey U.S. displeasures with the economic, military, and political situations. Bowing to U.S. pressure, President Marcos pledged elections. The elections were held February 7, 1986, between Marcos and Mrs. Corazon Aquino, widow of assassinated opposition politician, Ninoy Aquino. Responding to charges of fraud and manipulation in ballot counting, Republican Senator Richard Lugar, then chair of the U.S. Senate Foreign Relations Committee, headed a team of official observers to monitor the elections. He reported to President Reagan that there was widespread fraud in the elections that returned President Marcos to office. On February 19, 1986, the U.S. Senate voted 85–9 to condemn the Philippine elections. Ambassador Philip Habib went to Manila as the personal representative of the White House and reported back that Marcos was finished. A million civilians, "people power," demonstrated in the streets of Manila, and the Philippine defense minister as well as the deputy chief of staff resigned and called on President Marcos to resign. President Reagan urged President Marcos to resign on February 24. One day later Marcos left for Hawaii and Cory Aquino became president.

The above should not suggest the United States "pulled the strings" to oust Marcos. It suggests that at critical junctures the United States had input in returning democracy to the Philippines. In the case of Eastern Europe, the role of the Soviet Union in advancing political pluralism is more direct, as the description of events in Box 2.1 shows.

Supports can be divided into two basic types: *tangible* and *symbolic*. Tangible supports are actions that show or promote loyalty and identity with the political system. Examples include voting as an act of citizenship, paying taxes because of a feeling of commitment and identity, or flying the flag in front of your home. Symbolic supports are states of mind, such as attitudes of loyalty, patriotism, and commitment. These attitudes sometimes become tangible supports; at other times they remain simply a psychological orientation that creates emotional support.

Supports evolve because governments and regimes have responded over several decades and generations. Supports hold a political community together, even though there are sharp differences over particular policies or individuals in office. When the widely shared supports are few, the political system is threatened and radically different political arrangements may be imposed. During the closing days of Weimar Germany (1918–1933), shortly before Adolf Hitler assumed full power in 1933, the Communists and Nazis together were winning 50 percent of the votes. (In the November 1932 Reichstag elections, the Nazi party won 33 percent of the vote and the Communists 17 percent.) This lack of support for constitutional democracy made it easier for the Nazis to achieve power and transform the German government from a representative to a totalitarian political system.

Apathy, or indifference, can be either a support or a potential reservoir from which revolutionaries can mobilize support. For example, in the United States over 30 percent of the eligible electorate is consistently apolitical. Some people are apathetic because the electoral process involves so many people that they feel one vote makes no difference; others are uninterested because "things will not get

Box 2.1 **Soviet President Gorbachev Encourages Reform in Eastern Europe**

Negotiations between Poland's Communist leaders and Solidarity over the new coalition government in Warsaw were at an impasse last August. . . .

Then, at the peak of the crisis, on Tuesday, August 22, a telephone call came from Moscow, from Communist party headquarters, from Mikhail S. Gorbachev, the Soviet president and the party's general secretary. For 40 minutes, Gorbachev talked with Mieczyslaw Rakowski, the first secretary of the ruling Polish United Workers' Party, and counseled him on the need for compromise.

The Polish Communists must understand, Gorbachev told Rakowski bluntly, that the time had come to yield power. The party had lost the confidence of the people . . . Polish Communists should participate in the new coalition government, Gorbachev said, and they would have the understanding and support of their Soviet comrades. . . .

Four days later, Vladimir A. Kryuchkov, the head of the KGB, arrived in Warsaw to confer with Tadeusz Mazowiecki, the Solidarity nominee for prime minister, and to give the new coalition government Moscow's blessing. . . .

Gorbachev, setting out the Soviet Union's new foreign policy at the United Nations last December, had declared: "The principle of freedom of choice is mandatory. Refusal to recognize this principle will have serious consequences for world peace." . . .

And through all this, the Soviet Union, surprising itself as much as any Western observer, has supported and even helped promote the transformation.

The old leadership in Berlin, Prague, and Sofia were directed by their comrades in Moscow that the time had come for a change, that reforms could be delayed no longer, and that they could expect no Soviet support in clinging to power.

Source: Quoted from Michael Parks, "Gorbachev Unleashes the Forces of Reform," *Los Angeles Times* (December 17, 1989), p. Q5. Copyright 1989, Los Angeles Times. Reprinted by permission.

better," or they lack the mental ability to understand and organize political information. In some political systems fear and coercion encourage apathy. For others, apathy reflects general satisfaction with the political system and the feeling that there is no need to become concerned with political matters. A major survey of American households by the Bureau of the Census revealed that a plurality, 35 percent, of unregistered voters said they did not register because they were not interested in doing so. Under 1 percent of the unregistered said the reason was that one vote was too insignificant to make a difference.[5]

---

[5]U.S. Department of Commerce, "Voter Participation in November, 1974," *Current Population Reports*, Series P-20: 275 (January 1975), p. 5, Table 2.

Apathy, positively viewed, reflects the right of a person to be apolitical and also that the political stakes are agreeably low. Sometimes intense participation by too many citizens can mean the political stakes are too high, and the results are disheartening. In two German presidential elections in 1932, just before Adolf Hitler assumed power, 86.2 and 83.5 percent of the eligible voters went to the polls. In 1933, 88.8 percent voted in the legislative elections that the Nazis won.

Political apathy also can result from a sense of hopelessness and withdrawal from the political system. Apathy in an authoritarian state is commonly a defense mechanism. It does not directly challenge the regime, but it seeks to preserve in one of the few ways possible a degree of individual privacy and personal safety. It prevents the complete politicization of the individual in the name of the country. Given the proper circumstances, such apathy may be interrupted by spontaneous antiregime demonstrations, as happened in Eastern Europe in 1989–1990. Apathy based on a sense of hopelessness or an underlying hostility is not a support, and it can become a violent input when triggered.

Apathy, as we have seen, can provide support for the political system or it can be a potential source for mass agitation against the system. If a government is struggling against an insurgency, the apathy of the population just to stay alive is a disadvantage for the government. A government under this type of stress needs the positive support of its citizens and not an inclination to see the guerrillas as no better than the government.

Outputs

Outputs are government decisions. They can be laws, court rulings, executive-administrative orders, or conscious refusals to make a decision. Public administration is the subfield of political science that studies how decisions are implemented and if implementation is efficient, often with more concern for procedures (such as budgeting and personnel policies) than substance of decisions. No-decisions, the refusal of government to intervene or take an action concerning a problem or dispute in society, is also a form of output. Examples include the refusal of Canada to develop nuclear weapons and the refusal of the U.S. Congress to pass gun-control legislation.

Laws as output are apparent: Eighteen-year-olds are enfranchised by constitutional amendment, social security benefits are raised, or the speed limit is set at 55 miles per hour by act of Congress. One of the most famous judicial outputs in the United States was the Supreme Court decision in *Brown* v. *Board of Education of Topeka* (1954), in which racial segregation in public schools was declared unconstitutional. The implementation of that decision since 1954, though slow, has had a tremendous impact on society.

Unfortunately, most political science writing is not concerned with the output side of the political system. Relatively little research is done on the impact that output decisions have or on the question of whether they actually accomplish their purpose. Most political science literature focuses either on inputs or the government decision-making process and devotes little time to the effect of government policy.

Political Culture

The more people participate freely in making demands, the more effort required by government to balance, modify, approve, or reject some claims and convert the vast number of inputs into outputs. Much of what political scientists study is concerned with government institutions: history, organization, and functioning. Government is crucial because of its ultimate sanction—the legal use of physical force—and because of its decision-making and conversion roles.

As government decisions are made and policies carried out, they pass through a feedback process that affects the political culture, as well as the more immediate input side. **Political culture** (discussed in detail in Chapter 4) is shaped in part by outputs and affects the input process. Political culture refers to those aspects of our social heritage concerned with beliefs, attitudes, values, and behavior patterns influencing the way people perceive and behave in the political system. For example, American political culture generally believes key government officials should be chosen through competitive elections. This attitude toward electorally choosing leaders begins in our primary schools, when the sixth-grade or earlier students elect class officers. Other societies, such as the Soviet Union, which have a long-standing authoritarian tradition of rule by the few have accepted until recently that a small minority of the adult population will choose the rulers.

Political culture often emphasizes the study of beliefs and values and how they influence the thinking and actions of those actually making government decisions. Political culture also influences the type of claims and the style (voting, letters, demonstrations, riots, or apathetic obedience). For example, during the Tokugawa period (1603–1857) in Japan, the emperor was a figurehead and military lords, or *daimyo,* controlled the government. Rule often was arbitrary. The political culture enforced uniformity and self-conscious apolitical behavior. There were few popular demands. An in-depth study of the period by an anthropologist shows how the samurai warriors enforced detailed government rules by instantly decapitating anyone whose actions were "other than expected." Those Japanese who survived in the Tokugawa political system "learned in early childhood to keep their own counsel, trust no one, and conform fanatically to whatever might be ordered."[6]

Feedback

Feedback is a result of the changing opinions and actions of citizens, usually in response to government output. It may increase or decrease support for the system. It may affect the types of inputs or claims that are made from lowering taxes to ending the war in Vietnam or insurgents overthrowing the Soviet-backed government in Afghanistan. Feedback can range from voting to violence. Feedback in an authoritarian political system, as in the case of Tokugawa Japan, may be prohibited by the government so as to compel obedience, with the result that popular input is nonexistent.

---

[6]Douglas G. Haring, "The Formation of National Character in Tokugawa and Meiji, Japan," reprinted in Thomas J. Bellows, Stanley Erikson, and Herbert R. Winter, eds., *Political Science: Introductory Essays and Readings* (Belmont, Calif.: Duxbury Press, 1971), p. 166.

Relative satisfaction with output leads one to support the political system or even particular candidates and political parties. Often there is a fairly obvious feedback loop (see Figure 2.1).

The election of Republican George Bush in 1988 illustrates feedback. The election indicates voters (in this case 54 percent) supported the winning candidate, partly because they appreciated the way the economic and political systems were working. We were not at war, and, more importantly, there was no potential war visible. A majority of Americans seemed satisfied, or at least not dissatisfied. By September 1988, just over 50 percent of the adult American public said they were satisfied with the way things were going; those dissatisfied had dropped to 45 percent. A CBS/*New York Times* poll in August revealed that by a 69 to 26 percent margin Americans considered themselves better off than they were eight years ago, at the end of Democrat Jimmy Carter's administration. A sense of economic well-being and movement toward peace internationally led to feedback that helped Vice President George Bush succeed President Reagan. Among those who thought the future economy would get better, Bush won 61 percent of the vote; Bush won the votes of 58 percent who believed the economy would remain the same.

Another example of feedback affecting general political orientation is the case of postwar Japan, which underwent one of the most successful land-reform programs in this century. The American occupation required the Japanese Diet (legislature) to enact far-reaching land-reform legislation in October 1946. The number of farmers owning all their land increased from 36 percent to 62 percent within three years, and the number of farmers owning less than half their land dropped from 17 to 7 percent. The new agrarian policy and the feedback related to these reforms were accomplished. The mass of peasants were no longer dominated by a few landlords. Radical agrarian movements now found little support among the new peasant-owners. Political attitudes and input were greatly influenced. The peasants became interested mainly in conserving their new gains. The new peasant-owners "became the chief support of the conservative political parties."[7]

Communications and information are also part of the feedback loop. The presumption is that, with more information, governments are more effective. Feedback through elections, political polls, newspapers, interest groups, and the like provides information about the impact of outputs. Nevertheless, in this information-explosion era we live in, we often do not have sufficient information and are unable to utilize fully what we potentially have access to. Even in an open system with a wide range of competing inputs the amount of information moving through the feedback loop often is inadequate or cannot be retrieved at the moment it is required. Former Secretary of State Henry Kissinger, who achieved success as a government decision maker and as an eminent political scientist at Harvard University, spoke on the difficulties confronting political leaders as they must make complex and rapid choices. Kissinger says that under these pressures, which are common for political leaders, there is little time for reflection. Officials are so hard

---

[7]Franz H. Michael and George E. Taylor, *The Far East in the Modern World* (New York: Henry Holt, 1956), p. 546.

pressed that most of them "leave office with the perceptions and insight with which they entered."[8]

We are suggesting that even when all parts of the political system appear to be functioning adequately, the system always will be less than "perfect." Even in a democratic political environment with considerable subsystem (interest groups, parties, individual freedom) autonomy—resulting in a broad flow of claims and information feedback—policies and choices are subject to the "human factor." Anthony Downs, in his analysis of the civil servant as a decision maker, discusses several inevitable limitations to decision making.

1. Each decision maker can devote only a limited amount of time to decision making.
2. Each decision maker can mentally weigh and consider only a limited amount of information at one time.
3. The functions of most officials require them to become involved in more activities than they can consider simultaneously; hence, they must normally focus their attention on only part of their major concerns.
4. The amount of information initially available to every decision maker about each problem is only a small fraction of all the information potentially available on the subject.
5. Additional information bearing on any particular problem can usually be procured, but the costs of procurement and utilization may rise rapidly as the amount of data increases.
6. Important aspects of many problems involve information that cannot be procured at all, especially concerning future events; hence, many decisions must be made in the face of some ineradicable uncertainty.[9]

We believe an understanding of the principal characteristics of the political system enables the student to understand better the vast amounts of often-unrelated political information available every day. It allows the student to organize much of the information into understandable categories (what events involve demands, supports, conversion). Systems analysis alerts us to the fact that while everything may relate to everything ultimately, during a given period of time some things relate more than others. For example, we now are aware that we live in an age of scarce natural resources. Economic stagnation rather than growth could characterize the United States, Western Europe, and in fact much of the world for several years. This scarcity has led suddenly to important political inputs. Individuals and groups are demanding lower gasoline and fuel oil prices. Groups and rallies are organized to oppose nuclear power plants as a substitute for oil in favor of solar or water power. Others argue that we should limit the number of cars and engine size because we are consuming so much gasoline and pollution continues.

A declining natural resource—oil—led to all varieties of claims on governments

---

[8]Review of Henry Kissinger's *White House Years* by Daniel Southerland, in *Christian Science Monitor* (November 2, 1979), p. 15.

[9]Anthony Downs, *Inside Bureaucracy* (Boston: Little, Brown, 1967), p. 75.

to deal with this new problem. Various governments have adopted different policies. A knowledge of what we mean by the term "political system" should help us in identifying important issues and the most important groups or individuals involved in the political system or arena during a given period of time. Beyond this, there are limitations.

Criticisms of the Systems Approach

Not all political scientists agree with the systems approach to the study of government and politics. Some of the major criticisms are the following.

1. It is difficult to test the whole systems model because it is too mechanical and theoretical. It is easier to study parts or subsystems that are performing important functions, such as political parties, interest groups, or the bureaucracy. The components of a political system are distinct and different from each other and easier to analyze. Too much theory provides no answers.

2. Adjustments between parts and/or processes may not be what is intended. It often is difficult to predict response or determine with any degree of accuracy what a change in one part of the system (higher literacy, greater freedom of speech, lowered voting age) may have on another (increased political support, growing popular opposition, the creation of revolutionary parties). Moreover, government responses to a problem often fail to achieve what is intended.

   For example, the 1960s "war on poverty" in the United States was intended to involve the poor in planning and carrying out the program in their neighborhoods. Elections were held in poor neighborhoods to choose representatives to local Community Action Programs. Turnout was dismal, ranging between 1 and 5 percent of those eligible. Individuals elected often helped only their friends and their handful of political supporters. Within a few years there were numerous indictments of antipoverty workers for forgery, kickbacks, and embezzlement.[10]

3. Some critics argue that systems analysis is biased toward the status quo and is sympathetic only toward limited change. We cannot assume all parts are working toward survival (for example, a revolutionary party), nor have any measures been constructed to determine when a system is being adequately maintained or being exposed to too much stress and is about to collapse.

4. Systems theory frequently fails to guide us to anticipated results in specific cases. President Woodrow Wilson campaigned in 1916 to keep the United States out of World War I. President Lyndon Johnson campaigned in 1964 as the Vietnam peace candidate and implied Barry Goldwater, his opponent, was a dangerous war hawk. In both cases the presidential vote, or input, was for peace, not more war; in both cases the self-identified peace

---

[10]George E. Berkley, *The Craft of Public Administration* (Boston: Allyn & Bacon, 1975), p. 305.

candidate was elected, but more war was the result. Even in a democracy, popular input may lead to an opposite result. Systems theory provides scant information as to why at a particular moment in history, a lifelong Communist such as Soviet leader Mikhail Gorbachev calls for radical reform of the political system and the economic system as he did at the June 1988 Soviet Party Conference. Many of the key decisions and policies occur within government and systems theory often minimizes the predominant role of government.

CONCEPTS AND STRUCTURES

The second part of this chapter deals with basic concepts and structures. You are already aware of the terms discussed next. We believe, though, you should have precise definitions and explanations. This will make it easier to study politics, organize your information effectively, and have shared understanding with your classmates as you study political science. These terms are lighthouses that should serve as a guide and illuminate the material you are reading and discussing.

Political Analysis

The business of political scientists is **political analysis.** Most adults are aware of and discuss some political happenings. The political scientist, however, brings systematic training to bear on the study of politics. At its simplest, analysis is work undertaken by a trained person that requires studying a problem, decision, policy, or situation by organizing the data into categories or elements and then relating these to one another. Basic to the analytical process is *selective perception*—choosing the elements or variables that are of primary significance as opposed to those of secondary importance or even irrelevant to the study. Analysis should lead to generalization, explanation, and the offering of hypotheses for further study. Scientific analysis seeks to relate two or more political phenomena (type of political leadership, for example, and effectiveness of government decisions) with one another.

Analysis requires training and a basic knowledge of the subject matter. The determination of crucial variables and identification of nonobvious patterns, such as channels of recruitment to political leadership, the policy role of the bureaucracy, and cultural fragmentation, are analyzed most effectively by individuals who have spent a good deal of time studying these problems. Expectations and insights based on prior study and research are fundamental to sophisticated political analysis. Extensive study is required before a political scientist can become very knowledgeable about Japan, the Soviet Union, or Germany, for example. One objective of this book is to help the student acquire basic political science principles and data for effective political analysis in order to better understand the political world he or she lives in.

Robert Merton's analysis of American political machines in the late nineteenth and early twentieth centuries is quoted as an excellent example of political analysis. Merton pointed out the "human" side of the political machine, which saw its roots in the local neighborhood, where residents were principally concerned with personal problems and needs. The machine won its elections in the precincts through elaborate networks of personal ties and obligations.

> The precinct captain is forever a friend in need. In our prevailingly impersonal society, the machine, through its local agents, fulfills the important social function of humanizing and personalizing all manner of assistance to those in need. Food baskets and jobs, legal and extra-legal advice, setting to right minor scrapes with the law, helping the bright poor boy to a political scholarship in a local college, looking after the bereaved—the whole range of crises when a feller needs a friend, and above all, a friend who knows the score and who can do something about it—all of these find the ever-helpful precinct captain available in the pinch.[11]

Political machines were corrupt. They often used public money to benefit the leaders and their friends. But they also helped new migrants to the big cities to adjust to the problems of urbanization and industrialization. The machines helped these immigrants, some of whom could not speak English, to survive in an alien environment. Merton's analysis shows how political machines helped to integrate people into society through welfare services and similar programs aimed at individual adjustment. These were latent functions, or functions not originally intended by political machines, which were created to win elections. His excellent political analysis goes on to suggest that in our study of organizations we should be alert to the importance of latent functions in a social or political system.

Power and influence, discussed next, are related to most political functions.

Power and Influence

We can say that **power** permeates politics. Robert Dahl says all political systems involve "control, influence, power, or authority."[12] We are not so much concerned with power, rule, and authority as they may affect family relationships, the selection of a church official, a business reorganization, or the selection of a college president, except if some of these activities influence the public political system. We restrict politics in this text to the political system. We do not use it in the more popular sense, which refers to any situation (such as the election of a student body or club president or a new chair of the board in Corporation X) that involves **influence**, power, authority, and rules or regulations.

Power, some say is what politics is all about. Harold Lasswell's often-quoted analysis of politics is entitled *Politics—Who Gets What, When, How.*[13] The "who" in the title refers to who has power or who has access to those holding

---

[11]Robert Merton, *Social Theory and Social Structure*, 3rd ed. (Glencoe, Ill.: The Free Press, 1968), pp. 127–129, passim.

[12]Robert A. Dahl, *Modern Political Analysis*, 4th ed. (Englewood Cliffs, N.J.: Prentice-Hall, 1984), pp. 9 and 10.

[13]Harold Lasswell, *Politics—Who Gets What, When, How* (New York: McGraw-Hill, 1936).

power. Those with power are most able to control the allocation in society of all resources for which there is competition.

We define power in the following way: One person or group exercises power over another when it is intentional and done in such a way as to affect in a predictable way the action(s) of others. Power is the ability to get people, groups, or even another country to act in a certain way or to refrain from acting. Three aspects are involved: relationship, intention, and predictability. Power often involves penalties or rewards, but the instruments of power also can be rational persuasion or emotional appeals.

The difference between influence and power is predictability. Power suggests that the intended outcome will occur. Thus, the penalties and rewards are considerably more severe or greater in the hands of the person or group exercising power. A teacher can influence a student to study. Frequently, the penalty or reward, as the case may be, is the grade. For some students the grade is an important influence; for a few it is relatively insignificant because it is regarded as having only short-run consequences. In terms of grading, teachers generally have influence, not power.

The *power base* is composed of a few or many assets. The power base requires some but not all of the following: wealth, social status, control of force (military/ police), office, skills (legal, managerial, technical), personal magnetism, and friendships and other forms of extended personal relationships (family, ethnic group, religion). A person exercising power has one and usually more of the preceding. A public official has not only the office (legislator, judge, mayor) but also several other assets that enable him or her to achieve office. In the case of most democracies, a typically successful candidate will possess wealth, social status, education (legal training, for example), as well as some measure of personal magnetism. The following description of President Franklin Roosevelt indicates the importance of personality.

> His flashing smile, his cigarette holder set at a jaunty angle, his ready humor and booming laugh were the trademarks of his self-possession against the pressures of crisis. A brief exposure to Roosevelt was enough to repair the panicky, quiet the agitated, and inspirit the downhearted.[14]

Power is relational and reciprocal. It is affected both by the exerciser and the recipient. A country with adequate energy reserves is not nearly as dependent on the goodwill of the petroleum-producing countries as a nation that must import 90 percent of the energy resources it consumes. A poor person may be more responsive to the demands of a rich person than a rich person to another rich one. A person may be willing to endure severe penalties for a cause to which he or she is committed. Joan of Arc was not swayed by violence, even when she was under sentence of death and eventually executed.

Power-motivated change (PMC) refers to the efforts the exerciser must expend if power is to be exercised. When President Lyndon Johnson sent several hundred

---

[14]Louis W. Koenig, *The Chief Executive* (New York: Harcourt Brace, & World, 1964), p. 373.

troops to the Dominican Republic in 1965 to prevent what he said was a possible Communist takeover, relatively little effort was expended by the United States. Compare the Dominican case with American involvement in Vietnam. The American objective was to prevent insurgents, supported by North Vietnam, from winning control of South Vietnam. Beyond that, one can only debate the extent to which the United States desired to influence the policies and choice of political leaders of the Republic of Vietnam. American interests in Vietnam extended back to President Truman's second administration (1948–1952).

Many PMCs occurred as the United States sought to influence developments in Vietnam. The PMCs that occurred would not have taken place if we were not attempting to exercise power or influence in this ravaged Southeast Asian country. Examples in the Vietnam case are higher taxes, an expanded military draft, larger defense budgets, increased military and civilian aid to the Republic of Vietnam, and troop dispositions—at one point more than 500,000 U.S. military personnel were assigned to Vietnam. Eventually, these efforts became so burdensome and unpopular that the U.S. government reduced its efforts to exercise power or influence and agreed to a truce agreement in Vietnam in January 1973. The ultimate result was a Communist takeover in South Vietnam during the spring of 1975.

Pluralism and Elitism

There are various ways to analyze how power and influence are dispersed in a political system. Pluralism in some form has existed for two centuries, even though the term became common in political science only during the past 30 years. Pluralism assumes a fragmentation or division of power and influence. According to this theory, it must be present if a democratic society is to exist. Pluralist systems have no homogeneous, ruling elite class. Pluralists believe that political research since World War II confirms pluralism is how democracy actually works in the real world.

Politics is a constant struggle for advantage. Competing groups autonomous of government control keep any one group from becoming all-powerful. Majorities at any moment are temporary coalitions of interests that agree on the issue at hand. There is no permanent, cohesive majority.

Pluralism is extensive participation in the political process through competing and autonomous groups and hence competing viewpoints. Pluralism recognizes that many, though not all, important political decisions are influenced most effectively by organized groups (interest groups) concerned with the political question at hand. Pluralism requires that there be various competing, autonomous groups that are not government sponsored or manipulated. Most of all, the right to organize means freedom to oppose both individuals and policies and to support individuals seeking to replace incumbent office holders. The greatest number of groups and the greatest freedom they possess are found in pluralistic societies.

The right to participate and organize free of government control means there are innumerable organized groups in pluralist systems: churches, trade unions, cultural and sports organizations, neighborhood groups, business groups, and so on. Many of these groups regularly seek to influence government, others can be mobilized when their interests seem to be threatened either by government or other interest groups.

The individual is not overlooked, but an important part of one's political participation is as a group member who joins a group and behaves as he or she does because of group identifications. Groups can effectively organize and give expression to political demands, represent individual and often public interests, check other groups, check concentration of power, and often check or modify government policy. A pluralist government frequently is responding and adjusting to myriad group interests representing a broad range of opinions. Pluralism evolved as society became complex and technical, government became more active, and large bureaucratic organizations (industries, trade unions, etc.) came to dominate individual lives. Groups protect individual interests and are one of the most effective means by which individuals can express themselves and have access to important decisions. Groups do not discourage individual action but, among other things, help to protect individualism and serve individual needs. Bargaining, compromise, a widely shared consensus about the political rules of the game, and generally a superficial feeling of satisfaction with the political system characterize pluralism.

Pluralism presumes that resources are widely shared and that no segment of society is angrily and constantly alienated. A civic political culture and economic well-being reinforces pluralism. Robert A. Dahl, a dominant figure in political science, has studied political conflict and cohesion in a wide range of countries. He concludes

> Among the countries of the world, the frequency of competitive political systems and polyarchies [popular governments] is higher, the greater the Gross National Product and other variables associated with per capita GNP.[15]

Pluralism does not assume everyone is equal in terms of political knowledge, access, and influence. These are distributed unevenly among citizens. In an age of specialization where politics is at the margin of most people's interest in a pluralist system, some individuals have more clout than others. Specialization means in a sense there are many specialized elites linking society together. Not everyone is a lawyer, machinist, artist, neurosurgeon, TV star, teacher, farmer, or government official or has considerable influence on government decisions. Specialized positions in a complex society mean in effect there are many clusters of elites. Pluralism accepts specialization, but is committed to competing elites.

Elitism presumes that a few people control most of the economic, social, and political resources in society and use these resources to benefit themselves. Some, especially the rulers, believe the few are ruling for the benefit of most of the population. This ruling elite is also called an **oligarchy**—rule by the few for the benefit of the few. These are the top influentials, the movers and shakers who determine public policy and reap most of the benefits. Pure elitism is a pyramid, with a small elite at the top making all decisions and the subjects or masses below. A single ruling elite governing for their own benefit have characterized most

---

[15]Robert A. Dahl, *Modern Political Systems*, p. 84.

political systems throughout history. Twentieth-century variations include fascism, nazism, and communism, as well as innumerable dictators. Modern elitism, in this era of mass mobilization, has substituted rule by the few for the benefit of the few with rule by the few in the name of and supposedly for the benefit of the masses. The modern version still exploits and abuses; however, it seeks to justify its rule.

Historically, agricultural societies have been especially subjected to ruling elites, often made up of clusters of religious leaders, landed nobility, the educated, and warrior kings. Even today countries that are predominantly agricultural promote cumulative inequalities, especially in the absence of land reform or family-type farms. The principal or only source of wealth is the land and production thereof. Those who monopolize the large estates control the single source of wealth and are the only ones to have access to education and other acquired skills such as administrative, military, and political. These elites are a closed group. They alone determine who may become a member: through family inheritance, issuing titles of nobility, awarding a lucrative government contract, admission to an elite military school, or a scholarship to a university education. Advanced industrialized societies also have experienced ruling elites, as Russia after 1917, Czechoslovakia (1948–1989), Fascist Italy, Nazi Germany, and Imperial Japan.

Successful revolutionary elites quickly become ruling elites and use the government to create or assign rewards to themselves and exploit the masses. A former high-ranking Communist party leader in Yugoslavia, who spent many years in prison for his liberal views, described traditional Communist leaders as a new ruling class. Recently, he explained the monopolistic features of communism as it existed in eastern Europe until the late 1980s:

> The essence of any Communist system is the monopolistic rule of society by the Communist Party. Communism is about the possession of power. It is, moreover, about the possession of totalitarian power. Communism looks upon itself as fully entitled by the design of history to change and to control *not only* man's allegiance and his behavior as a political being, but also his readings, his tastes, his leisure time and, indeed, the whole of his private universe.[16]

A ruling elite assumes a monolithic ruling class where factions either yield or win, and the loser may be eliminated in more authoritarian systems. The ruling elite's power is comprehensive, dominating the economic as well as the political system and monopolizing all key social positions. Pure elitism does not involve competing elites, publicly struggling with each other for popular support.

Today, the debate between pluralism and elitism centers around the allegation that most pluralistic systems or democracies are actually variations of elitism. Elitists argue that small group of political activists run most of the groups as oligarchies. The group's interests often yield to what is advantageous to a leadership who propagandizes and hoodwinks the members. A handful of people still call the tune in so-called democratic countries, even though they may not be readily

---

[16]Milovan Djilas and George Urban in conversation, "Djilas on Gorbachev," *Encounter* (September–October 1988), pp. 3–4.

identifiable to the general public. Political, military, economic, and media monopolies are intertwined. The average citizen does not even know an overlapping but monopolistic elite exists.

A writer who forcefully articulated this viewpoint was the Harvard sociologist, C. Wright Mills, whose most famous book dealt with the U.S. political system and was entitled *The Power Elite.* Mills concluded that there was a single American elite from the corporations, the military, and the political world who dominate all important decisions made in the United States. The power elite cooperates among themselves, they recognize they are a ruling elite, they are self-serving, and political competition is over minor issues that do not threaten in-group cohesiveness. Most of society's rewards go to a few on top of the pyramid. Mills described the structure of the power elite:

> They rule the big corporations. They run the machinery of the state and claim its prerogatives. They direct the military establishment. They occupy the strategic command posts of the social structure, in which are now centered the effective means of the power and the wealth and the celebrity which they enjoy. . . .
>
> To be celebrated, to be wealthy, to have power, requires access to major institutions, for the institutional positions men occupy determines in large part their chances to have and to hold valued experience.[17]

We conclude that many political systems are or have been governed by a ruling elite. Even in the United States at the state and more commonly at the local level, there may be only slight political competition. A relatively few influential people in these instances may make most of the decisions whether it involves a new sports stadium, higher or lower public educational funding, or whether to discourage a new union industry that would push up prevailing wage rates and pluralize influence.

Political as well as economic and social competition does exist in the 40 to 45 democracies or pluralist political systems in today's world. We do not believe these are closet, elitist systems posing as pluralists. There is no pure pluralism, as there has been elitism over the centuries, but there are fairly close approximations— Western Europe, Australia, New Zealand, the United States, Costa Rica, Venezuela, and, in many ways, even contemporary Japan, to name a few. A relatively small number of people are finally involved in political decisions; but this represents more functional specialization discussed earlier than a monolithic ruling elite. The differences, for example, between the British Labour and Conservative parties are significant on topics such as nuclear weapons and nuclear disarmament. Open discussion and competitive election are crucial to political pluralism, and they are real in the 35 to 45 democratic countries. The degree to which pluralism is present in democracies can only be determined through country-by-country studies, but it exists.

Another way to look at power is the geographic distribution of power among levels of government, which is discussed next.

---

[17] C. Wright Mills, *The Power Elite* (New York: Oxford University Press, 1959), pp. 3–4 and 10–11.

Geographic Distribution of Power

Geographic distribution of powers is an important way to classify government depending on which powers a particular level of government (national or state) has. Is the power concentrated in the center at the national capital (unitary), or does the national government have some power with some powers constitutionally distributed to lower levels of government such as states and provinces (federal), or is the power concentrated in the state capitals (confederal)? The distinctions between these three types of government is not always sharp and these types of government overlap in practice. Nevertheless, these three types are distinguishable, and it is useful to know the principal characteristics of each.

Unitary government characterizes over 140 of the approximately 170 countries in the world today. All the power that the government possesses is in the central or national government. All dictatorships are unitary in practice, but not all unitary governments are dictatorships. For example, both France and Great Britain have unitary governments, but both are democracies. Great Britain has a strong local government tradition that was administratively consolidated in the late nineteenth century. City, town, and the more rural subdivisions of British counties, the districts and parishes, having taxing power and have elected governing councils. Local government powers and rights in a unitary country are delegated by the national government and can be taken back or changed simply by changing the laws affecting local government. In the British case, Parliament would pass a new law.

Federal governments divide power between the national government and the constituent parts—states in the United States, India, and Malaysia, provinces in Canada, cantons in Switzerland, and Länder in Germany. Altogether, approximately 20 nation-states have a federal type of government. Without exception, a constitution distributes power among the two levels of government. Which level has what powers can only be changed legally by amending the constitution, a much more complicated procedure in a country than enacting a new law. In the United States, the Constitution assigns powers or responsibilities to the national government (commonly called the *federal government*) and reserves to the states those powers not given to the federal government nor reserved to the people. The Canadian case is the reverse. The provinces have enumerated powers and the residual powers go to the national government. Under federalism, the two levels of government are supposed to be legally supreme within their respective spheres of activity. Formally speaking, the Soviet Union is a federal system, including 15 union republics. These union republics on paper have powers greater than the 50 American states, but actually these republics, until 1989, had little or no power.

One advantage of federalism is that it makes possible the building of a united country when there are important regional differences. These differences may be historic in origin, economic (rural versus industrial), or ethnic as when minorities are concentrated in certain areas such as several states in India or the French-speaking Canadians in Quebec. Local autonomy in certain policy areas may avoid unnecessary conflict with the central government and allow better response to local needs. In Germany, for example, where there are substantial historical differences, the Länder have their broadest powers in education, religion, and cultural life. Federalism also allows experimentation. If a policy is tried and found to be successful by one local government, it may be adopted by several others. If a policy fails, then the negative consequences are limited to one local government area. Federalism may also nurture democracy. It was adopted in the United States in part to disperse power and to prevent its concentration in the central government. The United States was the first modern political system to adopt federalism in 1789, with the establishment of the Constitution.

Confederations are the most decentralized of these three types of government and are the least common. Power in confederations is dispersed and resides in the regional or constituent governments. Whatever authority the central government has is delegated to it by the regional units. Under the Articles of Confederation and Perpetual Union Between the States (1781–1789) the United States was a Confederation. The articles required 9 of 13 votes (one vote per state) to pass legislation and unanimous consent, all 13 states, to amend the articles. Because the central government was unable to act on important national economic issues, the articles were replaced by the federal Constitution. Generally in a confederation individual units have the right to secede. The European Economic Community (EEC) in some ways resembles a Confederation. The final decision-making body is the Council of Ministers and each of the 12 member countries has a number of votes according to size. For example, France, Germany, Italy, and the United Kingdom have ten votes each while Greece has five and Ireland three votes. Where common policies are required of all countries, a qualified majority of votes is necessary. The qualified majority is 54 of a total 76 votes; although no country can veto, 22 votes is a blocking minority. Any member state can of course withdraw from the EEC. The United Nations is sometimes referred to as a confederation, although there is not a government, as defined above, in this organization. The United Nations is more a voluntary association of independent governments.

Another aspect of power and influence is **authority,** which in turn is related to **legitimacy.**

Authority and Legitimacy

Authority is one type of power. Authority is power that people regard as generally rightful or legitimate. This does not mean that one agrees in every instance with the decision by the person in authority. There is, though, a general belief in the rightfulness or appropriateness of the authority. The greater the authority of the person or group exercising power, the less need there will be to use force.

Legitimacy is the principle upon which authority rests in a political system. Legitimacy has three dimensions:

1. Procedural norms should be used in acquiring power. In democracies such procedures most commonly are competitive elections in which all adult persons may vote. "Legitimacy" is a relative term. What is legitimate in one political system may not be regarded as legitimate in another. In some societies rule by a council of elders (gerontocracy) has been considered appropriate. Age, experience, and wisdom are considered interdependent traits, and age is the criterion for membership on the council. For many centuries blood descent (as in a king or emperor) was regarded as the procedure for qualifying for office and power. Political systems with a monarch as the head of state actually exercising power (as opposed to a constitutional monarchy in which the king or queen is a figurehead) were based not on election or age but on the fortuitous circumstances of birth. Age or blood descent obviously are not regarded as legitimate in democratic political systems, but they were legitimate in many other countries.

2. Generally accepted procedures should be followed in exercising power. In constitutional systems, where a constitution and laws restrain government officials, even those at the highest level of power and discretion must follow the legal procedures expected of the office. This is contrary to some political systems where there are relatively few limitations on a ruler. For most of recorded history, it was regarded as an act of treason for subjects to remove even the most cruel and incompetent ruler.

Only during the last few centuries have we made progress toward a commitment to limited or constitutional government. This means that in some political systems the rulers and other government officials will lose legitimacy, as happened to President Nixon as a result of Watergate, if they flagrantly violate the basic procedural norms in exercising their political office.

3. Legitimacy also involves the notion that government and the political system should function so that government generally performs the tasks citizens expect of it. Popular expectations of the functions, if not obligations, of government have changed measurably during the last 200 years. During the nineteenth century the most common political system was the "night watchman state." Governments were expected to maintain domestic security; protect the borders; and construct and maintain communication and transportation networks. For example, immediately after the American colonies won their independence, two of the most important cabinet departments were the State Department and the Post Office Department. Expectations about government responsibilities have evolved worldwide in the last 100 years. People now turn to government to solve inflation, unemployment, land reform, energy shortages, retirement benefits, protection of the environment, zoning, and so on. A recent concern is fear of the greenhouse effect. Governments are asked to correct the rapid warming up of the earth because too much carbon dioxide (CO_2) is spilled into the atmosphere by burning fossil fuels. The increased CO_2 traps much of the heat radiating from the earth, creating a "greenhouse." To avoid crises predicted by such headlines as "Warming Spells Disaster," governments are challenged to move quickly against pollution in order to reduce CO_2. Popular expectations of government outputs vary among political systems, but there is a general worldwide consensus that governments must do more.

Where governments do not provide the minimal outputs the prevailing values deem necessary, the government and the rules of the game may be completely changed. Restructuring and reform are words too limited to describe events in Eastern Europe in 1989 and 1990. Czechoslovakia, the former East Germany, Hungary, and Poland engaged in replacing almost in toto bankrupt political and economic systems. Bulgaria and Romania are now moving in this direction (see Figure 2.2). There is an inexorable movement toward political pluralism as Com-

Figure 2.2 Pre-1989 Europe.

munist parties change names just to survive as viable political entities—realistic enough not to hope to maintain a monopoly on power, but idealistic enough to want to participate in a coalition government. Decades of political repression and economic mismanagement eroded the legitimacy of East European Communist political systems. Governments did not deliver the services and goods expected as the revolution of rising expectations swept through Eastern Europe as it also has many **Third World** countries (discussed in Chapter 11).

A **postindustrial society** (Western Europe, the United States, Canada, Japan, Australia, and New Zealand) seems to be what most East European and Third World countries aspire to—at least in terms of material standards of living. Many citizens in these societies also are struggling for some form of democracy, and democracy is characteristic of all postindustrial societies thus far. Therefore, because postindustrial societies are synonymous to date with political pluralism, we will discuss briefly some features of this postindustrial phenomenon.

Postindustrial Society

Once a country passes the point where under 50 percent of its labor force is in agriculture, it generally is moving toward an industrial society where an increasing percentage of the work force is engaged in the manufacturing sector. Since World War II most countries of the industrial world (United States, Canada, Western Europe, and Japan) have been moving into what is called postindustrial society. These societies also constitute nearly all of the 40 to 45 democratic political systems in the world today. Postindustrial societies are the wealthiest and most democratic political systems of the world.

Certain elements appear to stand out. The service sector (including transportation, communication, insurance, retail, trade, education, health care, and public administration) increasingly dominates in contrast to agriculture and industry. In 1970, service occupations in the United States, for example, employed 62 percent of the labor force.[18] Only 20 percent of the labor force works in manufacturing industries in 1985 compared to 31 percent in 1950.[19]

The pace of declining jobs in the industrial sector varies, but some figures are striking, particularly in the United States. During the month of January 1990, the U.S. Bureau of Labor Statistics reported 112,000 manufacturing jobs lost, whereas service jobs grew by 282,000 positions.[20] We note that some service occupations pay well such as physician, lawyer, or successful realtor, but a majority of these jobs pay moderately to poorly such as nurse's aid, fast-food worker, custodian, retail clerk, secretary, and so forth. This could create a growing income inequity in a political system and might threaten political pluralism.

---

[18]Samuel P. Huntington, ''Postindustrial Politics: How Benign Will It Be?'' *Comparative Politics*, 6:2 (1974), p. 171.

[19]Federal Reserve Bank of San Francisco Research Department, *FRBSF Weekly Letter* (January 16, 1987), p. 3. Because of increasing productivity, the share of manufacturing in national output remained at approximately 22 percent between 1950 and 1985.

[20]*Christian Science Monitor* (February 7, 1990), p. 1.

When industrial society replaced agricultural society in what are now demo-cratic political systems between 1830 and 1930, market demand and consumer goods were core elements of economic growth. To meet demands for cheap, availa-ble goods, large industrial organizations emerged. Competition among the numer-ous small companies in the open market was replaced by control through a small number of corporations. For example, in the 1870s, 35 to 40 percent of the labor force was self-employed, whereas by the 1970s, between 93 and 94 percent of the work force worked for others, not themselves.[21] There emerged a complex interde-pendence between the government (such as military procurement), scientific/educational institutionals (often in terms of grants for research and development), and industrial organizations. The interaction of these various institutions, often highly technical and complex, meant that in many instances, power, influence, and decision making became even less visible and understandable to the average citizen, though the impact on the public may even be greater. Interdependence is not just limited to what happens within a political system. A country's very prosperity may depend on how well its industry sells products abroad. The chair of the U.S. International Trade Commission warned that for every $1 billion in America's trade deficit 25,000 jobs are lost because when imports increase some American jobs are lost and others never created.[22] The magnitude of the American problem is shown by the fact that our trade deficit for several years has been above $100 billion annually.

Politically, postindustrial society suggests certain emerging trends, not all of them clear, and some contradictory. We will list a few examples.

1. Political alienation could become more common. Public participation in highly complex decisions far removed from the average citizen is difficult to ensure. Because experts with years of training have difficulty resolving problems, the conflicts and various proposed solutions seem far beyond the average citizen, who does not have the time or knowledge to understand the causes of problems such as the money supply and its effect on inflation.

2. The influence of political parties and even mass-participation interest groups may decline as individuals are less involved in these organizations. Those that do exert influence may be dominated increasingly by the lead-ers and career bureaucrats in the organization. The latest television com-munication techniques can be utilized by magnetic personalities with heavy financial backing appealing directly to individuals. A growing reli-ance on television for political information can lead to an impressionistic and superficial political involvement and further erosion of factual knowl-edge and the significance of choices presented.

3. Frustration and confusion also may be encouraged by the communications media (radio, newspapers, television). As one political journalist con-cluded, "The national media have put themselves into the role of perma-

---

[21]John B. Gurley, *Challenges to Communism* (San Francisco: W. H. Freeman and Company, 1982), p. 82.

[22]*Today*, 6:2 (September 16, 1983), p. 6. The magnitude of the American problem is shown by the fact that our 1988 trade deficit was $120 billion.

nent critical opposition to any government which does not instantly clean up the unfinished business of our time." Consequently, "no government will satisfy them."[23] It is in the nature of the mass media to have an interest in exposing, criticizing, and highlighting disagreement and inaction in government. An editor of the *Washington Post* observed, "we of the media like conflict, tension, the suspense of contest. We like these things because they make good copy. Our banner might well carry the motto 'Let's You and Him Fight.' "[24]

4. Postindustrial society has not produced identical results in every country. From 1970 to 1986 overall employment in the United States grew 36 percent, but declined nearly 1 percent in the Common Market countries. Interdependence means competition, and this may lead to economic problems for the United States and Canada as well as Europe.

   In the United States, for example, the Department of Commerce reported in 1985 that 70 percent of U.S. industry faced foreign competition compared to 30 percent of U.S. industry in 1969.[25] Others warn that today more jobs are lower-paying jobs and democracies face a falling standard of living, particularly as populations age and require more health care and pensions. The chair of the Houston-based Productivity Center warned

   > Household income [in the United States] is now 8 percent less than in 1973 in real dollars. Real compensation per hour is equal to that of 1969. And real weekly earnings are *less* than they were in 1962.[26]

Europeans face variations of the same problems that Americans face. Significant, highly technical economic shortfalls confront most postindustrial societies, except Japan, as we move into the last decade of the twentieth century. Slower economic growth and an eventual plateauing of expectations can shift the types of inputs and limit government outputs (see Box 2.2). Often these issues are sufficiently complex and uninteresting to be pushed aside by both voters and politicians.

Political issues not on the horizon ten years ago are beginning to challenge the postindustrial democracies. These societies now must deal not with improving life through growing economic abundance, but a coming age of selective growth that may last for several decades.

Some form of postindustrial society is a goal for many throughout the world. We have seen, though, it has its shortfalls and major problems.

Conflict and Adjustment

Up to this point we have provided you with a basic overview of the underlying concerns of politics and the academic discipline that studies it—political science.

---

[23]Quoting Theodore H. White in Huntington, *"Postindustrial Politics,"* p. 185.

[24]*Time* (November 19, 1979), p. 116.

[25]Bill Kroger, "Is American Losing the Global Economic Battle?" *Higher Education and National Affairs,* 34:3 (February 25, 1985), p. 1.

[26]Laurent Belsie, "Interview on Productivity," *Christian Science Monitor* (July 3, 1987), p. 5.

Box 2.2   **Postindustrial Slide: A Political Warning**

. . . In "The Reckoning," David Halberstam documents the 30-year decline of the American automobile and related industries, showing how this crisis occurred for the same reasons given for concern in the race to commercialize superconductors. Primarily, industry was—still is—unwilling to invest in developing economical, high-quality products because such investments did not pay off in immediate returns and stock benefits. . . .

The "service" economy, unlike one in which goods are produced for ourselves and the world, provides work for those with higher education and for those with almost no vocational skills at all, reflecting an equally sharp difference in pay scales. Mr. Halberstam points out that the salaries of those in the lower service economy, when adjusted for inflation, "are barely comparable to those of the pre–New Deal period."

. . . Wall Street continues to value the stock of companies based on immediate profits alone, setting the stage for those companies to shun reinvestment in products or plant improvement.

Should a particular company dare to attempt reinvestment, its undervalued stock makes it ripe for a hostile takeover by another company that will bypass such development for short-term paper gains. Furthermore, there are few meaningful tax incentives for industry to make or care about products, rather than paper, and even less tradition for equitable profit-sharing ventures that would involve workers, as well as management, in the long-range fate of the company. . . .

Instead, at Presidential election time, we can continue to focus on the private lives or love lives of candidates, on whether to mandate that teachers lead the Pledge of Allegiance, on an inarticulate and fuzzy nostalgia for traditional "family values," and on all the other issues peripheral to the basic health of this nation. We should, however, be aware that regardless of how often we repeat that "it is morning in America," a faint glow appears not only at dawn, but also at twilight.

Source: Quotes from a Letter to the Editor by Judith Chiti, *New York Times* (October 26, 1988), p. 21. © 1988 by the New York Times Company. Reprinted by permission.

We also have discussed certain basic approaches and have summarized key terms. We believe this is the best way to assist your introduction to political science. We do not believe there is one approach or a single key to understanding politics. There are writers who adopt an exclusive theme. One example is Hans Morgenthau, a distinguished author in the international politics field. Morgenthau believes all people share drives to live, reproduce, and dominate. He expands this assertion by declaring that all political life is a struggle for power.

> Both domestic and international politics are a struggle for power, modified only by different conditions under which this struggle takes place in the domestic and international spheres.[27]

We believe there is no single, underlying principle, such as a struggle for power, that is the basis for understanding politics. We believe that a broader approach will enable a student to understand better the ever-changing political world.

Our final point is implicit in much of what you have read so far. Change, transition, and competition are basic to what we are studying. The history of politics is development, adjustment, or regression. Seldom, if ever, is there a period that can be described as a time of no change.

Change, power, and competition are ever-present in contemporary politics. When we study political activities we inevitably deal with a constant state of flux. Many changes are consistent with the existing political and social institutions: One president is elected and another leaves office; one party replaces another as the majority party in parliament; the social security deduction or the income tax is raised or lowered. Institutions and the political process are not fundamentally altered by these changes.

A second type of change is more substantial and may fundamentally affect the functioning and organization of the political system: A semipresidential type of government replaces a parliament-dominated political system, as occurred in 1958 when the French Fifth Republic replaced the Fourth Republic. A hereditary conservative monarch has his powers removed and in his place a junta of young, radical, military officers makes government decisions, as happened in Ethiopia in 1974. Years of a militarily-imposed rule in El Salvador are now interrupted by insurgency. Atrocities are regularly committed by both the insurgents and death squads supposedly supported by the government. Change may be peaceful or violent, but it always is pervasive. A never-ending objective of political science is to attempt to explain the nature and types of change that are occurring.

Throughout the remainder of this text you should analyze carefully what you consider to be those institutions that encourage the peaceful adjustment of disagreement in the most reasonable and fair manner. We offer no solutions, except to note that political conflict probably will always exist, even with the best of intentions. John Stuart Mill stated it ably:

> As soon as any part of a person's conduct affects prejudicially the interests of others, society has jurisdiction over it, and the question whether the general welfare will or will not be promoted by interfering with it, becomes open to discussion. [It begins to be politically debated.][28]

We believe political science should make it possible for the student to understand better today's world. The student is being trained to perceive selectively and to focus on the key factors in the political system; to organize data; to retrieve

---

[27]Hans J. Morgenthau, *Politics Among Nations*, 5th ed. (New York: Alfred A. Knopf, 1973), pp. 34–35.

[28]John Stuart Mill, "On Liberty," in Marshall Cohen, ed., *The Philosophy of John Stuart Mill* (New York: The Modern Library, 1961), p. 272.

previously learned and relevant information as he or she interprets contemporary political events. Perception, organization, retrieval, and explanation as they relate to the political process are the capabilities you will acquire as you read this book.

SUMMARY

Despite its limitations, systems analysis provides the political scientist with a useful framework for analysis. It is the beginning point for a study of one or more individual political systems or for a study of international politics. It provides a general orientation and reminds us that there are certain basic processes, such as inputs, decision making, conversion, outputs, and feedback, that are performed in all systems. Which parts are important, how they interact, and what functions each performs can be determined only by analyzing specific cases.

The real political world is complicated. One objective of this book is to help you develop skills of political analysis as you study political conflict and adjustment. Certain terms and concepts are important as you develop your analytic skills. These have been discussed in the second part of this chapter.

RECOMMENDED READINGS

Cantori, Louis J., and Andrew H. Ziegler, eds. *Comparative Politics in the Post-Behavioral Era.* Boulder, Colo.: Lynne Rienner Publishers, 1988. This is a collection of essays by leading political scientists. Topics include institutions, public policy, and change. The book should be of interest in many of the discipline's subfields.

Dahl, Robert A. *Democracy and Its Critics.* New Haven, Conn.: Yale University Press, 1989. This capstone work is written by a distinguished political scientist. Dahl discusses the evolution of democracy from ancient Greece to the present. There is insightful analysis of why some countries adopt democracy and others do not. It provides a solid base for empirically analyzing countries moving toward or attempting to move toward democracy.

Easton, David. *A Systems Analysis of Political Life.* New York: John Wiley, 1965. The leading exponent of the systems approach is David Easton. This book is a well-written, comprehensive statement of his theories.

The Europa World Year Book, 2 vols. London: Europa Publications, Ltd., published annually. This is a valuable reference bringing together political, economic, geographic, and social data on most countries. Students also are referred to the six regularly updated regional books for more detailed information: *The Middle East and North Africa; Africa South of the Sahara; The Far East and Australia; South America, Central America, and the Caribbean; Western Europe;* and *The U.S.A. and Canada.*

Friedrich, Carl Joachim. *Man and His Government: An Empirical Theory of Politics.* New York: McGraw-Hill Book Company, Inc., 1963. Here is a well-organized and heuristic effort to review the political experience of mankind. It is full of insights and concepts that make it valuable to students interested in almost any area of political science.

Greenstein, Fred I., and Nelson W. Polsby, eds. *Handbook of Political Science,* 8 vols. Reading, Mass.: Addison-Wesley Publishing Company, 1975. These volumes contain essays and bibliographies on most of the terms and concepts used in this chapter. They are valuable for the evolution of political concepts, generalizations, and theory.

Harrington, Michael. *Socialism: Past and Future.* New York: Arcade, 1989. This is the last work of a leading proponent of democratic socialism. It argues that with appropriate humane policies socialism can occur. There are thought-provoking insights, even if one does not agree with many of the theses.

Huntington, Samuel P. *Political Order in Changing Societies.* New Haven, Conn.: Yale University Press, 1968. This classic study remains relevant to this day. Western and non-Western, historical and contemporary examples appear throughout the book. Theoretical insights, including the significant contributions to orderly change of institutions, are discussed.

Kornhauser, William. *The Politics of Mass Society.* New York: The Free Press, 1968. This is a distinguished study of mass political movement that can threaten democratic political systems. It follows a multidisciplinary approach to past events and is a relevant study of authoritarian societies moving toward pluralism.

Lane, Robert E. *Political Life.* Glencoe, Ill.: The Free Press, 1965. This well-organized and interesting analysis of how people behave politically is delightful to read. It has stood the test of time and is still useful.

Lipset, Seymour Martin. *Revolution and Counterrevolution: Change and Persistence in Social Structures,* rev. ed. Rutgers, N.J.: Transaction Books, 1988. This collection of essays looks at change and persistence in developed and developing countries. It includes excellent theoretical suggestions for further research and carefully considers the impact of historical experiences.

Williamson, Peter J. *Corporatism in Perspective: An Introductory Guide to Corporatist Theory.* London: Sage, 1989. This is a well-organized and readable explanation of corporatism. Corporatism sees societies rather differently than pluralism. What has been essentially a European doctrine becomes relevant to understanding the United States today.

Chapter 3

Political Theories and Ideologies

POLITICAL THEORIES

The study of political theory and political ideology are integral parts of political science. Both are ways of looking at important political phenomena. They are closely related because political theories provide the basis for political ideologies. As noted in Chapter 1, values and value arguments are part of politics and are among the most important features studied by political theorists. Moreover, in reviewing the development of political theory, we are looking at the origin of both political science and many of our basic institutions and values. For this reason, we turn now to political theory and ideology to help provide the foundation for understanding the political phenomena that make up the heart of subsequent chapters.

First, we look briefly at the political theories born in ancient, medieval, and early modern times and then turn our attention to the theories and ideologies of the modern era.

Political theory deals with government and people. It seeks to evaluate, explain, and predict political phenomena. From early times on people have pondered about their relationship to the political system and how to attain good government and a just society. The Western political tradition is the source of much wisdom, and many basic concepts of modern political life had their origin in the Greco-Roman world and in the Middle Ages.

In developing their theories, great political thinkers have attempted to find an answer to some political problem or crisis of their day. An example is Karl Marx, who made the evils of the industrial revolution in the middle of the nineteenth century the basis of his philosophy. In this sense, political theorists are dated, philosophers are dated, but all the great thinkers, in developing answers, have raised issues and come forth with answers that transcend the problems of their day. It is this feature that gives their work a timeless quality.

That political thought influences actual political institutions is unquestionable. The relationship between Karl Marx and the political and economic developments in the Soviet Union is obvious. This is not to suggest that the present-day Soviet Union is a blueprint of Marx's ideas, *for it obviously is not.* There are many developments that Marx did not anticipate, yet it would be hard to think of the Russian Revolution without Karl Marx.

There is also a close relationship between the ideals of John Locke, the English philosopher of the late seventeenth century, and political principles and practices in the United States. Not only is the American Declaration of Independence a restatement of Locke's philosophy, but such concepts and practices as limited government, a written constitution, and a bill of rights are derived from Locke and similar theorists.

In this brief survey of leading Western political philosophers, we should not ask which one is "right," for none has provided a complete answer to all the perennial problems of politics, although some developed a metaphysical system they believed was final. Rather, the question should be what insights these people offer in helping us to understand the great issues of politics.

Ancient and Medieval Background

Political theory begins in ancient Greece with Plato and Aristotle. Plato (427–347 B.C.) was an Athenian aristocrat. He was influenced greatly by his friend and teacher Socrates, whose death, decreed by the Athenian state, led Plato to distrust Athenian democracy, which was at its height in the fourth century B.C. In Athens citizens were entitled to participate directly in the government of the city by voting in the assembly of all citizens or serving on a jury. Selection for office was very democratic. The procedures employed were by lot and rotation in office. Although the Athenians prized their democracy and citizenship highly, there was also a dark side to their political system. Only a minority of the inhabitants of Athens were citizens, and slavery was accepted as natural.

Plato was opposed to democracy for various reasons:

1. The fear that majority rule can become a tyranny exercised by the majority over the minority.
2. Advancement in society is open only to those who are willing to please the majority, thus stifling many a superior mind.
3. Democracy may turn to "mob rule," a change instigated by a few demagogues.

Thus, in his major work, *The Republic,* he developed the blueprint for a nondemocratic ideal state. His Utopia consists of three classes: (1) the Guardians (rulers), (2) the Auxiliaries (soldiers and lower-rank civil servants), and (3) the Workers (farmers, craftspeople, and unskilled workers).

The Guardians govern society in a hierarchical fashion. The ruling Guardians (philosopher-kings) are the absolute leaders. The class structure is not hereditary but is based on the abilities of the members of each generation. Future elites are recruited for training at a very early age. While the ruling Guardians stand above the law, they must be, according to Plato, skilled in the arts of government and be good and wise rulers. Because of the wisdom of the leaders, there is no need for elections, political parties, or popular discussion of political issues. Thus, the citizenry-at-large is not involved in the political process.

To make sure that the ruling Guardians commit all their energies to the process of governing, Plato proposed that they live a communal life, *without* having private lives and families.

The society that Plato proposed is a contended, consensual, and just society, without economic extremes. Each citizen would be able to develop his or her potential in full. On this point there is a commonality of thought between Plato, Jean-Jacques Rousseau, and, especially, Karl Marx.

Plato's outline of the ideal state raises a number of questions to which he does not provide clear answers. Among these are: Will the ruling Guardians be always in agreement on major issues? Will factions develop? Will there be coup d'états? Will material possessions become tempting to the Guardians?

Aristotle (384–322 B.C.) believed, like his mentor Plato, that people are rational, moral beings and that they could attain a good life when living in a good state. Aristotle is referred to often as the first political scientist. His major work, *The*

Politics, is based on a detailed study of 158 governmental systems. Aristotle's ideal, in contrast to Plato's Utopia, is a constitutional society in which law, arising from the collective wisdom of the citizens, rather than Plato's philosopher-kings, is supreme. The constitutional ruler, according to Aristotle, rules by and with the consent of the citizens. Aristotle's preferred type of political society would be a monarchy, followed by an aristocracy, and, in third place, a moderate democracy, which Aristotle calls *polity.* He cautions that these forms can become perverted into a dictatorship, oligarchy, or extreme democracy (mob rule).

While Aristotle states that a monarchy would be the best form of government—as long as a wise and virtuous king can be found—he ponders at some length as to whether this king should be completely subject to the law, too. This is one of the few incongruities in Aristotle's political theory. This aside, however, Aristotle postulates that the prime features of a good society must be constitutional government, buttressed by the sovereignty of law and the equality of the citizens. It is to be a society of political moderation, where divergent views are balanced by the presence of a large middle class whose ideas and virtues would permeate the other classes.

Both Plato and Aristotle laid the basis for a science of politics. Both accepted the civic ideal of a state based on reason and aimed at the good life. Aristotle in particular established a logical method of political inquiry. Plato also accepted the complete equality of the sexes.

Following the death of Aristotle in 322 B.C. and with the advent of world empires in the Western world—for a brief time Alexander's empire and subsequently the Roman Empire—political thought showed a marked change as the independent city-state became obsolete. Now, the dominant school of thought was that of Greek and Roman Stoics. **Stoicism** was a school of thought rather than a philosophy identified with a particular individual. The Stoics equated God with universal reason, which they believed to be imminent in nature and in humanity. Politically, the Stoics emphasized the basic equality of *all* people, regardless of differences in wealth or social position. Gone was any distinction between Greeks and barbarians. Even a slave was a "laborer hired for life." The individual was a citizen not only of the secular state into which he or she was born but of the community of all humanity as well.

The Stoics also introduced the concept of **natural law**, which was to dominate Western political thought through the eighteenth century. Just as God was regarded as the reason governing the universe, so the souls of human beings were part of that reason. Natural law, in the words of the Roman philosopher and politician Cicero, a great popularizer of Stoicism, was "right reason in agreement with nature; it is of universal application, unchanging and everlasting; it summons to duty by its commands, and averts from wrongdoing by its prohibitions."[1] This law was considered the foundation of the state as it existed from eternity, and the state or commonwealth existed to promote ethical purposes or it was nothing.

---

[1]Michael B. Foster, ed., *Plato to Machiavelli: Masters of Political Thought,* vol. 1 (Cambridge, Mass.: The Riverside Press, 1964), p. 188.

Christianity as a body of thought was consistent with Stoicism in stressing the basic equality of all people. It also believed government to be of divine origin and stressed the duty of obedience, but it introduced a dualism unknown to the ancient world. A person is not only a citizen of an earthly kingdom but also, potentially at least, a member of the kingdom of God. Thus, there exists a divided loyalty as illustrated in the Gospels—a loyalty to Caesar and to God.

The idea of divided loyalty was unknown to the Greeks. To Plato and Aristotle the state served a moral purpose, and people could achieve their complete development only through the state. The state was considered before the individual, and the idea of the individual asserting rights against the state was unknown to the citizens of ancient Greece.

The concepts of human equality and of natural law were discussed further during the Middle Ages by St. Augustine (354–430 A.D.) and St. Thomas Aquinas (1224–1274). Though living eight centuries apart, these theorists developed their ideas within a framework that included politics and religion—a system of political theology. Both distinguished between the earthly city and the city of God, with the earthly city—whatever its political system may be—remaining a second best to the city of God. Both cities are part of the divine universe. People, according to St. Augustine and St. Thomas Aquinas, are rational beings with the God-given ability to live together peacefully. The main obligation of the earthly rulers is to establish and to maintain orderly societies in a just manner. St. Thomas Aquinas built on the premises made by St. Augustine and stated clearly that the prosperity and well-being of a community was based inexorably on the preservation of peace and unity. Centuries later the founders of democratic theory continued the discussion of some of the major thoughts advanced by St. Augustine and St. Thomas Aquinas, especially those having to do with the concept of legitimate power, the rationality of humankind, and the role of natural law.[2]

Early Modern Political Theory and the Rise of Individualism

One of the characteristics of the modern age, which began in the sixteenth century, is the rise of **individualism,** which was manifested in all walks of life. In religion, individualism is identified with the Protestant Reformation, which stressed individual salvation made possible by God's grace without the intervention of the Catholic Church. The modern age was associated with the rise of capitalism, which emphasized individual endeavor and financial rewards for those who were successful. Another influence was the Renaissance, which was characterized by a revival of interest in the Greek and Roman classics. The result was a new humanism centering on humanity as the "measure of all things." Fundamentally, the new individualism was a rebellion against the existing restraints of the traditional social order and a movement toward personal autonomy. The two leading political theo-

[2]See Andrew Hacker, *Political Theory: Philosophy, Ideology, Science* (New York: Macmillan, 1961), Chapter 5, for a more detailed discussion of political theology as expounded by St. Augustine and St. Thomas Aquinas.

rists of the early modern age were Niccolò Machiavelli and Thomas Hobbes. Both influenced the growth of individualism, though in contrasting ways.

Machiavelli   Machiavelli (1469–1527), a Florentine, was one of the most important figures of the Renaissance.[3] He introduced a new type of political thought. Before Machiavelli, all political philosophy dealt with the state as a means to the good life. Machiavelli ignored theories about the state as such. He was an individualist in his admiration of the successful but absolute ruler who makes power an end in itself.

The Prince, Machiavelli's chief work, is an accurate description of politics in the Italian city-states of the fifteenth century, a period characterized by low political morality and factional strife among the Italian leaders. According to Machiavelli, the able ruler must make the safety and success of the state superior to all considerations of morality or religion. The latter he accepted as facts of life to be used if they advanced the interests of the state, but to be disregarded if they did not serve the interests of the ruler. Machiavelli believed it better for a prince to be feared rather than loved. To Machiavelli, the success of a ruler's policy was determined by his ability to control *fortuna* and *virtu.* By *fortuna* he meant the uncertainty of history. *Virtu* referred to the ability to show mastery amid the uncertainty of events.

Machiavelli saw himself as an Italian patriot and scientific historian who sought the unification of Italy. Although he had a romantic and idealized vision of the Roman Republic, he believed that the Italians of his era were too corrupt to make a republic practical. Therefore, he advocated the absolute ruler, who, by exercising power politics, would bring about a more orderly society and achieve the unification of Italy.

Thomas Hobbes   Thomas Hobbes (1588–1679), an Englishman, gave considerable stimulus to the new individualism. In his famous work *Leviathan* he developed a social contract theory of government, which began with the autonomous individual rather than the state. According to this approach, the individuals created the state through the social contract. Although the later, more advanced social contract theory, as advocated by John Locke, stressed limited government and the right of revolution, these features were absent in Hobbes's thought. Instead, Hobbes's theory emphasized the dangers of anarchy and the need for a strong government to make life tolerable. Hobbes's philosophy reflected the social and political turmoil of his age characterized by the struggle between Charles I and the Puritan majority in Parliament, the subsequent civil war between the king and his supporters and the Puritans, the execution of Charles I, the rule of Oliver Cromwell, and the royalist restoration.

Hobbes was an individualist in the sense that the starting point of his philoso-

[3]For an excellent discussion of diverse evaluations of Machiavelli, see "Machiavelli: Cynic, Patriot, or Political Scientist," in De Lamar Jensen, ed., *Problems in European Civilization* (Boston: D. C. Heath and Co., 1960).

phy was the state of nature, a presocial state, characterized as a condition in which life was "solitary, poor, nasty, brutish, and short." To make life tolerable, people created an "artificial" community, the state, to which they turned over all power. As the state was the beneficiary of the contract and not a party to it, there was no possibility of asserting rights against the state.

Hobbes was also a materialist who ridiculed the traditional, natural-law philosophy and revealed religion. To him the only law was that made by the sovereign of a state. For example, it was the sovereign who would determine the religion of the state. In every state, according to Hobbes, there was a sovereign in whom ultimate power rested. What liberty there might be in a state existed only at the sufferance of the sovereign, whether the latter was a king or a democratic parliament.

To Hobbes, monarchy was the best government. Despite his preference for a strong monarchy, Hobbes should not be considered an advocate of modern dictatorship as exemplified in twentieth-century Fascist or Communist countries. Hobbes's monarch would preserve order and suppress any movements leading to possible anarchy, but he did not expect the monarch to engage in thought control and purges as contemporary dictators do. The ideal monarch would provide security and presumably a limited area of intellectual freedom for enlightened men like Hobbes.

Hobbes's overemphasis on the dangers of anarchy is in part a product of the age in which he lived. Without doubt, Hobbes was overly pessimistic about the possibilities of limited government, and he overstressed the role of force in maintaining order; yet, today in a period characterized by revolutions, riots, and social unrest, we may find some insights in Hobbes. Even in a democratic country force is the ultimate weapon in maintaining order when the community is threatened by lawlessness.

THE ROOTS, DEVELOPMENT, AND FEATURES OF CONTEMPORARY IDEOLOGIES

As we turn our attention to Hobbes's theoretical successor, John Locke, we find the beginning of a new development, namely, the establishment of roots for an ideology—democracy.

In an earlier publication we defined ideologies as "systematized sets of ideas that describe and promote the economic, political, and social orders and values of particular societies or groups."[4] Ideologies are clusters of political theories. For example, although John Locke laid the basis for liberal (or capitalist)[5] democracy, Jean-Jacques Rousseau, Adam Smith, Jeremy Bentham, John Stuart Mill, and a

---

[4]Thomas J. Bellows, Stanley Erikson, and Herbert R. Winter, *Political Science: Introductory Essays and Readings* (Belmont, Calif.: Duxbury Press, 1971), p. 51.

[5]The labels "liberal democracy" and "capitalist democracy" are used interchangeably by many Western scholars. We shall do likewise.

number of other political theorists have added to the Lockean base and thereby shaped democratic theory as we know it today.

Democracy, in its liberal (or capitalist) form, was the first major modern ideology to arise. It was followed by Marxism-Leninism (the philosophical framework for communism), fascism, and social democracy. Ideologies are utopian, that is, they prescribe what is envisioned as a perfect political order. In no instance will government in practice be able to match its ideological foundation. Some political systems are further removed from their ideological base than others.

Marxism-Leninism (communism) is associated with revolutionary change. In all the countries that were or are under Communist control, the system was brought about by revolution or Communist military intervention. Communist regimes have tried to move their societies ahead rapidly in the economic realm without regard to cost in human lives.

Democracies, social and liberal, are based on the ballot rather than the bullet. Although both types of democracy are concerned with improving their societies politically, economically, and socially, social democratic governments have moved more rapidly to bring about a greater degree of economic and social equity than the liberal democratic (or capitalist) governments.

Like communism, fascism is an antidemocratic movement using the bullet rather than the ballot to bring about change; but, in contrast to the revolutionary nature of communism, fascism is reactionary in the sense that it tries to turn society back to the totalitarian past.

Political scientists place ideologies and political parties on a scale called the "political spectrum." Communism, because of its revolutionary nature, appears at the extreme left, the democratic forces in the middle, and fascism, because of its reactionary nature, on the extreme right. Figure 3.1 shows the spectrum of the following ideologies.

Starting with John Locke, we shall discuss the major contributing theorists within the framework of the respective ideologies. Obviously, no theory or ideology develops in a vacuum. John Locke drew from the ideas of Aristotle, the Stoics, and Thomas Hobbes. Some students may be surprised to find that Karl Marx incorporated some Lockean ideas into his theory (the concept of majority rule, for example). With this introduction in mind, we shall now turn our attention to the founders and the roots of liberal democracy.

Liberal Democracy

The foremost founders of liberal democracy were John Locke (1632–1704), Adam Smith (1723–1790), both Englishmen, and Jean-Jacques Rousseau (1712–1778) a

Communism (revolutionary)	Social democracy (progressive reformist)	Liberal democracy (reformist)	Fascism (reactionary)
Antidemocratic	Democratic		Antidemocratic

Figure 3.1 A general spectrum of the major ideologies.

Frenchman. Their ideas laid the base for Western democracy and its early proto-types in Britain and the United States.

John Locke   The core of Locke's philosophy centers on two primary features that have served as the theoretical underpinning of Anglo-Saxon politics for the past three centuries: (1) government by consent of the citizenry and (2) government by constitution. Government, according to Locke, has an obligation to protect the

John Locke.

natural rights and the properties of people. The preservation of property rights was the primary reason for Locke to propose the Social Contract. According to him "the great and chief end . . . of men's uniting into commonwealths and putting themselves under government is the preservation of their property."[6]

Locke, like Hobbes, assumed that humanity originally lived in a state of nature; however, Locke's primitive state was prepolitical rather than presocial like that of Hobbes. Locke accepted the traditional philosophy of natural law. To this he added the concept of inherent **natural rights,** the rights to liberty and property that people enjoyed in the state of nature. To better secure these rights, people entered into a social contract, thus creating a political society.

The next step is the formation of a government by majority decision, as contrasted with the unanimity necessary for the social contract. To Locke, the government was trustee of society's rights. A government that failed to protect the individual's rights to liberty and property violated the trust and could no longer claim the obedience of its citizens. For a flagrant abuse of power, the people could resort to revolution.

Locke's philosophy not only justified the English Revolution of 1688, but the American Revolution as well. In the Declaration of Independence, Thomas Jefferson restated the essentials of Locke:

> That, to secure these Rights, Governments are instituted among Men, deriving their just Powers from the Consent of the Governed: that, whenever any Form of Government becomes destructive of these Ends, it is the right of the People to alter or abolish it, and institute new Government, laying its Foundation on such Principles, and organizing its Powers in such Forms, as to them shall seem most likely to effect their Safety and Happiness.

The United States Constitution, with its emphasis on the powers of government being limited to those delegated and implied, reflects strongly Locke's influence, and the Bill of Rights is a practical application of the idea of natural rights.

Today the philosophy of natural law and natural rights is not as strongly held as formerly. Few, if any, now believe in the social contract as a historical fact; nevertheless, Locke's philosophy is still of great significance. It is a way of explaining the importance of the individual and his or her priority to the state and the state as a constitutional relationship based on consent.

Locke's concept of government by consent was reinforced by the writings of the French philosopher Charles de Montesquieu (1689–1755), who is best known for his advocacy of the principle of separation of powers, an important doctrine that the Founding Fathers incorporated into the first three articles of the United States Constitution. Locke's and Montesquieu's espousal of limited government was followed by Rousseau's strong advocacy of the concept of popular sovereignty.

Jean-Jacques Rousseau   The Frenchman Rousseau lived at a time when political thought in his country was influenced greatly by the Era of Enlightenment. The

---

[6]John Locke, *The Second Treatise of Government,* Thomas P. Peardon, ed. (Indianapolis: Bobbs-Merrill, 1952), p. 71.

Signing the Declaration of Independence, July 4, 1776.

political philosophy of the Enlightenment undermined the foundations of the absolute monarchy in France. The basic assumptions of the Enlightenment were

1. Confidence in the ability of human reason and science to cure the social ills of humanity.
2. The belief that social evils are the result of bad government, but that human nature is essentially good.
3. Belief in the idea of progress.
4. Opposition to revealed religion.
5. Glorification of nature and worship of the God of nature.

Rousseau shared many of the tenets of the Enlightenment, but he was atypical in stressing the primacy of feelings and emotion over reason. Rousseau was a romanticist who disliked the abstract, deductive reasoning characteristic of the Enlightenment.

"Man was born free and everywhere he is in chains," states Rousseau in his famous book, *The Social Contract.* Paradoxically, the freedom of the state of nature, according to Rousseau, can be regained only through the establishment of a legitimate civil society in which citizens give up their natural freedom, in return for which they participate in the **general will** of the community. As each individual agrees to be ruled as well as to rule, all are made free. This is the social contract.

One of Rousseau's basic contributions is the concept of popular sovereignty. The political community created by the social contract alone possesses supreme power or sovereignty. All legitimate governments, according to Rousseau, are basically democratic. In a democracy the people rule directly. Even a monarch rules only as long as the sovereign people permit. Rousseau did not approve of representative institutions, for they violated his idea of direct rule by the people. He also believed the only state that could be based on his philosophy was a small one comparable to the Greek city-state.

The concept of the general will is another important contribution of Rousseau. As he sees it, the general will is an expression of what the common good requires. Although the general will is central to Rousseau's political philosophy, it is a mystical and somewhat illogical concept of what the common good requires. It is more than an expression of the majority viewpoint, which is merely the sum of private interests. In Rousseau's opinion, as humankind is naturally good, the general will is uncorrupted. Thus, the general will represents the common interests of all people.

The weakness in the idea of the general will is that Rousseau failed to safeguard minority rights. Only in the creation of the political community is unanimity required. Otherwise, the will of the majority prevails. The people are never wrong according to Rousseau, but he acknowledged that they might be misled. In democracies there will always be dissent, but Rousseau believed that dissenters, if they are not in agreement with the general will, must acknowledge their error. They may be "forced to be free" if necessary—that is, coerced. This is clearly not democratic and suggests the confusion inherent in the concept of the general will. Although Rousseau was a democrat, his philosophy, with slight modification, can lead to totalitarianism.

Rousseau's influence has been tremendous. The Declaration of the Rights of Man of the French Revolution stresses popular sovereignty. American democratic thought in the nineteenth century also reflects Rousseau's philosophy that all power is derived from the people. Yet Rousseau presents a utopian conception of democracy. For Locke the highest value is the individual; in contrast, Rousseau's guiding star was the community.

Adam Smith   While Locke and Rousseau provided the major political roots for liberal democracy, its economic base was cast by Adam Smith. A political economist, well known for his major work *The Wealth of Nations,* he advocated strongly the free market economy system. His theory was based substantially on the notion that people will act rationally in terms of meeting not only their own needs but the needs of society at large as well.

Smith developed the system of ideal capitalism. He believed that a **laissez-faire** type of economy, where individuals could pursue their economic efforts freely, unhampered by governmental regulations, would be the best system for promoting wealth for individuals as well as the country. Free competition, according to Smith, would produce a high degree of economic and social harmony, and the economy would run like a "self-winding clockwork."

According to Smith, the functions of government should be limited basically to the maintenance of domestic order and the protection of the country from foreign invasions. He spoke out strongly against all efforts of state intervention in the economic realm, including tariffs, and also against the establishment of labor unions.

Smith's philosophy had considerable impact on economic thinking and planning in Britain and the United States during the nineteenth century. However, there never existed a pure laissez-faire economy. Some degree of governmental control over aspects of the economy has existed from the beginning of political societies. These controls have grown substantially in the twentieth century, in the case of the United States, especially with the inauguration of the New Deal program. Nowadays people in all democratic societies look to the government for leadership and help to alleviate inflation, unemployment, and other undesirable features connected with the economy.

Principles of Liberal Democracy   Having discussed the major ideas of John Locke, Jean-Jacques Rousseau, and Adam Smith, we would like to focus briefly on the major political and economic principles that have emerged from the liberal democratic theories and have become operative in those countries we tend to label democracies. The political principles fall into two large categories:

1. *Provisions to provide broad-based citizen involvement in the public decision-making process.* The word "democracy" comes from the Greek words *demos* (people) and *kratos* (government), thus meaning "government of the people." Locke and Rousseau stressed that citizens must be able to participate extensively in the political process. Contemporary democracies have constitutionalized a number of principles to assure citizen involvement. The first of these is the principle of *political equality*, meaning that all citizens may participate on an equal basis in the affairs of society. As pointed out in Chapter 7, by 1945 almost all adult citizens in good standing (except those in penal institutions) had received the right to vote in the democratic societies. Only in Switzerland and Liechtenstein did women receive the right to vote at a later date. The next major principle is that of an established *electoral system*, providing for regularized periodic elections. This has enabled the citizenry to decide who should serve in legislative and elective executive offices. Related to the above have been the establishment of a *fair system of representation* (see Chapter 7 for a detailed discussion), and constitutional support for *political pluralism*, the legalized presence of competing interest groups and political parties. The above features are all operational in today's democracies.

2. *The presence of a high degree of freedom (or liberty).* These freedoms, although often taken for granted by citizens in democratic societies, are very important and tend to distinguish democracies from totalitarian societies. The most important freedoms, from our Western point of view, are those of assembly, press, religion, speech, movement (within the country and beyond the boundaries of one's country), and freedom from arbitrary treatment by the public authorities. Although these freedoms are *not* absolute in any society, the constitutions of present-day democracies guarantee and protect a high degree of these freedoms, in contrast to the more limited freedoms prevailing in other countries.

The two major economic characteristics that have emerged in the democracies are: (1) Most agricultural, industrial, and service-type properties are held in *private* hands, with few governmental limitations on the amount of accumulation, and (2) the presence of a **mixed market economy.** Twentieth-century democracies have departed substantially from the laissez-faire concept advocated by Adam Smith. Although present-day democratic governments *do not control* their countries' economies, they *intervene increasingly,* and quite often by public demand. This intervention may be aimed to regulate certain areas of exports or imports, may be designed to curtail inflation and/or unemployment, or regulate safety measures in industries. Increasing government intervention in the economy, we believe, is here to stay.

After having examined the basic roots and features of liberal (or capitalist) democracy, we would like to focus our attention now on an ideological movement which, in recent decades, has become a kind of a twin (though not an identical twin) to liberal democracy, namely, social democracy.

Social Democracy

Social democracy, labeled democratic socialism by some and socialism[7] by still others, developed in the late nineteenth century in reaction to the excesses of the industrial revolution and capitalism as well as revolutionary Marxism. The main objective of the social democrats has been to attain, in addition to political democracy, a high degree of economic and social equality. These aims have been pursued with persistence by the social democratic parties in the democratic societies. Nowadays there are substantially more commonalities between liberal democracy and social democracy than differences. The United States can be considered as perhaps the best example of a liberal democracy and Sweden serves as a good example of a social democratic one.

The roots of social democracy are threefold: (1) pre-Marxian utopian socialism; (2) revisionism; and (3) Fabianism. *Pre-Marxian utopian socialism* carried a strong tenet of humanitarianism and aimed to improve the conditions of the working class. Utopian socialists include, among others, François Emile Babeuf (1760–1797), a Frenchman who was strongly influenced by the writings of Rousseau. Perhaps the most radical among the utopian socialists, he promoted the idea of establishing a communal type of society in which all people would be totally equal. Babeuf proposed that all private property be abolished and become the property of all society. Another French utopian socialist was Claude Henri Saint-Simon (1760–1825). He spoke out strongly in favor of modifying the capitalist system so that it would become more humane. In addition, he was a strong advocate of universal

---

[7]The term "socialism" has led to a good deal of confusion, because it has been used to describe a variety of ideological and political movements. Some people in the United States have employed it to label the social democratic movement as well as attempts to move society toward the welfare state (for example, proposals to give the national government a greater role in the administration of health services). Others have utilized the term to describe both social democracy and communism. The various ideologies present in the developing societies are often lumped into one category and labeled "Third World socialism." Communist leaders use the term "socialism" to describe their economic and social system, indicating, presumably, that they still consider themselves to be in the Marxian-coined socialist transition period.

education. These and other French utopian socialists were joined by Robert Owen (1771–1858), a wealthy British industrialist. A staunch humanitarian, Owen improved considerably the lot of the workers in his New Lanark mill. He was firmly convinced that the improvement of working conditions had a corresponding positive effect on the profitability of the industry and the well-being of all people. Among other features, Owen supported the establishment of trade unions and producer cooperatives. In sum, underlying all of utopian socialism was a strong humanitarian trend.

A second major root of social democracy, and perhaps the most important, is *revisionism,* namely, Marxism as revised by Eduard Bernstein (1850–1932), a German writer and party activist. Bernstein was aided in his efforts by the Frenchman Jean Léon Jaurès (1859–1914). Bernstein found that economic and historical developments in the latter part of the nineteenth century had invalidated a number of Marxian assumptions and predictions. More specifically, Bernstein argued that

1. Marx's predictions concerning the collapse of capitalism were wrong because Marx had greatly underestimated the inherent strength of capitalism. Bernstein argued that capitalism was here to stay, and the role of the social democratic forces was to humanize it from within.
2. Bernstein stated that socialism must eschew the Marxian-proposed "dictatorship of the proletariat" as well as any other type of dictatorship in the name of a particular class or party. He conceived social democracy as "the fulfillment of the theory and practice of democracy in all social relations, the abolition of all class privileges, and the elimination of arbitrariness and unreasonable discrimination and inequality in human relationships."[8]
3. Lastly, Bernstein argued that

> The socialist movement must, in the formulation of its program, purge itself of the remaining elements of [Marxian] Utopianism. It must stop conceiving of itself as fulfilling a "final goal," and constantly realize itself in the myriad daily tasks, small or large, which confront the movement towards greater democratization. Whatever the ends of socialism, the means to achieve them must be continuous with these ends. This interrelatedness of means and ends requires no belief in a predetermined goal to guide it, but only a sense of direction in which the socialist movement is going.[9]

Bernstein did not mean to be completely indifferent to the ideals of socialism, but proposed an evolutionary course of action. He rejected the Marxian dictum that revolutionary means were needed to achieve a socialist society. Bernstein advocated the utilization of the existing political processes and institutions to attain the goals of the socialist movement.

Bernstein should be considered the founder of today's social democracy. After World War I his ideas became the guideline for the social democratic movement,

---

[8]Eduard Bernstein, *Evolutionary Socialism,* introduction by Sidney Hook, Edith C. Harvey, trans. (New York: Schocken Books, 1961), p. xii.

[9]Ibid., p. xiii.

guiding it along the reformist, evolutionary path. Bernstein influenced not only reformist socialist leaders in Europe, but also Eugene Debs and Norman Thomas in the United States. To give an example of the extent of the reformist process, let us mention that in 1959, when the German Social Democratic Party met at a special party congress in the picturesque city of Bad Godesberg, the color of the tablecloth, the curtains, and other cloth-type furnishings was blue (rather than the former red), a symbolic indication that the party had rid itself of the last vestiges of Marxism.

The third root leading to the growth of social democracy, largely though not exclusively in Britain, is *Fabianism.* The Fabian movement, non-Marxian in nature, was established by a number of British intellectuals, including such towering figures as Sidney Webb (1859–1947), Beatrice Webb (1858–1943), George Bernard Shaw (1856–1950), and H. G. Wells (1866–1946). The aim of the Fabian Society was to establish evolutionary socialism in Britain. Less politically active than their continental European counterparts, the Fabians spread their message through articles, pamphlets, and books. The success of the Fabian message is found in the establishment of the British Labour Party (1900), whose platform was based largely on Fabian ideas. In 1922 the Labour Party replaced the Liberals as the second largest political party in Britain.

The Principles and Aims of Social Democracy   Since the 1920s social democratic parties have played an important role in the politics of a number of European countries, as well as in Australia and New Zealand. Social democratic forces have been in control of the government at various times in most of the democratic societies. When controlling the government, their composite policies have been fairly similar to those of Western countries ruled by conservative governments. *Social democracy has been a staunch defender of political democracy as well as political pluralism and has spoken out strongly in favor of a high degree of freedom for the citizenry* as much as the forces of liberal democracy.

In additional, social democratic parties, although being subject to substantial diversity with regard to their origins, development, and the roles they have played in their respective countries, *have been strong advocates of establishing substantial economic democracy in their countries.* Social democracy favors a fair distribution of wealth that includes a steep progressive income tax and, as a consequence, a smaller income differential between the more prosperous and the less prosperous than, for example, found in the United States. Social democratic welfare programs have taken the form of national health programs, adequate public pension payments, fair health and housing provisions for the elderly, generous unemployment payments, and the nationalization of some key industries. In Finland and Norway, approximately 10 percent of the industrial and service sectors are nationalized. The corresponding figures for France and Sweden are about 9 percent and 7.5 percent for the United Kingdom. We should note, however, that parts of some of the programs mentioned above have been instituted in democratic countries ruled by liberal democratic forces, too.

Sweden is often cited as the democratic country having the most comprehensive welfare program. The primary reason for this is that the Swedish Social Demo-

Swedish Prime Minister Ingvar Carlsson, an eminent Social Democratic spokesperson.

crats were continuously in control of the government from 1932 to 1976. During those 44 years the Swedish government was able to introduce a far-reaching series of welfare programs. In no other country has the social democratic party ruled, uninterrupted, for this long a time.

The movement of social democracy has found relatively few adherents in the United States. In contrast to Europe, most of the leaders of the growing union movement in this country in the late nineteenth century gave their support to the Democratic party instead of establishing a labor-orientated Social Democratic party. The Socialist party, U.S.A., did best in the 1912 presidential election, when it received nearly 6 percent of the popular vote. Later, a number of European-born intellectuals joined its ranks, including such towering figures as Albert Einstein, Erich Fromm, and Reinhold Niebuhr. Many of the ideas espoused by Eugene Debs and Norman Thomas, the early twentieth-century leaders of the American Socialist party, were incorporated into Franklin D. Roosevelt's New Deal platform and were put into practice during his administration. The social security program is one case in point. Finally, U.S. socialists have served in recent decades as mayors of Bridgeport, Connecticut; Milwaukee, Wisconsin; and Burlington, Vermont.

Before leaving the subject, however, it should be recognized that all democratic societies, whether liberal or social, have moved toward the welfare state.[10] The point to note is that some have started earlier and have moved further than others. For example, the German government introduced a social security program in the 1880s (under the conservative Chancellor Bismarck). In contrast, a social security program was not implemented in the United States until 1936. At the present time, difficult economic conditions have made it necessary for all democratic governments to husband their monetary resources more carefully than in earlier decades. As a consequence, liberal democratic as well as social democratic governments have commenced with selective cutbacks in social welfare programs.

Next, we shall turn our attention to the revolutionary ideology of Marxism-Leninism.

Marxism-Leninism

No political theorist is more famous than the legendary Karl Marx. He has inspired political movements around the globe, and more than one-fourth of the world's population is governed today by Communist regimes, which allege that they rule on the basis of the ideas provided by Marx and revised some decades later by Vladimir Ilich Lenin.

Karl Marx (1818–1883) was born and raised in Trier, in the Mosel valley in Germany. In 1835, he enrolled at Bonn University to study law, but he soon shifted his interest to philosophy. The major school for the study of philosophy at that time was the Humboldt University in Berlin, where the famous Friedrich Hegel (1770–1831) had established the foremost center for the study of philosophy in Europe.

After two semesters in Bonn, Marx moved on to Berlin and became deeply involved in the study of Hegel's theories. Following the completion of his doctorate, Karl Marx turned to journalism. He wrote with considerable success for the *Rheinische Zeitung* and became its editor-in-chief in 1842. However, the conservative Prussian government took a dislike to his radical-liberal articles, and Karl Marx moved to Paris in the summer of 1843. The Prussian government continued its

---

[10]See Arnold J. Heidenheimer, Hugh Heclo, and Carolyn Teich Adams, *Comparative Public Policy: The Politics of Social Choice in Europe, America, and Japan*, 3rd ed. (New York: St. Martin's Press, 1990). The book provides a number of comparative data on welfare expenditures and taxation in the democratic societies.

pressure and urged the French government to expel him. Thus, in 1845 Marx moved to Brussels and, in 1849 to London, where he settled permanently. Marx had entertained ideas to move to the United States, but financial problems forced him to give up this thought.

In Paris, Marx had made the acquaintance of Friedrich Engels (1820–1895), the son of a German industrialist. Engels became a lifelong friend, literary collaborator, and banker of last resort for Karl Marx. Commissioned to write a party platform for the young Communist Internationale, Marx and Engels produced in 1848 the famous *Communist Manifesto.* Besides many other publications, Marx wrote the monumental *Das Kapital (The Capital).* The first volume of this work was published prior to Karl Marx's death. Friedrich Engels edited volumes 2 and 3 later on. Nobody but Engels could have done this complicated task. The ideas of Karl Marx were put first into practice, in a revised fashion, by Vladimir Lenin (1870–1924) in the 1917 Russian Revolution.

The core of Marxian philosophy focuses on the dialectical unfolding of history. The concept of the dialectic, a three-part process consisting of thesis, antithesis, and synthesis, was developed by Friedrich Hegel. He applied this process to the unfolding of ideas as the moving force in history. The dialectic process can be explained as following: A doctrine is advanced about some subject, but such a doctrine is necessarily partial and one sided because of human fallibility and is

Karl Marx.

Cover of *Manifesto of the Communist Party,* first edition.

limited by the historical perspective of the period. Critics develop an opposite doctrine to correct the errors in the initial thesis. As this second doctrine, or antithesis, also will be one sided and only partial in its truth, it will lead to a third doctrine, or synthesis, of the true elements in the original thesis and its opposite antithesis. However, the synthesis is not the complete truth and the dialectical process will start again with another antithesis. To Hegel this dialectical process was more than a way of acquiring knowledge, it was the essence of reality itself and its unfolding was the will of God or the Absolute.

Karl Marx turned the Hegelian dialectic "upside down," applying it to economic phenomena. Thus, this part of his philosophy became known as **dialectical materialism.** For Marx the mode of production became the key to societal development. Agrarianism was the basis of feudalistic society. The rising commercialism of sixteenth- and seventeenth-century Western Europe set the stage for the industrial revolution and the development of capitalism. According to Marx, capitalism was characterized socioeconomically by two classes, the bourgeoisie (those who owned the means of production) and the proletariat (the workers). The contradictions between the two classes would lead to the revolution that would set the stage for the coming of communism. Marx's major aim in his writings was to explain the working of the dialectic, the contradictions inherent in capitalism, the demise of capitalism, and the coming of the Communist era.

The following will explain these fundamentals of Marxian theory in more detail. The *Communist Manifesto,* written by Marx and Engels in 1848 to serve as a kind of party platform for the recently founded Communist Internationale, provided the starting points of Marxist doctrine. Based on the dialectical principle of the unfolding of history, Marx and Engels explained all of history as a series of class struggles that propelled society perpetually toward improvement. The ruling class of a given dialectical period determines the features of society. Under capitalism, it is the bourgeoisie that determines the economic, political, and social order of society. The advance of capitalism would lead to ever-worsening economic crises and a constantly widening gulf between the bourgeoisie and the proletariat. With the fate of the proletariat going from bad to worse due to perpetually increasing exploitation and constantly declining purchasing power, the historically predestined stage for the revolution is set. The now united proletariat will follow the famous Marxian battle cry "workers arise" and overthrow the bourgeoisie. As stated by Marx in the first volume of *Das Kapital,* "the expropriators are expropriated."

The successful revolution will be followed by the *socialist transition period,* a time during which society would be prepared for *pure communism.* In his earlier writings Marx stated clearly that the revolution would be a violent one, because the bourgeoisie would not surrender its properties peacefully. As he states in volume 1 of *Das Kapital,* "Force is the midwife of every old society pregnant with a new one." There is some evidence, however, that in his later years he became more mellow on this matter. In a speech that he gave in The Hague, Holland, in the early 1870s, he pointed out that the most advanced industrialized countries, mentioning Britain, Holland, and the United States specifically, could possibly move into the socialist transition phase and ultimately that of pure communism by fairly peaceful means.

The socialist transition period, we mentioned earlier, would prepare society for pure communism. More specifically, agriculture and industry, expropriated during the revolution, would become now the property of all of society. Remaining remnants of bourgeois behavior would be eliminated, and the masses would be educated toward the future Communist Utopia. At no time did Marx or Engels state explicitly how long the socialist transition period would last, though some of their hints seem to indicate that they envisioned it to be of short duration. We should note that no Communist leader has stated so far that his society has arrived at pure communism.

According to Marx and Engels the main features of pure communism would be as following:

1. It would be a completely egalitarian society, with everybody enjoying equal social status.
2. People would be paid according to their needs, in the famous words of Marx, "from each according to his ability, to each according to his needs." This implies that people would behave with complete altruism in pure communism; they would render their labor gladly and to the best of their ability.
3. The government would wither away. Under capitalism the government was the tool of the bourgeoisie. Its job was twofold: To protect the bourgeoisie and its property and to coerce and suppress the proletariat. Because the revolution had established a classless society and the last vestiges of bourgeois behavior had been eliminated during the socialist transition period, there was no further need for government to exercise coercive force. Furthermore, because private property has been abolished, the former inequities of exploitation and profit making had ceased. Therefore, no further clashes of interest would occur. Communist society, according to Marx and Engels, would be without politics. The function of government would shift from that of protecting one class and coercing the other to one of administering the nonhuman aspects of the economic sector.
4. As Engels pointed out, communism would take over the technology from capitalism, improve upon it, and establish highly industrialized societies. Public ownership and public service will endow the productive process with a kind of self-evident rationality.
5. Communist technology will be so far advanced that the former division of labor will disappear. Each person will be able to employ his or her talents in a variety of endeavors.

What happens to the dialectic once society has arrived at pure communism? At no time do Marx or Engels state that communism constitutes the finite stage of human and societal development. Rather, their point is that communism would be the societal order in the near future, *but not the final goal of human development.* The dialectic will grind on and communism would be succeeded by a superior form of human society.[11] However, they did not speculate on what that would be.

The systematic scheme put forth by Marx and Engels is the most comprehensive theory advanced to explain societal development. It includes a tremendous faith in the potentially absolute altruism in humankind. Yet, Marxism includes some fundamental errors.

1. Marx, in arguing that capitalist society consisted of two classes only and that the proletariat made up the large majority of society (at one point he speaks of 90 percent), misjudged the complexity of modern society. His simplistic two-tier system was anything but scientific, rather it was Marx's goal and based on conjecture.

2. Marx's theory of the state, which stipulated that after the revolution society would be transformed into a full participatory democracy, focused exclusively on economic phenomena, mainly the nationalization of agriculture and industry. Political phenomena such as constitutionalism, representation, and the nature of government, so important in liberal and social democracies, received no consideration. This vacuum in the Marxian theory of state provided Lenin, Stalin, Mao Zedong, and other Communist leaders with the opportunity to develop the political structures and processes as they saw fit.

3. Marx's basic assumption that the terrible living and working conditions of the proletariat during the early stage of the industrial revolution would further deteriorate with the advance of capitalism was clearly false. Contrary to Marxian prognosis, social reforms—a part of the move toward the welfare state—have improved considerably the lot of many workers in capitalist societies. The road toward the welfare state, concurrent with the rise of labor unions and collective bargaining, counteracted a heightening of class conflicts in the advanced industrialized countries.

4. Marx was wrong in predicting the collapse of capitalism due to overproduction and steadily diminishing markets. Although capitalism has experienced some scares, the Great Depression of the 1930s, for example, it has shown an endurance that Marx did not foresee.

5. Contrary to the expectations of Marx and Engels, the "revolution" proclaimed in the *Communist Manifesto* did not take place in the advanced capitalist societies in the later part of the nineteenth century but decades later in the feudalistic agrarian societies of Russia and China, *countries that clearly did not meet the prerequisites stated by Marx.* In the backward societies that adopted communism it became the tool to move them forcibly, and at great human cost, into the industrial age.

---

[11]See, for example, Hans-Joachim Lieber and Peter Furth, eds., *Karl Marx: Frühe Schriften,* vol. 1 (Stuttgart, Germany: Cotta Verlag, 1962), p. 608, for Marx's clear statement regarding the above. His key words are "Der Kommunismus ist die notwendige Gestalt und das energische Prinzip der nächsten Zukunft, *aber der Kommunismus ist nicht als solches das Ziel der menschlichen Entwicklung.*" ("Communism is the necessary form and active principle of the near future, but communism as such is not the final goal of human development"—author's translation.)

Despite all these errors of judgment, which could be attributed to human frailty—namely, the impossibility of predicting with absolute certainty the socio-politico-economic developments in future decades—Marx and Engels have left a most definitive mark in history, more so than any great thinkers before them.

Lenin's Contributions   Vladimir Ilich Lenin (his original name was Vladimir Ilich Ulyanov), the son of a czarist administrator of education, spearheaded the Russian Revolution of November 1917, which led to the establishment of the first so-called Communist society. Lenin was an unusual combination of active revolutionary and political and economic theorist. His philosophy was based on that of Marx, but it was a Marxism modified in the light of developments in Russia. Lenin differed from Marx in a number of respects. First, because Russia was not a developed capitalist country, it was not a likely candidate for the type of revolution Marx had predicted. Lenin explained the Communist victory in Russia as a result of the country having experienced capitalism "vicariously," through contact with the more advanced capitalist countries of the West. Second, he believed that capitalism had entered the imperialist phase, because the European powers were engaged in a worldwide imperialistic war in a struggle for world markets. Consequently, revolutionary activity would occur everywhere.

Third, Lenin also differed from Marx in his interpretation of the role of the proletariat in bringing about revolutionary activity. Unlike Marx, Lenin believed the working class by itself was not capable of developing a revolutionary consciousness. A revolution according to Lenin could come about only through a vanguard of dedicated revolutionaries, the Communist party, who would supplant the old regime as rulers. Thus the dictatorship of the proletariat became the dictatorship of the Communist party in Russia. The party ruled in the name of the proletariat.

Fourth, Lenin introduced the concept of *democratic centralism,* a principle that combines some freedom of discussion with centralized control. Democratic centralism implies that before the party adopts a position on a certain issue, this issue can be discussed and debated widely among the party membership. However, once a decision has been made by the party leadership, everybody is required to accept that decision and to adhere to it.

Fifth, Lenin was more explicit than Marx about the period of transition following the revolution. He believed that an extended period of time was necessary before the attainment of communism was possible. Following the revolution, there would be a period of revolutionary transformation during which time suppression of the minority of exploiters still remaining would be necessary. The state would continue, but would rule in the name of the proletariat. During the period of transition, inequalities of wealth would still exist but exploitation of the many no longer would be possible, for the means of production would cease to be in private hands. Only when society was capable of attaining the formula of "from each according to his ability—to each according to his needs" would the state disappear. At what time this stage would occur was not clear.

The combined ideas of Marx, Engels, and Lenin have become known as Marxism-Leninism, the ideological base underlying today's Communist systems. Communist leaders have stated many times that Marx, Engels, and Lenin have developed the true scientific theory for social development. For example, Nikita Khrushchev, when addressing the National Press Club in Washington, D.C., in 1959, stated "We believe that Karl Marx, Engels, and Lenin gave scientific proof of the fact that the system, the social system of socialism, would take the place of capitalism. We believe in that."[12] Twenty-seven years later, Mikhail S. Gorbachev, in his address to the twenty-seventh CPSU (Communist Party of the Soviet Union) Congress stated:

> Formulating the long-term and fundamental tasks, the Central Committee [of the CPSU] has consistently taken guidance in Marxism-Leninism, the truly scientific theory of social development."[13]

But are there still many "true believers" in the Soviet Union?

The Development of Communist Systems The 1917 Russian Revolution led to the establishment of the Union of Soviet Socialist Republics (USSR), the first society based on Marxism-Leninism. It was followed by China several decades later. Under Lenin, dictatorial power was vested in the leadership of the Communist party, with Lenin being the "first among equals." His successor Joseph Stalin (1879–1953), however, concentrated all power in his hands, establishing an absolute dictatorship in the Soviet Union and also over the Communist movements abroad. His successors (Khrushchev, Brezhnev, Andropov, and Chernenko) have followed a more moderate style of leadership than Stalin, although keeping the Soviet Union a closed society with a highly centralized economy.

The present leader of the Soviet Union, Mikhail Gorbachev, has embarked on a very ambitious program that, if fully implemented, would change life in the Soviet Union considerably. Under the labels of **glasnost** (openness) and **perestroika** (restructuring of the economy), Gorbachev is trying to invigorate Soviet society.[14]

The three leading aberrations from the Soviet style of communism are **Maoism** (as revised by Deng Xiaoping) in China, **Titoism** in Yugoslavia, and **Eurocommunism** in some of the democratic societies.

In contrast to the urban proletarian base of Soviet communism, Mao Zedong (1893–1977) developed Chinese communism by using the peasantry as the revolutionary force. He achieved control of China by way of guerrilla warfare rather than urban insurrection. Mao's agrarian-based road to Communist control has served as a guide for Communist guerrilla forces in Third World countries. Differences of view existed between Mao Zedong and the Soviet leaders since the 1920s and led to a full break in relations in 1960. Only recently have relations between the two major Communist countries improved.

Tito (1892–1980) split from the Soviet-ruled Communist Commonwealth in

---

[12]*New York Times* (September 17, 1959).

[13]Translated from the speech as reported in *Pravda* (February 26, 1986).

[14]See Mikhail Gorbachev, *Perestroika: New Thinking for Our Country and the World* (New York: Harper & Row, 1987).

Old and new in the People's Republic of China.

1948. Slowly but surely, he liberalized communism in his country. Two key features distinguish Yugoslavia from the other Communist countries:

1. A decentralized economy based on supply and demand. Yugoslav workers' councils in the factories have a substantial say in regard to production, management, and personnel policies.
2. Yugoslavia is a fairly open society. Most Yugoslavs may travel quite readily to democratic countries. Many Yugoslavs work in West Germany, France, or Switzerland. Also, Yugoslavia has become a favorite vacation place for many West Europeans.

The movement labeled *Eurocommunism* developed in the 1960s. Spearheaded by the leadership of the large Italian Communist party, it was joined soon by the French and the Spanish Communist parties, as well as factions within the Communist parties in other democracies. The movement received its first large-scale attention in 1968 when Italian Communist leaders spoke out publicly against the Soviet invasion of Czechoslovakia.

Eurocommunism is based on three major facets:

1. Complete independence from the Soviet leadership.
2. The commitment to support the democratic order and to obtain political office through participation in competitive elections.
3. Its readiness to form electoral alliances with democratic parties of the left and the center.

Since the development of Eurocommunism, adherents have participated only once in a national coalition government, namely in France during the 1970s.

The Communist movement shrank in the late 1980s when Poland and Hungary began to move toward political pluralism. Still more surprising were, in 1989, the reformist coup d'états in East Germany, Czechoslovakia, Bulgaria, and Romania. These changes were possible because, in contrast to past practice, Soviet troops did not intervene. Poland, Hungary, Czechoslovakia, Bulgaria, and Romania are on the road toward democracy.

Fascism and National Socialism

The last major ideological movement we should discuss is that of fascism and national socialism, especially because of the tremendous amount of harm to humanity it caused during the earlier part of this century. Fascism became the ideological creed for Mussolini's regime in Italy and national socialism, the political philosophy buttressing Hitler's regime in Germany. The two creeds are closely related to each other and are at the extreme right of the political spectrum, meaning that they are reactionary movements. In recent years, the word "fascism" has been used often to label both of these ideological movements. One basic component, among others, that fascism and national socialism have in common with communism is that both feature the concept of supreme rule by the *one* political party—which in the instances of Mussolini, Hitler, and Stalin amounted to a one-person dictatorship.

Fascist writers do not contribute a great deal to an explanation of the ideology of the movement. Mussolini stressed the "will to power" and the supremacy of the state over the individual. German writers like Alfred Rosenberg stressed the myth of Aryan racial superiority. The basic elements of Fascist ideology, however, include the following.

1. *Irrationalism*—the notion that people are not rational and that they have to be led by way of manipulation.
2. *An extreme type of social Darwinism*—as reflected in the systems' fatally discriminatory racial policies.
3. *Supernationalism*—the notion that one's country is superior to all other countries.
4. *The leadership principle*—society is made up of a single hierarchy. Each subordinate owes absolute obedience to his or her superior, and all owe absolute obedience to the ultimate leader.
5. *Strong opposition to democratic principles and practices;* they are weak and inefficient.
6. *An avid anticommunism,* which was conveniently forgotten, however, temporarily in the case of the 1939 German-Soviet Nonaggression Pact.[15]

Nazi leaders stressed Aryan supremacy and used it as a justification for the extermination of "inferior" races, such as the Jews, whom the Nazis blamed for

---

[15]For a detailed discussion of some of the points above see Lyman Tower Sargent, *Contemporary Political Ideologies,* 7th ed. (Homewood, Ill.: The Dorsey Press, 1987), pp. 161–174.

the ills of Germany. The nationalism of both the Italian and German versions of fascism glorified war as the climax of human achievement.

Very important, too, was the leadership principle. The demented Hitler, as *Führer*, presumably embodied within himself the ability to speak for the entire German nation. Only he could express the will of the German people. This might be considered a perversion of Rousseau's concept of the general will. Hitler as leader provided all values to the regime. Hermann Göring, a high-ranking Nazi leader, claimed that Hitler was infallible.

How does one explain the coming about of fascism, a system of government that is responsible for so many atrocities against humanity? The following theories attempt to answer the question.

One interpretation, the Marxist, holds that fascism is the final stage of capitalism, in which capitalists conspire to save themselves by establishing a dictatorship. In support of this view, it is pointed out that a number of German capitalists subsidized Hitler financially, because he promised to save the country from communism. Although many of these financiers regarded Hitler as a demagogue, they believed that he could be managed so that their economic interests would be protected. Hitler was strongly anticommunist and appealed to the fear of communism not only among the industrialists but the middle class as well. Supporters of this view point out that Germany was in a state of severe economic crisis when Hitler came to power and that a probable alternative regime was a Communist one.

This interpretation has elements of truth but ignores the fact that Hitler's dictatorship encroached upon property rights to such an extent that many industrialists were reduced to the status of paid managers of their own enterprises. Some business people had their property seized by the Nazi government. The Marxist interpretation also ignored the strong popular support for Hitler among various segments of the population.

Fascism also has been described as essentially a personal dictatorship comparable to the rule of Napoleon. This view ignores the mass support of the Nazis and obscures the totalitarian character of the dictatorship, which goes beyond the realm of the political and includes all aspects of individual life.

Another interpretation stresses the fact that Hitler's movement grew out of the strong military tradition that had roots deep in German history. According to this theory, the Nazi dictatorship was basically a new and extreme version of German militarism. This explanation overlooks the fact that Hitler differed considerably in kind as well as in degree from such earlier militarists as the German Kaiser Wilhelm II who ruled Germany before and during World War I or Frederick the Great. These men were militaristic and authoritarian, but they did not repudiate the basic values of Western civilization as Hitler did. They did not believe in the Nazi racial theories or seek military domination to the same extent as the Nazis.

A fourth view of fascism interprets it as a political manifestation of a crisis of Western civilization that occurred in Germany and Italy because of special circumstances in those countries. These conditions, however, could develop anywhere. The basis of fascism, according to this view, is despair caused by the loss of faith on the part of the German and Italian people in the ability of their political and economic institutions to solve their social problems. As a result, they accepted a tyranny that promised to restore some degree of order and provide a meaning to life; however, the new order was the embodiment of naked power, and it repudiated reason and all Western values. The last court of appeal in a fascist system is the will of the leader, who is not influenced by reason or justice. This explanation contains elements of truth the other three ignore.[16]

Germany and Italy have been the only two advanced countries that have been ruled by Fascist regimes. Both societies paid dearly for it in World War II in terms of the loss of human lives and destruction of their cities. Approximately 10 percent of the German population was killed during World War II and the immediate months following the war (in the case of the Soviet-occupied areas). It also lost a substantial amount of territory in the East and, in addition, became a bifurcated society for forty-five years.

However, these points do not mean that fascism was present in these two societies only. The Fascist cause received a good deal of support from the Franco government in Spain and smaller Fascist-type groups that existed during the 1930s in all European countries, with the exception of the Soviet Union. Furthermore, Fascist-type groups have existed already for some time in practically all American countries—with considerable strength in Argentina, Chile, Paraguay, and Columbia—as well as in South Africa.

In 1945, the Fascist governments of Germany and Italy were completely defeated and destroyed. Denazification programs, undertaken by the Allied occupation forces, were aimed to punish the war criminals and to liquidate the fascist movement per se. The success of the program was incomplete at best in that a number of war criminals succeeded in fleeing to South America or other areas that provided a safe haven for them.

Since 1945, Fascist forces have not played an important role in Western democracies. In the case of West Germany, a small extremist right-wing party was outlawed by the High Court in 1952, and succeeding right-wing movements, which were semifascist at best, have suffered defeat at the polls. Italy is the only country where a neofascist party, the Italian Social Party (MSI), has been and still is represented in the Parliament, having received between 2 (1948) and 5.8 percent (1953) of the vote. More recently, the MSI merged with the Monarchists. In other countries of the West small Fascist or neofascist groups have continued to exist in the form of extralegal groups. Staffed originally by Fascist survivors of World War II, they have been joined more recently by a number of younger people (especially males) who find that fascist symbolism boosts their ego. These are the people of the George Lincoln Rockwell, Maynard Orlando Nelson, and Matt Koehl type (three leading neofascists of recent vintage in the United States) and their supporters.

Though mention has been made in recent years of a resurgence of fascism and the growth of extremist components within the **New Right**, evidence on this is rather spotty.[17] The groups mentioned are rather small in size, and their most

---

[16]See John H. Hallowell, *Main Currents in Modern Political Thought* (New York: Henry Holt, 1950), for a more extensive discussion of these points.

[17]See Dennis Eisenberg, *The Re-emergence of Fascism* (New York: A. S. Barnes, 1967), for a comprehensive analysis of the state of Fascism during the first two decades following World War II.

unfortunate statements and pranks are all too often attempts to seek public attention. However, German national socialism and Italian fascism started as small movements, too. Thus, it is impossible to say with absolute certainty that similar developments might not occur again. The state of the economy in the Western world in years to come will have a great deal of bearing on the degree of satisfaction or dissatisfaction that exists among the citizenry, and the more satisfaction that exists the less political extremism there is likely to be.

One of the more recent books on fascism starts with the sentence, "Fascism is on the rise in the contemporary world." However, the author's focus is on the developing countries, which he finds quite prone to adopt extremist regimes, rather than on the postindustrial societies.[18] Let us hope that democratic societies can improve democracy to the point that the populace will not fall prey to fascist ideological appeals.

SUMMARY

Throughout the ages, the great political theorists have dealt with the question, What is a good government and what kind of society will provide the base for it? Their theories were influenced substantially by the type of society they lived in, be it the Greek city-state system at the time of Plato or the early phase of the industrial revolution whose excesses provided the stimulus for the writings of Karl Marx and Friedrich Engels.

Political ideologies are sets or clusters of ideas that promote a given type of economic, political, and social order. In a pure sense, ideologies consist of the ideas of a number of theorists who have built on each others' ideas. These ideologies have been modified, more or less, by those who have put them into practice. Further, prevalent ideologies have been integrated into the framework of policies pursued by governments. One of the fascinating occurrances of our time is that Marxism-Leninism, as applied in practice, is losing a great deal of ground, whereas democracy, as we conceive it, is gaining influence by leaps and bounds.

RECOMMENDED READINGS

Bernstein, Eduard. *Evolutionary Socialism,* Edith C. Harvey, trans. New York: Schocken Books, 1961. This work is the classic statement providing the basis for democratic socialism.

Bracher, Karl Dietrich. *The German Dictatorship: Origins, Structure, and Effects of National Socialism,* Jean Steinberg, trans., introduction by Peter Gay. New York: Praeger, 1970. The most authoritative work on national socialism is written by Germany's foremost political scientist.

[18]Anthony James Joes, *Fascism in the Contemporary World: Ideology, Evolution, Resurgence* (Boulder, Colo.: Westview Press, 1978).

Dahl, Robert A. *Democracy and Its Critics.* New Haven, Conn.: Yale University Press, 1989. This country's leading scholar on the subject of democracy examines its basic assumptions, states why it is important, and considers its future prospects.

Dahl, Robert A. *A Preface to Economic Democracy.* Berkeley, Calif.: University of California Press, 1985. This is an important essay in favor of "workplace democracy." Dahl proposes that the vitality of democracy would be strengthened substantially by extending democracy to the economic realm.

Leonhard, Wolfgang. *Eurocommunism: Challenge for East and West,* Mark Vecchio, trans. New York: Holt, Rinehart & Winston, 1978. The book features the most comprehensive discussion of the origin and development of Eurocommunism.

Macridis, Roy C. *Contemporary Political Ideologies: Movements and Regimes,* 4th ed. Glenview, Ill.: Scott, Foresman/Little, Brown, 1989. This is a highly readable text that discusses in detail the major ideologies of our time.

McLellan, David. *Karl Marx: His Life and Thought.* New York: Harper & Row, 1973. This book is by far the best and most detailed biography of Karl Marx in the English language.

McLellan, David. *Marxism After Marx.* New York: Harper & Row, 1979. This is an excellent introductory discussion of the progression and diverse interpretations of Marx's ideas from the 1880s to the raucous 1960s.

Nelson, Brian R. *Western Political Thought: From Socrates to the Age of Ideology.* Englewood Cliffs, N.J.: Prentice-Hall, 1982. The author presents an informative and comparative discussion of the "great thinkers," from Socrates to Karl Marx.

Ozinga, James R. *Communism: The Story of the Idea and Its Implementation.* Englewood Cliffs, N.J.: Prentice-Hall, 1987. This is a thorough discussion of Marxism and its implementation in twentieth-century societies.

Paterson, William E., and Ian Campbell. *Social Democracy in Post-War Europe.* New York: St. Martin's Press, 1974. The book features an informative discussion of the post–World War II social democratic parties in Western Europe, with special focus on their clientele and platforms in terms of domestic and foreign policy.

Smith, Dennis M. *Mussolini's Roman Empire.* New York: Viking, 1976. This is a detailed study of the rise and demise of fascism in Italy.

Input Agencies

The Process of Political Socialization

Political socialization refers to the process by which people acquire their political beliefs. It is a complex and continuous development. **Political culture** provides the basic framework for the people of a society. Several agents such as the family, peer groups, formal education, occupation, and the mass media play an important role in the socialization process. It is very difficult to assign precise or exact weight to each of these agents, for some have more influence on an individual than others.

POLITICAL CULTURE

If a student were asked to learn all about the political system of Japan, Italy, or some other country, how should the student proceed? One way would be to read Japan's constitution in its entirety very carefully. Perhaps the student could even memorize key sections of the Italian Constitution. How well would the student then understand the political system of Japan or Italy? If you guessed hardly at all, you guessed correctly.

Or imagine an Indonesian or Saudi Arabian college student whose only grasp or contact with the American political system was a thorough reading of the United States Constitution. Political parties are not even mentioned in the United States Constitution. How much does he or she then know about the political system?

Simply learning all the facts and details about governmental institutions, structures, and procedures of elections will not shed very much light on a country's political life. There is a critical underlying psychological dimension that includes another aspect or orientation, the *political culture.* The political culture consists of attitudes, beliefs, values, and skills that are held by an entire population as well as various separate patterns found in smaller sections of the population.

The idea of a political culture has appeared in various forms from early times. Aristotle's writings hint at the concept. The French philosopher Montesquieu, anticipating modern political science, wrote that a given climate, soil, economy, form of government, commerce, religion, and customs will evolve into a unique political system. He believed that there had to be a "fit" between the people and the government that he called the "Spirit of the Laws." Montesquieu tried to show how the various environments people must adapt to will lead to different types of governments. He defined the law as the "necessary relations arising from the nature of things."[1] Although his works are often vague and imprecise, they are still useful and provocative.

Today, political culture is not so rudimentary an idea as it was in Montesquieu's time. It is possible through rigorous analysis to identify and even to measure the concept. Public opinion polls and in-depth attitude surveys are two principal instruments used to reveal and measure attitudes, beliefs, and values making up political culture.

---

[1]See, for example, George H. Sabine and Thomas L. Thorson, *A History of Political Theory,* 4th ed. (Hinsdale, Ill.: Dryden Press, 1973), pp. 509–511.

A country's political culture is composed of various aspects or components. There is the factual or data aspect. How much does the individual know about the government, for example, who is the prime minister, the names and programs of the major political parties, and the functions of the various branches of government? This is known as the *cognitive* component of political culture. Another part of political culture, the *affective* component, concerns the feelings an individual has about the political system, such as pride, fear, trust, or contempt.

Finally, there are the judgments about how well the political system is performing. Does the citizen rate the government as doing a good job, a poor job, or an improving or worsening job? This is known as the *evaluative* component.

To summarize, a country's political culture is a composite of cognitive (facts), affective (feelings), and evaluative (judgment) orientations. For example, an individual may know the names and officials of the political parties (cognitive). He or she may also have a feeling of warmth and loyalty (affective) toward the government. Finally, the person may consider the leaders and their policies to be faulty and failing (evaluative).

An understanding of the political culture is useful when one is trying to bridge the gap between the individual on the one hand and the government on the other. By gathering a large collection of responses and case studies, one can generate a data base from which to proceed toward the concept of political culture. As a result of studying the profile of a country's political culture, it becomes possible to understand the political orientation of a single individual. Reading a country's constitution and principal laws can hardly shed any light on this entire area.

Almond and Powell have classified political cultures according to how much people feel they should or can be involved in politics. Are the citizens engaged in the political process actively, or are they spectators? The first type, the *parochials*, are found in many developing countries, especially those that have gained independence after World War II. There are large groups who lack awareness or even consciousness regarding the national government, although the ever-expanding availability of modern electronic communications has widened the circle of awareness. These people are left out of the government or untouched by its full powers. The parochial knows very little about the political system and expects nothing from it. There is almost total detachment.

A second major type of political culture does know about the government and expects something from it, but mostly as a passive recipient. This is called a *subject* political culture. There is a connection between the government and the people, but it is mostly one sided, the citizens (the subjects) being on the receiving end of government policies. The British political system with its tradition rooted in feudalism and aristocracy leans toward a subject political culture.

Even though the British maintain a democratic system with free elections, there persists a mind-set of deference and submission. Consequently, the British still refer to themselves as British subjects of the crown and not citizens.

The last category of political culture is **participatory**, which, as its name suggests, means the people are actively involved in determining government policies. Here, the people are actively involved in an ongoing basis with the governmental process. The citizen knows about the government and tries to influence policy output. The United States is said to have a *participant* political culture.[2]

Political Subcultures

Studies have found significant differences in the attitudes and political knowledge of different parts of the population. This argues for further studies that break the political culture down into what political scientists call *subcultures,* or parts of the wider culture. Geographic region, religion, nationality or ethnic identity, social class, and urban or rural locations can all affect what people believe and how they vote.

In Japan there is a well-documented existence of important social and cultural differences between urban and rural sectors as well as higher frequencies of political participation found in rural districts than in the urban sectors. We know from the findings of various sociological and anthropological studies that social relationships differ markedly in rural and urban Japan. Apparently, there are practices and outlooks in the rural area that foster political culture beliefs that encourage the development of popular government (voting) more so than in the urban sector.[3] Clearly, the reasons for the rural subculture in Japan are complex. Advances in the economic positions of typical farm families have been remarkable. Indeed, the scale of rural affluence in recent years is a highly believable contribution to some of the subcultural norms in Japan.[4]

Most societies experience some sort of fundamental division in the values and aspirations of different groups in the system. For example, the political cultures in Italy and Austria would seem to share much in common, being fragmented into three major divisions: A rural, agricultural, catholic subculture; a modernizing, middle-class subculture; and an anticlerical, lower-class, urban subculture. Are these political cultures indeed similar?[5]

What we do and do not define as a separate political subculture depends largely on the concerns and problems in question. An observer of American politics may be concerned with the liberal and conservative wings of the Democratic party as policy subcultures, whereas a comparable analyst might dismiss them as being so firmly within the more general American political culture as to be unworthy of separate classifications.[6]

However, there is no question of the importance of the subcultural differences that exist in certain countries. France is the classic case of a country whose political

---

[2]Gabriel A. Almond and G. Bingham Powell, Jr., *Comparative Politics: A Developmental Approach* (Boston: Little, Brown, 1966), pp. 50–72.

[3]Bradley M. Richardson, *The Political Culture of Japan* (Berkeley: Calif.: University of California Press, 1974), p. 17.

[4]Ibid.

[5]Gabriel Almond and G. Bingham Powell, Jr., *Comparative Politics: A Developmental Approach,* p. 111.

[6]Ibid., p. 64.

culture, although manifesting a strong national identity in some respects, appears to be so fragmented as to make effective political performance almost impossible at times. In many of the countries of the Third World, this problem of political subculture is also crucial. In India, the differences of language, religion, class, and caste pose enormous problems for the political regime. Lebanon offers an example of a country that has been effectively ripped to pieces in a tragic confrontation of clashing political subcultures.

So far we have learned that simply knowing the various articles of the constitution or the names of the prominent government officials or how a bill becomes law only gives a flat and unidimensional understanding of politics. By studying the psychological orientation toward the government, that is, the political culture, the political system comes to life, and we can begin to understand what is really happening politically in a country.

POLITICAL SOCIALIZATION

To many analysts, the study of political culture begins with the premise that a person's political behavior is learned behavior. They assert that a person's political orientations are profoundly shaped by the individuals and institutions that influence him or her early in life, particularly by the home, school, and friends.[7] Political socialization is a process by which political cultures are transmitted as well as maintained and changed. Political socialization is thus concerned with the origin of political awareness and attitudes.

In the perspective of political socialization, an individual is born, psychologically at least, the citizen of no land. He or she does not know what government is "his" or "hers"; is ignorant of the officials, symbols, rituals, and values he or she is supposed to honor or despise; and must be taught his or her political identity.[8] Citizens within a given country eventually share a common sense of national identity and loyalty that distinguishes them from the people of other countries. At the same time, they may have diverse feelings about the effectiveness of their political leaders. Political socialization helps to account for both the commonalities and diversities of political life.[9]

Changes in the patterns of political culture come about through political socialization. When the totalitarian state revises the account of history in school textbooks or when a new country expands the school system, the political elites are attempting to shape and control the process of creating political orientations. An extreme example of a country trying to develop a new political culture through political socialization is Vietnam. When North Vietnam took control of South Vietnam a determined and tireless effort was made to retrain the people. Many

---

[7]Walter A. Rosenbaum, *Political Culture* (New York: Praeger, 1975), p. 13.

[8]Ibid.

[9]Richard Dawson, Kenneth Prewitt, and Karen Dawson, *Political Socialization* (Boston: Little, Brown, 1977), p. 11.

former members of the previous government and armed forces and those who associated with the Americans were sent to camps to be "reeducated" into "correct" political thinking. Capitalist and "bourgeois" attitudes were considered antigovernment.

How and why do most people come to identify with a country? Why do some persons develop a sense of involvement in politics while others do not? How, when, and why do people develop commitments to particular parties or ideologies? These are basic questions for understanding political life. They are especially important for those seeking to understand relationships between political systems and their individual constituents. These issues are the focus of political socialization.[10]

Political socialization, in short, is that part of the political process that forms political attitudes. Almost all children acquire distinctive political orientation and behaviors at an early age. Socialization is an ongoing process, one that takes place over time. Of course, individuals "learn" about politics throughout their lives and, in varying degrees, alter political perspectives. Virtually no one enters adulthood with a fixed and unchangeable political mind-set. It is in reference to this continuous or developing process that the study of political socialization differs most sharply from opinion polls or similar surveys.

In this respect, socialization can be compared to time-lapsed photography, such as a film showing a flower opening, whereas a public-opinion poll can most easily be compared to a single snapshot frozen in time. Political socialization is the way one generation passes on political standards and beliefs to succeeding generations, a process called *cultural transmission.* [11]

In a sense the socialization process is never completed but goes on continuously throughout life. Attitudes are always being adapted, questioned or reinforced as the individual goes through his or her life experiences. Early family impressions can create a favorable image of a political party, for example, but subsequent education, job experience, and the influence of friends may alter that early image into an unfriendly or even hostile one.[12]

Socialization focuses our attention on how and when a person acquires political ideas and feelings. We have observed that it is an ongoing, continuous process that is never fully finished. As David Easton explains it:

> Identification of time as a determinant, therefore, inevitably leads to a development perspective. We look not at a given moment in the past but at a sequence of time periods so as to be able to appreciate the extent to which current behavior or orientation are the outcome of characteristic pattern of development.[13]

For political science any detailed attention to political socialization is an acknowledgment that the present has evolved from many previous experiences.

---

[10]Ibid., p. 3.

[11]Almond and Powell, *Comparative Politics: A Developmental Approach,* p. 16.

[12]Ibid., p. 65.

[13]David Easton and Jack Dennis, *Children in the Political System* (New York: McGraw-Hill, 1969), p. 8.

Horizontal and Vertical Socialization

Every society must provide for the fulfillment of certain elementary or basic functions such as the goods and services necessary for survival, the reproduction of its numbers, a certain degree of law and order, and some form of defense from foreign encroachment.[14] Each generation must learn what is expected or required of its members if these functions are to be fulfilled. If the socialization process were to fail, no society could maintain itself, and disintegration would be the result.

To express the process more clearly, David Easton draws a distinction between vertical and horizontal socialization. By vertical socialization he means the transmission of cultural values from the older to the younger generation—from grandfather to father to son. Horizontal socialization, on the other hand, expresses socialization within a single generation—brothers, sisters, classmates, peers, and friends. In other words, members of the same generation also influence one another.

If a political system is to maintain itself, the existing generation must repeat itself in the younger, maturing generation. This is the vertical dimension of a stable political system. When one is looking at a dominant or ruling class in a stable society, there exists a similarity of its members' views. A function of socialization works toward a harmony in outlook and behavior within a generation.[15]

Where different ethnic groups, social classes, regional groups, and even educational systems implant contrasting political attitudes, concepts, and patterns of behavior in the children, the rising generation will be more likely to develop diverse and conflicting points of view. If the process of vertical socialization (older to younger) results in a new generation having seriously divided and antagonistic attitudes about the structures and operation of the government, it may be assumed that some political instability and conflict will result. Thus, examples of a younger generation seriously divided from the dominant structures and processes of government are the Catholics of Northern Ireland and the Palestinians on the West Bank and the Gaza Strip. The governmental authority has been seriously challenged by the youth.

From the beginning of its multiethnic immigration and the heritage of a melting pot country, Americans have followed politics that would tend to erase many cultural and linguistic differences over the generations. In contrast, Canada has pursued policies that perpetuate ethnic, cultural, language, and, to a degree, political divisions across the generations. As a consequence, the province of Quebec has teetered on the verge of secession from the rest of Canada. Most polls conducted in French-speaking Canada show about 40 percent support some sort of independence from the Canadian Confederation.

If the socialization process raises children who upon reaching adulthood have

---

[14]Ibid., p. 28.

[15]Ibid., p. 31.

among themselves conflicting hopes, conceptions of the rules of the system, attitudes toward compliance and feelings about legitimacy, it can be assumed that social and political tensions will result that can lead to unrest. The Soviet Union's Baltic Republics offer striking examples. After 50 years of Russian incorporation and domination, Lithuania, Estonia, and Latvia are rejecting the legitimacy of Moscow's control. Obviously, the young demonstrators of Lithuania were brought up with a pride in their distinct heritage, religion, and independence. Indeed, the difficulties facing the Soviet leaders in numerous ethnic border regions such as Armenia, Georgia, and Moldavia, as well as the Baltic republics, all offer examples of a faltering or failed russification and Communist indoctrination policy. Deep-seated and unshakable values, attitudes, and beliefs were conveyed through the generations in a vertical way to arrive at the predicament in which the Soviet Union now finds itself. These strong nationalist feelings were developed outside the official channels of communication and education. In January 1990, when Gorbachev first visited Lithuania to mediate the growing tensions, his fears were not lessened when he saw the flags of Estonia, Latvia, Moldavia, Georgia, Armenia, and the Ukraine at a rally he attended. These are some of the republics where separatist and nationalist sentiments have survived many years of Communist party suppression and propaganda.

The Soviet Union has been identified by both popular opinion and scholars as a country that has engaged in considerable **political indoctrination**.[16] The Soviet principles of pedagogy, first formulated in the 1930s, accept as their aim the formation of behavior, character, and traits of personality necessary to the Soviet state.[17] The most important teaching agents have been the schools. A major part of this indoctrination is done through the curriculum. The chief goal of the educational experience has been to inculcate loyalty and support for the polity, its leaders, and their policies. Songbooks, readers, and textbooks have been designed to convince the students that the accomplishments of the Soviet people are unequaled anywhere in the world.[18]

The developments within the USSR's border republics in the late 1980s and early 1990s prove that other socialization processes were taking place outside of the governmentally controlled channels. Over time, the centrally directed Soviet empire has not been able to replicate or reproduce itself intact (vertical socialization) very effectively.

People living in a society must be trained and educated to fit into the political, cultural, and social institutions that they inherit (vertical), but they must also learn to "fit" with each other at the present time (horizontal). A person is said to be "well socialized" if he or she fits into the overall pattern in a harmonious way, but "poorly socialized" if he or she deviates beyond some unspecified range. Some of the deep and nagging divisions based on race in a number of American urban areas might be examples of weak horizontal integration.

---

[16]Frederick C. Barghorn, *Politics in the USSR* (Boston: Little, Brown, 1966), p. 84.

[17]Ibid., p. 85.

[18]Dawson, Prewitt, and Dawson, *Political Socialization*, p. 145.

Congruence Theory

In most countries the government has the most power. Indeed, the political system has a monopoly over the use of power. This power is also known as **authority**. If a government has authority, then it also has control. When we speak of *authority patterns*, we refer to a relationship between a superior and a subordinate. The government official is superior and the individual is inferior in regards to direction and control. When one studies authority patterns, then, in effect, one is studying government and politics.

A national society is often the largest and most comprehensive unit with which an individual citizen identifies. Consequently, for a person living in Japan, Japanese society is the largest unit with which he or she relates. Societies are themselves "social units" of governments.[19] Put another way, the target of the government's authority and power is the national society. Societies are made up of large-scale networks of relations in which subordinate social units (e.g., families, schools, clubs, and corporations) all build up to a national government. Consequently, it is likely that the general characteristics of societies will also affect authority relations in these lower units.

Besides authority there are a number of traits that cut across all parts of society. One example is language: Most members of most societies speak a common language. An example related to authority is the class structure, which is also called **stratification**. Stratification signifies a kind of ranking and the ways in which people in a society are vertically divided. There is a higher and lower level in terms of prestige, respect, worthiness, and dignity.[20] Societies have usually relied on two different bases of stratification. One basis is inherited such as race, caste, titled aristocracy, or ethnic group; this basis is also called *ascribed*. Another basis is merit or achievement, such as level of education, professional competence, or skills.

A modern industrial political system must operate on the basis of merit and achievement in order to become most productive and competitive. Awarding jobs and career opportunities on the basis of class, religion, gender, or ethnic basis alone is antithetical to a modern, rational, industrial society. A democratic government based on the ideal of equality functions most easily in a society that leans toward achievement and not ascribed characteristics.

In any society there are countless situations where authority besides the national government is involved. For purposes of distinction we will call the political system *public government.* Where we find authority elsewhere, such as the family, school, place of work, and other places, we will call it *private government.*

Authority patterns have varying degrees of consistency, or "fit," so to speak, among its elements. When something is congruent, it is in harmony or agreement with something else. The congruence of authority suggests the authority patterns of separate social units resemble one another. The attitudes and practices are

---

[19]Harry Eckstein and Ted Robert Garr, *Patterns of Authority* (New York: John Wiley & Sons, 1975), p. 412.

[20]Ibid., p. 414.

similar rather than different from one subunit (e.g., family) to another (e.g., school).[21]

The concept of congruence of authority patterns is very useful for the study of political socialization and the political stability of a country.

The way a child is raised in the family, followed by the experience in school, continuing on to adulthood and the circumstances of work and personal experience, should mold or shape an individual who is appropriate or "fits" in a particular political system.

In Imperial Germany (before 1914), working-class families were disciplined by the father, the patriarch. All the children's activities were monitored, and enforcement was rigorous and even violent at times. Orders for the children were specific (not "help your mother," but "wash the dishes" or "get some potatoes"). These orders were detailed even when the children knew exactly what was expected of them.[22] Regarding formal education, there can be little doubt that, in Germany, the family had precedence over the school.[23] The material taught was originally in the possession of the teachers and was dished out to the pupils like a meal. The teacher's monopoly provided him or her with an overpowering authority, and the students were in a subservient position.[24] After World War I, a democratic government was established in Germany, the Weimar Republic, with free election and civil liberties. The Germans now had a government whose "fit" was incongruent, because German authority patterns were basically authoritarian. Eventually, the Weimar Republic fell with the dire economic conditions of the late 1920s and early 1930s, destroying any remaining hopes of democratic survival.

AGENTS OF POLITICAL SOCIALIZATION

Political socialization is achieved through a wide variety of institutions and agencies. Some of these agents are direct and deliberate, such as a civics class extolling the virtues of a political system. Other agents are more subtle and indirect, such as childhood play groups. The entire political socialization process is complex and impossible to comprehend fully; nevertheless, we will attempt to separate and explain the principal agents of political socialization, bearing in mind that socialization is a continuous process.

Primary groups are particularly significant in forming political ideas. A primary group is usually small and informal. The family, close friends, peer groups, and some acquaintances at work are examples of primary groups. **Secondary groups** are generally larger, more formal, and structured. Interactions within secondary groups are less personal and more superficial. Some examples of second-

---

[21]Ibid., p. 403.

[22]Ibid., p. 57.

[23]Ralf Dahrendorf, *Society and Democracy in Germany* (New York: Doubleday, 1967), pp. 313–314.

[24]Ibid., p. 141.

ary groups would be students in a college classroom, members of a large club, and an occupational association, such as a labor union or professional society.

Primary groups play a particularly strong role in the socialization process. The family, close **peer groups**, and work associates are important sources of political learning. Throughout life some friends and trusted colleagues will continue to serve as a source of information and ideas. Secondary groups act as agents of political learning in ways paralleling the family and school; however, not all secondary groups get involved in politics to the same degree. Being a member of the American Civil Liberties Union (ACLU) obviously involves much more political learning and experience than membership in the local poetry club. A major contribution of secondary groups is to provide experience and training in large group situations and leadership skills that can be transferred to the political world.[25]

Family

Throughout the world, in all cultures, the family is a major source of socialization. Various reasons help to explain this primacy. Two major ones are: the unlimited access to the individuals being socialized and the strength and intensity of the ties that exist among members of the family.[26] The stronger the links and the closer the ties, the more impact a given association will have.

A note of caution is needed here. Although the family has a powerful role in the overall socialization of the individual, political learning and political attitudes are only a small part of all social learning. There are a number of other reasons why the family often plays a low-key role in transmitting political values, such as a lack of knowledge on the part of the parents or lack of interest and salience.

The agenda of the parents is already quite full. Preparing one's offspring for a productive, social, and economic life is no easy task. For most parents, having children with adequate social, educational, and occupational skills in adult life is more important than getting them ready for the political world. It is not surprising that little direct political training is done by the parents. Some scholars have even argued that other agents, such as the schools, are more influential than the family in contemporary American society.[27]

Nonetheless, the family still plays a formative role in the political socialization of its children. Whether it be through conversations or participation, or nonparticipation, parents do hand down their political outlooks. The children are first-hand observers of the amount of trust, fear, loyalty, support, or resentment displayed by the adult members of the family toward the political systems. It is precisely because parents are in such a unique position that their influence, however indirect it may be, is so significant.

---

[25]Dawson and Prewitt, *Political Socialization,* p. 186.

[26]Ibid., p. 115.

[27]See Robert Hess and Judith Torney, *The Development of Political Attitudes in Children* (Chicago: Aldine, 1967).

There are merits both to arguments that stress the primacy of the family and those that play down its impact. Rather than try to resolve the question of whether the family is relatively more or less important than other agents, let us judge each national society on its own.

A comprehensive study of American high school seniors found a high level of correspondence between parent and children with respect to party identification and support for particular political leaders.[28] Although parent-offspring congruence is not perfect, the level of correspondence and the consistency of findings in this area are impressive.

The basic political outlooks and attachments for which parental transmission is greatest are the beliefs that tend to be acquired early in life, at the point when the impact of the family looms particularly large. Inasmuch as positions on specific issues are formed throughout life, and in contexts far removed from the early years when the family impact is so strong, it is not surprising that the imprint of the family is less apparent as the years go by. Issues for which early family positions have little relevance may confront the adult. Other agents of socialization will have had a chance to exert influence by the time the adult citizen, and maybe even the high school senior, forms preferences on specific issues.[29]

School

Every country has some type of educational system. In most developed societies schooling begins around age 5 and ends at about 17 or 18. The obvious reason for the educational system is to prepare the new generation with the technologies and skills needed to foster and perpetuate the country. No political system is willing to leave to chance this critical function.

There is a distinction between school and education. Education can take place anywhere and at any time. We are educated by our parents, peers, our church, and the news media. School, on the other hand, is a structured and formal institution. Schools have a twofold task. They provide knowledge and skills, but they also teach obedience and discipline. The discipline received in the family is more personal, whereas in the schools it is more regimented and formal. When first entering school, the student learns the alphabet, but he or she also learns obedience to authority. We are more interested here in schools as they relate to political learning and political life.

The educational system provides the students with knowledge about the political world and their role in it. The curriculum is one of the principal tools of political socialization. Materials are selected for the classrooms with an eye toward reinforcing and instilling the cultural values and standards of the national society. The country's history and past achievements are especially filtered so as to reflect the glory and honor of its past. Whether the country has a democratic or dictatorial

---

[28]M. Kent Jennings and Richard G. Niemi, *The Political Character of Adolescence* (Princeton, N.J.: Princeton University Press, 1974), pp. 51–62.

[29]Dawson and Prewitt, *Political Socialization*, p. 25.

form of government, the schools must transmit the knowledge and values necessary for good citizenship as defined by the rulers. Whether it is deemed political indoctrination or civic training depends on who is doing the judging. An American businessperson would describe classroom instruction in the Soviet Union about the merits of Marxism as political indoctrination and not civic training. A Communist party official would probably label a class about capitalism and free enterprise in the United States as political propaganda.

When the values being taught in the school curriculum are in harmony or closely resemble the values prevailing in other socializing agents, then the political values are intensified and their influence is deepened. However, if the political norms being taught in the classroom diverge sharply from other important agents of political learning, then the impact is reduced. To summarize, the better the "fit" or congruence, the more successful the political training.

Using the erstwhile Communist East European regimes as an example (Poland, East Germany, Romania, Czechoslovakia, Hungary, and Bulgaria), the explicit Communist party socialization and indoctrination in the schools, in the workplace, and the communication media was not reinforced at all by other agents of socialization such as the family, religion, and western media penetration. Consequently, the world witnessed the total lack of legitimacy of the Communist governments and their speedy collapse in 1989.

Political values are also handed down to the students through the ceremonies of the classroom such as pledging allegiance to the flag, singing the national anthem and related patriotic songs, celebrating national leaders and victorious wars, along with portraits and commemorative holidays. In every country educational leaders expect that such exposure will lead to greater respect and affection for the society and its form of government. During these rituals, the collective nature of patriotism is stressed and the group experience can be compelling for an impressionable young student.

Schools also affect political socialization through the teacher's official position. The teacher is a formal authority figure. Other than a police officer or a fire fighter, who is more remote, the teacher is the first state-connected figure a young citizen is compelled to encounter. Although the child has experienced the authority and direction of the parents, the schoolteacher's position is noticeably different. Parents are personal and permanent. In the preschool years, the emotional and intimate care and concern of parents is blurred and fused along with their authority. Teachers, on the other hand, are soon viewed as authority figures much like political authority. The teacher is playing a structured role. In time, the child begins to get a sense of the hierarchical order and rank within the school itself, e.g., such as the teacher, principal, and superintendent. The child is taught to obey any incumbent who is filling a particular role at a given time in the educational system.

A classic example of the system of education acting as a handmaiden to the political regime is Britain in the nineteenth and early twentieth century. In Britain, a strong elitist principle has been one of the main guiding posts, which has meant that education has been seen as a scarce resource to be doled out to the masses in sparing quantities. This influenced both the structure and content of education, with the elite receiving a different kind of education in separate institutions from

U.S. schoolchildren pledging allegiance to the flag.

the masses.[30] Indeed, there was some fear that if the state expanded educational opportunities, this could stimulate revolutionary fervor. Certain members of the British aristocracy and bourgeoisie dreaded the idea that the excesses of continental European revolutions would spread to their "tight little island."

The solution was to educate individuals for their station in life, so the schools had the task of confirming a class and political structure by teaching the kind of behavioral patterns that a hierarchical set of class relations demanded. The dominant feeling may have been that only those from higher-class backgrounds were

---

[30]Ted Tapper, *Political Education and Stability* (New York: John Wiley & Sons, 1976), p. 42.

The authoritarian approach: Chinese schoolchildren in their required uniform.

capable of benefitting from the more elevated forms of education. The Newcastle Commission, which studied British education in 1861, received the following testimony from the Reverend James Fraser:

> Even if it were possible, I doubt whether it would be desirable, with a view to the real interests of the peasant boy, to keep him in school till he was 14 or 15 years of age.

But it is not possible. We must make up our minds to see the last of him, as far as the day school is concerned at 10 or 11.[31]

Occupation

Adults spend most of their lives at work. Jobs and the groups and experiences connected to the workplace are settings for the development and transmission of political information and values. A trade union, a professional association, and even social groups such as the company softball team can help to shape an individual's political attitudes. Studies of opinions and political preferences have found that individuals tend to share common opinions with those people with whom they spend a lot of time and have close relationships. Husbands and wives, friends and neighbors, and work associates tend to look at the political and social world in similar ways.[32]

Heightened collective activity at the workplace such as bargaining for a new contract or a strike can have a profound socializing effect. The lessons learned by the Polish workers who became members of the Solidarity Labor Union and their participation in strikes in the early 1980s can be seen in their success with the reforms and elections of 1989.

Mass Media

Modern societies are becoming increasingly a single global network. The **mass media**—radio, television, newspapers, and magazines—have become vital channels for transmitting political information and values within the country and beyond its borders. Current events and evaluations of these events are conveyed to the people through the news media. The information may be directed from the government to the citizen, from one group to another group, or from a group to private citizens and from the citizens to the government.

Modern communication media play an increasingly significant role in the political developments of countries as diverse as the United States, the Soviet Union, and China. As societies advance technologically and as the people become more geographically and socially mobile, the traditional structures like the extended family and community-based ties weaken, and the mass media gain in prominence. Few societies can escape. In the spring of 1989, 200 million Soviet citizens were hypnotized by the spirited live televised debate in their Supreme Soviet. There is some evidence that fax machines and computers linking the United States and China played some part in generating public sympathy and attention regarding the students' plight in China during the student unrest in spring of 1989.

One must be wary when weighing the effects of the mass media on political

---

[31]J. Stuart Maclure, *Educational Documents: England and Wales 1816–1963* (London: Chapman & Hall, 1965), p. 75.

[32]Angus Campbell, Gerald Gurin, and Warren Miller, *The Voter Decides* (New York: Harper & Row, 1954), pp. 199–206.

socialization. On the whole, studies have shown that the media usually tends to reinforce or reaffirm preexisting attitudes. The media channels are not always effective at converting the people to new ideas. There is evidence suggesting that those who pay the closest attention to a particular message are already predisposed in their orientation. Those groups that are most hopefully regarded as the target of communication are often least likely to be in the audience.[33]

Before leaving the topic of political socialization, let us note the following point. Most of the literature and research regarding political socialization has proceeded on the assumption that the person being socialized plays only a passive role in the process of absorbing the values of the agent. This view of the individual's role is a natural outgrowth of a definition of socialization as a mechanism of transmitting cultural values to new members of a society, a definition shared by the cultural anthropologists and sociologists who did so much to shape the study of political socialization.[34] Yet there can be no political socialization without a "socializee" (a person to socialize), a living, breathing individual who seeks, screens, and selectively avoids certain sensory stimuli. Far from being merely passive recipients of information and cues, most people can be assumed to be actively seeking certain kinds of information from specific kinds of courses (e.g., the Voice of America and Radio Free Europe) under identifiable conditions and to be consciously avoiding other kinds (e.g., government-controlled publications and broadcasts).

In summary, people who evaluate the messages transmitted by socializing agents are not always in harmony with the views characteristic of those agents. Thus, the socialization process is not a transactional one, but an interactional process in which two-way exchange and influences can occur.

The tendency to downplay the effect of the socializee on the socialization experience was probably reinforced by the perception of politics as essentially an adult prerogative that, coupled with the research focus on children, led to the assumption that adult and elite socialization agents simply fed political information and values to the "formless child" and "ignorant masses."[35]

SUMMARY

The politico-psychological dimension of a country's political system plays a central role in the entire political process. The attitudes, beliefs, orientations, and values that the citizens possess regarding the government are known as the political culture.

A political culture is a particular distribution of political attitudes, values, feelings, information, and skills. Just as people's attitudes affect what they do,

[33]Elihu Katz and Paul Lazarfeld, *Personal Influence* (New York: The Free Press, 1955), pp. 21–22.

[34]David Schwartz and Sandra Schwartz, *New Directions in Political Socialization* (New York: Free Press, 1975), p. 8.

[35]Ibid.

likewise, a country's political culture affects the conduct of citizens and leaders throughout the political system. Political cultures may be consensual or conflictual on issues of public policy and on their views of legitimate governmental and political arrangements. In a consensual political culture, citizens tend to agree on the appropriate means of making political decisions and tend to share views on major problems and solutions. Leading examples of consensual political cultures are the United States and Great Britain. In more conflictual cultures the citizens are sharply divided on both the legitimacy of the regime and solutions to major problems. France and Italy have displayed conflictual political cultures. It follows, therefore, that the political culture of a country can contribute either to stability (consensual) or instability (conflictual) in the political system.

In the process of political socialization one generation passes political standards and beliefs on to succeeding generations. Most people, at a relatively early age, acquire distinctive political attitudes and behavior patterns. The development of political beliefs results from taking cues and examples from such sources as family, school, peers, and the communications media.

Where all the agents of political socialization support and reinforce each other (congruence), the country is more likely to have political stability. The people and the government have a comfortable "fit." On the other hand, if the individuals experience conflicting and confusing values from the various agents of political socialization (incongruence), political unrest may follow.

RECOMMENDED READINGS

Almond, Gabriel, and Sidney Verba. *The Civic Culture.* Boston: Little, Brown, 1963. This is a rich analysis of political culture using a cross-national approach. The attitudes of people in five countries are compared: the United States, the United Kingdom, West Germany, Mexico, and Italy.

Dawson, Richard E., Kenneth Prewitt, and Karen S. Dawson. *Political Socialization,* 2nd ed. Boston: Little, Brown, 1977. The authors present a brief and well-written introduction to the subject of political socialization. There is an especially good investigation of the impact of the family upon political learning.

Ippolito, Dennis S., Thomas G. Walker, and Kenneth L. Kolson. *Public Opinion and Responsible Democracy.* Englewood Cliffs, N.J.: Prentice-Hall, 1976. The emphasis is on the political consequences and effects of public opinion in the American political system. The book focuses on elite opinion and the linkages between the public and political elites.

McClosky, Herbert, and John R. Zaller. *The American Ethos.* Cambridge: Harvard University Press, 1984. The authors offer a comprehensive study of the basic political values of the citizens in the United States, especially their attitudes about capitalism and democracy.

Niemi, Richard G. *How Family Members Perceive Each Other.* New Haven, Conn.: Yale University Press, 1974. This is an extensive study of high school students and their parents. A prominent feature of the book is to match students with their parents and husbands with their wives.

Pye, Lucien W., and Sidney Verba, eds. *Political Culture and Political Development.* Princeton, N.J.: Princeton University Press, 1965. A classic collection of articles that show how political style and activity have been influenced by political culture in ten countries.

Renshon, Stanley A., ed. *Handbook of Political Socialization.* New York: The Free Press, 1977. This is an advanced level study of political socialization. It looks at the boundaries of current research and promising roads for subsequent inquiry.

Schwartz, David G., and S.K. Schwartz, eds. *New Directions in Political Socialization.* New York: The Free Press, 1975. The authors identify and describe some new directions in theory and research. For example, there is a chapter on popular music as an agent of political socialization.

Stacey, Barrie. *Political Socialization in Western Society.* New York: St. Martin's Press, 1977. The author looks at childhood, adolescence, national identity, class, and age and their relationship to political socialization.

White, Stephen. *Political Culture and Soviet Politics.* New York: St. Martin's Press, 1979. This is good study of nondemocratic political culture. The author focuses on the country's centuries of previous political experience and the persistence of traditional beliefs and practices.

Interest Groups

Most people are social, at least in some of their activities. As society grows and people interact and depend on those beyond their immediate families, they often form groups to promote or protect their interests. Chapter 3 noted a principal reason democratic theorists believe organized government came into being was to protect and facilitate private interests. Much of politics, at least pluralistic or democratic politics, is about conflict, negotiation, and government decisions, which often represent a compromise. Many people get involved in politics for reasons of self-interest, or join groups they believe will watch out for their interests. A great deal of political participation is through membership in an organized group, and interest groups are a principal input mechanism.

Robert A. Dahl of Yale University lists 20 conditions that are required if a democratic political system is to exist. The first "requirement" listed is the "freedom to form and join organizations."[1] Fifteen years earlier, the same author noted that through groups (and other means) democracy extends "the number, size, and diversity of minorities whose preferences will influence the outcome of governmental decisions."[2]

British political party specialist, R. T. McKenzie, observes that, in a pluralist system, interest groups, not political parties, *represent* the people by expressing their demands. Political parties "are teams of potential decision makers who offer themselves as prospective governors of the country between whom the voters have an opportunity to choose at a general election." Groups are the ever-present representing institutions. Once in office, government officials must "contend with the *real* on-going expressions of group demands through the organized interests in the society."[3]

INTEREST GROUPS

All pluralistic political systems have interest groups. If anything, interest groups, like government budgets worldwide, continue to expand. The word "interest" has also come to connote organized interests and often special interests. Interest groups are a source of activity in all democracies, and they have been major sources in moving the previously **authoritarian** Soviet Union and Eastern Europe toward political reform.

Since World War II, we have discovered that the more specialized and technologically advanced a society is, the more significant organized groups become in the political process. Groups are key institutions in formulating and making demands in a political system. Strident group claims and group leaders unwilling or unable to compromise may also fragment the political system and threaten its stability or

---

[1]Robert A. Dahl, *Polyarchy: Participation and Opposition* (New Haven. Conn.: Yale University Press, 1971), p. 3.

[2]Robert A. Dahl, *A Preface to Democratic Theory* (Chicago: University of Chicago Press, 1956), p. 133.

[3]R. T. McKenzie, "Political Parties Revisited," *Government and Opposition*, 12:4 (Autumn 1978), p. 528.

even survival. Political fragmentation is more likely in societies that are becoming less politically restrained; and new as well as old ethnic, religious, linguistic, and regional claims suddenly and vocally arrive in the political arena. Groups need to operate within some rules of the game if they are to be eufunctional (contribute to functioning) in a democratic political system or in a country transiting to democracy. Should generally agreed upon rules not exist, the very survival of the system can be threatened.

The Definition of Interest Groups

Interest groups are made up of people who share common traits, attitudes, beliefs, and/or objectives and who organize or join to promote and protect these interests. An interest group is in most cases an advantage group; it is to an individual's advantage to join. It is an organized body that is supposed to look after the interests of its members. Organized groups have bylaws, formal membership requirements, meetings, and elected officers and thus have continuity. They provide information and other services to members and maintain a communication flow through such things as newsletters that publicize the organization's objectives and the efforts to further these objectives.

Although the terms "interest groups" and "pressure groups" often are used interchangeably, we distinguish between the two. A pressure group is one whose predominant or sole aim is to influence public authorities. Some groups are organized specifically for this purpose, such as the Vietnam Veterans against the War or Concerned Citizens opposed to a state income tax. Other interest groups may primarily look after the welfare of their members and only occasionally attempt to influence a public issue. One example would be the American Automobile Association, which provides insurance, tour information, towing, repair services, and bail bonds; but may engage infrequently in political activity, such as opposing an increased gasoline tax or initiating legal action against a well-known and persistent speed-trap operation. We use the term "interest group" (which includes "pressure groups") because almost all organized groups at one time or another attempt to influence government on some issue. Interest groups attempt to influence government decisions and even support political candidates. They do *not*, however, nominate candidates for public office. Political parties nominate candidates, which will be discussed in Chapter 6. Most interest groups usually have restricted concerns, such as minimum wages, textile tariffs, gun control, milk supports, and the like, whereas political parties are concerned with all aspects of public policy, both domestic and international.

The Evolution of Interest Groups

The twentieth century witnessed a rapid increase in the number of interest groups. Two reasons are (1) functional specialization leading to the evolution of very specialized groups (such as the General Confederation of Beet-Growers in France, the Milk Producers Federation, the Burley and Dark Leaf Tobacco Export Association, the American Hot Dip Galvanizers Association in the United States, and the

British Road Haulage Association) and (2) the fact that governments throughout the world are taking on more activities and responsibilities, as discussed in Chapter 1.

As the number of people allowed to participate legally in politics (usually through voting rights) increased and the scope of government activities expanded throughout society, it was natural that organizations were created to respond to the new conditions. Interest groups also are found in many developing countries. Regardless of the stage of industrialization-urbanization, like-minded people have attempted to influence political behavior by joining together. Organized interest groups also are called **secondary groups** to distinguish them from primary, face-to-face associations, such as family, schoolmates, or fraternities or sororities.

Private groups now have much more to gain or lose as a result of government policies or potential policies. In an effort to influence government decisions, a group is increasingly likely to encounter other organized interests with conflicting objectives, and this leads to greater activity. For example, on one Texas university campus Students for Animal Welfare posted flyers prepared by the New England Anti-Vivisection Society. These flyers described and pictured the use of animals in painful scientific experiments. Within days, other flyers appeared announcing an imminent rally at the entrance to the Health Science Center, sponsored by the Incurably Ill for Animal Research to defend scientific experiments on animals.

Government is more pervasive and is more likely to affect the private lives of persons than it was 30 or 50 years ago. In an excellent study of the British Medical Association (BMA), Harry Eckstein found the growth of government an important reason for political activity by the BMA:

> The state of Britain today [1950s and 1960s] disposes directly of 40 percent of the national income; and that fact speaks for itself. We may regard political and actual groups . . . drawn into politics chiefly through the impact of public policies, either policies actually adopted or policies which are "threatened" [by government].[4]

Canadian provincial governments and the national government account for 43 percent of gross national expenditure. In the United States many business organizations, foreign companies and countries, as well as other associations now employ full-time lobbyists in Washington, D.C., because of the expanded scope of government programs and regulations. Many Washington-based lawyers work principally as professional lobbyists for numerous clients. One measure of growing input activity as government activities increase was the tripling of Washington lawyers between 1973 and 1982.

As a society becomes more economically differentiated, groups organize to represent specialized interests. When one interest group begins to make claims on government, new groups are organized, or existing groups take on new tasks to counter these claims. The growing complexity and interrelatedness of today's world leads to the growth of interest groups. The longer a democratic political

---

[4]Harry Eckstein, *Pressure Group Politics: The Case of the British Medical Association* (Stanford, Calif.: Stanford University Press, 1960), p. 27.

system enjoys stability and experiences gradual change, the more interest groups it accumulates.

Sometimes groups temporarily form to deal with a particular issue. Once the issue has been settled, the group disbands. For example, the Wing Airport Resistance Association (WARA) in Britain shows what can happen when change and "modernization" confront basic home and neighborhood concerns. WARA's struggle was described as "a classic example of a protest pressure group of the 'I don't want it in my back garden or flying over my house' type."[5]

WARA did not direct its efforts mainly at the various ministries or the cabinet in London as might be expected. Rather, it focused on selected Members of Parliament (M.P.s), the media, popular opinion, and local government. WARA's objective was to keep London's third airport away from the North Buckinghamshire area. A lawyer was chosen to represent WARA before a commission appointed by the minister of technology to make the final decision. M.P.s became vice presidents of the association, and 60,000 dues-paying members were recruited from the North Buckinghamshire area. A professional public relations firm was hired, and two publicity efforts involved hundreds of agricultural vehicles, cars, and trucks parading through all the threatened villages. Thousands of newsletters, pamphlets, newssheets, and protests from local government groups and M.P.s ultimately led the ministry of technology to select Foulness, where the main public objection was upsetting the wildlife balance.

Broadly speaking, this was an environmental issue, at least for those living near the proposed North Buckinghamshire airport site. It is an example of interests and inputs that would not have occurred 60 years ago because there were few public airports and minimal commercial air travel. It also is an example of mass input, seeking media attention rather than negotiations with government bureaucrats held behind closed doors. Residents organized WARA for the specific purpose of pressuring the government to change its mind, and they won.

Most interest groups are more durable than WARA. For example, hand gun control becomes an intense public policy issue after an assassination or a well-publicized mass murder. Public outrage calls for stricter handgun legislation. The National Rifle Association, however, claims it can immediately swamp Washington offices with 500,000 letters opposing any gun control legislation.[6] This medium-sized lobby has generally been very successful in blocking such legislation when demands for gun control intensified. Public opinion is often transient, but the National Rifle Association endures "forever."

Not all interest groups work within the system. Some groups emerge to challenge the political system to change itself fundamentally. The Southern Christian Leadership Conference, discussed in Box 5.1, is an interest group that made such claims.

---

[5]W. N. Coxall, *Parties and Pressure Groups,* 2nd ed. (London: Longman, 1985), p. 138. The summary of WARA is from ibid., pp. 138–140.

[6]Dennis S. Ippolito and Thomas G. Walker, *Political Parties, Interest Groups, and Public Policy: Group Influence in American Politics* (Englewood Cliffs, N.J.: Prentice-Hall, 1980), p. 335.

Box 5.1 **Martin Luther King, Jr., and the Emergence of a New Interest Group**

Martin Luther King, Jr., and the civil rights movement became household words in the late 1950s. Events began in December 1955, when Rosa Parks, a black woman, refused to give up her seat on a Montgomery, Alabama, bus for a white passenger who was standing. Mrs. Parks was arrested and released on bail. Her lawyer consulted with an English professor at Alabama State University who served on a newly organized political affairs committee at Dexter Avenue Baptist Church. The church's pastor was 26-year-old Martin Luther King, Jr. At a meeting in the church basement a few days after Mrs. Parks's arrest, 50 black leaders, including Reverend and Mrs. King, approved plans for Montgomery blacks to boycott city buses until segregated seating ended.

The evening Rosa Parks was convicted of violating a Montgomery statute, a meeting in another Baptist church elected Reverend King president of the Montgomery Improvement Association and voted to extend the bus boycott indefinitely. Speaking before an audience of 15,000 that night, Reverend King declared

> There comes a time when people get tired of being pushed out of the glittering sunlight of life's July, and left standing amidst the piercing chill of an Alpine November. . . . [Quoting from Amos] And we are determined here in Montgomery—to work and fight until justice runs down like water, and righteousness like a mighty stream![a]

A recently published book on Martin Luther King, Jr., concludes "King would work on his timing, but his oratory had just made him forever a public person."[b] Support for the boycott rapidly spread nationwide among civil rights activists, northern blacks whose buses were not segregated, and among non-bus-riding blacks in the South. Twelve months after the boycott began, the Supreme Court declared in December 1956 that the Montgomery bus segregation law was unconstitutional.

Martin Luther King, Jr.'s presence and oratory turned this boycott into a broad-based, nonviolent attack on segregation generally. Soon King was heading up the Southern Christian Leadership Conference, and nonviolent protest against legal forms of discrimination became the dominant input mechanism for civil rights progress. Martin Luther King, Jr., rose from obscurity to become the national leader and organizer of American civil rights interests and nonviolent protest until his assassination in 1968. King's entreprenurial skills and vision, as well as being at the right place at the right time (situation), and a clear understanding of benefits by members led to more than a decade of intense and sustained civil rights/interest group input in the political system.

[a]Taylor Branch, *Parting the Waters: America in the King Years 1954–63* (New York: Simon & Schuster, 1988), pp. 140–141. Events surrounding the Montgomery boycott are drawn from Chapters 4 and 5 of this book.

[b]Ibid., p. 142.

Organizations are created by leaders who develop a package of advantages that benefit both the member and the leader, and the organization takes shape and grows. Self-interest obviously leads to the formation of most interest groups. Self-interest as first cause has been labeled the "exchange theory of interest groups." Exchange theory emphasizes the roles of specific individuals (entrepreneurs), whose efforts bring about the first visible signs of a new interest group. An example is Ralph Nader, founder of Public Citizen, a consumer protection group. Many democratic interest groups were based on a distinction between the entrepreneur, or organizer, and the individual member, or customer. People belong because they receive some benefits. The creative and innovative role of the entrepreneur-organizer offers future customers (potential members) benefits if they join the organization. When people join, the group is in business. The important fact about this explanation is that it provides specific examples of why and how formal associations are created by the organizer.[7]

Organizations generally survive if members have dues and donations to invest in their cause. Members are compensated when they believe benefits received exceed costs. Sometimes outside money keeps a group going. Britain's Genetic Study Unit, an interest group that condemns the use of oral contraceptives but supports condoms, receives funds for research and other needs from the London Rubber Company.

Interest groups emerge and grow for a variety of reasons. For example, as manufacturing increases, unions will expand when the political system permits. The growth of white-collar employment and the service sector means fewer union members. About 50 percent of manufacturing workers belong to unions in the United States, while only about 10 percent of white-collar workers carry union cards. There are usually a combination of factors including social, economic, and political conditions interacting with the motivations and abilities of individuals who initiate the organizations.

Why do people join interest groups? Because different groups may offer such important benefits as improved working conditions, better medical care, lower transportation fees, or a sense of moral rectitude. Benefits are the glue that holds interest groups together in democratic political systems.

Types of Interest Groups

Quite common is the restrictive interest group that speaks principally for the narrow interests of its members; the National Rifle Association; the Real Estate Brokers Association; and the Edison Electric Institute, a research and lobbying group for investor owned utility companies, are examples.

Many groups go beyond the specific interests of their members. These groups are *multi-issue interest groups* that also promote broader interests they believe will benefit society in general, as well as their members. Two examples are

---

[7]See Robert Salisbury, "An Exchange Theory of Interest Groups," *Midwest Journal of Political Science*, 13:1 (1969), pp. 1–32.

1. The American Chamber of Commerce and the National Association of Manufacturers, who take public positions on matters of general concern, such as foreign aid, the United Nations, and civil rights.
2. *The People's Lobby,* a 1985 book reporting on the 1983–1984 U.S. Congress by the AFL-CIO Department of Legislation, including sections on restoring civil rights enforcement and the adoption of the metric system. More recently, the AFL-CIO's Free Trade Unions Institute has been active in supporting the Solidarity union movement in Poland and in 1989 began assisting free trade union groups in Hungary.

A more recent phenomenon on the political scene is the *single-issue group* that emerges in response to a controversial public question. Often, ad hoc groups will organize to support or oppose specific bond issues or urban renewal projects. Others are of a more permanent nature. They have had their greatest growth in the United States but are expanding rapidly in most postindustrial societies. These single-cause groups are devoted uncompromisingly to supporting or opposing such causes as abortion, the use of animals in scientific laboratories, tax reduction, nuclear power plants, environmental pollution, and so forth.

Many interest groups, however, are not organized to represent specific material interests of the membership. These are public principle or *promotional groups.* In fact, a sizable number of these groups—such as the American Civil Liberties Union, the League of Women Voters, the British Royal Society for the Prevention of Cruelty to Children, or the Voluntary Euthanasia Society—support positions they believe will improve society in specific ways. These groups are not organized primarily to promote interests unique to their members. A group that has become increasingly active, for example, is the World Society for the Protection of Animals.

Antiabortion forces rally near the Capitol in Washington, D.C.

Interest-Group Benefits

Interest-group members generally receive one or more benefits from membership. One is material benefits—personal rewards such as higher wages, an industrial park that will increase the general business volume in the community, or higher prices for the farmer. Material benefits do not only come from claims made on the government. Many interest groups offer their members group rates (lower rates) for such things as medical insurance and life insurance. Many membership cards provide motel, auto rental, book, and pharmacy discounts, special money market funds, and so forth. Groups also offer personal social *values,* in which psychological and social nonmaterial needs are realized. These would include such needs as affiliation, social interaction, sense of personal identification and belonging, status, fun, and congeniality. A third benefit is cause or promotion. These do not directly promote a participant's special interests. The goals, it is typically claimed, will benefit many people if not all humanity. Examples of such goals would include saving the environment, opposing the spread of nuclear power plants, promoting freedom of expression or civil rights, opposing increased defense spending, and encouraging patriotism and national loyalty. The expression and support of these "good" values are often personally satisfying. Benefits that result may accrue to large numbers of people who have not joined the organization or may not even be aware a group exists promoting the objective. People belong for a sense of social conscience or to establish or confirm a sense of direction to one's life.

Individuals may belong to an organization and receive more than one type of benefit, or one person may perceive one type of benefit, whereas another person perceives a different benefit. Member benefits also may change over the years. Veterans' organizations are one example of such variations in benefits. The late V. O. Key concluded that "every war has been followed by the establishment of a society of veterans to bring pressure for the creation of conduits from the Federal Treasury to the pockets of the veterans."[8] One of the most successful veterans' organizations in the United States, founded at the end of World War I, is the American Legion, which has nearly 3 million members. The Legion and other veterans' groups have been highly successful in securing such material benefits as bonuses, medical care, educational allowances, and the veterans' ten-point test preference when applying for federal jobs. As these benefits have been secured, solidarity values have become more relevant. For many veterans and their families the American Legion building is a center of social and recreational activities. Purposive benefits are also an aspect of veterans' organizations. Various patriotic contests are held and awards made to high school students and others. In 1921 the Legion was a founding sponsor, with the National Education Association, of American Education Week (now also cosponsored by the Department of Education and the National Congress of Parents and Teachers). During American Education Week, programs are undertaken that alert communities to the achievements and needs of the local schools. A strong America and loyalty to it are important objec-

---

[8]V. O. Key, Jr., *Politics, Parties, and Pressure Groups,* 5th ed. (New York: Thomas Y. Crowell, 1974), p. 106.

tives of most veterans' groups. Material benefits were emphasized initially after major wars when millions of new veterans returned home. Other benefits became more important as material objectives were achieved. Although no survey has been taken, we may assume that veterans belong for different reasons. Some may be most interested in the social benefits, whereas others may believe membership is the most effective way to identify with and support educational and patriotic goals. Different benefits are seen as important by different individuals.

Functions of Interest Groups

The first, if not always obvious, political function of an interest group is to influence public policy in an effort to provide benefits to its members. In so doing, it helps to communicate popular feelings and demands to the government. Where a competitive party system exists, part of an interest group's political effort is devoted to influencing one or more of the political parties. A political party in turn attempts to reconcile as many conflicting interests as the party judges ideologically practical in order to win electoral support. Interest groups lobby or seek to persuade government officials, including bureaucrats, and they often contribute time, money, and people to support political candidates (electioneering). Many interest groups also function as a source of information to bureaucrats and lawmakers. This information generally must be "straight" and not obviously manipulated if a group is to build up and retain trust and prestige.

Decentralized parties, such as those found in the United States, Japan, sometimes in France, and in several Latin American countries, leave candidates susceptible to interest-group demands at election time. In such parties, candidates often rely on the support of various groups to finance and man the election campaign. Representatives in the legislature carry obligations to interest groups, which must be paid off eventually. These obligations further reduce party cohesion and discipline in a legislature. The most striking example is the United States, where Congress often appears as an every person for himself or herself scramble. Members of Congress vote first of all to satisfy district or parochial interests and concentrate on providing local services to constituents. There is little reason to stress party identification or association with a president if this conflicts with the district connections that a winning candidate has built up and must continue to nurture. Strong, centralized parties, such as the major parties of Great Britain and Germany, however, are likely to have institutionalized relations with interest groups primarily with the state or national party organizations. Financial support is channeled from the central headquarters, rather than given directly to individual candidates as in the United States. Centralized financing increases the disciplinary powers of party leaders and the unity of the party.

Interest groups also function as another "circuit of representation" in pluralistic societies. Interest-group membership in a pluralistic society may be relatively low, but the number of individuals belonging to groups is much larger than the number belonging to political parties. One circuit of representation is elections, but these occur every two years at the most and generally there are intervals of three to five years between elections. New issues arise and party manifestos are vague.

Interest groups, to use one author's phrase, supply "emotion."[9] They react, communicate opinions, and provide some measure of public response to officials on a regular basis, year-round.

In a 1959 study, which has become a classic, William Kornhauser warned against the dangers of **mass society**. Mass society is a potentially dangerous outcome of the industrial, mobile, technologically sophisticated environment of the postindustrial world. The end result is that "intermediate relations," which are principally interest groups, break down. A mass society can be manipulated by elites with the technology available to them. One example was Nazi Germany, where the ministry of propaganda under Joseph Goebbels played a key role in brainwashing the masses. George Orwell's classic work, *Nineteen Eighty-Four*, published in 1948, shows the worst possibilities of a mass society where anyone showing evidence of "thought-crime" is taken to the ministry of love to be tortured.[10]

Based on Kornhauser's concern that we avoid the evils of mass society, he lists several positive functions performed by **intermediate groups**, or interest groups.

1. Independent groups assist in dealing with many local problems. For example, in the absence of such associations as the PTA, which provides channels of communication between parents and schools, parents are less likely to develop or maintain interest and participation in aspects of the school program.
2. Most interest-group leaders, irrespective of their particular aims (unless they seek to transform radically the political system), help to legitimize the larger system of authority because they work within the system.
3. A large number of stable and independent groups mean diverse and competing interests. Opposition between groups restrains each group's power. This discourages concentrations of power dangerous to both decision makers and the masses.
4. Autonomy prevents a concentration of power. Groups are more or less autonomous in their own spheres of activity. Group membership and activities are not dictated by government. Group independence is also known as *subsystem autonomy.*
5. There are some overlapping memberships among groups. Because each group is concerned with only limited aspects of its members' lives, groups generally do not seek total domination over their membership. Many people belong to more than one group, and sometimes these groups disagree on specific issues.[11]

---

[9]An elaboration of this point and a general discussion of interest groups in Great Britain is on a cassette, "Parties and Interest Groups," by Samuel Finer (New York: Holt, Rinehart and Winston, 1972), side 2.

[10]For a useful contemporary analysis of *Nineteen Eighty-Four* by a political scientist, see Robert C. Tucker, "Does Big Brother Really Exist?" *Wilson Quarterly*, 8:1 (1984), pp. 106–117.

[11]See William Kornhauser, *The Politics of Mass Society* (New York: The Free Press, 1959), pp. 76–78.

TACTICS AND EFFECTIVENESS OF INTEREST GROUPS

Interest-group tactics vary considerably. Interest groups do not confine their activities to lobbying public officials and electioneering. They engage in strikes and boycotts on occasion. They also seek to build support through education and information campaigns, attempt to influence the civil service, and, through court action, seek to correct what they consider illegal or inequitable practices. For example, the National Association for the Advancement of Colored People (NAACP) has been especially active in litigation. Much of the civil rights progress in the United States has been achieved by NAACP court-initiated actions, where the organization used the Fourteenth Amendment to argue that many forms of racial discrimination allowed or required by state laws were unconstitutional.

With the federal form of government and separation of powers in the United States there are numerous points of influence for an interest group. A negative response from one agency, one branch, or one level of government will turn the group toward another target. Many interests have found more response from American state legislatures than from the Congress, and vice versa. Interest groups concentrate their government lobbying at the most responsive points in the decision-making process.

The United States, Great Britain, and France

The U.S. Congress has been a special target of interest groups, whereas in Great Britain greater success has been achieved at the cabinet and bureaucratic levels. There also is increased lobbying of the executive branch and the bureaucracy in the United States. The ever-widening scope and technical character of modern economic and social policies has increased the power and responsibilities of the executive/administrative branch. A majority of legislation, even in the United States, is drafted in the executive branch. Bills that become laws tend to be legal frameworks that must be "fleshed out" by administrative interpretation and implementation. Even if an interest group has "lost" and a legislative act has been passed, it may seek to further a relationship with the administering body to secure a congenial interpretation of policy.

One institutional arrangement that has evolved this century and is based on mutual interests is called an **iron triangle.** When administrative agencies, interest groups, and congressional subcommittees interact for many years in shared areas of concerns, close cooperation frequently occurs. In fact, the cooperation is so close that the triangles tend to dominate policy-making in their areas of interest.

There are iron, or cozy, triangles involved in both legislative and bureaucratic policy-making. Often the general public is unaware of this sectional power. Sometimes the ensuing legislation benefits the public interest, other times not. One example of an iron triangle are senior citizen groups, such as the powerful American Association of Retired Persons, who work closely with legislative subcommittees on aging and health, and both often draw on the support of the Social Security Administration. Similar agency-group-committee triangles exist in dozens of other

© 1978 by Sidney Harris.

policy areas. Sectional power benefits group interests, because they usually do not have to win over the whole political system.

Under the British system, the cabinet dominates policy-making, and the civil service has much latitude in drafting and implementing laws and regulations. Consequently, most British interest groups focus on the executive branch. Moreover, statutes often require such consultation. In the 1970s, more than 600 advisory committees consulted with the British government in specific areas. The groups were legally built into the system to look after the interests of their own members. In his pioneering study of British interest groups, Samuel Finer observed that "on a host of official committees civil servants sit cheek by jowl with representatives of interested associations." For example, the Trades Union Congress is represented on 60 permanent committees, including the Standing Committee on Building Material Prices, the Duty-Free Machinery Imports Committee, and the Joint Advisory Panel for the Decontrol of Fat Stock.[12] It is at these points of contact that much of the influence of interest groups occurs in Great Britain. Not only in Great Britain but in many other countries are there such committees composed of representatives

---

[12]Samuel E. Finer, *Anonymous Empire* (London: Pall Mall Press, 1966), pp. 31–32.

from the government and interest groups. Interest groups that are closely identified with a particular political party frequently may apply excessive pressure. The trade union leadership in Great Britain is closely associated with the British Labour party. A former Labour party prime minister reportedly once shouted at a union official who was trying to change British government policy to suit his preferences: "Get your tanks off my lawn."[13]

British interest groups generally concentrate input on those who make most of the decisions: the government (cabinet) or the bureaucracy. Interest groups are so closely interlocked in the decision-making process that frequently they do not have to take the initiative. Prior consultation with affected interest groups is normal procedure. Before a bill is introduced into Parliament, the ministry working on the bill will discuss the general principles with relevant groups. This is important because before the government has publicly committed itself to specific legislation it is more willing to accept requests to modify its proposal. Thus, the principal channels of British interest-group activity lead to the executive branch.

Extensive day-to-day use of administrative channels in democratic political systems means that a high proportion of interest-group activities are not readily visible. This emerging emphasis on interest-group representation with the bureaucracy is a new variation of pluralism—administrative pluralism. New problems require technical expertise and ongoing consultation. A result is that interest groups have a continuous impact on government policy-making and implementation in the executive branch.

The growing phenomenon of interest-group and administrative interaction is criticized by some who see this as weakening democratic principles and procedures. If the principal representative institution, the legislature, delegates broad responsibilities to a less visible and publicly accountable bureaucracy administering laws and depends heavily on the executive for drafting bills, broader popular input is eroded. Some political scientists see the growing network of alliances between interest groups and administrative agencies as subverting the legislative role and thus democracy. These alliances favor broad discretionary authority for the bureaucracy so that if problems arise they can be worked out without going back to the legislature. This new concept of representation may restrict input and decision making to those interests directly concerned.[14]

An example of the problems that can be caused by this close relationship between interest groups and government can be seen in the history of the French Fourth Republic (1947–1958). Under that system, most interest groups in France were allied with political parties, for example, the General Confederation of Workers with the Communist party and the French Confederation of Catholic Workers with the Popular Republican Movement (MRP), the middle-of-the-road Catholic party. It was not unusual for groups to be more concerned with pushing the

---

[13]Quoted in Alex N. Dragnich and Jorgen Rasmuseen, *Major European Governments*, 7th ed. (Homewood, Ill.: The Dorsey Press. 1987), p. 87.

[14]An exposition of this viewpoint is Theodore J. Lowi, *The End of Liberalism.* 2nd ed. (New York: W. W. Norton & Co., 1979).

interests of the party than the specific concerns of members. This partly explains why only 12 percent of the French work force was unionized in the mid-1980s, compared to 20 percent in the United States. Because parties were relatively weak in the Fourth Republic's parliamentary system, many interest groups had considerable leverage lobbying the National Assembly (legislature) or the bureaucracy.

The specialized legislative committees in the Fourth Republic often substituted bills written by interest groups for bills submitted by a long string of coalition governments. The Constitution of the Fifth Republic (1958 to date), launched by Charles de Gaulle and his supporters, strengthened the independent power of the president and deliberately weakened the National Assembly and the committee system, which often had been colonized by powerful interest groups. The architects of the Fifth Republic and the interest groups subsequently expanded the system whereby groups went to advisory committees—growing centers of access and influence. French governments find it expedient to consult with interest groups, particularly when proposed legislative or administrative action will impinge directly on a group. In the 1980s there were 3,000 commissions, 1,200 committees, and 500 councils bringing together interest-group representatives and bureaucratic offices. For example, the ministry of finance "consults" with more than 130 advisory committees.[15] Other favorite interest-group targets are the private staffs of the ministers and the highly compartmentalized and vertically organized divisions of the national government administration.

The influence of an interest group varies according to situation, administrative officials involved, and the political disposition of the government in power. There is evidence that French governments have consistently maintained a dialogue with pertinent groups. The most institutionalized input under the Fifth Republic is at the executive/administrative level. This is another example of administration pluralism. As one student of French interest groups observed, however, measuring group influence is "like finding a black cat in the coal bin at midnight."[16]

One example of "backroom dealing" that can occur under administrative pluralism is described by British author Anthony Sampson, an expert on international oil companies and the Organization of Petroleum Exporting Countries (OPEC). In the following quote he charges many Western business groups influenced their respective governments to keep oil prices up, despite the fact all these countries imported oil.

> But it was not only the new oil producers [countries that only recently began to export oil] who were now siding with OPEC. It was a vast network of oil companies, arms companies, construction companies and, above all, bankers. The banks had loaned billions to such countries as Mexico, Venezuela and Nigeria, who were suddenly

---

[15]These numbers are taken from Henry W. Ehrmann, *Politics in France*, 4th ed. (Boston: Little, Brown, 1983), p. 204.

[16]Frank L. Wilson, *Interest Group Politics in France* (Cambridge: Cambridge University Press, 1987), p. 221. Wilson is quoting an American lobbyist first cited in Allan J. Cegler and Burdett A. Loomis, eds., *Interest Group Politics* (Palo Alto, Calif.: Stanford University Press, 1983), p. 22.

impoverished by a new drop in [oil] revenues. And so the banks used their lobbying powers to support the high oil price.[17]

Nevertheless, legislators still play an important role in decision making, and many issues are too controversial to be handled quietly through interest-group/administrative channels; for example, gun control, social security benefits, and the Equal Rights Amendment.

Strategy, tactics, relations with administrative officials, and the capability of the group's leadership are not the only factors that contribute to the political effectiveness or ineffectiveness of an interest group. Size can be important, but if the membership is not cohesive or does not focus on specific objectives, the group may carry little political influence. The American Medical Association (AMA) usually has been more politically effective than the much bigger National Congress of Parents and Teachers. The cohesive 1 million-plus membership of the National Rifle Association (NRA) has been highly effective on the single issue of opposition to national gun control legislation. In several close congressional races it has helped to defeat candidates who supported gun control. The political effectiveness, cohesion, and determination of an interest group are affected by the intensity of concern among the members of the group. The size of the NRA membership has been encouraged in fact by executive action. A federal judge finally ruled in 1979 that the Pentagon's policy of selling surplus military firearms *only* to members of the NRA was discriminatory on the grounds that this subsidized and thereby bolstered the membership of a private organization. NRA activities have led to the creation of a counter interest group, Handgun Control, whose efforts to date have not been successful.

The first objective of a candidate or a party in a competitive political system is to win elections. Ways that an interest group can have a voice in later policy are by contributing money to candidates, giving key campaigns organizational support, or if many members live in electorally close constituencies. The last assumes that group members will vote nearly en bloc. Through various means, interest groups can participate in the electoral process.

Lobbying

Lobbying is an attempt by special interest groups and their representatives to influence policymakers. The function is highly visible in the United States and is common in most democracies. It is the best-known, and probably most criticized, method of group influence. It has been called the *invisible government.* Traditionally, the word "lobbyist" connotes undue influence and strong-arm tactics. Americans have long enjoyed denouncing lobbyists as unscrupulous and corrupt. With the Regulation of Lobbying Act of 1946, this perception is slowly fading.

Lobbyists in the United States today are often full-time professionals who are neither as glamorous nor as dishonest as the media suggests. There are between

---

[17]"Ten Years of Oil Crisis," *Newsweek* (September 12, 1983), p. 60.

Opponents of gun control march on the New Jersey Capitol.

50,000 and 80,000 people employed in the more than 2,000 registered lobbying organizations listed in the *Washington Information Directory.* This directory is published annually by the Congressional Quarterly, Inc.

Access is the buzzword used by thousands of lobbyists. To successfully influence any policy, you must first make contact with the appropriate members of Congress and then persuasively state your case. Lobbyists become experts in political influence and legislative technique. They make themselves—their accurate information, their contacts, their political savvy—indispensable. Some lobbyists even draft legislation, write speeches, and help plan legislative strategy. The more indispensable lobbyists become, the more access they will have. The more access they have, the more likely their interests will be accommodated.

Lobbyists also know the value of their "grass roots" supporters. The 1960s, with the civil rights movement and the Vietnam War protests, saw a massive grass roots phenomenon associated with lobbying efforts. Professional lobbyists have refined this strategy and use it with increased frequency. When Washington decision makers are inundated with letters, telegrams, and petitions from concerned voters, they listen. As you have already learned, power and influence are closely related. The American lobbyist has no legal power, but he or she cultivates and uses a high level of influence.

Mrs. Sarah Brady, a leading spokesperson for gun control, is shown guns taken from drug dealers in Washington, D.C. during a news conference on handgun-control legislation. Mrs. Brady is the wife of former presidential press secretary James Brady, who was seriously injured during the 1981 assassination attempt on President Reagan.

Table 5.1   LOBBYING THE BUREAUCRACY

	Percentage of bureaucrats reporting "regular" contacts with	
Country	Members of legislature	Representatives of interest groups
Germany	74	74
Italy	50	59
United States	64	93

Source: Adapted from Joel D. Aberbach, Robert D. Putnam, and Bert A. Rockman, *Bureaucrats and Politicians in Western Democracies* (Cambridge, Mass.: Harvard University Press, 1981), p. 230.

Lobbyists in other countries as well as the United States contact both bureaucrats as well as legislators, as shown in Table 5.1. Interest groups also cross national boundaries and are active in areas where there was limited activity before. For example, in 1987, Japanese companies and trade associations had 109 registered lobbyists in the United States. Hundreds of other lobbyists consult with U.S. subsidiaries of Japanese companies, and these are not registered as lobbying for a foreign company. Much Japanese lobbying goes on with the executive branch rather than with Congress, which is increasingly unhappy with Japanese trade surpluses and practices. As of mid-1988, there were over 900 agents registered under the U.S. Foreign Agents Registration Act representing foreign associations, corporations, individuals, and governments.[18]

Lionel Olmer, a former undersecretary of commerce and then vocal critic of Japanese trade practices, served as a consultant to the chair of Nippon Telephone and Telegraph Company after he retired from the federal government. Robert Gray, an advisor to the 1980 Reagan campaign and Robert Straus, former chair of the Democratic National Committee, also have represented Japanese companies. After the Reagan administration announced plans in 1987 to impose trade sanctions on $300 million worth of Japanese products, "lobbyists packed a commerce department auditorium for two days to argue for exemptions for 100 firms. Most succeeded." One lobbyist explained, "On the macro issues of trade, we fail miserably. But when it comes to arguing for specific companies, specific products, we shine."[19] Japanese and other foreign companies and even countries have learned the value of hiring American lobbyists to provide information and promote detailed, case-specific interests. A Michigan member of Congress observing all of this warned "the

[18]*Current American Government* (Washington, D.C.: Congressional Quarterly Inc., Spring 1989), p. 48.

[19]Both quotes from Jeffrey L. Sheier, "How 'Japan Inc.' Pleads Its Case in Washington," *U.S. News and World Report* (May 4, 1987), p. 22.

[U.S.] government has become a finishing school for lobbyists for foreign interests.''[20]

Money and Political Action Committees

Money is the lubricant of politics as it is in so many other systems. A major source
of money for legislators seeking election are the political action committees (PACs)
or their equivalent in other countries.

The U.S. political system witnessed an upsurge of PACs between the mid-
1970s and today. There were 600 PACs in 1975 and over 4,200 at the end of 1988.
Their purpose is to raise and distribute campaign funds to those running for
political office. The 1974 Election Campaign Amendment Act attempted to curtail
campaign abuses by limiting the amount of money a few ''fat cats'' could donate
to candidates. At the same time, the legal rights of PACs were spelled out, including
the right of businesses and corporations to set up PACs. PACs are associated with
individual companies, corporations, or trade unions. PACs also solicit funds publicly, such as the recently organized Beer Drinkers of America to fight higher beer
taxes and a proposed ban on television beer commercials.

Two case examples will be discussed: one in Japan, the other in the United
States.

In 1988–1989 an influence-peddling scandal in Japan made headlines worldwide. The scandal grew and the Liberal Democratic party (LDP) leaders (the LDP
has governed Japan since 1955) found it difficult to cope with important domestic
and international policy matters for months.

Former Prime Minister Takeshita admitted in April 1989 that he received
$377,000 from the Recruit Company through ticket sales for two fund-raising
parties in May 1987. When Mr. Takeshita received the money he was secretary-
general of the LDP and the leading contender for the position of prime minister
(the ruling LDP elected him to that position later in 1987). The scandal began to
unravel publicly when a Japanese newspaper revealed that administrative advisers
to top LDP rulers had made profits of more than $100,000 each. These advisers
bought unlisted shares in Recruit Cosmos, a real estate subsidiary of the conglomerate, Recruit Company. The shares were quickly sold at great profit after they were
publicly listed on the Tokyo Stock Exchange.

The donations or purchase of blocks of tickets to the fund-raising parties does
not violate the Political Donations Restrictions Act as long as the ticket price is
within a commonsense range and the company purchases are within a reasonable
limit—constraints that are both vague and subject to loose interpretation. The
simultaneous revelations of legal Recruit Company political contributions and a
subdivision, Recruit Cosmos, providing personal gain through turn-around profits

---

[20]Rich Thomas, ''Trading on Good Connections: Japan Hires Former U.S. Officials to Plead Its Case,''
Newsweek (December 22, 1986), p. 48. The details on foreign lobbying are drawn from the Sheier
article and the Thomas article.

Table 5.2   SELECTED 1987–1988 POLITICAL ACTION COMMITTEE CONTRIBUTIONS TO
POLITICAL CANDIDATES IN U.S. FEDERAL ELECTIONS

Political Action Committee	Total dollar amount
Aircraft Owners and Pilots Association	$ 290,089
American Federation of State, County, and Municipal Employees	1,658,386
American Medical Association	2,315,646
Association of Trial Lawyers of America	1,919,558
Auto Dealers and Drivers for Free Trade	1,158,700
Carpenters' Legislative Improvement Committee	1,357,998
Committee on Letter Carriers	1,732,482
Machinists Nonpartisan Political League	1,492,780
National Education Association	2,104,689
Realtors Political Action Committee	3,045,769

Source: Federal Election Commission, *FEC Reports on Financial Activity, 1987–1988* (Washington, D.C.: Federal Election Commission, September 1989), Vols. 3 and 4, passim.

in the stock market caused an uproar in Japan. Business financial input for political leaders and their legislative factions has always been assumed. The description of the legal contributions while simultaneously revealing individual profiteering, all facilitated by the same company, caused popular approval of the LDP government to plummet to a record post-1948 low of 5 percent in mid-1989, and Prime Minister Takeshita's resignation announcement in April 1989.

A sample of major PAC contributors in the U.S. 1987–1988 federal election campaigns is shown in Table 5.2. You may be surprised by the variety of specialized interest groups that take an active interest in national political campaigns.

A recent book, *The Best Congress Money Can Buy*, crusades against massive interest-group donations by highlighting some of the dangers and abuses. Senator Robert Dole (R) of Kansas is described as the Senate champion when it comes to raising PAC money, having collected $3,366,305 from 1972 through 1986. The U.S. House of Representatives allows members elected before 1980 to keep political campaign contributions, after all expenses have been met, for personal use *after* one has retired from the House or been defeated. Contributions pour into the political war chests of incumbents, even when the political challenge is minimal and it is a safe seat. Representative Ronnie Flipper (D) of Alabama has built a retirement fund of $600,000 and Representative Stephen Solarz (D) of New York has amassed nearly $1 million. Senator Robert Dole observed: "When these political action committees give money, they expect something in return other than good government."[21]

All competitive political systems have interest groups and depend on the money and other contributions made to political candidates by these groups. Inter-

[21]R. Cort Kirkwood, "Congressmen, War Chests, and the Influence of PACs," *Christian Science Monitor* (September 28, 1988), p. 20, reviewing Philip M. Stern, *The Best Money Congress Can Buy* (New York: Pantheon Books, 1988). The quote and fund information were drawn from this article.

est groups are not just interested in supporting winners; they are even more interested in influencing the winner after the votes have been tallied. All contributions are not nefarious, corrupting, illegal, or designed to buy the vote of an elected candidate, but abuses can and do occur. The most honorable form of interest-group financial input that would satisfy a majority of political practitioners and observers has yet to be devised.

Finally, we want to make clear that the composition of the total political system is crucial. In a pluralistic environment autonomous input is allowed and even encouraged. Large numbers of people with various points of view can organize claims and promote their special concerns. In authoritarian systems, this is not the case.

INTEREST-GROUP INPUT IN THIRD WORLD AND AUTHORITARIAN/TOTALITARIAN SYSTEMS

Political systems of the developing world manifest substantial variation in their tolerance of interest groups. Countries such as Malaysia, Taiwan, India, or Venezuela have numerous autonomous interest groups. Other political systems, such as Laos, Burma, Nepal, Paraguay, Saudi Arabia, and many of the African countries have few if any interest groups with freedom of input. In authoritarian political systems, where power is concentrated in the hands of a small group (Soviet Union before 1989, North Korea, Iran), some interests are represented by individuals or factions within the leadership. Inevitably, there also are the *institutional* interest groups that originally came into being to perform functions other than interest articulation, such as the military, bureaucrats, religious leaders, and so forth. Too often, though, objectives promoted by institutional interest groups are intended primarily to enhance the position of one segment of an already too-powerful elite.

Interest groups in developing countries, where a degree of autonomous group organization is allowed, can play especially crucial roles. Historically, the rulers in these areas have not been expected to consult or respond to the wishes of their subjects. Reliable information about public concerns and attitudes is not available. The newly independent governments, in order to remain in power for very long, must respond to the more urgent claims and demands of a citizenry conscious of the revolution of rising expectations. There is a danger here because most of the political arrangements are new in the developing countries. Frequently there is serious disagreement over what the political rules of the game should be. Many groups, such as those in Iran, Afghanistan, and Lebanon, do not push specific or particular interests directly related to their group but support, often violently, comprehensive issues they believe will create a political arena disposed to favor them. This we call **system conflict**—when people battle over whether there should be a theocratic constitution controlled by religious leaders, a republic, a monarchy, or a Communist system; who can organize for political purposes; or what groups can be citizens or exercise some local regional autonomy. When groups uncompromisingly pursue their objectives without self-restraint, turn to assassination and mass terrorism, press for mutually exclusive objectives (which, if successful, restrict the basic values of other groups), then the political system is unstable or ruled by an oppressive dictatorship.

The other type of conflict is called *issue conflict* because the basic institutions and rules of the game in the political system are not the central issues of competition. Issue conflict is limited to the types common in the developed, pluralist systems, on issues such as government defense policy, tax relief, rural uplift programs, housing, industrialization versus pollution, new universities, and so forth.

Third World governments often have great difficulty acknowledging the rights of issue groups while at the same time seeking to control or eliminate the activities of the system-oriented groups. Persistent ignoring of issue groups and failure to initiate responsive programs and policies may lead to instability or the beginnings of reform.

Mexico, a Third World country where autonomous interest groups are slowly emerging, provides an example. Mexico is among the most politically stable of the Latin American countries. PRI, or the Institutional Revolutionary party, has ruled the country without break since 1929, winning a 71 percent landslide in the 1982 presidential race.

Mexico under the PRI has created a system whereby individuals or social groups relate to the government through one organization licensed by the state. These represent segments of society such as teachers, trade unions, peasants, businesspeople, and so forth. The Mexican Workers Confederation (CTM) dominates the labor movement (approximately 3.5 million workers), although there are other officially sanctioned unions, such as the Union of State Workers and Teachers' Union. Interest groups are much more subject to government control in Mexico than in pluralist systems. The leaderships of these groups have exerted exceptional influence on government, and some allege groups such as the CTM represent primarily the interests of the privileged leaders rather than members.

Mexico's current president, Harvard-trained Carlos Salinas, inaugurated on December 1, 1988, for a six-year term, received an unprecedented low popular vote of 50.7 percent. Particularly unhappy was Fidel Velazquez, the then 88-year-old head of the labor movement, who traditionally delivered votes to the PRI and had no sympathy for President Salinas's moderate pluralism and talking with non-PRI groups. Velazquez complained that negotiations with various autonomous groups as well as with opposition parties under the more open, accomodationist approach Salinas adopted was handing over power step-by-step to non-PRI groups. Velazquez is described as one of the *dinosaurs* who support the interest-group system and PRI domination as it has existed for 50 years. One observer described Velazquez as Mexico's most important labor leader for nearly 40 years and as "one of the PRI's main power brokers, a man who could demand cabinet posts and senate seats for those loyal to him and who was consulted on presidential successions."[22]

---

[22]Larry Rohter, "Can He Save Mexico?" *New York Times Magazine* (November 20, 1988), p. 93.

President Salinas has balanced his cabinet with "dinosaurs" and "smurfs." *Smurfs* are young technocrats, most holding graduate degrees from top schools in the United States, with little political experience and who support political reforms, including a more open input process. Several years will pass before we know if consequential, independent labor and business groups will emerge, and groups autonomous from the government and the PRI will begin to exert meaningful influence. There was one small sign of hope, for example, when President Salinas ordered the arrest of the head of the notoriously corrupt Oil Workers' Union and PRI stalwart, the domineering Joaquin Hernandez Salicia. Subsequently, in April 1989, 500,000 teachers struck for better wages and to rid themselves of their corrupt PRI leader, Carlos Jonguitud. Elementary school teachers earn $150 a month, and there are widespread reports that many must pay union officials several hundred dollars to be assigned a job.

Mexico is an interesting example of rule by a small elite slowly yielding in the 1980s to a more pluralist system. Many of the old-line interest-group leaders are also PRI leaders and thus a part of the ruling power structure. What appears to be slowly happening is that members of many hitherto government-sponsored interest groups are trying to expel dishonest, dinosaur leaders and to articulate independent demands.

A developing society with new responsibilities and problems might find useful some form of interest-group development, if for nothing else, to alert the rulers of the more prevalent concerns of the population. Authoritarian and totalitarian regimes that are publicly committed to conformity reject the existence of autonomous groups and the input of such claims into the decision-making process. So-called interest groups, taken over or created by the state, serve principally to mobilize, regulate, and extend the control of government. Any form of independent, popular expression is prohibited.

One function of a formally organized group in an authoritarian system is to be a government channel, explaining to members what their true interests are and how government is meeting these interests. Interest groups also regiment and monitor individuals and help enforce government policy.

An example of an authoritarian political system undergoing irregular reform is the People's Republic of China (PRC). The PRC is tightly and often brutally controlled politically. However, since 1978 it has gradually developed a market economy and participated in educational and other exchange programs with democratic countries. (About 28,000 PRC students study in the United States each year.) Progress in the aforementioned areas, especially economic pluralism, is irregular. These developments plus the fact the PRC no longer actively exports revolutionary ideology places mainland China in the authoritarian rather than totalitarian category since the late 1970s.

One method of manipulating the population was to enroll as many persons as possible in one or more state-controlled interest groups. In this case, these groups propagandized and controlled the most populous nation (1.1 billion) in the world. One organization, the Women's Union, has over 80 million members. Much emphasis is placed on equality, and a major objective is to get women out of the home and into production and defense work. The Communist Youth League, with over 25 million members, is the "reserve force of the party" and is open to all young people between the ages of 14 and 25. The Youth League sponsors a junior group, the Young Pioneers, for the 9- to 14-year-olds. During the 1950s these two groups were urged to learn and practice the "five loves": love of fatherland, people, labor, science, and public property. Love of parents and family were not mentioned. The Communist Youth League and Young Pioneers mold the minds of the young and reflect ever-changing government policy. These groups support government policy and do not articulate popular demands. They act as a recruiting device for future party leaders by spotting those with leadership abilities. They strive to create in the youth an enthusiastic devotion to the party and its goals.[23]

Communist-ruled mainland China began initiating economic reforms in 1978, eventually permitting the sale of 1800 items at market prices, many of these farm products. Communes were broken up in the rural areas; now peasants can "own" land through 50-year leaseholds and even sell a lease to another farmer. In the urban areas small businesses are permitted to develop. In a growing number of factories the workers are being paid according to the value of their work and training, and a few successful factories have introduced profit-sharing. The gradual introduction of a market economy and modified free enterprise has not, though, been matched by political reform.

The first independent interest group emerged in 1989—university students. Student demonstrations at universities in 1986–1987 were put down, with many students expelled or arrested. The new wave of demonstrations that began early in 1989 has increasingly symbolized popular frustration. Protests began in March and April with 10,000 persons, and, by May, daily demonstrations were calculated to involve over 1,000,000 persons, including cheering onlooker-supporters. The demonstrations generally began in Tiananmen Square, the largest square in the world, located in Beijing, capital of the PRC. There were numerous sit-ins with lists of demands read outside the Great Hall of the People, where the National People's Congress meets when in session. Several times students demonstrated before the front gate of Zhongnanhai Compound where government leaders live, a brazen and unheard of challenge since Communist rule began in 1949.

University students make up less than one-fifth of 1 percent of the PRC's population. Since the late nineteenth century, student demonstrations have been the catalysts of major political movements and upheavals in China. In contrast to the 1986–1987 student demonstrations, which some now say were vague calls for democracy or simply unstructured discontent, the new demands started out to be more feasible and less politically threatening—freedom of the press and assembly, lift the ban on demonstrations, more funding for education, and disclosure of the

---

[23]The material on the PRC is taken from Richard L. Walker, *China under Communism: The First Five Years* (New Haven, Conn.: Yale University Press, 1955), pp. 36–42, and James R. Townsend, *Politics in China*, 2nd ed. (Boston: Little, Brown, 1980), Chapter VI.

incomes of top leaders. More sensitive demands, such as calls to release political prisoners, were not made. Leaders from two student groups (but not including leaders from an umbrella organization representing 40 different campuses) met with officials from mainland China's State Council and the State Education Commission in April. Part of this meeting was broadcast on Chinese television. This suggested a tacit approval at that time of a sporadically functioning, sometimes independent critic of the state. Student leaders sought to influence leadership policies, not overthrow the ruling China Communist party, and this may be why they were grudgingly tolerated for several weeks.

Although interpretations may differ over the reasons why, the beginnings of political pluralism—vital to the survival of interest groups—ended on "Bloody Sunday," June 4, 1989. Tanks, troops, and armed vehicles fought their way to Tiananmen Square, and by 7:00 A.M. the square was cleared. As many as 3,000 Chinese students lost their lives, shot or crushed, as the 27th Division of the People's Liberation Army moved against what were officially described as counter-revolutionary elements. Absolute party control was returned. The Communist leadership saw this ultimately as system conflict, challenging the monopoly of the Chinese Communist party, and this could not be allowed.

The PRC is an example of where economic liberalization led an authoritarian

Osrin in the *Plain Dealer*.

regime to tolerate reluctantly some autonomous interest group input but then decisively pull back to restore an outward political conformity. The political right to organize and have input is crucial to autonomous interest-group development.

Although interest groups in authoritarian and totalitarian systems are a mechanism for government control of the population, there is an indication that within the elites there is some competition. This competition can be over issues, or it may involve leadership struggles, that is, support for one faction, opposition for another faction. By faction we mean a group of individuals seeking to increase their influence or power where the principal objective is to serve personal interests and status. Frequently it is difficult to know whether conflict within the elite is issue conflict or whether an issue is simply a means that one faction may use to criticize another faction.

Sometimes there are genuine policy differences between government ministries or even disagreements within ministries, for example, jurisdiction of the security police versus the military; increased military expenditure versus public housing; expand heavy industry versus more consumer goods; product competition and workers' bonuses versus traditional Marxist industrial policy. One Soviet specialist summarized the nature of interest groups among those exercising authority in a Communist system: "A striking feature of political interest groups in the Soviet Union is that normally they are not formally organized, but are more often loose groupings of like-minded or like-interested persons."[24]

General Secretary Mikhail Gorbachev took over the reins of power in the Soviet Communist party in 1985. He found a collapsing Soviet economic system. Since then, he has vigorously called for *glasnost* (openness, publicity) in the political and communication systems in order to effect *perestroika* (restructuring, rebuilding) the economy. *Perestroika* would decentralize the economy, introduce market forces, and increase the production of consumer goods. The only way to introduce far-reaching structural reforms was by winning popular support for the government. *Glasnost* would make *perestroika* possible. It is now clear even the general secretary did not realize the depth of popular alienation brought about by Stalinist communism.

What is happening in Eastern Europe seems to be a precursor of what may happen in the Soviet Union, at least in terms of interest groups. One example is Czechoslovakia where between November and December 1989 a Communist dictatorship was replaced with a coalition government (Communists included) and a leading human-rights activist, Vaclav Havel, was chosen as president of the country. The Circle of Independent Intelligentsia, a reformist interest group, evolved into the Civic Forum, which has become a permanent factor in Czech society enunciating a broad program of political reform and may even become a political party.

The demand for market economies also prepares the groundwork for producer interest groups. For example, the Society of Entrepreneurs was created in late 1989

---

[24]H. Gordon Skilling, "Groups in Soviet Politics: Some Hypotheses," in H. Gordon Skilling and Franklin Griffiths, eds., *Interest Groups in Soviet Politics* (Princeton, N.J.: Princeton University Press, 1971), p. 27.

Drawing by Jeff Danziger in the Christian Science Monitor, © 1989 TCSPS.

in Prague to provide advice and solidarity to hopeful entrepreneurs. Its initial problems were to raise cash, rent an office, and secure typewriters and a fax machine to better serve its 100,000 members.

Spontaneous demonstrations sometimes act as consumer input. On New Year's Eve 1989, in Sverdlovsk in the Soviet Union, citizens filled the streets to protest shortages in wine and vodka. "Within hours, wine, cheese, fish, sausage, and other food products appeared on the shelves."[25]

On the dark side, as pluralism evolves, groups held back by an authoritarian party whose first objective were order and discipline will quickly emerge, drawing on old resentments. Once some form of competitive politics emerges, groups with irreconcilable differences may organize, compete, and even attack one another. Some of these groups may have world views so different that in the Soviet Union we may see democratizing fragmentation and danger of chaos.

The emergence of ethnic interest groups has been murderous as in the 1990 massacres between Azerbaijanis and Armenians. Various groups organized, two of the most well known being the Azerbaizan Popular Front and the Armenian Karabakh Committee. Much of the conflict has centered on the future of an Armenian enclave inside the Soviet Socialist Republic of Azerbaijan.

---

[25]"Gorbachev's Challenge: Soviet Hot Spots," *Christian Science Monitor* (February 1, 1990), pp. 10–11.

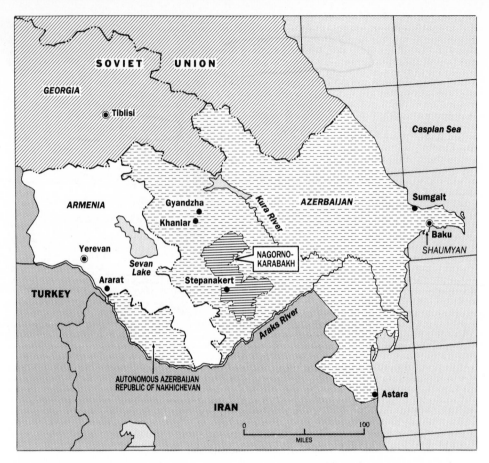

Separatism and strife in the Soviet Union. (Nagorno-Karabakh is the Armenian enclave.)

Religious bigotry and ethnic hatred are at the top of the list of issues separating the two people. The Armenians—mainly Christian for centuries—see the Turkic-speaking Muslim Azerbaijanis as relatives of the Turks they hold responsible for a series of Armenian massacres, including the 1915 genocide in which more than 1 million Armenians were killed. For the Azerbaijanis, Islam is a central part of their national identity, and they regard the Armenians' profession of Christianity as an assertion of unwarranted superiority.[26]

One Soviet journalist reported from the region:

We have seen murders here of the cruelest sort. Men, women, and children, the young and the old alike, were attacked and often killed because they were Armenian. That alone—to be Armenian in Azerbaijan—was a virtual sentence of death.[27]

---

[26]"A Land Divided: The Armenia/Azerbaijan Crisis," "A Times Special Report," *Los Angeles Times* (February 1990), p. S3. Copyright 1990, *Los Angeles Times.* Reprinted by permission.

[27]Ibid, p. S2.

Antigovernment interest-group activity in Poland: Lech Walesa addressing a Solidarity gathering.

Pluralization, tragically, can also release irreconcilable ancient hostilities, aroused and shaped by modern organization techniques.

Infrequently, as far as we know, groups in the Soviet Union attempt to make independent demands. Workers' demonstrations and strikes were reported in 1980. One major strike, protesting food shortages, involved 70,000 workers for two days at an auto plant. Other strikes occurred through 1981. Although these demonstrations were quickly crushed, steps were taken to prevent further occurrences. Local union responsibilities were increased and the next national Party Congress urged trade union officials to more vigorously represent worker interests.[28] To show the impact of *glasnost,* Soviet trade unions were given the legal right to strike in 1989.

Interest groups in authoritarian and totalitarian systems are in an early stage of development as compared to pluralistic systems. They only vaguely resemble Western-style interest groups, and the range of their input activities is limited strictly by what an autocratic leadership will allow. For decades, formal organized groups in Communist countries such as the Academy of Sciences, the Writer's Union, the Lenin-Communist League of Youth, and the Central Council of Trade

[28]Marshall I. Goldman, *USSR in Crisis* (New York: W. W. Norton, 1983), p. 111.

Unions, were principally instruments of the ruling elite to control the population. These groups possessed little independence and had little input, and this only now is beginning to change slowly.

INTEREST GROUPS AND PLURALISM IN ACTION

Without pluralism there can be no autonomous interest groups. The reverse is also true: Without interest groups, pluralism cannot exist. Some form of pluralism is necessary if a political system is to achieve the optimum level of human progress and freedom.

We noted in Chapter 2 that pluralism exists only in relatively open, democratic societies. The basis of pluralism is competitive and autonomous groups are predominant in the input process and have important influence in policy-making. It presumes most persons join groups voluntarily, and these groups are not instruments of the state. Political systems that are becoming less authoritarian often move gradually toward pluralism. An example is the USSR.

In addition to a multiplicity of associations, there should be some multiple affiliations: "Individuals belong to several groups, no one group is inclusive of its members' lives."[29] In a pluralist system, often called a *democracy*, many groups have members with a variety of social characteristics (class, education, age, religion, ethnic, or racial identifications) and a majority of individuals belong to more than one organization. The various organizations serve different needs and are independent of each other. No group dominates a person's thinking. Several memberships give the individual a variety of perspectives and sometimes even conflicting signals. It is hoped that various memberships will not be cumulative in a monolithic, doctrinaire way that gives the individual a rigid and closed view of the political world as, for example, the Communist who belongs to the Communist trade union, reads a Communist newspaper, and belongs to a social group whose members are all Communists.

Pluralism encourages individual action, such as voting, and collective action through group membership. These two types of participation are not necessarily contradictory. **Classical democratic theory** of the eighteenth and nineteenth centuries stressed individual responsibility and individual choice based on rational evaluation of the issues. Individual participation is still common in a pluralist system, as in the private act of voting, writing a letter to a government department or a public official, or meeting with an elected official. The individual also may participate collectively through interest groups. Groups with an organized membership, monetary resources, administrative skills and contacts, and offices in the state, provincial, or national capitals are often successful in influencing policy.

A group of Yale University scholars, led by the chair of the political science department, studied and refined the concept of pluralism in the late 1950s. This classic work analyzed the power structure and policy process in New Haven,

---

[29]William Kornhauser, *The Politics of Mass Society* (New York: The Free Press, 1959), p. 80.

Connecticut.[30] The analysis concluded that no single group dominated politics. Each issue provoked coalitions among different individuals and groups. Pluralism means limited participation in many issues because of specialized interest or limited time. When issues affecting a large number of people are involved, or when wide publicity is given the issue, broader participation occurs. One participant in the study concluded that political decision makers were relatively free to deal with issues that were routine or minor. "Other kinds of decision-making—of a non-routine, un-bureaucratized, or innovative variety seem to require special consent by citizens who fall outside the small decision-making group."[31]

The pluralist view of interest groups support a division of power and a series of checks and balances so that no group, not even a popular majority, can exercise unlimited power. Robert Dahl summarized the basic principle of political pluralism:

> Since even legal and constitutional arrangements will be subverted if some citizens or groups of citizens gain disproportionate opportunities for power in comparison with other citizens, the potential power of one citizen or group must be balanced by the potential power of other citizens.[32]

At the national level in the United States, for example, this balance and division of power was achieved by the Constitution: Certain powers are denied to Congress (Article I); Congress is bicameral and legislation must be approved by both houses (Article I); the president can veto laws passed by Congress (Article II); the federal judiciary is largely independent of the president and Congress (Article III); and the national government is prohibited from undertaking certain acts, and rights are guaranteed to the citizens (Amendments 1 through 9).

Pluralism regards concentrations of power as dangerous, whether in government, large corporations, powerful trade unions, or landed estates. Pluralism sees competing centers of power as allowing broad inputs and checking the consolidation of private or public power. Competition and regulated conflict are accepted as inevitable. Important functions of government are maintaining the rules of the game, preventing undue accumulation of power in private organizations, and maintaining individual freedoms. Interest groups should organize and express opinion, provide information to the public and government officials, and act as a check on government officials or other interest groups. Interest groups must negotiate and compromise. Decisions are reached more slowly and may not always be as logically consistent because of the need to accommodate diverse inputs. Multiple centers of power mean various groups may have the power to dilute, delay, or veto. Ideally, no affected group should be ignored in the solution, even if no group entirely

---

[30]The first of several books to appear based on this study was Robert A. Dahl. *Who Governs? Democracy and Power in an American City* (New Haven, Conn.: Yale University Press, 1961).

[31]Nelson W. Polsby, *Community Power and Political Theory* (New Haven, Conn.: Yale University Press, 1963), p. 128.

[32]Robert A. Dahl, *Pluralist Democracy in the United States: Conflict and Consent* (Chicago: Rand McNally, 1967), p. 40.

realizes its objectives. Coalition building around specific issues and bargaining, negotiating, and accommodating different viewpoints are key aspects of pluralism.

CRITICISMS OF INTEREST-GROUP POLITICS

Interest-group politics, as it has evolved in postindustrial political systems, has its critics, and objections have been raised to this type of political system. We now will discuss the eight bases for these objections.

1. Classical democratic theory emphasized the rational, informed, and thoughtful political participation of the individual. Emphasis on political competition among groups and the resulting competition among leadership elites implicitly rejects classical individual participation. Pluralists generally consider the typical voter uninformed and only occasionally interested. Meaningful political competition and participation is among group elites. The individual exercises some power because of the right to vote among alternatives at regularly held elections. However, individual input for the average person is limited essentially to elections.

2. Pluralism assumes that individuals identify with and belong to associations that advance individual as well as group interests. It anticipates that many individuals will belong to more than one interest group. Multiple memberships expose a person to various opinions and thus increase political information and political tolerance. In actual practice group memberships may not be as extensive as often assumed.

   Critics of pluralism point to the fact that more than 40 percent of the adult population in the United States and Canada has no organizational membership. Furthermore, those who do voluntarily belong are the better educated, the wealthier, and predominantly from the middle and upper classes. Group membership is even lower in most other democratic political systems. A significant strata of the population is thus on the periphery of a functioning pluralism.

3. Many groups are dominated by the leaders; the average association member has little influence on the organization's policies. Robert Michels was the first modern scholar to conclude that the **iron law of oligarchy** was an inherent trait of organizations. Michels alleged that whoever "says organization says oligarchy," and he claimed that domination of organizations by the full-time professional staff was inevitable. Michels saw organizations as unrepresentative in many ways. Leaders dominate because of

   a. *Superior knowledge.* They are privy to much information that can be used to secure assent for their program.

   b. *Control over the formal means of communication with the membership.* They dominate the organization press; as full-time salaried officials, they may travel from place to place presenting their case at the organization's expense; and their position enables them to command an audience.

c. *Skill in the art of politics.* They are more adept than nonprofessionals in making speeches, writing articles, and organizing group activities.

d. *The nature of their positions.* Those who become full-time officials of unions, political parties, or who serve as parliamentary representatives, "whilst belonging by social position to the class of the ruled, have in fact come to form part of the ruling oligarchy." Leaders of the masses become part of the "power elite." Leaders develop perspectives and interests derived from their position among the more privileged elements, often contrary to the interests of many of their members.[33]

4. Pluralism assumes checks and balances resulting from group conflict, with no group or coalition emerging permanently victorious. Critics claim that too often there is inequality of bargaining power among groups. Many times, well-led groups representing narrow interests have acquired much political expertise in achieving their goals. Producer groups, especially those producing essential products, even when the number of individuals involved is not large, achieve too much success under a pluralistic system. Consumer groups tend to be more amorphous, poorly organized, and less successful in the political system.

5. Narrow interest groups work toward a redistribution of benefits toward themselves. In relatively stable postindustrial societies the number of special interest groups grows steadily. A business cartel will limit production in order to enjoy higher prices, or a labor union will oppose modernizing a plant because it may reduce the number of jobs or compel employees to work harder. Distribution of economic benefits is the principal conflict area in developed economies; the country's best talent and energies concentrate on winning the distribution game rather than increasing productivity and fostering economic innovation.[34] Stagnation, rather than growth, often results.

6. The issues interest groups address are often very technical and discourage popular participation or even opposition by other interest groups, thus destroying the competition between groups so relevant to pluralism. Benefits to be achieved are important to the group concerned but may imply no specific penalty on any particular group, except possibly the "public interest." Sometimes, even when simplified, the issue is unclear to the intelligent reader, as in the following case: "Dow Chemical Co., which generates some of its own electricity, circulated a proposal to give cogener-

---

[33]Seymour Martin Lipset, "Introduction," in Robert Michels, *Political Parties,* Edan and Cedar Paul, trans. (New York: The Free Press, 1962), pp. 16–18.

[34]Mancur Olson, *The Rise and Decline of Nations* (New Haven, Conn.: Yale University Press, 1982). For another point of view, see the critique of Olson's book by Robert B. Reich, "Why Democracy Makes Economic Sense," *New Republic,* 189:25 (December 19, 1983), pp. 28–37.

ation equipment the same tax treatment that utilities would receive under the Administration's user plan, rather than the harsher treatment that industrial boilers would get."[35]

7. Another criticism is the "no government leadership" hypothesis, which maintains that the public interest, representing the essential concerns and needs of the whole society is not promoted in a pluralist system. Government does not advance specific **national interest** policies; rather, it plays an umpire role and maintains the rules of the game in the political arena. The bargaining, negotiation, and compromises that result produce some benefits for the groups involved, but no group completely achieves its objectives. Equilibrium is a principal objective and government plays a key role in maintaining the dialogue, monitoring the competition, and through laws and regulations implementing the eventual compromises. Government rarely initiates policy or promotes policies that respond to a broad public interest beyond the narrower concerns of competing group interests. A politician's first commitment, it is said, is to get elected, and often this means balancing the demands of narrow special interests to build a majority.

8. Hyperpluralism is pluralism carried to extremes. The relationship between innumerable interest groups, various administrative officials and agencies, and elected officials means politics is basically a process of parceling out decisions among the various collaborating groups. Hyperpluralism believes government regards almost all interests as legitimate and therefore should advance them all. Government becomes excessively expensive, and the idea of public interest, distinguished from the sum of special interests, disappears.

   This condition exists when groups become too powerful and too vocal. When the government tries to support every cause, policies become confusing and contradictory. One of the most obvious examples is the government providing substantial funds to promote cancer research while also subsidizing tobacco growers.

   Hyperpluralism is not unique to the United States. When the French Fifth Republic came into being in 1958, both President Charles de Gaulle and Prime Minister Michel Debre were determined to replace the regime of special interests they believed had dominated the Fourth Republic. Reformers described the powerful French interest groups of years past as "the feudal forces which were dismembering the state."[36]

There are obviously many criticisms of interest groups that we have not dealt with in detail. The quiet negotiations through personal contacts between interest

---

[35]Richard Corrigan, "Lobbyists are Putting the Blitz on Carter's Energy Plan," *National Journal* (November 26, 1977), p. 1837.

[36]Vincent Wright, *The Government and Politics of France*, 3rd ed. (London: Unwin Hyman, 1989), p. 254.

group representatives, government bureaucrats, and political leaders, which take place away from the public limelight, may lead to secret deals. Unfortunately, these decisions too often culminate in payoffs and kickbacks to government officials as a reward for a favorable ruling. Leaving aside the corruption issue, there also is a widespread feeling that a political decision based on the intense pressure of one or two groups means that one "part" benefits to the disadvantage of the general public interest. Producer groups organize more frequently and effectively than consumer groups. Many believe these are narrow, selfish interests intent upon "ripping off" the general public. It is also commonly observed that not all members support the politics of the group with equal zeal. Some members are hardly aware of the group's political positions. Interest group leaders often are not regularly accountable to their members.

Nevertheless, autonomous interest groups are a principal means by which to pluralize a political system and to divide power. They frequently provide the citizen with a means to affiliate in an organized and effective manner and voice demands and opinions independent of the government.

Interest groups are objects of much justifiable criticism; nevertheless, they are the lifeblood of democratic politics. They are the most effective means to date to prevent the concentration of power in the hands of a single, ruling oligarchy. Autonomous, often competing activity of many interest groups strengthens democracy and reduces authoritarianism.

SUMMARY

The politics of interest groups, which characterizes most modern democracies, has evolved; it was not constructed or deliberately planned. Interest groups have proliferated in the last two centuries as social and economic life became more specialized, complex, and interdependent. Autonomous interest groups make possible organizational and individual freedom in the political system. The pluralism of interest-group politics has many virtues as it actually functions. It seems to be one means by which authoritarian politics can move toward more personal freedom and citizen input. A proponent of pluralism, Robert A. Dahl, has observed how we must deal with the empirical political world we live in, not an ideal model that can never be realized.

Dahl first concludes that there are no students of modern politics who deny the proposition "that leaders do, as a matter of fact, have great weight in large, modern representative systems." Dahl goes on to state:

> At the empirical level, experience with and systematic study of political life in cities and countries with democratic governments has turned up evidence that, if valid, raises interesting and important empirical questions. . . . This evidence seems to demonstrate rather conclusively, I think, that rates of participation vary widely, that a rather large fraction of adults participate in political life barely at all, and that a small

proportion of adults participate a very great deal. Confronted by this evidence, political scientists have had either to reject it as factually false, which it is increasingly difficult to do, or to accept it provisionally as correct.[37]

Active, autonomous interest-group politics is not a utopian blueprint. It exists today in fewer than 45 political systems. Pluralistic systems are concentrated in North America and Western Europe and scattered haphazardly in the rest of the world, for example, in Japan, Costa Rica, India, Israel, Singapore, Malaysia, Taiwan, Venezuela, and a few others. There are important signs that such systems are also evolving in Eastern Europe and the Soviet Union. In terms of interest-group politics, for better or worse, pluralism is the environment in which interest groups, free of government domination, function most effectively. Finally, like it or not, it is characteristic of most modern political systems commonly labeled "democratic."

RECOMMENDED READINGS

Ball, Alan R., and Frances Mullard. *Pressure Politics in Industrial Societies.* Atlantic Highlands, N.J.: Humanities Press International, 1987. First published in Great Britain, this is a straightforward account of contemporary interest-group systems in several developed societies.

Beer, Samuel. *Britain Against Itself: The Political Contradictions of Collectivism.* New York: W. W. Norton & Company, 1982. A specialist on British politics analyzes modern Great Britain. His thesis is that the competition between interest groups produced inflation and the loss of control over public expenditure.

Berry, Jeffrey M. *The Interest Group Society,* 2nd ed. Glenview, Ill.: Scott Foresman/Little, Brown, 1989. This is a quick yet thorough introduction to interest groups at the national level in the United States. It covers all standard areas including networks and subgovernments.

Ehrmann, Henry, ed. *Interest Groups on Four Continents.* Westport, Conn.: Greenwood Press, 1983. This work first appeared in 1958 and has been reprinted several times. This classic anthology of interest groups outside the United States includes theoretical insights.

Jackson, Brooks. *Honest Graft: Big Money and the American Political Process.* New York: Alfred A. Knopf, 1988. Tony Coelho is the major figure in this book by a *Wall Street Journal* reporter. Coelho is treated sympathetically, almost a victim of the PAC system. On a broader level, the book intends to show how money dominates so much of Washington politics.

Lowi, Theodore J. *The End of Liberalism: The Second Republic of the United States,* 2nd ed. New York: W. W. Norton & Company, 1979. This is a critique of an expanding liberal government and the increasing presence and power of interest groups. The author argues that interest groups have too much power in the United States. This book is a good foundation to analyze the growth of interest groups worldwide.

---

[37]Robert A. Dahl, "Further Reflections on the Elitist Theory of Democracy," *American Political Science Review,* 60:2 (June 1966), pp. 298–299.

Olson, Mancur. *The Rise and Decline of Nations.* New Haven, Conn.: Yale University Press, 1982. The author draws widely on history, economics, sociology, and political science to suggest interest groups can be very damaging in democratic societies. He develops stimulating hypotheses, even if the reader does not always agree with the conclusions.

Truman, David B. *The Governmental Process: Political Interests and Public Opinion,* 2nd ed. New York: Alfred A. Knopf, 1971. This is the standard point of departure for post–World War II books on U.S. interest groups. The first edition was published in 1951. Truman believes interest groups are the raw material of politics and basic to understanding democratic political systems.

Wilson, Frank L. *Interest Group Politics in France.* Cambridge: Cambridge University Press, 1987. Case or county studies about interest groups are once again being published. This is a particularly good study of a political system often written about but insufficiently studied in depth.

Zamosc, Leon. *The Agrarian Question and the Peasant Movement in Colombia: Struggles of the National Peasant Association 1967–1981.* New York: Cambridge University Press, 1986. This book is based on a seven-year study of peasant organizations in a developing country. The author analyzes why there was such limited success due to group characteristics, changing peasant society, and external variables.

Chapter 6

Political Parties

One of the briefer definitions of democracy states:

> Democracy exists where the principal leaders of a political system are selected by competitive elections in which the bulk of the population have the opportunity to participate.[1]

A democratic political system requires **political parties**. Political parties first emerged in countries that were pluralizing or democratizing. The virtues of popular participation have been debated and fought over since at least the fourth century B.C., when Plato and Aristotle were writing as the Greek city-state system collapsed. It is only in the last 200 years, though, that some variation of democracy has emerged in more than a handful of countries, approximately 40 to 45 today. When the opinions and desires of a substantial number of citizens began to be taken into account by the political elite—either because of philosophical commitment or practical necessity—political parties organized. Parties brought organization to mass participation. Enfranchisement was a relatively slow process during the nineteenth century, but the pace increased in this century. In the American presidential elections of 1824, for example, when blacks and women were not permitted to vote and tax and property qualifications still existed in many states, 3.8 percent of the total population voted.[2] In Japan, a mere 1.1 percent of the population was eligible to vote in the first national election held in 1890; subsequent lowering of the tax qualification meant that by 1920 the eligible electorate represented 5.49 percent of Japan's population.[3]

Most political scientists believe political parties in a pluralistic system provide the maximum opportunity for popular influence on government. A competitive party system through free and competitive elections allows large numbers of people to have a voice in choosing political leaders and provides some direction to government policies. Many political scientists believe that the most important institution in a democracy is the political party:

> Political parties created democracy and . . . modern democracy is unthinkable save in terms of the parties. As a matter of fact, the condition of the parties is the best possible evidence of the nature of any regime.[4]

There are, of course, various types of political parties in nonpluralistic political systems. Party in some form of another is a nearly universal institution. Democratic parties, we contend, are the norm. Other variations of party are discussed later in the chapter.

---

[1]Samuel P. Huntington and Clement H. Moore, "Conclusion: Authoritarianism, Democracy, and One-Party Politics," in Samuel P. Huntington and Clement H. Moore, eds., *Authoritarian Politics in Modern Society* (New York: Basic Books, 1970), p. 509.

[2]Robert Lane, *Political Life* (Glencoe, Ill.: Free Press, 1965), p. 19.

[3]Chitoshi Yanaga, *Japanese People and Politics* (New York: John Wiley, 1956), pp. 281–282.

[4]E. E. Schattschneider, *Party Government* (New York: Rinehart, 1942), p. 1.

POLITICAL PARTIES DEFINED

We define democratic, competitive parties first because this is the original type of party. Only in this century have groups called parties emerged as instruments of revolution and authoritarian control.

A *political party* in a democracy is a group of voters organized for the purposes of nominating and electing candidates legally to public office in order to influence and/or control personnel and policy. A *party* is distinguished from an *interest group* in that a party nominates candidates for public office, while interest groups do not.

Even if a party wins few electoral victories, it still may have an impact on the political system and attract loyal supporters. In the United States, for example, third parties often act as "issue finders" for major parties. The late Norman Thomas, the leading American Socialist of the century, wryly observed many times that, although the Socialist party of America never won a national election, many Socialist proposals, such as minimum wage laws, a social security system, unemployment compensation, and a federal Department of Labor, were enacted by the Democrats and Republicans several decades after they were first proposed by the Socialists.

The points listed in Boxes 6.1 and 6.2 describe the democratically oriented party, which supports constitutionally guaranteed political competition. History shows us political parties that were dedicated to the overthrow of a political system and eliminated competitive elections once they acquired power, either by working through the electoral system (the Nazi party at the end of the German Weimar Republic, 1933) or by working outside the existing system (the Bolsheviks as a subversive movement in the 1917 Russian Revolution). When these parties were allowed to compete, as the Nazis were in Weimar Germany (1918–1933), they adopted electoral strategies that disrupt and cripple the political system. In the declining years of the Weimar Republic, as Depression conditions weakened the ruling democratic parties, the party system collapsed into street brawls. Uniformed bullyboys of the Nazi and Communist parties made it impossible for other political parties to appear in public without the support of a gang of hoodlums. Pitched battles between party militia were difficult to control and helped to destroy German democracy.

Frequently, a totalitarian party became the "organization weapon" to launch a revolution.[5] Such a party has few democratic party traits. V. I. Lenin (1870–1924), the architect of the October 1917 Russian Revolution that brought the Communists to power, first described the principles upon which a totalitarian party is founded. His prescriptions continue to be mainsprings of action for such groups. As Lenin explained to his followers:

> And this promise I shall defend no matter how much you instigate the crowd against me for my "anti-democratic" views, . . . 3. that the organization must consist chiefly

---

[5]Phillip Selznick, *The Organizational Weapon: A Study of Bolshevik Strategy and Tactics* (Glencoe, Ill.: Free Press, 1960).

Box 6.1 **Organizational Features of Political Parties in Democracies**

1. Associations of leaders and members seeking to win elections.

2. Local organizations, committees, or branches that maintain some relationship (communication, provide election workers, and so on) with the central headquarters. The organization may be highly centralized as the British Conservative Party or decentralized as in the United States.

3. Institutionalization or permanency of the party organization, which is only established when there is a procedure by which party leaders can succeed one another and a new group or generation of leaders has replaced the founding members.

4. Subject to regulation by government rules. The organization is influenced in part by the party's own bylaws and the customs and traditions of the political culture.

Box 6.2 **Political Party Functions in Democracies**

1. Campaign to win elective offices.

2. Aggregate receptive interest groups in order to win electoral and financial support for the party.

3. Simplify the issues and emphasize a few to obtain public attention and support. By transmitting information to large numbers of people, parties encourage interest and participation.

4. Establish itself as a symbol in the minds of people (or a reference group). Simply put: Build voter identification. (Reference groups are groups that are important in a person's thinking. They may evoke positive or negative responses.)

5. Influence the organization of government (personnel) and participate in and influence policy formation.

6. Numerous other functions: Legitimize and stabilize the political system by providing an organization through which the more vocal and compelling claims can influence government; act as a two-way communication process between elected officials and the average citizen; contribute to the orderly succession of political leadership; and provide an avenue by which ambitious persons can achieve political elite status.

The end of political parties in Germany: Nazi SS troops parade before Hitler.

of persons engaged in revolution as a profession; 4. that in a country with a despotic government, the more we restrict the membership of this organization to persons who are engaged in revolution as a profession and who have been professionally trained in the art of combatting the political police the more difficult will it be to catch the organization. . . .[6]

If the revolutionary party succeeds, it is the end of competitive politics, and the victorious party becomes an instrument of domination and the elimination of all

---

[6]V. I. Lenin, *What Is to Be Done?* (New York: International Publishers, 1929), p. 116.

personal rights. The types of parties that emerge in a country are partly a result of historical conditions that led to party development. Changing conditions can help change the nature of parties, as we see in the Soviet Union and Eastern Europe today.

ORIGINS OF POLITICAL PARTIES

Parties in the organized, mass participation sense first emerged in the United States during the late eighteenth century, almost immediately after the 13 colonies achieved independence. Not everyone supported these new organizations. George Washington warned in his Farewell Address on September 19, 1796, "against the baneful effects of parties generally including opening the door to foreign influence and corruption."[7]

From 1797 onward many political leaders throughout the world have been suspicious of parties. The refusal to permit more than one party usually is based on one or more of the following: (1) to perpetuate rule by an oligarchy; (2) to preserve domestic tranquility and avoid unnecessary quarreling; and (3) to prevent the infiltration of foreign influence.

The origins of political parties can be traced to five historical causes that will be discussed in order of their appearance. All types of political parties appear in an environment where traditional institutions and practices are declining and new ideas and techniques are appearing.

In Response to Competitive Elections

Political parties first came into being as a consequence of specific constitutional arrangements and laws that provided for or encouraged competitive elections. Political parties in the United States appeared in the 1790s because state laws encouraged this type of organization by "defining the rules of the game"[8] and providing for election contests.

Key persons sympathetic to the importance of parties strengthened a party system. Thomas Jefferson, America's third president, placed himself indisputably at the head of the newly emerged Democrat-Republican party. Cabinet posts were carefully allocated to qualified Republicans where he and the party needed support. A student of this period has noted:

> Jefferson believed that the party was a vehicle for people's expression and therefore relied upon it for grass roots feelings. The geographical distribution of the Cabinet provided access to the people's opinion throughout the young country.[9]

---

[7]U.S. House of Representatives, *Washington's Farewell Address to the People of the United States,* House Document No. 504, 89th Congress, 2nd Session, 1966, pp. 15–16.

[8]Paul Goodman, "The First American Party System," in William Nisbett Chambers and Walter Dean Burnham, eds., *The American Party Systems: Stages of Political Development,* 2nd ed. (New York: Oxford University Press, 1975), p. 65.

[9]Agnes Rose Burton, CSJ, "Political Parties: Effect on the Presidency," *Presidential Studies Quarterly,* 11:2 (Spring 1981), p. 292.

Likewise, in other countries, mass parties evolved because the **suffrage** was expanded and groups organized to contest elections. In Great Britain, prior to the Reform Act of 1832, members of Parliament rarely were challenged in an election. Many, if not a majority, came from constituencies under the domination of a wealthy landlord, known as *pocket boroughs.* A *rotten borough* was a parliamentary district where the population was virtually nil. The most famous was Old Sarum, which in 1800 had only seven inhabitants and returned two members of Parliament (M.P.s). The seven voters regularly auctioned their votes to the highest bidder.

There are two stages in the historical development of British parties. First, there were factions or alignments of M.P.s. Before the 1830s parliamentary groups organized for debating and voting purposes. Lines were clearly drawn, for example, over the intense controversies surrounding debate and passage of the 1832 electoral reform. During the constitutional and religious conflicts of the seventeenth century, Royalists supporters were called *Tories* (a Tory being an Irish brigand), because the King's supporters used Irish troops to secure the success of the Stuart King, James II, in 1679. The other group, often opposed to the Crown, was called the *Whigs* after the Whiggamores who were Scottish Presbyterian rebels in the seventeenth century. These names stayed until the nineteenth century when the Tories became the Conservatives and the Whigs became the Liberal party.[10] The second, or external, stage of party development occurred after 1832 as mass party organization began to evolve outside of Parliament.

Prior to 1832 the number of voting constituents per M.P. averaged 330. The Reform Act eliminated some of the worst inequities, such as providing the city of Manchester—population of 180,000—with representation in the House of Commons for the first time. The Reform Act was a modest effort, increasing the eligible electorate by 50 percent, to between 650,000 and 700,000 people, or about 3 percent of the adult population. This numerical increase in the electorate led like-minded groups of M.P.s to initiate external party electoral organizations after 1832.

Political parties organized in Japan in 1881 as mechanisms of protest. The leadership of these groups was composed largely of ex-*samurai* (warriors) and former members of the government who resented the domination of the Choshu and Satsuma clans in the government. The appearance, combining, and disappearance of many organizations was partly a result of the fact that no constitutional or other legal guide provided an appropriate outlet. With the appearance of the Emperor Meiji's constitution in February 1889, party organizations were provided with a logical focus. Article 35 of the new constitution described the House of Representatives as "composed of Members elected by the people according to the provisions of the Law of Election." Elections were held first in July 1890, and within ten years the dominant group in Japanese politics—the Genro, or Elder Statesmen—concluded that the most effective way to influence government was to

---

[10]For an explanation of party names and the term "party" in the early British context, see R. M. Punnett, *British Government and Politics,* 5th ed. (Chicago: Dorsey Press, 1988), pp. 74–75.

Socialist leader Ms. Takako Doi celebrates electoral victories in Japan, 1989.

form a political party that could win a majority of seats and organize the popularly chosen House of Representatives. The earlier manipulation and corruption of individual legislators and party cliques by the executive had brought increasing discredit to the government. The Diet (a bicameral legislature) depended on a party system in order to function properly, and the previous techniques could not be relied upon in the future to produce the desired results.

In his study of Western party systems, Maurice Duverger refers to those who have a "parliamentary origin" and those "externally created" or "extraparliamentary" in origin.[11] In both instances the party seeks to influence or control government because of and through the electoral process. In the first instance are groups of representatives in parliament who have joined together on certain questions and established ties with electoral committees as the suffrage is extended and new groups win the right to vote. Examples would be the Conservative and Liberal parties in Great Britain and the American Federalists and Jeffersonian Republicans. The external party usually originates among groups who have not participated in an organized manner in the electoral process but now see the time as opportune because many potential supporters have gained the franchise. The activities of the Fabian Society and the Trades Union Congress, which led to the creation of the British Labour party in 1900, is an example.

To Encourage Unity

Although democratic party systems emerged as a result of constitutional legal prodding, one-party or authoritarian party systems generally have different beginnings.

Nationalist movements against a foreign colonial power frequently led to a single-party system. Successful anticolonial movements were not inclined to tolerate political opposition after gaining independence. The need for a monolithic unity to deal with the numerous economic and political challenges that threatened to overwhelm a poor, economically underdeveloped system was the reason commonly advanced to justify a one-party system. A reason given by a West African party systems' analyst is that "single party" systems emerged because "it was a goal set by a political elite which then worked self-consciously for its achievement."[12] Political elites presumably were first and foremost concerned with remaining in power, and the means to accomplish this was the single party, which could help control the population. A sure way to stay in power is to prevent effective competition.

Another reason advanced for the creation of one-party states in former colonial territories is that this type of political system is in accord with revered historical-cultural traditions. An elite working through a single party is in harmony with traditional practices. Many non-Western traditional societies generally were inclined toward some form of extended deliberation that would result in a consensus, not toward a jarring count of votes with public losers. Majority rule and representative government have no roots in most traditional societies where "the voice of the elders, the wise, and the specially qualified was entitled to extra or even decisive weight"[13] and should not be subject to open, public criticism.

---

[11]See Maurice Duverger, *Political Parties: Their Organization and Activity in the Modern State,* 3rd ed., Barbara and Robert North, trans. (New York: Methuen, 1969), pp. xiii–xxxvii.

[12]Aristide R. Zolberg, *Creating Political Order: The Party States of West Africa,* (reprint, Chicago: University of Chicago Press, 1985), pp. 35–36.

[13]Rupert Emerson, *From Empire to Nation: The Rise to Self-Assertion of Asian and African Peoples* (Boston: Beacon Press, 1964), p. 284.

As Revolutionary Weapons

Beginning with the Russian Communist party, numerous political parties were founded in this century as revolutionary weapons. Some, such as the Nazi party, adopted a quasi-constitutional strategy. The Nazis pursued their goal within the existing party system, manipulating and disrupting the system in the name of their totalitarian blueprint for the future. Adolf Hitler proclaimed that the Weimar constitution gave the Nazis "the ground on which to wage our battle." Too many ignored Hitler's warning that when the Nazis captured power, "we shall then mould the state into that form which we consider to be the right one."[14] Most revolutionary parties were, however, required to adopt a conspiratorial posture because they were illegal. The Communist party of the Soviet Union (officially founded in 1898 as the Russian Social Democratic Labor party), for example, seized power through underground conspiracy, revolution, and finally civil war, which did not end until 1920.

Another revolutionary weapon was the Chinese Communist party (CCP), founded in July 1921 when the First Party Congress was held in a Roman Catholic girls' school in the French concession at Shanghai—outside the jurisdiction of Chinese law. Thirteen Chinese, including Mao Zedong, attended this meeting; two Comintern agents—a Soviet citizen and a Dutchman—also attended. The First Congress established the party as a revolutionary weapon that refused to cooperate with any existing political group. One document adopted at the Congress urged "aggression" toward existing parties and declared "no relationship with other parties or groups."[15] Today the CCP rules 1.1 billion people in the most populous country in the world.

In Response to Liberal Ideas

Political parties also were created as a response to the spread of liberal ideas from the West. Many Japanese parties before the 1890 constitution were partly a consequence of Western ideas and writings, which were widely circulated among the Japanese elites.

The agitation for more openness and the right to organize now occurring in the Soviet Union and the People's Republic of China (PRC) are partly based on reading Western political literature and on direct observation of democratic political systems. For example, during the late 1980s, nearly 28,000 PRC students were in the United States each year studying in colleges and universities. By mid-1989, 60,000 American-trained students had returned to the PRC.

As a Means of Control

A final point of origin for political parties is the need to mobilize and control the growing political consciousness of the masses. Samuel P. Huntington has noted,

---

[14]Frederick Mundell Watkins, *The Failure of Constitutional Powers under the German Republic* (Cambridge, Mass.: Harvard University Press, 1939), p. 53.

[15]Stuart Schram, *Mao Tse-tung* (Baltimore, Md.: Penguin Books, 1966), p. 66.

Table 6.1 **GROWTH OF THE COMMUNIST PARTY OF THE SOVIET UNION**

Year	Total membership
1917	335,000
1927	1,148,000
1939	2,478,000
1952	6,882,000
1967	11,350,000
1986	19,000,000

"significantly, when authoritarian regimes with weak parties confront crises, the party tends to reemerge as a more important actor."[16] When a new group of leaders seizes power, a political party is created or expanded to penetrate the grass roots and control the population.

A traditional political system is often a no-party country. However, a new, revolutionary government that attempts to bring about fundamental changes in the social and economic systems generally turns into a single, monopolistic party. A dictatorial government attempting far-reaching and radical new programs must penetrate all of society and harness, persuade, and dominate it. Thus, the creation of a key instrument to accomplish this transformation—a ruling political party.

The single, monopolistic party is created to indoctrinate and control the masses and strengthen the position of the ruling elite. For nearly 60 years, the secretary of the Communist party of the Soviet Union (CPSU) supervised all party, government, and economic decision-units in his district (except security), sometimes setting goals and establishing procedures that overrode existing policies. Supervision, control, and coordination often lead to day-to-day administrative involvement and give the monopolistic party pervasive authority, especially as the political system becomes institutionalized. Table 6.1 shows the growth of the CPSU as its control responsibilities, justified by its ideology, expanded prior to the launching of *perestroika* and *glasnost* after 1985.

Party origins and ideology profoundly influence the objectives and organization of parties. Parties established to seize power by any available means and/or to harness a population are unlikely to assume a democratic character at a very early date.

TYPES OF PARTIES AND PARTY SYSTEMS

Political parties are classified according to a number of criteria. We will discuss four of the more useful classifications.

---

[16]Huntington and Moore, eds., *Authoritarian Politics*, p. 9.

An Early Classification

One of the earliest and most heuristic attempts to classify political parties in the post-1945 period was by Maurice Duverger. Professor Duverger recognized the need for profound case studies of individual parties, but argued there must also be a general theory of parties. He recognized that such a theory would be preliminary, but it was essential. Duverger noted that parties were fundamentally different in their basic organizational units. He used these differences to form the basis of his classification theory of cadre party, mass party, and devotee party.

The *cadre party* emphasizes quality at the top, notables who have contacts, money, and expertise. It has few members, does not seek a mass membership, and stresses winning elections. Party doctrine and the enthusiasm of most party identifiers is low. Party discipline is weak and its appeal is to the middle class especially. U.S. parties and a majority of European conservatives and middle-of-the-road parties fit this category.

The *mass party* sees recruiting and educating members as fundamental activities. Its first level organizational unit is the branch. The mass party draws its finances not from a few wealthy donors, but from mass membership. Party ideology and discipline are strong. Enthusiasm, at least in the initial decades, was high. These parties focus on the working class and are Socialist.

The *devotee party* is more open than the mass, but more closed than the cadre party. It is the vanguard of the class, ethnic, or national group it represents. The inner party members are the elite, while the large group of outer members are the followers, or implementers, of the party line. It is the inner circle who are the enlightened, fighting vanguard and monopolizers of power. Fascist, Nazi, and traditional Communist parties fit in this category.[17]

These categories are not a comprehensive set of characteristics that every party in each category must possess. The categories do, though, provide a broadly marked path to help illuminate the study of specific parties or cluster of parties.

Pragmatic, Absolute-Value, and Particularistic Parties

Pragmatic-bargaining or *broker-type parties* are typical of the Canadian and American systems,[18] though this form of party appears to be spreading, even to some Communist parties in Western Europe. This party type is highly voter conscious, is hungry for votes, and attempts to respond to the maximum number of interests by policies and campaign statements with the widest appeal. The party appeals to all strata of society and usually attracts support from identifiable social groupings. Britain's Conservative party attracts upper- and middle-class voters especially, but approximately one-quarter of British labor union members vote Conservative. Bar-

[17]Maurice Duverger, *Political Parties*, 2nd ed., Barbara and Robert North, trans. (New York: Science Editions, John Wiley, 1959). For a review of this approach, see Aaron B. Wildavsky, "A Methodological Critique of Duverger's *Political Parties*," *Journal of Politics*, 25:2 (May 1959), pp. 303–318.

[18]Gabriel Almond was one of the first to set forth a scheme based on party style or behavior in the political arena. See Gabriel Almond and James S. Coleman, eds., *The Politics of the Developing Areas* (Princeton, N.J.: Princeton University Press, 1960), pp. 43–45.

Table 6.2   **1988 PRESIDENTIAL VOTE PERCENTAGE BY GROUPS NORMALLY ALIGNED WITH DEMOCRATIC PARTY**

Group	Voted for Republican George Bush	Voted for Democrat Michael Dukakis
Blacks	12	86
Hispanics	30	69
Jewish	35	64
Family income under $12,500	37	62
Liberals	18	81
Unemployed	37	62
Democratic primary election voters	21	78

Source: Voter exit poll, *New York Times* (November 10, 1988), p. 18. Nationwide the total percentage of popular vote for George Bush was 53% and for Michael Dukakis, 45%. © 1988 by The New York Times Company. Reprinted by permission.

gaining, compromise, accommodation, responsiveness, and a marketplace atmosphere dominate party strategy. This type of party functions in a system with a broad political consensus, where intense doctrinal issues do not divide society. The bargaining, broker party is criticized for failing to present the voters with clear-cut alternatives and for failing to lead on the critical issues of the day. One expert on British parties, writing early in this century, criticized British parties for their overriding concern to win "by picking up votes from every quarter. Parties did not lead, but built blocs of votes and were often obligated to conciliate even the representatives of the fanciful movements and the fads" in order to win votes.[19]

Table 6.2 illustrates how the pragmatic-bargaining parties in the United States draw support and hence make appeals to groups that traditionally support the other party. The umbrella party seeks votes from all groups and generally acts accordingly.

Absolute-value-oriented or *ideological parties,* such as the Nazi party or all Communist parties until the last few years, push a rigid, comprehensive program and usually regard compromise and negotiation as weakness. Party members often are recruited from among the most alienated groups in the population. Appeals for support are limited by the fact that potential members must convert to a highly structured party doctrine. Parties that fit into this category usually are revolutionary or reactionary.

Enemies of the party are numerous, and many are killed. A rather extreme but not untypical example is Cambodia (Kampuchea). Between 1975 and 1979, Prime Minister Pol Pot's Communists, often called the *Organization,* deliberately murdered approximately 1 million people in a total population of 7 million. Anyone who had worked with the previous non-Communist government, including all of their family members, were executed. Individuals with a high school education or

---

[19]M. Ostrogorski, *Democracy and the Organization of Political Parties,* vol. 2 (New York: Macmillan, 1902), p. 684.

above and their families were brutally killed (throat slit, beaten to death, or buried alive). This Asian holocaust occurred because the Communist rulers believed those murdered could never be trusted, and it was "safer" and cheaper (in many cases execution squads were ordered not to use bullets) to destroy them rather than attempt to brainwash or imprison them. These events were dramatically recorded in the movie *The Killing Fields*.

Deviation from the "official" ideology is treason or an act of resignation from the party. Challenging the current leadership—and hence party doctrine—can produce fatal results. Leon Trotsky, Lenin's most influential comrade, eventually clashed with Stalin and left the Soviet Union in 1929. After living in several countries and maintaining constant public criticism of the Stalin regime, Trotsky settled in Coyoacán, Mexico, in 1937, where he kept up his attacks against Stalin's leadership. Trotsky was assassinated on August 20, 1940, by a trusted supporter, Jacques Monard. It was soon alleged that the killer was an agent of the Soviet secret police.

Some parties, such as the Prohibition party in the United States, are inflexible in only certain policy areas, but would negotiate in other matters. Most absolute-value-oriented parties operating in a competitive party system vigorously oppose whatever party or parties are in power. Some Communist parties do become more flexible and bargaining-minded as they come closer to power, particularly after they see an opportunity to form a coalition government with non-Communist parties. This is the case in the Italian Communist party (PCI) and other Eurocommunist parties. For example, the PCI leader, Achille Ochetto, proclaims the PCI is a Western European party of the left and not an ideological party of the East, embraces the North Atlantic Treaty Organization, and seeks to be a contributing pillar of the Western alliance.[20]

Particularistic parties are self-limiting, because they combine their appeals to specific ethnic, linguistic, or religious groups, such as the Hindu Maha Sabha, a conservative Indian party that restricts its membership to Hindus. These are communal parties dedicated to traditional values or to what Clifford Geertz has described as **primordial sentiments**, which are given facts, "such as being born into a particular language or religious community, ethnic or racial group, kinship, geographic region, etc."[21]

At times these particularistic parties are willing to work within the larger political system and pursue a strategy of negotiation and compromise as the best means of protecting the group's interests. Frequently, though, the party's emphasis on traditional identifications intensifies divisions in society to the point that political negotiation becomes unlikely. One of the causes of the Nigerian Civil War (1967–1970) was that political distrusts and misunderstandings increased after

---

[20]Karen Wolman, "Italy Communists Go Mainstream," *Christian Science Monitor* (May 16, 1989), p. 4.

[21]For an analysis of such identifications in contemporary politics, see Clifford Geertz, "Primordial Sentiments and Civil Politics in New States," in *Old Societies and New States; the Quest for Modernity in Asia and Africa* (Glencoe, Ill.: Free Press, 1963), p. 109.

independence. Independence and a new government offer a new prize to be won by ambitious individuals. Often it is the primordial sentiments that are appealed to and politicized by aspiring leaders as they seek to build popular support. For example, one of the best organized Nigerian parties in the pre—Civil War period was the Action Group, whose support was drawn almost entirely from the Yoruba tribe.

Single-Party, Two-Party, and Multiparty Systems

Political parties can be classified and analyzed according to a number of criteria. One of the most common classifications when considering the party system as a whole is by number of parties; single-party, two-party, and multiparty systems.

An analysis of *single-party systems* reveals wide variations among them. There are monolithic, authoritarian parties, such as the Chinese CCP and the Workers' Party of Vietnam, which traditionally penetrate all of society. Parties such as Mexico's Institutional Revolutionary party completely overshadow the several legal opposition parties, but they do not monopolize society to the degree the ruling parties in mainland China and the Democratic Republic of Vietnam have done.

The American South for a century after the Civil War was described as a single-party system. The term "one party" in the United States defines a condition where meaningful two-party competition is absent. The South was not a case where a highly authoritarian political organization monopolized the selection of government officials. The states are required constitutionally to hold elections, and hotly contested electoral battles regularly occurred in the primaries, if not in the general elections.[22] Japan is often described as a dominant or one-party system because the Liberal Democratic party has held power without a break since 1955. For a discussion of a special type of single party, see One-Party Revolutionary Regimes.

Two-party systems are limited to a few countries, principally the United States, Great Britain, New Zealand, and Australia. (As we later note, no competitive electoral system has *only* two parties.) The opposition is sufficiently united that they can coalesce into a dominant opposition party, which can, if the electoral winds shift, remain united as a governing party. A general mass consensus on the political rules of the game undergird the system. Both parties concentrate on competing for the dominant bloc of the middle-of-the-road voters. Multiparty systems can tolerate an extremist party, but representative elections cannot continue in a two-party system if one of the two parties is extremist or totalitarian, determined to destroy its competitor when it comes to power.

One of the first two-party systems was the British, where the opposition was, and is, an integral part of the political process. Being in opposition is regarded as a legitimate public service, and since 1937 the leader of the opposition has been paid a special salary by the government.

No two-party system has *only* two parties, but in a two-party system there are

---

[22]A fascinating, though somewhat dated, analysis of one-party American states is V. O. Key, *Southern Politics* (New York: Vintage Books, 1949).

only two major parties that have a chance to control the national political system. The smaller third party is common to American national politics. In the 1968 presidential election, George Wallace's American Independent party (AIP) garnered 13.6 percent of the popular vote, but no AIP candidate was elected to office. Between 1945 and 1987 in Great Britain, the Liberal party vote plus the popular votes of minor parties in general elections have ranged between 3.2 percent and 30 percent. In the 1987 general election, the Alliance (Liberal and Social Democrats) received 22.6 percent of the popular vote, yet the Alliance won only 22 of the 650 seats in the House of Commons. Never since World War II have the Conservative and Labour parties combined controlled less than 94 percent of the seats in the House of Commons, and the average share of the two major parties has been 97 percent of the seats. Both Great Britain and the United States have single-member districts with plurality election (the election winner is the contestant with more votes than any other candidate, but not necessarily a majority); therefore, unless a party's strength is concentrated in a few districts (as Alliance support is not) a party may win 20 or even 30 percent of the vote in a district but not elect a candidate.

In the American two-party system, the Democratic and Republican parties are decentralized, with state and even county organizations autonomous of the next higher level in the party hierarchy. Party candidates compete in elections, but the parties do not remain strictly competitive after the elections. Presidents and governments invariably depend on bipartisan support for many proposals, because members of the chief executive's own party sometime vote against him or her on major issues.

Great Britain has a disciplined two-party system. The term "disciplined parties" means that commonly there are no crossovers when the House of Commons votes. Each party usually can depend on its M.P.s to support the party position.

There also is the two-plus system such as in Germany. The two dominant parties are the Christian Democrats and Social Democrats; but there are two smaller, relevant parties, the Greens and the Free Democrats. The United States and Great Britain are not two-plus because third and fourth parties seldom win elective offices. Third-plus parties, however, remind the two major parties of emerging issues or substantial popular discontent.

In *multiparty systems,* one party rarely wins an absolute majority of seats in the legislature. Consequently, in a parliamentary regime, a coalition government (one made up of several parties) must be formed. In multiparty systems parties often represent limited-appeal interests and seek to advance these interests by participating in a coalition government. It may seem surprising, but in trying to build a coalition, only one or two parts of the party program may be accepted by other members of the coalition. The compromises on party doctrine occur in the legislature, after the election. The negotiations are decisive. It is at this time that the critical bargains are struck and ministries divided among the parties. The number of parties and the amount of party cohesiveness and government stability vary among multiparty systems. The Netherlands has a parliamentary system of government in which five or six parties have dominated the political scene in the post-1945 period. These parties generally receive 80 percent or more of the popular vote. The country becomes a single constituency when national elections are held, and a party's representation in the popularly elected Second Chamber of 140 members is determined by its proportion of the national popular vote.

The continuity of popular support for most parties has been a postwar feature of Dutch politics. A poll taken after the 1956 elections revealed that 85 percent of the persons interviewed had voted for the same party they had supported in 1952. Following the elections held in October 1981, the four largest parties controlled 135 of 150 seats (48, 44, 26, and 17 seats, respectively). The government formed in 1977 was composed of three parties, representing 109 seats in the Second Chamber. Of necessity, any government must be a coalition government, and while it may require many weeks of negotiation to form the coalition, governments normally remain in office for several years. After the 1981 elections, for example, a four-month bargaining process occurred before a majority coalition government could be formed. However, a multiparty system has not prevented government stability and the capacity to develop and implement policy in the Netherlands, once a coalition has been arranged.

The French multiparty system was a contributing factor to the *immobilisme* of French politics during the Fourth Republic (1946–1958). Cabinets or governments were approved and fell with an unhealthy frequency. Between 1946 and 1958 there were 26 different cabinets. Governments became unable to deal with critical issues, such as the Algerian revolution, and important social and economic policies. The Fourth Republic was a parliamentary regime. In 1956, 150 Communist deputies were elected to the 597-member National Assembly. The Communists consistently opposed the government, and cabinets had to be formed from the remaining groups: the Mouvement Populaire Republicain—a social reformist Catholic party with 83 deputies; the Socialists with 95 deputies; and a host of smaller groupings. Some parties other than the Communists, such as the pro-Gaullists and the Poujadists, with approximately 70 seats, also pursued an antigovernment policy. The parties in the middle, which sought to form governments, were limited by the number of parties with which they could realistically negotiate. Throughout most of the Fourth Republic, 350 to 400 of the 597 votes in the National Assembly were available to form a government, but all 400 votes were not available at the same time. Another weakening factor was the absence of party cohesion. On 72 crucial votes between 1946 and 1956 in the National Assembly, only the Communists and Socialists maintained party discipline. On numerous votes, from 10 to 40 percent of the parties' deputies voted against the parties' majority. During this same period, ten governments were forced to resign because of split voting in parties that originally had voted for installing the cabinet.[23]

In a multiparty system the common denominator is the presence of three or more political parties with relevant electoral support. The ability of the executive branch to govern in a multiparty system varies, depending on the number of parties, party cohesion, and party ideologies. Recent studies suggest that in Western

---

[23]David S. McLellon, "Ministerial Instability and the Lack of Internal Cohesion in French Parties," *World Affairs Quarterly*, 28 (April 1957), pp. 3–24.

Europe, when there are five or less parties, politics is moderated and stabilized because most of these parties focus their campaigns on the moderate center. When the number of parties exceeds five, at least some of the parties move to extremes, increasing campaign shrillness and divisions in the political system.

Reasons for two-party, two-party-plus, or multiparty systems are still debated among political scientists. Many are based on long-standing cleavages involving class, region, ethnicity, language, or religion. Single-member districts (SMD) where a plurality produces a winner, such as in the United States, Great Britain, and Australia, facilitate two-party or two-party-plus systems. The most frequent explanation for two-plus or multiparties in an SMD system is the regional concentration of minority or ideological groups. Proportional representation (PR) requires multimember districts. For example, in the Netherlands and Israel, the whole country is one district. Parties win seats in parliament pretty much in line with their proportion of the popular vote. PR in several countries has encouraged the splitting of parties. Postwar Germany and France are good case studies of changes in the electoral laws facilitating minor parties or favoring a two-plus system or two-party blocs, depending on whether some variation of PR was used or single-member districts were introduced.

One-Party Revolutionary Regimes

The first single-party political regimes appeared in the Soviet Union in 1917, in Italy in 1922, and in Germany in 1933, when the Communist, Fascist, and Nazi parties, respectively, came to power. Of these three, original one-party systems, only the Soviet system survives today.

As we noted, however, the variation among one-party systems has been substantial. To speak of a single-party regime today refers to a wide variety of practices. The common factor that most single-party countries share is their authoritarian character. There are regimes, however, that are single-party systems but are not highly authoritarian, such as Mexico's Institutional Revolutionary Party.

Many one-party systems arise out of a historical experience with severe and prolonged divisions that led to internal war. The party's first objective is to create order and organize the country. In a century when mass political consciousness has become a fact of life, the single party restrains and organizes this consciousness in order to control the population. After the seizure of power the victors carry forward a struggle to purge society of the "enemy." Among totalitarian one-party regimes this is a brutal period in the nation's history, as during the first five years (1949–1954) of the PRC when 10 to 14 million "enemies of the people" were eliminated.

Samuel P. Huntington has analyzed revolutionary one-party systems in depth.[24] Successful revolutionary parties are determined to create a monolithic social and political order. Change, mass mobilization, terror, and absolute loyalty are the hallmarks of a newly established revolutionary one-party system. Those

[24] Samuel P. Huntington, "Social and Institutional Dynamics of One-Party Systems," in Huntington and Moore, eds., *Authoritarian Politics*, pp. 3–47. This section is based on Huntington's chapter.

unwilling to convert or those whom the leadership deems unworthy of being converted (for example, Jews or landlords) are destroyed. The revolutionary single party's tentacles touch all parts of society and the individual's existence. Huntington suggests such a ruling party goes through three stages:

1. **Transformation** occurs as the old order or aspects of it are destroyed. This is a most brutal period. Purges, executions, summary imprisonments, and confiscation plague the population. The enemy is identified and destroyed or driven out. The systematic snuffing out of human life on unprecedented scales occurred during the years of the party dictatorship in Nazi Germany, the Soviet Union, the PRC, and the Democratic Republic of Vietnam, when millions of people were executed or sent to concentration camps from which only few returned. Recent estimates suggest that 40 million people were killed in the Soviet Union between 1929 and 1939 as Stalin established his monolithic political order.

2. In the **consolidation stage**, the old order has been destroyed and the regime legitimizes itself on the basis of the institutions and performance of the new order. Ideology begins to erode. In the consolidation stage support or tolerance of the regime rests on the institutions and the performance of the system. Ideology becomes rote chant by the ambitious.

   The consolidation stage is the period of institutionalization. A common result is to limit the power of the leader and establish an oligarchic system in which power is divided among several individuals.

3. Assuming that the founding leader is no longer on the scene and the party has surmounted the succession crisis, the institutions of the new order have taken hold, the party enters the **adaptation stage**. In this stage the party must relate itself to four social developments: (a) the emergence of highly trained technicians and managers who are (b) responsible for the operation of an economically rewarding society; (c) the appearance of intellectuals trained under the new order who frequently criticize the regime; and (d) various groups in society demanding a role in the decision-making process.

Glasnost and *perestroika,* as advocated by Mikhail Gorbachev, suggests that a fourth stage may occur—*political pluralism* (at least it has in Eastern Europe and the Soviet Union). Debate, claims, rallies, and demonstrations may call for political and economic reforms that even reformist leaderships had not anticipated.

In some pluralizing authoritarian regimes there is evidence of a willingness to become more responsive, through legalizing opposition parties or at least through the inclusion of more than one officially certified nominee per office.

Such trends are not always present in all Communist political systems. For example, mainland China, after the death of Mao in 1976, embarked on a comprehensive development program known as the *four modernizations:* modernization of defense, agriculture, industry, and science and technology. A drive was launched to popularize educational quality. During the Mao-instigated Cultural Revolution (1966–1969), teachers who valued knowledge over politics were labeled "bourgeois'' and replaced by young, usually uneducated Red Guards. The four modernizations reinstated the dismissed teachers and stressed diligent study, competitive exams, and discipline in the classroom. Related to this was the emergence in 1977 of the two-block-long "democracy wall" in Peking where those critical of government policies posted their protests. For two years the government continued to waver on how much criticism could be allowed. The editor of the most popular antigovernment magazine, *Exploration,* was sentenced to 15 years in prison in late 1979, and democracy wall was effectively closed down.

The role of "expert" over "Red" (following the party line but with no technical expertise) now predominates in decision making. Critical groups are demanding more voice in order to avoid past mistakes, but the Communist regime gradually is silencing dissent as the government seeks to mobilize and control all national resources for the four modernizations.

During the past ten years the Chinese mainland economy was rapidly liberalized. Collective farms were replaced by nearly autonomous peasant farmers. Profit incentives and pay according to the value of work were introduced in the industrial sector. Political reforms have not kept pace with economic reforms, however. The PRC leadership sees popular demands for democracy and human rights running well ahead of any possible, positive government response. The massive, May 1989 demonstrations by over a million people in Tiananmen Square produced negligible political results, the exception being the June massacre, when more than 3,000 students and bystanders were killed and 10,000 were seriously wounded. The

The tanks stop for a moment: Tiananmen Square, June 5, 1989.

danger of political drift on the Chinese mainland has led a cautious party leadership to reject gradual political liberalization in favor of political repression. Political order remains in order in post-1979 China.

The Chinese Communist party is shoring up its dominant role and resurrecting party slogans, heroes, and propaganda campaigns. These are all measures that gave the CCP pervasive control of society in the past. The party began cleansing itself of reformers in 1990 by requiring its 47 million members to submit new, detailed membership applications.

Political Parties in the Third World

Many political systems in the Third World are dominated by a single party and some may be expected to move through the stages just outlined. Countries such as Costa Rica, India, and Venezuela have competitive elections and cannot be classified as single-party systems. In other political systems, such as North Korea and Vietnam, the leaders use the party as an instrument to control and mobilize the population. Newly independent countries face the fact that two or more parties with substantial support could lead to political divisions that would threaten the unity of the country or weaken a government's attempt to develop and carry out programs. In many developing countries a major party function is to convey the wishes of the government to the citizens.

One heritage developing political systems share is **avoidance politics**. In traditional political systems, the masses did not participate in governing. The best that could be hoped for was a condition in which one could avoid government rules or modify government regulations and requirements through an understanding with local officials. Taxes, peace and order, and military conscripts were the traditional government requirements, which on occasion were brutally enforced. Beyond these, governments limited their involvement in the local community. Participant systems (for example, the United States, Canada, Japan, and Western Europe), on the other hand, have responsive governments that remain in office because they successfully build coalitions of interests that can command an electoral majority. Participation emphasizes input factors at the electoral and policy-making stages.

Transitional systems in the Third World—countries such as Nigeria, Taiwan (Republic of China), Mexico, and Singapore—combine the need for nation building (security, stability, economic development, and often national integration) with a movement toward a participatory culture. In other cases, leaders whose nations are undergoing internal and external stress may believe that only discipline and maintaining a subject-oriented political system can build a social and economic base necessary for national development.

Subversive involvement by foreign powers, traditional divisions in society, and the limited capacity of the government to solve problems are ingredients that shape developing party systems. The presence of one or more of these factors plus the determination of a ruling elite to monopolize political power inclines a government toward some form of one-party solution.

History suggests that a bureaucratic, often isolated single ruling party that has monopolized politics for years leads to inefficiency, little interest in massive popular discontent, and a predominant concern with holding onto power. This is a major reason there are increasing demands for democracy and the right to organize politically in countries such as the PRC.

PARTY ORGANIZATION

Any political party must have an organization, even if the organization is as limited as a few legislators consulting one another under a shared party label. Party organization ranges from the decentralized and open-entry arrangements where anyone can join and try to be nominated as a candidate, as found in many parts of the United States, to the hierarchical and centralized pattern common to authoritarian parties.

Many democratic parties have a reciprocal deference-type organization where both leaders and supporters-followers defer to one another depending on the situation or the issue involved. In this type of organization there are numerous leaders and power is scattered among several levels of the organization. The national leaders depend on the goodwill and support of the organization below them, and party leaders at lower levels depend on national leaders for advice, guidance, and rewards. Independence, initiative, or indifference at the local and middle party levels are tolerated by the leadership in order to maintain or expand the working and financially contributing party membership, since this is essentially a voluntary organization.[25]

A democratic party is usually "greedy" for supporters. If a party consciously seeks to expand its electoral appeal, it attracts the support of various interests, some of which inevitably have conflicting objectives. The effort to manage intergroup rivalries and maintain a broad coalition causes a party to mediate the demands made by the groups that support it. No group gets everything it wants; tension arising from conflicting claims always is present. Both the Democratic and Republican parties in the United States receive support from business interests and trade-union members. It requires considerable skill by party leaders to balance the claims of business and labor so as to satisfy some members from each group and maintain maximum electoral support.

Tension, conflict, and bargaining are ever-present in this type of party, and most party leaders are unable and unwilling to establish an effective chain of command. This "downward deference" results from the need for votes, the voluntary nature of party support, the few persons interested in working for a party, and the general absence of penalties that can be applied by party leaders to party workers who occasionally are indifferent or recalcitrant. Both the upper- and lower-echelon party workers mutually depend on one another.

---

[25]For further discussion of these points see Harold Lasswell and Abraham Kaplan, *Power and Society* (New Haven, Conn.: Yale University Press, 1950), pp. 219–220; and Samuel J. Eldersveld, *Political Parties: A Behavioral Analysis* (Chicago: Rand McNally, 1964), especially pp. 1–13.

The opposite of the loosely organized party is the organization based on Robert Michels's iron law of oligarchy. We discussed the principal features of the iron law in Chapter 5. We simply note here that Michels declared that "who says organization says oligarchy," oligarchy being control of an organization by a few people at the top.

We can now discuss the Liberal Democratic party of Japan as an example of a decentralized party and the CPSU as an example (until the late 1980s) of a hierarchical party.

Decentralization in Japan

Japanese political parties, especially the ruling, conservative Liberal Democratic party (LDP), rest on the ties and loyalties of the boss-follower *(oyabun-kobun)* system of traditional Japan. The LDP has ruled Japan since 1955. Parties are federations of follower-leader groups. Local organizations are the responsibility of the local candidate and the faction that supports him or her. Political parties per se receive only moderate political loyalty. The Japanese voters' commitment to the faction's local associations is the means through which the LDP has won all but one election to both houses of the bicameral legislature or Diet since 1955.

The lower house of the Diet, the House of Representatives, officially chooses the prime minister. Actually, the individual selected as LDP president by LDP members of both houses of the Diet is chosen prime minister by the House of Representatives.

Party identification among Japanese voters remained weak during the 1980s. Upward of 40 percent of the voters do not have any party identification. Many of those who identify with a party are nominal or weak party identifiers.[26] Faction boss, the candidate, and faction remain key elements in LDP organization. Leaders take care of the faction's interest, and candidates and their supporters accept the authority of the faction leader or boss. Japan is divided into 130 election districts, each returning three to five representatives, depending on the population size of the district. A voter has only one vote. A party must estimate carefully its vote-getting ability to decide, for example, in a five-seat district, whether to run three, four, or five candidates, or seats will be lost to another party that concentrates its votes on one or two candidates. Factional rivalry is intensified because the most formidable opponent in the district sometimes is an individual from one's own party, although a different faction. The Communist party's insistence on fielding a candidate in every district helps the LDP by splitting the opposition vote in close contests.

The organizational and monetary support a candidate can expect is drawn principally from the faction leader. Each leader has local associations and, more importantly, has built up a network of financial backers, the only source of adequate funding. Representatives are to show loyalty and support to their leader as coalitions form among factions to choose a party president/prime minister from among faction leaders and to secure faction representation in the cabinet.

---

[26]Bradley M. Richardson and Scott C. Flanagan, *Politics in Japan* (Boston: Little, Brown, 1984), p. 83.

Since revision of the fund-raising law in 1975, fund-raising receptions have become a major source of financing for factions. These receptions are to cheer on a political leader, celebrate a birthday, publication of a book, or appointment to the cabinet or high party position, and so forth. Businesses purchase a block of $150 to $250 tickets. These qualify as business expenses, not political contributions. Former Prime Minister Takeshita, who resigned because of the Recruit Company scandal (see Chapter 5, Money and Political Action Committees), was unexcelled at arranging receptions for his faction. In May 1987, he became the first Japanese politician to collect more than $15 million in gross receipts from a single fund-raising party.

LDP faction leaders have access to substantial funds. It generally is accepted that 90 percent of business contributions are given to the LDP. The bulk of the contributions go to faction leaders who then distribute the money to their followers in the Diet. The system holds together at the top because party leaders recognize that the various factions forming the party, which in effect is a federation, must receive rewards. In the late 1980s, there were six factions in the House of Representatives, each faction identified by the name of the leader, or *oyabun*. The six factions ranged between 12 and 72 members. Factions are organized formally, with a headquarters, staff, and regular meetings independent of the party. Within each faction, power is centralized. The cooperation of three or more factions is necessary

The 26th CPSU Congress (1981) in session.

for the LDP to nominate a party president who then becomes prime minister. Representatives of all factions rally behind the prime minister and serve in the cabinet. Rotation of the party presidency among factions is encouraged because of the two-term, four-year limit for LDP presidents.

Prime ministers usually coordinate policy, but rarely lead. Faction leaders or their close associates often dominate particular areas of policy, such as agriculture, education, or trade. The winning candidate for prime minister, through extended bargaining among faction leaders, determines which cabinet posts each faction will control. Each faction, however, chooses who will serve in each ministry it is allocated.

The Liberal Democrats organizationally combine hierarchy and reciprocal deference. The viability of the LDP is apparent, however, because LDP dominant-party democracy has controlled Japan since 1955.

The LDP's one loss at the national level occurred in July 1989, when half of the House of Councillor's members, or 126, were up for election. The LDP had their negative political burdens going into the campaign: (1) the unpopular 3 percent sales tax; (2) Prime Minister Uno's publicized personal indiscretions; and (3) the Recruit money scandal discussed in Chapter 5. Moreover, the Japanese Socialist party (JSP) leader was the personable Takako Doi, the first woman ever to lead a political party in Japan. A record total of 146 candidates out of 670 were women, twice the number of women contesting the upper house elections in 1986. The preelection LDP majority fell from 145 of 252 seats to 109 seats. The JSP total jumped from 42 to 66.

Takako Doi is a popular political figure who actively courts and uses the media. She clearly projects a clean image: Take political decisions out from behind closed doors. In 1987, she launched "Operation Madonna," recruiting 187 politically inexperienced women to run for local political office; 177 were elected. The February 1990 elections for the more powerful lower House of Representatives saw Japan moving toward a 1.5 party system, although confirming continuing LDP control of government. The LDP garnered 275 seats out of a total 512, 18 more than a bare majority; plus there is the likely support of 11 independents. This is close to the 295 seats held by the LDP before the election. The JSP won 60 percent more seats, from 83 to 136 seats. The Japanese people are not yet ready to trust another party to govern. The JSP is limited by its left-wing ideology, a vague program of reform, and a 40-year image as a left-wing debating society. A television poll after the election showed a majority of Japanese wanted Takako Doi as prime minister, but an even larger majority opposed the JSP leading the government. Japan has a parliamentary system, and a distrust of the JSP organization and history, as opposed to the party leader, hurt Ms. Doi's bid. Opposition control of the House of Councillors and the JSP challenge have, however, given the LDP a series of challenges not faced in 35 years of unbroken rule.

Hierarchy in the Soviet Union

Lenin, the founder of the CPSU, stressed organization as the "kernel" of his doctrine. Lenin and his successors have accepted the dogma first stated by Lenin that "Marxism is fortified by the material unity of organization which welds millions of toilers into an army of the working class."[27] Without organization, ideology would fail; an army of disciplined communicants was the means to achieve power and then to govern. The term the Communists use to describe their party organization is **democratic centralism**, which in practice means all power is in the hands of a few party leaders, with the democratic component nonexistent. Key features of democratic centralism are

1. Election of all party executive bodies at all organizational levels from below.
2. Regular accountability of party executive bodies to their party organizations and to higher party bodies.
3. Strict party discipline and subordination of the minority to the majority.
4. The absolutely binding character of the decisions of higher bodies upon lower bodies.[28]

The Party Congress, scheduled to meet every five years, elects a Central Committee. There were 4,993 delegates at the Twenty-Seventh Congress of the CPSU held in February–March 1986. A Central Committee of 307 members and 170 nonvoting candidate members was "elected." The Central Committee "elected" the top party decision-making body, a Politburo of 12 members and 7 candidate members.

Power is effectively centralized in the Politburo and progressively dominated by party General Secretary Mikhail Gorbachev who came to power in 1985. (Gorbachev also was elected president of the Soviet Union, unopposed, by the Soviet legislature in October 1988.) The general secretary and some members of the Politburo, with the assistance of the party's top administrative apparatus, the Central Committee Secretariat (headed by the general secretary), decide who will attend the Congress and who will be selected to the Central Committee and the Politburo.

Traditionally, the CPSU has functioned as a military hierarchy, with subordinates trying faithfully to carry out orders from above. The tyrannical Joseph Stalin, who ruled the Soviet Union from 1928 until his death in 1953, tolerated no dissent and unmercifully purged his opponents. Conservative estimates are that between 1930 and 1953, including the Great Purge of comrades (1934–1938) and the Stalin-induced famine during collectivization, upward of 40 million Soviet citizens were killed. Of the 1,966 delegates attending the Seventeenth Party Congress in 1934, 1,108 had been arrested on counterrevolutionary charges by the time the Eighteenth Party Congress met in 1939.[29] The party became a tool for Stalin's meglomania and maintaining absolute control.

---

[27]Selznick, *The Organizational Weapon*, p. 8.

[28]Merle Fainsod, *How Russia Is Ruled*, rev. ed. (Cambridge, Mass.: Harvard University Press, 1963), p. 208.

[29]For details on these developments see Robert Conquest, *The Great Terror: Stalin's Purge of the Thirties*, rev. ed. (New York: Macmillan, 1973).

Gorbachev's *glasnost,* or openness/publicity, described in Chapter 5, made the 1988 Extraordinary Party Congress (the first since 1941) unique in terms of open expression. Gorbachev emphasized that economic restructuring depended on political change, declaring the economy had hit a dead end. The total reform program depended on political change. He warned: "I will tell you outright if we do not reform the political system, all our initiatives, the whole massive tasks we have undertaken, will grind to a halt."[30] An example of the free-wheeling openness was a member urging his fellow delegates to remove those who had promoted the policy of stagnation over the years. His list of those who should go included two Politburo members and the editor of *Pravda* (*The Truth,* the party newspaper).

In terms of the CPSU party organization, Gorbachev initially sought a dynamic party, guiding reform, with some intraparty liberalization substituting for multipartyism, and final decision making retained at the top. General Secretary Gorbachev declared at the end of the conference that the party should be relieved of the administration/managerial role it had followed since the 1920s and should focus its activities on political methods of guidance. This latter responsibility is still in the very early stages of development.

A strong leader and guided democracy are not antithetical to democratic centralism. Public criticism and criticism and competition within the party may be the means to provide input and feedback and to overcome the conservative, vested party interests who oppose change. At a 1989 Central Committee meeting, Gorbachev announced that 110 committee members had all signed letters withdrawing "voluntarily." Many of these removed or purged were elderly or in poor health, but others, such as the late President Andrei A. Gromyko opposed reform and had fallen from favor. More discussion, grass-roots–selected criticism, and the basic elements of democratic centralism seem to characterize the CPSU in 1990.

In conclusion, we believe the relevance for the student of the classifications discussed is not to memorize labels or categories. Rather, it helps to identify where specific parties might fit into a pigeonhole or why a party does not fit. It also alerts students who are studying a particular party or comparing parties to look at functions, appeals, organizations, and members. These classifications are to facilitate further study and are not an end in themselves.

PARTY MEMBERSHIP

When political parties were just emerging in the eighteenth century, the British political writer and statesman Edmund Burke defined a political party as "a body of men united for promoting, by their joint endeavors, the national interest upon some particular principle in which they are all agreed."[31]

Dedication to a particular political philosophy or set of political principles is

[30]"Moscow's Free-for-All," *Newsweek* (July 11, 1988), p. 34.

[31]Edmund Burke, *Burke's Works,* vol. I (London: Henry G. Bohn, 1855), p. 375.

not an important motivating factor for a majority of party members today. In the United States such an individual would be described as an "ideologue" who "weighs policy alternatives posed in a campaign, making his choice on the basis of agreement or disagreement with the candidates' expressed views on the crucial problems of the day." This person has "a reasonably self-conscious and overarching view of the good life, usually expressed in the form of a liberal or conservative philosophy."[32] The data available concerning the number of Americans who are predominantly issue oriented or "ideologues" indicate that they make up approximately 10 percent of the voters.

Democracies

People join political parties for many reasons in pluralistic systems. The more apparent motives include promotion of selected political policies or doctrines and securing economic or social benefits for a particular stratum or category of the population. People also join parties for reasons that are not immediately obvious from looking at the party and its political orientation. Moreover, the nature of party membership varies among political parties and even within the same party. In the United States, for example, members are not card-carrying Democrats or Republicans who have had their membership applications carefully screened. Two authorities on American political parties identifies U.S. parties as having three heads or three membership categories. Party organization includes those who serve on party committees, regular contributors, and those who work actively in campaigns. Paid party employees are in this group. Party in government includes candidates as well as national, state, and local government officeholders. Party in the electorate is the largest number. These are self-identified party members who range from intensely and regularly committed to the party to those who split their vote. Some in this group may occasionally work in a campaign or intermittently contribute money.[33] These three categories of membership also are common among middle-of-the-road, middle-class, or conservative parties in other countries.

The desire to exercise power, manipulate people, and receive deference motivates some. Harold Lasswell described *political man* as one who accentuates and demands power and orients himself toward experiences that involve power.[34] The need for power is the dominant need. Both Robert E. Lane and Harold Lasswell noted later, however, that a person with an overt desire for power is likely to achieve only a minor political status in democratic political systems. A person dominated by power needs will not have the interpersonal, broker-type skills that are required of successful politicians in democracies, although such a person may

---

[32]Fred I. Greenstein and Frank B. Feigert, *The American Party System and the American People*, 3rd ed. (Englewood Cliffs, N.J.: Prentice-Hall, 1985), p. 38.

[33]Frank J. Sorauf and Paul Allen Beck, *Party Politics in America*, 6th ed. (Glenview, Ill.: Scott, Foresman, 1988), Chapter 1.

[34]Harold Lasswell, *Power and Personality* (New York: W. W. Norton, 1948), p. 57.

do very well in authoritarian and totalitarian political systems. As Lane has noted, "In adult life the search for the jugular of power may very likely lead to the world of finance, journalism, or industry instead of politics."[35]

Without attempting to provide an exhaustive list of conscious and unconscious personal reasons that motivate persons to join a political party, we shall discuss selected motivations in order to give an indication of the needs served by political-party membership.

Social adjustment and social interaction are factors that encourage party affiliation. A survey of political leaders in Detroit, beginning at the precinct level, found that precinct leaders often were disillusioned with the political importance of their jobs, but at least 55 percent remained politically active because of "social contacts and association with friends."[36]

Desire for personal economic gain also prompts some to become party members or supporters. It is a political truism that it is not only *what* you know, but *who* you know that is important. The political arena provides the opportunity to make invaluable contacts with influential persons in the world of business and labor. Most of the improper activities that too often make the headlines result from special favors or "inside information" that one may obtain by knowing the right public official. Such networking is not necessarily improper or unethical. On occasion, however, the fine line between acceptable and illegal is crossed. One instance was the resignation of former Speaker Jim Wright (D.-Texas) from the House of Representatives effective June 15, 1989, ending a 34-year House career. He was the first Speaker in the history of the House of Representatives to resign because of scandal. In April, the House Ethics Committee reported it believed Speaker Wright had violated House ethics rules 69 times. These alleged violations included $145,000 in improper gifts from Fort Worth developer George Mallick and sales of his book, *Reflections of a Public Man*, to circumvent annual limits on speech-making fees. Another instance was the Recruit scandal in Japan, discussed previously. Special prosecutors began their investigation in September 1988, and it ended in May 1989. The charges included illegal campaign donations and bribery for expected favors for the large real estate and information service company. Nineteen government and business officials were arrested or indicted, including two members of the Diet. Prime Minister Takashita announced his resignation in April 1989, and his closest administrative assistant committed suicide. The previous prime minister, Mr. Nakasone, resigned his LDP membership in May to atone for his responsibility in the scandal.

Status and ego enhancement also obviously are available to the political activist who has the opportunity to meet various and sundry political personalities of the moment. The "inside information" that swirls throughout any political system enables a party member to stand out among his or her peers as a person especially knowledgeable and informed and a person to be listened to.

---

[35]Lane, *Political Life*, p. 127.

[36]Eldersveld, *Political Parties*, p. 290.

Robert Lane has suggested other needs that are served, including curiosity.[37] Curiosity is a result of the need to come to grips with and understand the environment. For a few, this may include joining a party and comprehending the political world. Lane suggests that the search for meaning may be a "basic" drive to be fulfilled after other basic requirements (temperature, thirst, hunger, sex, security) have been met. Persons with a highly developed curiosity probably will follow events in the political world closely and in some instances will become active political party members.

Unconscious, neurotic needs also lead some persons to affiliate with a party. This is not a common phenomenon, but it is a fact that one means of working out inner psychic tensions is to join a political party. Furthermore, it is not only the extremist right-wing and left-wing parties that attract this type of person. Parties in the political center also have members who are too intensely, unreasonably, and absolutely committed to party objectives. Such individuals develop their own rigid value system, and their irrational (sometimes neurotic) dedication prompts them to question the motives and credibility of those who politically disagree with them in the slightest way. The liberal-authoritarian or conservative-authoritarian who takes a middle-of-the-road political philosophy and distorts it to alleviate inner tensions is found in most democratic parties.

Single-Party Systems

The career advantages and elite status in a totalitarian political system are even more apparent. Certain jobs are open only to those willing and qualified to join the ruling party. A study of party membership in the Soviet Union classified selected occupations as "party restricted," where the number of nonparty members was 1 percent or less: heads of government departments, directorates from the city level up, and the directors of state-owned enterprises. "Virtually party restricted" occupations included those in which non-CPSU members ranged up to 5 percent: judges, army officers, and probably the police.[38]

Those who want power, influence, or access find active membership in the single ruling party generally an effective means to acquire these assets. The CCP has a membership of 47 million, about half of whom are cadre. Party membership, and even more so cadre status, requires careful investigation. The cadre are the ruling class in mainland China, with extensive and often unregulated power. The CCP stressed four factors for cadre membership: family background, class status, social connection, and seniority.[39] Party membership in the PRC is very different from being a Democrat or Republican in the United States.

People join political parties for many reasons. It appears that Edmund Burke's eighteenth-century appraisal of a political party as a group of individuals commit-

---

[37]Lane, *Political Life*, pp. 112–120.

[38]I. H. Rigby, *Communist Party Membership in the U.S.S.R.: 1917–1967* (Princeton N.J.: Princeton University Press, 1968), p. 449.

[39]For a useful discussion of party membership see Alan P. Liu, *How China Is Ruled* (Englewood Cliffs, N.J.: Prentice-Hall, 1986), Chapter 4.

ted to certain political principles no longer describes the principal motivation, but is only one among numerous reasons.

PARTY FUNCTIONS

Functions are key to defining and explaining institutions, including political parties. Party functions help shape and sustain the political system. Functions also can change, evolve, atrophy, or be discarded over time.

In Pluralistic Systems

Political parties in competitive political systems are first and foremost concerned with controlling or participating in government by electing candidates. Other functions related to this first one include: acting as mediators/negotiators and balancing competing claims or demands so that conflicting groups resolve their objectives in a peaceful and institutionalized manner; identifying and organizing public attitudes (gun control, reduced property taxes) in order to win votes and influence government decisions; educating and informing the citizenry on public issues; simplifying and reducing the number of issue alternatives; recruiting and selecting leaders; establishing and confirming procedural standards for the conduct of government, especially the means by which political leaders are chosen; and providing welfare services and social outlets for party members. Parties out of power provide a constant source of criticism, which should illuminate and influence government policy and contribute to maintaining personal and political liberties. In the American party system and some other party systems such as the French, members of the government party often are as active in criticizing the government as members of the opposition parties.

A political scientist and former president of Harvard University once observed that brokerage is the most "universal function" of parties in a democracy and that the broker role is "a new profession whose function consists of bringing buyer and seller together."[40]

> The process of forming public opinion involves, therefore, bringing men together in masses on some middle ground where they can combine to carry out a common policy. In short, it requires a species of brokerage, and one of the functions of politicians is that of brokers.[41]

Another term in vogue is **aggregation**, "the function of converting demands by interest groups into general policy alternatives."[42] Aggregation estab-

[40]A. Lawrence Lowell, *Public Opinion and Popular Government*, 2nd ed. (New York: Longmans Green, 1930), p. 60.

[41]Ibid., p. 62. Lowell first offered this analysis in 1909 in the James Schouler lectures at Johns Hopkins University.

[42]Gabriel A. Almond and G. Bingham Powell, Jr., *Comparative Politics: A Developmental Approach* (Boston: Little, Brown, 1966), p. 98.

lishes a few policy alternatives in order to build or maintain an alliance of support groups. It presumes the existence of numerous interest groups (trade unions, business organizations, etc.) whose claims are balanced, mediated, and combined by parties to gain votes. In competitive political systems, it is at the party level that this combining process labeled aggregation often occurs.

A critical party function is **electioneering**, although in recent years the ability of parties to sway opinion has been questioned. In the metropolitan Detroit area, where party organization is well developed and active, it is reported that approximately 60 percent of the adults in Detroit were "completely unexposed to party structure" and 44 percent had *never* been exposed personally to a party organization.[43] If voters are not contacted face-to-face or by phone, it suggests that immediate and significant electoral influence may have to come from another source. The political party no longer monopolizes the important skills or manpower a candidate requires to be elected. Today most candidates rely on public-relations specialists, who are experts in appealing to the electorate via radio, television, newspapers, and direct mailings. Ad hoc campaign organizations and a large number of personal volunteers (generally including many college students) for a popular candidate are the more common techniques used today. The importance of **primary elections** in the United States means that most candidates must construct their own organization, at least for purposes of winning the primary election and becoming the party's nominee in the general election.

If the parties' electioneering function has been modified in democracies, it has not disappeared. The Cook County "organization," or machine, of the late Mayor Richard Daley is but one example of an organization that until recently had great electoral clout. Mayor Daley had especially strong control over 11 wards, "the automatic 11" in Chicago. In the 1968 presidential election, for example, he "delivered" 205,000 votes to Hubert Humphrey as opposed to the 21,000 received by Republican Richard Nixon.[44] A British example gives further evidence that the electoral role of the party should not be disregarded, especially in close elections. Even though most minds may have been made up weeks or months before election day, parties can encourage those who are so busy they might not vote, stimulate the indifferent, and sway a few. The absentee ballot, or postal vote, as it is known in Great Britain, indicates how a party with superior organization can be decisive:

> What is significant is that in nine most marginally won Conservative seats in 1964 the average postal vote was 1772. . . . On the assumption that they split 2:1 in favor of the Conservatives, they would have been decisive in twelve constituencies; at any other election since 1950 they would have been decisive in at least six constituencies.[45]

[43]Eldersveld, *Political Parties*, pp. 442 and 526.

[44]Leon O'Connor, *Clout: Mayor Daley and His City* (New York: Avon Books, 1975), p. 212.

[45]Peter G. Pulzer, *Political Representation and Elections: Parties and Voting in Great Britain*, 3rd ed. (Winchester, Mass.: Allen & Unwin, 1975), pp. 88–89.

1988 U.S. presidential candidates George Bush and Michael Dukakis before a debate.

More recently, resurgent Republican party organization in the United States has emphasized the value of "trench-work" politics and the absentee vote. Absentee votes were encouraged with campaign packets that urged Republicans in California to "vote in the privacy of your own home and avoid long lines and parking problems." Republican George Dukmejian won the California governor's race in 1982 by less than 100,000 votes "on the strength of a massive Republican-financed absentee voter effort." The "Dukmejian Model" is now being implemented in all 50 states.[46]

In Authoritarian and Totalitarian Systems

Parties perform important, although changing, functions in democracies. In political systems where there are no competitive elections, the ruling political party

---

[46]"Republicans Plan Absentee Ballot Drive in All 50 States," *Today,* 6:13 (December 2, 1983), p. 5.

performs equally important but different functions: deciding policies and programs, overseeing the government bureaucracy and the implementation of policy, propagandizing and indoctrinating the masses, supervising the behavior of the population, and selecting and approving party leaders and persons in positions of influence at all levels of society.

Communist parties generally are based on the principle that all government agencies exist as the faithful executors of the general line of the party. Joseph Stalin expounded this exclusive position of the Communist party:

> The Party must stand at the head of the working class; it must see farther than the working class; it must lead the proletariat, and not follow in the tail of the spontaneous movement.[47]

A totalitarian party attempts not only to control the most influential people in society but also to colonize and win their positive support. Academic and professional groups are rapidly expanding segments of the Soviet population and the CPSU. Policy-making and supervision by the CPSU have been its most important functions, and these depend on the allegiance of the academic and professional strata. The power to fill important personnel positions, whether party officials, teachers, doctors, judges, high-ranking military officers, engineers or other important government administrative positions, is called the *nomenklatura* system. The extent of party control over appointments is not precisely known outside the Soviet Union. *Nomenklatura* is the third leg of the troika of control; the other two being policy-making and detailed supervision of policy implementation. Estimates are that the system extends to at least 3 million positions today.[48] One does not need to be a party member in every instance, but career mobility is enhanced by CPSU membership. Candidates for one of the 3 million-plus positions must have demonstrated consistent loyalty to the political system.

Recruiting and indoctrinating the highly trained groups is complemented by mobilizing and politicizing the masses. An important means by which the party can accomplish this is through elections, although elections are different from what we regard as normal because generally there is only one candidate per office. Elections are a time for propagandizing and indoctrinating the masses and justifying government policy. Electoral turnout and the percentage of valid votes in a district is also an indication of how well the party organization in that district has done its job and of whether any threatening discontent, as expressed through blank or defaced ballots, is present.

An authoritarian party system can, however, begin to evolve into a more pluralistic system, as is occurring in the Soviet Union. The Soviet Union had the freest election in March 1989 that it had experienced since the Communists seized

---

[47]Joseph Stalin, *Foundations of Leninism* (New York: International Publishers, 1934), p. 109, quoted in Merle Fainsod, *How Russia Is Ruled*, 2nd ed. (Cambridge, Mass.: Harvard University Press, 1963), p. 137.

[48]Gordon B. Smith, *Soviet Politics: Continuity and Contradiction* (New York: St. Martin's Press, 1988), p. 84.

power in October 1917. The election was for the new Congress of People's Deputies. The CPSU and other approved groups selected 750 deputies, while the remaining 1,500 seats were filled at the constituency level. A total of 2,895 candidates ran in 1,116 districts, while 384 constituencies had only one candidate. The commander of Soviet forces in East Germany was defeated by a lieutenant colonel advocating radical reform of the armed forces. Several high-ranking, unopposed party officials were defeated when more than 50 percent of the voters crossed out their names. Political parties other than the CPSU were not allowed. Many of the winning candidates were those advocating the most radical reforms in the political system, and there was substantial competition in the one-party elections.

General Secretary Gorbachev's political reforms include amending or repealing Article 6 of the Soviet Constitution. Article 6 assures Communist party dominance and identifies the CPSU as "the leading and guiding force of Soviet society and the nucleus of its political system."

The party chief of Leningrad, a symbol of oppressive party domination and a nonvoting member of the Politburo who was defeated resoundingly in the 1989 parliamentary elections, summed up conservative frustration with the reformers:

> It is no secret that things have gotten to the point where we have people with party membership cards openly speaking against the Communist Party of the Soviet Union, against its vanguard role in society, calling for transforming the party of action into a party of discussion clubs.[49]

Open divisions in the party are complemented by the rise of regional-nationalist groups. One in every six Soviet citizens lives in the breadbasket of the Soviet Union, the Ukraine. There is a growing organized movement there—Ruk—which is calling for autonomy, but which some observers believe really wants independence. A gradual emergence of openness or pluralism in the Soviet Union has led to divergent interests speaking out and organizing. At the worst, there is danger of a growing political chaos in a country of depressed economic conditions and all the differences that result from spanning 11 time zones.

Reducing the power of the Communist party and other democratic reforms including toleration of more organized opposition groups may work against the firm guidance even reformers need to effect economic and political change. Once an authoritarian party loses the will to maintain absolute power at any cost, it may find it difficult to hold on to power at all. Poland has had a Solidarity prime minister since mid-1989. During a three-month period in 1989, Czechoslovakia moved from a hard-line, neo-Stalinist regime to a coalition government with a formerly jailed, anti-Communist dissident as president. During the first round of Hungary's free parliamentary elections in April 1990, the renamed Communist party, the Socialist Workers party, won only 4 percent of the vote. This is under the required 5 percent a party must win to hold seats in the new parliament.

---

[49]Bill Keller, "In Soviet, Party Officials Rage at Changes Under Gorbachev," *New York Times* (April 28, 1989), p. 6.

In Third World Political Systems

Political parties in the Third World perform many of the same functions as in authoritarian and totalitarian systems, especially if there is only one party or if one party overshadows all others. Only a few Third World countries (for example, Costa Rica, India, the Republic of China, and Venezuela) have competitive elections.

Most developing societies possess only a short political heritage. Such traditional institutions as emperor, king, sultan, or shah, at least at the national political level, are of slight use in the contemporary world.

Samuel P. Huntington has noted that when "political institutions collapse or are weak or non-existent," stability and the beginning of political integration depend upon a strong party. The party becomes the one institution that can organize and develop the country. It becomes "the distinctive organization of modern politics" whose function is "to organize participation, to aggregate interests, to serve as the link between social forces and the government."[50]

Political parties, like most organizations, are subject to local customs and social institutions. Constitutions and laws provide the formal guidelines within which parties must operate, but the intraparty behavior patterns—including exercise of influence, the negotiation procedures, rewards, and patronage for one's supporters—determine the character of the party or party system.

Few political parties in the developing world are technologically and ideologically capable of achieving the monolithic character of the totalitarian parties in the West. The most notable effort in this regard was made by the CCP. This attempt began to show public signs of failure with the launching of China's Cultural Revolution in 1966. The revolution was launched to correct the behavior of party cadre who, after nearly two decades in power, were complacent, bureaucratically sluggish, and often more pragmatic, if not opportunistic, than properly revolutionary. The Cultural Revolution eventually was halted in 1969 when it became clear that the authority system of the Communist regime was being undermined.[51]

The Institutional Revolutionary Party (PRI), called the Mexican Revolutionary Party until 1946, is one of the more successful one-party regimes, in the developing world that has monopolized power. The PRI has ruled Mexico since 1929. Many observers believe the most striking feature of the Mexican political system is its stability, the most stable among Latin American countries in the past six decades. None of the PRI's nominees for president, governor, or senate was officially defeated until July 1989 (a PRI gubernatorial nominee was defeated in Baja California Norte). Ballot-box manipulation frequently is alleged by opponents.

PRI was founded in 1929 to ensure the power of the national government and end violence among competing candidates for public office. As one distinguished Mexican historian explained, "It was a party that was born not to fight for power,

---

[50]Huntington, *Political Order in Changing Societies*, p. 91.

[51]For a still useful overview of the Cultural Revolution, see John Gittings, "The State of the Party," *Far Eastern Economic Review*, 59:9 (February 29, 1968), pp. 375–380.

Table 6.3 SELECTED PRESIDENTIAL
ELECTIONS, PERCENTAGE OF
VOTES CAST FOR THE
INSTITUTIONAL REVOLUTIONARY
PARTY

Year	Institutional Revolutionary Party percentage
1934	98.2
1952	74.3
1970	85.8
1982	77.6
1988	50.7

but to administer it without sharing it."[52] The party has had two major functions: (1) mobilizing support during elections; (2) maintaining popular support and controlling the population. PRI has seldom functioned as an aggregator of diverse viewpoints or been a conduit for independent claims on the government. The party incorporated three major groups into its organization:

1. PRI-sanctioned labor unions, including the Confederation of Mexican workers and the Federation of Unions of State Workers.
2. The National Peasant Confederation.
3. Middle-class groups.

This attempted organizational monopoly of major interests and their incorporation in PRI generally serves party needs and can be viewed as a means to subordinate and often preclude independent input. These groups in more recent years have occasionally linked members' interests to government decision making.

A series of very gradual political reforms began with the popular President Lopez Mateos (1958–1964). These reforms have led to some seats for opposition parties in the Chamber of Deputies (the more powerful, popularly elected 300 member lower house in the bicameral legislature) as well as some mayoral electoral victories. More competitive elections and the inevitable cumulative frustrations with a party that has monopolized power for over 60 years has led to declining support for the PRI as shown in Table 6.3.

Chapter 5 noted that PRI under President Carlos Salinas may have to begin gradually to move from an organization of mobilization and control to a party that will begin to broker autonomous interests and compete for votes. There also is a tradition in Mexico of allowing an outlet for protest votes and permitting opposition leaders to compete in the electoral process. The more honest elections become, the more likely it is that a competitive party system will evolve in Mexico.

The role of the party in a developing country varies among political systems.

---

[52]Quoted in Gabriel A. Almond and G. Bingham Powell, Jr., eds., *Comparative Politics Today* (Glenview, Ill.: Scott, Foresman, 1988), p. 454.

The problems associated with developing party organization and its responsibilities are substantial. The struggle to establish government authority patterns that will make possible stability and orderly growth is the history of the developing world since 1945.

THE DECLINE OF POLITICAL PARTIES IN POSTINDUSTRIAL DEMOCRATIC SOCIETIES

The electoral function is an important party function. In the United States, however, the role of party in elections has declined, and this decline may also be occurring in several Western European countries. Beginning in the 1960s more people identified themselves as Independents than as Democrats or Republicans in the United States. In 1950, 80 percent of Americans voted straight party tickets; by 1970 this had dropped to 50 percent, and in the 1980s straight-ticket voting was below 50 percent.[53] As these figures suggest, party influence on electoral behavior has declined noticeably.

In the United States and other advanced countries, the use of mass media is slowly eroding party identification because of the candidates' own actions. When campaigns were conducted principally through personal appearances before partisan audiences and through the efforts of local party workers, party loyalty was stressed. Today, when a candidate appears on national or local television, she or he is speaking not only to party supporters but to supporters of the other party and independents as well. The candidate sometimes asks support on the basis of issues and more often on the basis of her or his personal characteristics—capable, qualified, trustworthy, and so on. Party identification in most elections other than a presidential election is played down, often not mentioned. Candidates increasingly campaign as individuals and promote themselves in terms of their own talents, rather than join with other office seekers from the same party in a combined effort. Basically, a candidate puts together his or her own organization, often depending heavily on a public-relations firm. If successful in winning office, the official stresses service to the constituents, helping them with information needs, assistance with government regulations, intercession with bureaucratic officials, and so on. It is the individual constituency that is of prime concern. The party has little influence on these officials and can impose few penalties.

Mass media in the postindustrial democracies is criticized for weakening parties and oversimplifying the political process. Television, it is alleged, "tends to focus on the colorful personality and the current crises. It appears to aim less at the minds of the viewers than their emotions . . . and is superficial and thin in facts."[54] Television's unblinking concentration causes politicians from presidents

---

[53]Frederick G. Dutton, *Changing Sources of Power: American Politics in the 1970s* (New York: McGraw-Hill, 1971), p. 228.

[54]The American Assembly, *The Future of American Political Parties* (New York: Columbia University, 1983), p. 5.

Box 6.3 **The 1988 Made-for-Television Election Campaign**

If 1960 was the year that television became a decisive factor in a national campaign, 1988 is the year that television *was* the campaign, a year in which one party, at its convention, deliberately muted the colors of the flag so they would televise better. To ensure that the news media would deliver the desired image, both campaigns shielded their men from spontaneous contact with the press, arranging instead a series of colorful, staged-for-TV events. . . .

. . . "Television has been been co-opted by the imagemakers and the media managers," says former network correspondent Marvin Kalb, director of Harvard's Shorenstein Barone Center on the Press, Politics and Public Policy. "The manipulators learned that by controlling the pictures you end up controlling the content." . . .

TV covers only three things, says Bush's media guru, Roger Ailes, "visuals, attacks, and mistakes." Broadcast news, agrees Michael Deaver, Ronald Reagan's former imagemaker, is "primarily concerned with entertainment values." . . .

Obligated to fill their nightly quota of Bush news, the network went with what the Bush campaign did offer: a choreographed scene of the Vice President framed against the flag, attacking his opponent with pointed barbs, tailored for TV. Meanwhile, Michael Dukakis was stuck in another era, holding almost daily press conferences. On TV he came across as defensive, weakly responding to Bush's assaults. After several weeks of losing out in the nightly sound-bite contest, he learned to play by the new rules: he withdrew. The video game was soon in full swing. Bush went to a flag factory; Dukakis rode a tank.

Source: Excerpts from Laurence Zuckerman, "The Made-for-TV Campaign," *Time* (November 14, 1988), p. 66. Copyright 1988 Time Warner Inc. Reprinted by permission.

down to emphasize looking good as much or more than doing good (see Box 6.3). The complex issues are reduced to a few seconds on television. People feel informed when in fact they are not. Because television news stories generally stress what is wrong, not what is right, distrust toward politics often grows. Certainly in the United States, as we previously noted, voter turnout is generally in decline. Doubts about the positive impact of television have not, however, diminished political use of it. A candidate for the Democratic presidential nomination, Senator John Glenn of Ohio, observed early in his 1984 campaign:

> People buy almost everything they need through television. They're not going to break that pattern when it comes to electing their leaders.[55]

---

[55]"Liftoff for Campaign 1984," *Newsweek* (October 3, 1983), p. 34.

Table 6.4 PARTY IDENTIFICATION AND FATHER'S PARTY
IDENTIFICATION

	Recalls father's party		Does not recall father's party	
	France	U.S.	France	U.S.
Has Party ID	79.4	81.6	47.7	50.7
No Party ID	20.6	18.4	52.3	49.3

Source: Phillip E. Converse, "Of Time and Partisan Stability," *Comparative Political Studies,* 2:2 (July 1969), p. 145.

Because of the emphasis on the media and direct-mail technology, the candidates create their own organizations. They seek out various interest groups and political action committees to finance campaigns generally with scant assistance from state or national party organizations. The most common election phenomenon today is the campaign consultant who has mastered such techniques as direct mailing, television, and other media exposure and raising money for the individual candidates' high-technology and expensive campaigning. The campaign consultants' backgrounds are almost invariably in marketing/advertising, not party politics. The bitterly contested 1983 mayoral race in Chicago brought out some of the most negative results of the decline of party and the emergence of the consultant and a babble of individual candidate voices urging only "Vote for me" and/or attacking the opponent. A perceptive political journalist entitled his analysis of the Chicago election as "Hired Guns: Consultants Bloodied Chicago Race." He explained:

> In the last 25 years, as television's role in politics has expanded, so has the influence of the "hired guns." Tearing down opponents is, for them, often the easiest way to win an election, and they bear a responsibility for the increasing negativism of our campaigns.[56]

The decline of party identity and party loyalty also is partly related to the decline of the family in postindustrial society. Party identification, like religion, is inherited in considerable measure from the family environment, as shown in Table 6.4. Weaker family ties mean weaker social and political inheritance.

The bottom line to the decline of parties, if it continues, is that democracy may become less effective. The positive things that political parties have done—in terms of identifying and structuring issues (e.g., meaningful party platforms), recruiting people to engage in political activities beyond the campaign of a particular candidate, aggregating diverse interests to come up with a limited number of public policy choices, and providing leadership beyond what an opinion poll says what is popular at the moment—will diminish. Bumper sticker campaigns are gimmicks to capture popular attention, but do not help educate the voters or allow at least

[56]David Broder, *Today,* 5:29 (April 22, 1983), p. 15.

some intelligent policy choices. Political parties have been effective supports and facilitators of democracy. Without their traditional eufunctional role, democratic political systems will be weakened.

SUMMARY

We should not assume that the emergence of competitive political parties in the 40 to 45 democratic political systems throughout the world has been a natural or easy evolution. It has not. Nor can we assume competitive party systems will emerge inevitably in most countries. The transition from intolerance of opposition to allowing dissent and finally to acceptance of diversity and disagreement has been slow and uneven. It is desirable but it is not easy to manage or nurture a political system in which the activities of competing parties facilitate effective government. Democracy and competitive political party systems cannot be exported very easily.

Competing political parties can be one—if not the most—effective means to reconcile peacefully and in an orderly way private rights and wants and public authority. Unfortunately, there is no blueprint based on past experiences that can reveal how this can be made to occur in other political systems. It seems fair to say that only when there is widespread agreement on fundamentals—such as the type of government, religious toleration, minority rights, or a consensus on rules of the game—will there be democracy and competing political parties. Political party competition requires self-restraint, moderation, and the ability to compromise. It is not surprising that democratic party systems are present in less than 30 percent of the world's approximately 170 countries.

In most other political systems, except a few that appear to be making an arduous transition to more open and competitive politics (Mexico, Nigeria, the Republic of China, and South Korea) political parties are designed to monopolize power. No other party is permitted to exist. The single party is used to strengthen and perpetuate rule by an oligarchy. Regretfully, although parties initially emerged to express popular opinion, in a majority of countries today they were created and refined to control and penetrate society for the benefit of a small ruling elite.

RECOMMENDED READINGS

Bellows, Thomas J. *The People's Action Party of Singapore: Emergence of a Dominant Party System*, Yale University Southeast Asia Studes, Monograph Series No. 14. New Haven, Conn., 1970. This analysis shows how a dominant party that has ruled Singapore for 32 years emerged out of a competitive party system. Electoral strategies, party organization, and the decline of party role are discussed.

Bialer, Seweryn, ed. *Politics, Society, and Nationality Inside Gorbachev's Russia.* Boulder, Colo.: Westview Press, 1989. A collection of essays on the contemporary Soviet Union is risky, but this is an excellent undertaking. The roots of change are discussed and reforms evaluated. The dangers of the nationality problem are considered.

Dahl, Robert A. *Political Oppositions in Western Democracies.* New Haven, Conn.: Yale University Press, 1965. This superior collection of theoretical and case study chapters considers why opposition parties emerged and "exotic" peaceful competition took root. It provides a still relevant foundation to analyze democratic development today.

Duverger, Maurice. *Political Parties,* by Barbara and Robert North, trans., 3rd ed. New York: Methuen, 1969. This ground-breaking study or political parties provides numerous theoretical insights and is still useful in studying contemporary party systems.

Downs, Anthony. *An Economic Theory of Democracy.* New York: Harper & Row, 1965. This book is especially useful for developing hypotheses. It analyzes political parties as if they were to follow rationally and consistently a policy of maximizing votes.

Huntington, Samuel P., and Clement H. Moore, eds. *Authoritarian Politics in Modern Society: The Dynamics of One Party Systems.* New York: Basic Books, 1970. Long before it was popular, this book analyzed the problems and sometimes successes of one-party systems adapting to social and economic changes. They provide excellent case studies ranging from the American South to Taiwan and Mexico and also include many theoretical insights.

Lawson, Kay, and Peter H. Merkl. *When Parties Fail: Emerging Alternative Organizations.* Princeton, N.J.: Princeton University Press, 1988. This book is concerned with the diminished viability of major parties all over the world. The focus is on the emergence of minor parties, single-issue groups, and movements. There are numerous case studies of democratic and nondemocratic political systems.

Panebianco, Angelo. *Political Parties: Organization and Power,* Marc Silver, trans. New York: Cambridge University Press, 1988. The author is interested in parties as organizations. He assumes party leaders are in search of power and are guided by the desire to maintain it. Although there is a useful evaluation of historical change and institutionalization, the parties studied are limited to Western Europe.

Sartori, Giovanni. *Parties and Party Systems: A Framework for Analysis,* vol I. New York: Cambridge University Press, 1976. This is a heuristic effort to develop a general theory of parties. The author discusses all varieties of parties and includes substantial data as well as concepts and theories.

Wolinetz, Steven B., ed. *Parties and Party Systems in Liberal Democracies.* New York: Routledge, Chapman & Hall, 1988. Case studies of political party systems are once again beginning to appear. This work provides basic data on which to test some of the macrotheories. The focus is on Western Europe and North America, including Mexico.

Chapter 7

Representation and Elections

In political systems where **elections** actually determine who will have the power to make political decisions, they are one of the most important inputs into the political process. They provide a link by which the governed can partly control their governors. Elections are also the chief institutional mechanism by which representatives are selected. **Representation** can provide an effective process for making demands and translating them into policy. Although the idea of representation developed independently of democracy, representation and elections are identified closely with modern democratic systems, so closely that many people erroneously think of them as the only means of popular participation and control in pluralistic countries. Nevertheless, elections and representation imply that power and authority come from the people, that they flow from the bottom up. Where this condition is missing, elections and representative-type institutions can exist—they are found under almost every form of government—but they do not decide who will govern or how.[1]

THEORIES OF REPRESENTATION

"No taxation without representation" is a well-known battle cry in Western politics. We all are familiar with taxes, but what is representation? Representation has many different, even conflicting, meanings. Politically, representation means having someone act in your place in governmental decision making. Representatives are people who act for or on behalf of other people in the decision-making process. They speak for and commit others to particular courses of action.[2]

There are many different ways in which a person can be understood as representing another politically. Many have nothing to do with either democracy or elections. Throughout history many people have claimed to be representative. Medieval and Renaissance kings claimed to represent their people regardless of what the masses of people thought. Leninist doctrine creates a role for the disciplined revolutionary party as the representative and embodiment of the proletariat's real interest. According to many Fascists, the leader, or Führer, somehow incarnated the will and interest of the people. Other theorists, such as Thomas Hobbes (1588–1679) argued that the people give up all their power to a sovereign whose will is then absolute and unchallengeable, but is understood as embodying the will of the people.

Such ideas, however, have nothing to do with democratic concepts of representation. These emphasize that representatives are selected by their constituents and are accountable to them, at least through elections. Elections are the key to modern

---

[1]We will use the phrase "representative institutions" rather than legislatures to indicate that many agencies may be involved in speaking or defending popular values and interests. In some circumstances these may include executives, judicial systems, bureaucracies, and even political parties. Legislatures, however, are the major representative bodies.

[2]This and many other meanings are discussed in Hanna Pitkin, *The Concept of Representation* (Berkeley, Calif.: University of California Press, 1967), pp. 1–13, 241–252, and passim; and Hanna Pitkin, ed., *Representation* (New York: Atherton, 1969), pp. 1–23.

concepts of representation. Linking elections, representation, and responsibility does not, however, tell us what the representative does or what the link or connection is between the representative and the represented. Since the eighteenth century, two persistent, conflicting, though plausible, theories have attempted to explain this relation. Variously called *delegate versus trustee, mandate versus independent,* or *delegate versus independent,* the argument centers on how much independence a representative can have from the wishes of the constituency. The following answers are typical of a continuing and unresolved debate. This discourse is alive today in current controversies in the United States over the extent to which members of Congress should mirror their constituents' demands on major issues.

Independent or Delegate?

Edmund Burke (1729–1797) best stated the argument that elected representatives should be independent of their constituents' wishes when those wishes conflict with the representatives' best judgment on an issue. Burke argued that we elect representatives for their good judgment, not merely as mirror images of our desires. The exercise of judgment requires independence of thought and action. As Burke stated:

> It ought to be the happiness and glory of a representative to live in the strictest union, the closest correspondence, the most unreserved communication with his constituents. Their wishes ought to have great weight on him. . . . It is his duty to sacrifice his repose, his pleasures, his satisfactions to theirs. . . . But his unbiased opinion, his enlightened conscience, he ought not to sacrifice to you or any set of men living. . . . They are a trust from Providence, for the abuse of which he is deeply answerable. Your representative owes you, not his industry only, but his judgment; and he betrays, instead of serving you, if he sacrifices it to your opinion.[3]

According to Burke, the representative's first duty was to look after the national interest. When local interests or opinions clash with national interest or tradition, representatives should ignore local opinion. For Burke, representatives could not be bound by local interests or instructions and still perform a deliberative function for the national interest. The representative is, therefore, a trustee, holding the people's power. As a trustee it is the representative's duty to work for the constituents' and country's real interest, not for temporary, often mad, opinions that may seize an unreflective and ill-informed public. Implicit in Burke's argument is the idea that representatives have superior wisdom, information, and expertise.

Many have challenged these assumptions and the idea that representatives can best perform their function if independent of their constituency's wishes. They have argued for and accepted the idea that a representative must reflect the expressed interests and desires of his or her constituency.

In its purest form the representative-as-delegate thesis argues that the repre-

---

[3]Edmund Burke, "Speech at the Conclusion of the Poll," Bristol, November 3, 1774, *Works,* vol. 1 (London: J. Duffy, 1854), pp. 446–447.

sentative has no independent function. He or she is merely a proxy, a stand-in, or a pipeline for the constituency. The representative follows only the instructions from the constituency and has no policy-making or deliberative function. His or her primary duty is to present the constituents' opinions and decisions, defend their interests, and vote according to their instructions. When new situations arise, the representative must return to the local constituency and receive new instructions.

Although he did not approve of representative government, Jean-Jacques Rousseau (1712–1778) came closest to expressing the delegate view. In the *Social Contract*, Rousseau argued that representation was tyranny, control of the sovereign people by their representatives, unless the representatives only conveyed the desires of the people. All they could do was transmit decisions, nothing more.[4]

Without going to this extreme, Thomas Paine, Thomas Jefferson, and John Adams proposed that at least one house of the legislature ought to reflect closely the interests and opinions of the people at large. Common attitudes in the United States indicate a strong belief that representatives should reflect constituent interests, yet reflecting constituent interests is far from serving as a pipeline for constituent wishes.

To be effective, the delegate theory would require small and/or homogeneous electoral districts where people would be very much alike. It also would require simple problems and highly informed voters. As such, we have no national examples of the delegate thesis in practice. The U.S. Congress under the Articles of Confederation, when members were instructed by their state legislatures, and the United Nations General Assembly are the closest examples of the delegate thesis in operation.

Obviously, there is a great deal of tension between these different theories. It is not simply a matter of choosing one or the other. There is no unequivocal answer as to which system would be superior. Your own answer must depend on your values, coupled with your expectations about government and interpretation of political traditions. Politicians are of many minds on this question. In Britain members of the House of Commons see themselves as being concerned with their constituency, but vote according to the determination of their party. In the United States,[5] legislators often say they respond to their constituents' interests, particularly in providing services, but they rarely find clear statements of those interests. On many issues the public is uninterested or poorly informed on both basic facts and how their representatives voted. Many people, as many as 50 percent in the United States, do not know who their representative is. Representatives have a great deal of independence of action on issues that have low visibility to the public. On most questions before a legislature, representatives follow their own minds or respond to interest groups simply because the public at large is not deeply interested in or informed about them. On highly visible, often emotional, issues, such

---

[4]Rousseau's arguments are collected conveniently in Hanna Pitkin, ed., *Representation*, pp. 51–72.

[5]John C. Wahlke, *The Legislative System: Explorations in Legislative Behavior* (New York: John Wiley, 1962), Chapter 12.

as arms control, foreign aid, inflation, taxes, and unemployment, representatives have less room to follow their own inclinations because their constituents have strong opinions on these issues and long memories at the next election.

In fact, these rival theories represent two ends of a continuum. How close to one or the other end a country or even a particular legislator will come depends on many things that may shift over time. These include the strength of the political parties, laws, customs, and traditions; the legislator's view of duty; the visibility of issues; and the obvious desire for reelection. Weighing these different factors, we can say that one representative is closer to being independent, whereas another is closer to being a delegate. Each, however, will exercise some elements of these rival theories.

WHAT DOES A REPRESENTATIVE REPRESENT?

Theories of representative/represented relations do not tell us exactly what a representative represents. Burke claimed representatives look after the fixed permanent interests of the country. Delegate theorists claim representatives defend their constituents' expressed interests. Assuming a fair apportionment and the right of everyone to participate, problems remain; it is useful to point out some of the relevant questions, even though we can give no concrete answers to them.

The larger countries become, the greater the distance and distinction between represented and representative. The more people a representative "represents," the less contact and control each person has over this representative. Representatives become more independent as size and pluralism in districts increase simply because there are more people to respond to. Not only are individual voices lost when many people speak, but in large districts representatives depend less on any single group for reelection than they do in small ones.

If increased size makes contact with individuals more difficult, perhaps it can be said that representatives represent a majority of their constituents. Leaving aside what this means for those who are in the minority, we must ask who or what a majority is. This is neither a flippant nor an easy question to answer. Majorities are rarely fixed and permanent. They shift from issue to issue. A person may be in the majority on one issue, in the minority on another, and in different coalitions on each issue. If the representative is to carry out a deliberative function, he or she cannot poll the constituency on every issue, even if the members of the constituency could be expected to have opinions and preferences on all issues.

Perhaps interest groups answer our dilemma. Can we say that representatives respond to and represent the expressed interests of organized groups? They do simply because organized groups are better able to offer programs, rewards, and threats than unorganized masses. But the question then becomes, whom do the interest groups represent and what do they seek? Moreover, many people are not organized or may never be part of a majority opinion or interest. The theory of representation holds that everyone is represented, but quite often major opinions and wishes are neglected. As will be noted later, proportional representation is one answer to this problem.

Finally, despite our political and institutional focus, representation is not confined to formal political institutions. Large private groups, such as professional organizations and labor unions, often maintain representative mechanisms. The American Medical Association has a House of Delegates, and elected representatives from local medical societies meet yearly to decide basic policy. Most large labor unions have similar mechanisms. Moreover, political parties and interest groups are representative of their members in shaping and influencing governmental policy. Often nongovernmental feedback agencies, such as television or the press, are also involved in "representing" opinions. Bureaucracies often "represent" particular clients or interest groups, but are these representative in terms of democratic values? Many argue that these organizations must be made accountable at least to their members. This demand faces all the problems that formal elected representative institutions face, coupled with the fact that the decision-making process of these organizations tends to be hidden from public view.

What a representative does and how he or she responds, therefore, is not always clear. Despite these problems, representation is still an important key to popular participation in states that are too big for direct decision making by all citizens. Along with interest groups and party activity, representation is one of the most important schemes for including the mass of people in decision making, at least in terms of helping choose who the formal political decision makers will be. Though it does not work perfectly, it provides people with a serious opportunity to influence and set limits to government.

REPRESENTATION IN THE CONTEMPORARY WORLD

The ideas, problems, and tensions discussed previously are peculiar to democratic countries because the concept of effective representation by elected officials is largely nonexistent elsewhere.

The theory and practice of representation developed in the West before the modern concept of elections. Representation is traceable to the thirteenth century, although only England has a more or less unbroken record of development. It was not until the seventeenth century in England that some theorists began to link representation and responsibility to constituents through elections. Successful institutionalization of this link through widespread adult male participation in moderately honest elections to select representatives did not develop until the late eighteenth and early nineteenth centuries, first in the United States and then in England. Universal adult suffrage was not achieved until the twentieth century, and even then many people could not participate because of prejudice and social pressures.

Efforts to make representative institutions effective and responsive continue today. In 1962, in *Baker* v. *Carr,* the U.S. Supreme Court ruled that reapportionment issues do not constitute "political" questions; therefore, federal courts could hear issues arising in this area. The decision gave rise to several landmark cases. In 1964, in *Wesberry* v. *Sanders,* the Court declared that the Constitution requires one person, one vote. According to the Court, congressional districts must be apportioned among the 50 states according to population. *Wesberry* v. *Sanders* pertained to congressional districts in Georgia. In a subsequent decision the same year, in *Reynolds* v. *Sims*, the Court ruled that state legislative districts must be substantially equal in population. These decisions helped to ensure that urban and suburban residents would have the same representation as rural voters.[6]

While the court decisions in *Wesberry* v. *Sanders* and *Reynolds* v. *Sims* focused on and resolved the issue of district population equality, other representation/reapportionment issues have remained. The most important of these issues centers on the need to apportion districts fairly and equitably. Fair and equitable apportionment, in this context, refers to the compactness and contiguity of districts, the preservation of politico-historical boundaries, the maintenance of partisan competitiveness, and the avoidance of partisan bias in the apportionment process.[7] According to Robert B. McKay:

> . . . there is absolutely no evidence that parties in power will do anything less than everything possible to maximize the political power of that party and to minimize power of the opposition.[8]

Unless substantial changes are made in this area, those who feel wronged in apportionment cases will rely increasingly on the judiciary to restore equality and fairness.

A good example of the above occurred in Rhode Island in 1982. For several decades, the Rhode Island state legislature featured a very large Democratic majority in both houses, with the Republicans holding only a few seats in each. In early 1982 the Rhode Island Reapportionment Commission came forth with its decennial redistricting plan, favoring the forces in power. The plan was challenged soon after in court by an independent Democratic senator and the state Republican party for allegedly violating provisions of both federal and state constitutions on account of gross **gerrymandering**.[9] The court, in *Licht* v. *Quattrocchi*, sided with the plaintiffs, stating that the 1982 Rhode Island Redistricting Act "constitutes an impermissible malapportionment of the Rhode Island Senate districts" and a violation of the fourteenth Amendment of the U.S. Constitution and the Nineteenth Amendment of the Rhode Island Constitution. In particular, the court pointed at the lack of compactness, the lack of contiguity, and the deviations from the natural and historical boundaries in the redistricting plan. On appeal, the state Supreme Court upheld the lower court's decision. Concurrently, by federal court order, the November 1982 state senate elections were postponed. Following these events, a second redistricting plan proposed by the commission was struck down by the court, too. Finally, a third redistricting plan was held to be constitutional, and the senate elections were set for June 21, 1983. The plaintiff Democratic senator was

---

[6]See Gordon E. Baker, *The Reapportionment Revolution* (New York: Random House, 1966), and Robert A. Goldwin, ed., *Representation and Misrepresentation* (Chicago: Rand McNally, 1968).

[7]This issue, as well as related ones, is discussed in considerable detail in Bernard Grofman et al., eds., *Representation and Redistricting Issues* (Lexington, Mass.: D. C. Heath, 1982).

[8]Ibid., p. 4.

[9]Politically speaking, the word "gerrymander" refers to a situation where a voting area has been divided in such a fashion as to give the majority party an unfair advantage.

readily reelected, and the Republican party, in part because of the more equitable reapportionment provided by the third redistricting plan, won a substantial victory by increasing its number of seats from the former 7 to 21 in the 50-seat senate. This is the largest number of seats the Republicans have held in the state senate for some decades.

Representative institutions exist in the Communist countries, too. In most of these countries, however, legislatures play a less important role than they do in democracies. We should note, however, that an important change in regard to the above has taken place in the Soviet Union. The large-scale revision of the Soviet legislative system, as initiated in late 1988, has produced a new Supreme Soviet that is substantially more involved in the policy-making process than its predecessor.[10]

There is no single way to characterize representative institutions in the developing countries. In terms of power and success they range from nonexistent in countries such as Saudi Arabia and a few of the one-man-rule countries of Africa to almost thriving as in Singapore. They have been most influential in former British colonies and in Latin America, but even here representative institutions are weak measured by democratic standards. Most developing countries have some form of representative institution, but almost everywhere they have little power and are dominated by strong executives. In countries such as Chile and India, where a tradition of strong representative institutions appeared to be developing, events of the last decade have virtually eliminated legislatures as effective political voices. As fragile and limited as representative institutions may appear in the West, they have more power and more opportunity to affect policy than anywhere else.

Having discussed the general nature of representation, we shall turn our attention now to the major electoral systems that are used to elect members of the **lower houses** of national legislatures. This will be followed by a section dealing with the selection of members of **upper houses.** We should keep in mind that not all countries have **bicameral** (consisting of two chambers) legislatures. Procedures for choosing chief executives are discussed in Chapter 9.

MAJOR ELECTORAL SYSTEMS

Different methods are used for electing people to representative office. The single-member district system and the proportional system are employed for electing the members of the lower houses. A larger variety of methods are used to select the members of upper houses.

The Single-Member District System

The **single-member district** system is used in the United States and Great Britain for choosing members of Congress and the House of Commons. The United

---

[10]See our discussion in Chapter 8.

States, for example, is divided into 435 congressional districts. The people in each of these districts elect only one candidate to the House of Representatives. Thus, a candidate must receive a majority of the votes cast (if there are two candidates for the office) or a plurality (if there are three or more candidates) in order to be elected. This system exaggerates the legislative representation of the winner and gives the second party a near monopoly of the opposition, as will be explained. Under the single-member district system, votes for minor party candidates usually become wasted votes, unless a candidate has a very large electoral support in his or her district. Such cases have occurred in Canada and the United Kingdom in recent years.

An American professor, E. E. Schattschneider, was one of the first political scientists to analyze the impact of the single-member district system.[11] As Schatt-schneider noted:

> If, for example, one were told merely that a given party received a total of 10,000,000 votes in all of the 435 [American congressional] districts taken together, out of a vote of 40,000,000 it would be impossible to guess even approximately the number of seats won by the party until something were known of the distribution of the vote.[12]

In a two-party system, votes usually are not evenly distributed geographically. Some districts will be won overwhelmingly; in other districts the popular vote will be extremely close. Each party has its geographical areas of support and is able to survive a major electoral defeat. The second party monopolizes the opposition and accrues support as the inevitable dissatisfaction with the winner occurs. **Third parties** enjoy electoral success only when they have considerable strength in one area of the country and receive a majority or plurality of the votes there. If the third party has no substantial pockets of support it is doomed, as happened in the case of the Liberal party in Great Britain. Relegated to third place by the Labour party in the 1920s, it retained some support of voters throughout the country. Today the Liberal party holds only a handful of seats in Parliament. In the 1979 parliamentary elections, the Conservatives won 43.9 percent of the vote (as opposed to Labour's 36.9 percent) and 53.4 percent of the seats in the House of Commons. The Liberal party polled 13.8 percent of the vote but won only 11 seats, less than 2 percent. We are citing the 1979 data, because the 1983 and 1987 British elections do not give a clear picture of the voting strength of the Liberal party on account of its electoral alliance with the Social Democratic party formed in the early 1970s. The point to note is that under the single-member district system, voters are usually limited to two viable alternatives.

The record of serious third parties in the United States indicates that the single-member district system has been an important factor in their lack of success. The only third party that replaced one of the major parties was the Republican party in the 1850s, but it was aided by the fact that the Whig party it replaced was

---

[11]See E. E. Schattschneider, *Party Government* (New York: Holt, Rinehart & Winston, 1942), pp. 69–84.

[12]Ibid., p. 70.

Prime Minister Margaret Thatcher leaves polling station after casting her vote.

already in a process of dissolution. The Populist party in the 1880s had some electoral success in electing members of both houses of Congress in the West, but its weakness was that it was largely a sectional party that could not replace the Democrats as the second party. Its failure also was aided by the fact that the Democrats in 1896 endorsed one of its main planks—the free and unlimited coinage of silver. The two major parties in the United States frequently "steal" proposals from minor parties.

The failure of third parties has been most apparent on the congressional level. Theodore Roosevelt's Progressive party had little success in electing members to Congress, even though Roosevelt was a popular figure who ran second in 1912 in the contest for the presidency. Only for a brief time in the early part of the century were the Socialists able to elect two members, one from a congressional district in Milwaukee, and the other from a district in New York City.

A modification of the single-member district plan is the **runoff election,** which is used in elections to the French National Assembly in the Fifth Republic. In France a second election is held for candidates who fail to receive majorities on the first ballot. In some districts only the two highest plurality candidates participate in the runoff. In others all candidates are on the ballot and occasionally even newcomers may enter the race. In these cases the runoff is decided by a plurality vote. Experience in France to date shows that only a minority of candidates receive a majority on the first ballot.

The dual-ballot system was adopted in France principally for two reasons: to encourage the emergence of a majority party in the National Assembly and to reduce the number of Communist deputies. The law does not work against any particular party, but the final results depend upon the relationships of the parties to one another. The first vote enables each party to secure an accurate reading of its popularity. The one-week interval between elections enables the parties to consolidate their votes and switch their support to the most likely winners in the second vote. If a party is unable or refuses to enter into electoral alliances or trade-offs, the number of deputies it elects is far below its nationwide popular vote.

In 1958, the year Charles de Gaulle became president of France, the French Communist party (PCF) did not enter into alliances with other parties of the Left. The alliances could have resulted in Left support for Communists in some districts, and in turn the Communists supporting the most popular Left candidate in other districts. Thus, while the PCF received 22 percent of the popular vote nationally, it won only 7 percent of the National Assembly seats. By the 1970s the PCF was participating with the Socialists and Radicals in a Union of the Left against the pro-Gaullist Union of Republicans for Progress. In the March 1979 elections for the National Assembly, only 14 percent of the parliamentary seats were won on the first ballot. The PCF received 20.6 percent of the popular vote in the first round. At the conclusion of the second ballot, 86 PCF candidates were elected—17 percent of the total seats in the National Assembly—a notable improvement over the earlier showing.

Proportional Representation

Proportional representation is designed to give each political party approximately the number of legislative seats as the party's voting strength justifies. The list system is the most common type of proportional representation. Prior to an election, the party draws up lists of candidates, equal to the number of seats contested in the multimember district, rank-ordering the names of the candidates. The larger the percentage of the party vote, the more people are elected from the list. The list system was used in Weimar Germany (1919–1933) and the French Fourth Republic (1946–1958) and is employed now in Israel, Italy, and the Netherlands, among others. List-proportional representation reduces popular control—the party, not the voters, selects the names on the list and their rank order. The lower the position on the list, the less likely it is the candidate will be elected. Power is in the hands of the party hierarchy. Also, the list is a simple device. The voters only need to identify with the party or its symbol; however, they may feel isolated from the government because they have no specific representative with whom they can identify and to whom they can turn. The immediate responsibility of the representative is to the party organization, not the voters.

In some countries the voters are allowed some degree of choice in rearranging the list according to their own preferences. Only in Austria are the voters allowed complete freedom in this respect.

Italy is one of the countries using the list system of proportional representation. The country is divided in 32 national election districts. All but one of these are multimember districts (i.e., the voters elect several deputies from each district).

The names of the party candidates appear on party lists, which are the result of lengthy intraparty bargaining and consultation.

On election day the voters mark on their ballots the party list of their choice with an "X." Furthermore, voters may, if they so desire, write on the ballot the names of their three or four preferred candidates from among those on the party list. The preference votes help to determine who from among the candidates will be elected. If a party in the first district is entitled to four deputies, the four list candidates having received the highest number of votes are elected.

After all the votes have been counted, the parliamentary seats assigned to each district are distributed among the parties on the basis of proportional representation. In other words, a district's number of seats are allocated to the parties according to the percentage of votes that each party polled. Remaining percentage fractions and unassigned seats from all districts are transferred to a national electoral pool in Rome and are distributed by that body proportionally to the parties. Thus, each party will receive a number of parliamentary seats generally in proportion to its percentage of the total vote.[13]

To exemplify this procedure, we show in Table 7.1 the results of the 1987 national election in Italy. Had Italy used the single-member district system, as do the United States and the United Kingdom, the two strongest parties (the Christian Democrats and the Communists) would have won nearly all the seats, with the Socialists gaining a handful, and the localized parties obtaining their seats as indicated.

Not all countries using the system of proportional representation have as fragmented a party system—and as much political instability—as does Italy. In Austria, for example, only three parties are represented in the *Nationalrat*, the lower house of the legislature.

Germany has a modified system of proportional representation. To avoid small splinter parties, the country has excluded from representation in the *Bundestag* (the lower house of the legislature) all parties failing to receive at least 5 percent of the countrywide party vote or three seats in one of the states by direct election. The German Basic Law provides also that half of the representatives are to be elected by majority (or plurality) vote in single-member districts, whereas the other half are chosen by party lists in each state, which is given a certain number of seats to elect. Under this hybrid system, Germany has approached a two-party system consisting of Social Democrats and Christian Democrats. A small liberal party, comparable to the party of that name in Britain, has often held the balance of power in the former West Germany.

Advantages and Disadvantages of Proportional Representation The distinguished nineteenth-century British philosopher John Stuart Mill presented the most important theoretical justification of proportional representation.[14] Sup-

---

[13]See Raphael Zariski, *Italy: The Politics of Uneven Development* (Hinsdale, Ill.: The Dryden Press, 1972), pp. 194–196.

[14]See his essay, "Representative Government," in John Stuart Mill, *Utilitarianism, Liberty, and Representative Government* (New York: E. P. Dutton, 1947).

Table 7.1 **RESULTS OF THE 1987 ELECTIONS IN ITALY**

Party	Votes	Percentage of total	Number of seats in the Chamber of Deputies
Christian Democrats (DC)	13,252,866	34.3	234
Communists (PCI)	10,284,975	26.6	177
Socialists (PSI)	5,510,567	14.3	94
Social Movement (MSI-DN)	2,280,222	5.9	35
Republicans (PRI)	1,430,945	3.7	21
Social Democrats (PSDI)	1,142,026	3.0	17
Radicals (P. Rad.)	990,150	2.5	13
Green List (LV)	971,728	2.5	13
Liberals	811,512	2.1	11
Democratic Proletarian	643,397	1.7	8
South Tyrolians (PPST)[a]	201,521	0.5	3
Sardinian Party (PSd'A)[a]	170,724	0.4	2
League of Lombarda (LL)[a]	186,254	0.5	1
Union Valle d'Aosta (UV-ADP-PRI)[b]	41,707	0.1	1
League of Veneto–United Pensioners (LV-PU)	299,450	0.8	0
Others[c]	400,535	1.1	0
Total	38,618,579	100.0	630

[a]Although the number of votes received by the South Tyrolians, the Sardinian party, and the League of Lombarda was below 1.5 percent each, these parties, nevertheless, elected 3, 2, and 1 deputies, respectively, because their votes were highly geographically concentrated.

[b]The Valle d'Aosta is a single-member constituency by virtue of its geographical isolation.

[c]This category includes 20 small parties.

Source: Italian Election Office, Rome.

porters of this system contend that it gives a more accurate picture of public opinion than the single-member district plan, because it gives minorities representation proportionate to their voting strength. It also is argued that proportional representation is the best method for independent voters to express their views. Another argument is that it will help eliminate lobbying because of the greater variety of interests represented.

Critics reply that although the majority and minority systems have defects, proportional representation may make it impossible for the majority to govern. Excessive representation for minority parties may divide the legislature into interest groups that prevent the enactment of legislation based on a majority consensus. Perhaps the most effective criticism is that the purpose of elections is to create a broad majority consensus in a parliament that will enable the government to act effectively. This cannot be accomplished, it is said, if every minority group is to have exact mathematical representation.

One of the leading scholars on this subject, Carl J. Friedrich, cites the experience in Weimar Germany as a leading cause of the collapse of the Republic in

1933.[15] He feels that the list system stratified party organizations and created new parties because of the ease with which they could be set up. Furthermore, parties were controlled by party bosses who emphasized creed and dogma. At the same time, moderate parties came to be identified with some special interest group. This combination of entrenched interests and radical dogmatism made the organization of stable cabinets very difficult.

On the other hand, Friedrich recognizes the stability of the Scandinavian countries, the Netherlands, and Belgium under proportional representation, but attributes this to the moderating influence of the monarchy in those countries. In these countries the monarch still exerts some political influence and the countries' smallness permits a degree of intimacy between the royal court and Parliament.

No conclusive answer is possible on the merits of proportional representation. It cannot be proved that proportional representation causes multiplication of parties, because most countries that adopted proportional representation already had multiparty systems. Yet frequently the tendency toward political fragmentation is intensified under proportional representation. In view of the political disintegration of the Weimar Republic and the undermining of popular confidence in the Fourth French Republic, the burden of proof would appear to be on the supporters of proportional representation.

SELECTION OF MEMBERS OF UPPER HOUSES

The manner of selecting members of upper houses of legislatures is usually different from that used for lower houses. Also, the upper houses frequently possess less power than the lower houses. The U.S. Senate is a notable exception in this respect. In Germany and the United States the upper house reflects the federal system.

The U.S. Senate is a result of the Connecticut Compromise at the Constitutional Convention, whereby it was agreed that the Senate would represent the states, with two senators from each state. The Senate is a continuing body with one-third of the members elected every two years for six-year terms. Because senators are elected from the state at large, the state serves as a single-member district. The powers of the Senate are substantially the same as those of the House of Representatives.

In many ways the British House of Lords is an anachronism. The great majority of its membership of approximately 1,200 hold their seats because each is the oldest son of a nobleman whose ancestor was given a title hundreds of years ago. Its membership includes princes of the royal blood and 16 peers representing Scotland. There are also members whose seats are not hereditary: the 26 lords spiritual of the Church of England; about 400 members appointed for life under an act of 1958; and the 9 "law lords" who constitute the House of Lords acting as the highest court of the land.

---

[15]See Carl J. Friedrich, *Constitutional Government and Democracy*, 4th ed. (Waltham, Mass.: Blaisdell Publishing, 1968), Chapter 15, especially pp. 302–306.

Although once equal to the House of Commons in power, the House of Lords has steadily lost power. Its chief functions today are to relieve the House of Commons of the burden of considering private bills and initiating bills of a noncontroversial nature that can pass the House of Commons with dispatch if previously debated in the Upper Chamber.

The upper chamber in France is called the *Senate*. Its powers are limited. The 283 senators serve nine-year terms, with one-third of the membership being elected indirectly by local electoral colleges every three years.

The German Bundesrat (the upper chamber) represents the territorial units of the German Republic. Unlike the U.S. Senate, which represents the people of the states, the Bundesrat represents the states or Länder as such. All members are appointed by their respective state governments and serve for indeterminate terms. Each state delegation casts a single vote determined by instructions from their governments. The Bundesrat can be overridden by an equivalent majority of the Bundestag (i.e., a bill passed by a simple majority vote in the Bundesrat can be nullified by a simple majority vote in the Bundestag).

VOTING BEHAVIOR

The significance of voting varies with the importance of elections in determining political decision makers. The percentage of people voting, however, does not always reflect the actual importance of elections. Thus, some Communist countries such as Albania report voter turnouts of 100 percent, and typical turnouts in other Communist countries are almost invariably in the 95-percent-plus range. Many democratic societies report turnouts in excess of 80 percent (see Table 7.2). On the other hand, U.S. congressional elections in nonpresidential election years have drawn between 30.1 percent and 46.1 percent during the past six decades. In 1984, 53.3 percent of the eligible electorate voted in the United States. This figure varied from a low of 40.7 percent in South Carolina to 68.2 percent in Minnesota.[16]

These differences force us to ask why there is such profound variation, not only among different countries, but also within the same nation-state. Political participation is a learned activity. The processes of political socialization and rewards and punishments for participation help to account for these differences. Yet what lies behind this political socialization? Who participates? Who does not? Why?

Characteristics such as race, age, sex, class, and education are correlated with voting. In the United States black people have had traditionally a much lower turnout than white people. In 1976, 48.7 percent of the black population of voting age reported they voted, whereas in 1984 55.8 percent reported they voted. Comparable statistics for the white population were 60.9 percent in 1976 and 61.4 percent in 1984.[17] The figures for black voting show an increase from previous years and can be expected to rise further. In the past, however, black citizens of voting age

---

[16]These figures are adapted from the U.S. Bureau of the Census, *Statistical Abstract of the United States 1988* (Washington, D.C.: U.S. Government Printing Office, 1987), p. 251.

[17]Ibid., p. 249.

Table 7.2 **PERCENTAGE OF ELECTORATE VOTING IN NATIONAL PARLIAMENTARY OR PRESIDENTIAL[a] ELECTIONS**

Country	Percentage	Year
Australia[b]	95[c]	1984
	94	1987
Austria	91	1983
	90	1986
Canada	75	1984
	76	1988
Denmark	87	1987
	87	1988
Finland	75	1983
	72	1987
Ireland	72	1982
	73	1987
Italy	89	1983
	88	1987
Japan	71	1983
	71	1986
Netherlands	81	1982
	86	1986
New Zealand	92	1984
	89	1987
Norway	79	1981
	83	1985
Sweden	90	1985
	86	1988
United Kingdom	73	1983
	75	1987
United States[d]	53	1984
	50	1988
West Germany	89	1983
	84	1987

[a]The only presidential elections included are those of the United States.

[b]In Australia voting is compulsory.

[c]Numbers are rounded off to the nearest whole number.

[d]The population figure from which the U.S. percentages are derived covers all civilian noninstitutional citizens and resident aliens 18 years and over. By law, resident aliens may not vote. The U.S. Bureau of the Census figured that in 1984 resident aliens made up 4.3 percent of the population of the United States. Thus, in reality the percentage of people voting in the United States is correspondingly higher than officially stated.

Sources: U.S. data for 1984 are from *Statistical Abstract of the United States,* op. cit., p. 251. The 1988 figure was obtained directly from the U.S. Bureau of the Census. The data for the other countries were gathered from the consulate general office or embassy of each country.

The Reverend Jesse Jackson leads a number of supporters to the Hinds County Courthouse in Jackson, Mississippi, to register to vote.

had a lower rate of registration than white citizens. This record of lower participation reflects the social, economic, and political environment of exclusion, threats, and punishments for voting that many black people have experienced. Before passage of civil rights legislation in 1964 and 1965, discriminatory literacy tests, delay tactics, and intimidation prevented large numbers of blacks from registering to vote. In 1960, before massive voter registration drives and federal intervention, 23.1 percent of the black population of the 11 southern states that made up the Old Confederacy[18] were registered to vote, as compared to 46.1 percent of the white population. In 1986, 60.8 percent of the eligible black population were registered as opposed to 69.9 percent of the white population.

Age and education have a positive correlation with voting. This is true for all races and groups. Here socialization probably accounts for greater participation. As people receive more education, they are exposed to more information about how the system works and their role in it, as well as increased exhortation to participate. Also, as people get older they tend to participate more, probably because they view themselves as having an increased stake in the political system. In the United States in 1984, 36.7 percent of the eligible 18- to 20-year-olds reported voting, as opposed to 54.5 percent of people in the 25- to 34-year-old category and 69.8 percent in the

[18]Alabama, Arkansas, Florida, Georgia, Louisiana, Mississippi, North Carolina, South Carolina, Tennessee, Texas, and Virginia. *Statistical Abstract of the United States 1989*, p. 261.

45- to 64-year-old category.[19] Low voter turnout among the young tends to be typical of most democracies.

If this book had been written 30 years ago, we would now include a somewhat pious and perhaps tongue-in-cheek discussion of how women vote at a much lower rate than do men. Given socialization patterns all over the world, women traditionally have been discouraged from and even punished for participating; "politics is man's work" symbolized this attitude. Moreover, women have been enfranchised only in the twentieth century.[20] Women have had less opportunity to learn participation. This situation has changed substantially. In the 1980 presidential election, for the first time in the history of the United States, a slightly larger percentage of females reported voting than males.

In the United States people with lower socioeconomic status tend to vote less than those with higher status. This is probably the result of less education, less apparent stake in the system, and less reinforcement by other groups that would encourage participation. In European democracies with class-based political parties that actively encourage people to vote, there are smaller differences in participation rates between classes than in the United States. In general, strong identification with a political party or candidate tends to encourage participation.

Many other factors affect participation. For some people political participation may seem threatening to their relation with family and friends. Others may feel it is futile to vote, a feeling that political forces are unmanageable, or that there is a large gap between democratic ideals and political reality. Many have weak spurs to political involvement, being concerned with their families and friends or seeing few links between political activity and satisfaction of their needs. A small number of people may simply be satisfied with their political system and see no need to participate. Others, feeling there is no effective choice between candidates or parties, do not vote.

Electoral procedures also may disqualify people from participating. Voter registration procedures and residency requirements prevent some of the potential electorate from voting in the United States. However, residency requirements are not the deterrent they once were because the Voting Rights Act of 1970 lowered most of them to thirty days. Problems with absentee ballots and difficulties in reaching polling stations disenfranchise some people. Even bad weather or a belief that one's candidate or party will win (or lose) may keep some from voting; in these cases the nonvoters probably have a low motivation to vote based on some other factor. The fact that elections are held on a Tuesday—a normal workday—may also lead to a lower voter turnout. In a number of other countries elections are held on a Sunday or a holiday.

One additional factor may discourage people from voting: the problem of choosing among candidates or parties. Although it is true that most people do not have well-developed and explicit policy preferences and may have relatively little

---

[19]*Statistical Abstract of the United States 1988*, p. 249.

[20]Complete franchise equality on a countrywide level: Belgium, 1948; Canada, 1920; France, 1944; Germany, 1919; Italy, 1946; United Kingdom, 1928; United States, 1920.

knowledge about issues, most people do have attitudes about politics. Many express preferred policy outcomes or prefer certain candidate characteristics. The problem is—how should a voter choose when two or more candidates present programs, each program having some policies the voter prefers and some he or she dislikes and rejects? Which candidate should the voter select? In such a case powerful cross-pressures are operating because one's vote may be for some issues one favors and others one may oppose. Some voters, unable to choose, may not vote at all.

Determinants of Voting Choice

Voting is a complicated act. How a person will vote depends on a number of factors. Some of the more important of these are class identification, education, occupation, parental partisanship, race, region, and religion. Although class identification in the United States has been weaker historically than in Britain and in parts of continental Europe, it has played a role in voting in this country in the sense that the more class conscious a person is, the more his or her economic position will influence the electoral choices.[21] Education and occupation are related in the sense that the degree of education a person possesses usually has a close bearing on the occupation the person holds.

Religion and ethnic considerations are two factors that have had more significance in some presidential elections in the United States than in others. Although John F. Kennedy received 82 percent of the Jewish vote and 78 percent of the Roman Catholic vote in 1960, according to some experts, the religious issue has become muted in American politics in recent years.[22] Nevertheless, religio-ethnic differences have deep roots in American political history. Jews and Roman Catholics are more likely to vote for Democratic candidates than are Protestants. There is more support for Democrats among Roman Catholics of Irish and Polish ethnic background than among Catholics of German and Italian ethnicity.[23]

There are similarities and differences among the voting patterns in the United States and the other democratic countries of the world. More economically well-to-do voters in Western Europe, Australia, New Zealand, and Japan are likely to vote for political candidates and parties to the right of the center than their counterparts in the United States. On the left, a number of West European countries, as well as Australia and New Zealand, traditionally have had strong social-democratic-type labor parties, such as the Social Democratic parties in Austria and Germany and the Labour Party in Britain. These have garnered the labor vote in their countries more completely than the Democratic party ever has been able to do in the United States. Much of this holds true also for Scandinavian electoral politics, with the

---

[21]See Gerald Pomper, *Voter's Choice: Varieties of American Electoral Behavior* (New York: Harper & Row, 1975), p. 42ff.

[22]See especially Albert J. Menendez, *Religion at the Polls* (Philadelphia: Westminster Press, 1977).

[23]Norman H. Nie, Sidney Verba, and John R. Petrocik, *The Changing American Voter* (Cambridge, Mass.: Harvard University Press, 1976), p. 213ff.

addition that politics in these countries has been influenced considerably by rural/urban contrasts and considerations, as evidenced by the presence of strong Agrarian parties in Norway and Sweden.

Religion as a factor in voting has been more prominent in some European countries than in others. The electoral support for the Christian Democratic movements in Belgium, Italy, the Netherlands, Switzerland, and Germany cuts through the whole range of occupational groups in these countries, though more in some provinces than in others. For example, a substantial number of blue-collar workers in Bavaria (Germany) are staunch supporters of the conservative Christian Social Union.

Some of the preceding criteria, such as the tendency to vote for the political forces to the left or the right of the center depending upon one's economic and class standing, apply also to those developing countries that have viable two- or multi-party systems, such as Barbados, Jamaica, or Venezuela.

THE SIGNIFICANCE OF ELECTIONS

Democracies

Free elections perform a crucial but limited role. They do not mathematically reveal popular sentiment about a long list of controversial public issues. At best, competitive elections are only a rough approximation of popular feeling. No electoral system goes beyond this indispensable yet restricted function, but in the absence of some type of election and a legislature, free or manipulated, few governments today believe the public will accept them as legitimate.

Even in competitive elections voters are not knowledgeable about all aspects of a party's program. A vote for a candidate or a party cannot be interpreted as support or even awareness of each item in the electoral program.

Survey research in the United States reveals the impressionistic and unstructured view of politics common to a majority of people. We need to understand that presidential elections in our country do not decide policy but at most determine who shall decide what government shall do. There is substantial lack of familiarity with even the most important political issues of the time. There is also considerable confusion in the public mind about what effect the election of one party over another would have on specific policies. As a result, it may be implied that the electoral outcome is necessarily ambiguous as to what specific policies government should pursue. Also, as a consequence of the public's limited understanding of issues, interpretations as to the meaning of elections are speculative.

Electoral systems never equitably represent every element in the community. Neither are they as revealing of specific popular feeling as reformers in the nineteenth century had hoped. Despite these qualifications, competitive elections are the best means we know of for the largest number of qualified persons to influence government. Popularly chosen legislatures are the institutions that include the bulk of elected officials; where the widest range of groups have a voice; and where interaction with, and accountability to, the public most frequently occurs.

The democratization of Soviet politics: Boris Yeltsin on the campaign trail.

Communist Societies

Prior to 1988, elections in the Soviet Union and most other Communist countries were noncompetitive and served mainly the purpose of providing legitimacy for the regime. Electioneering imparted a sense of mass participation and involvement. It gave the citizenry a feeling of civic importance. Communist leaders announced proudly election turnouts of 99 or even 100 percent.

Although, at the time of this writing, the aforementioned still holds true for such Stalinist holdovers as Albania and North Korea, drastic political changes have taken place in Eastern Europe. Bulgaria, Czechoslovakia, Hungary, Poland, and Romania are in the process of departing from the Soviet Commonwealth. Their recent elections have been as real and competitive as any elections in the countries we label democracies.

In the Soviet Union, too, substantial changes have taken place in regard to elections. When in the spring of 1989 the members of the Congress of People's Deputies were elected, a number of candidates for the first time ever faced opponents in their campaign. Subsequently, the campaign to elect 542 of the 2,250 Congress of People's Deputies to the new Supreme Soviet (the national legislature) depicted some election contests that were fought as vigorously as the campaigns we see here in the United States.

These rapid changes in the Communist orbit make it quite difficult for us to conjecture about further changes. What we can say with certainty is that in the

Soviet Union the one-candidate, noncompetitive election system has become a thing of the past.

Developing Countries

Depending on the nature of the political system, the functions of elections in developing countries range from some of those listed as democracies to the manipulated elections of dictatorial regimes.

Some political leaders contend that elections are an integral part of the "democratic" process, even in one-party countries. For example, former President Nyerere of Tanzania, one of Africa's foremost politicians, has spoken and written frequently on democracy in Africa.[24] Tanzania has only one political party, the Tanzanian African National Union, and seats are contested rarely in an election. President Nyerere, nevertheless, has claimed that Tanzania is a democracy. He argued that a national movement, open to every segment of the population, has nothing to fear from discontented and excluded factions because no such faction exists. If a country has two or more parties, each represents only a segment of the population, but a single party is identified with the country as a whole. Elections confirm that one party is a *genuine* national movement, representing the whole country and excluding none. President Nyerere has stated that frequently there are vigorous debates and the input of grassroots opinion at party meetings. He argued for free debate in private party conferences, but once a policy is decided party discipline prevails. Debate and input occur before elections, but elections are a necessary part of the policy-making cycle and affirm decisions that supposedly have been debated freely within the party.

Elections are also sometimes a means of psychologically reinforcing a leadership or, after a change in government, of ratifying the new leaders. These carefully controlled elections are intended to demonstrate the success of efforts to achieve national harmony and integration. Often elections are an effort to legitimize a political system by demonstrating that a government has wide popular support, even when some opposition groups are allowed to compete. A government that in some way can achieve a popular electoral majority is reinforced in its own sense of legitimacy and by the mandate it can hold before world opinion. In a few developing countries, elections are genuinely competitive, relatively honestly administered, and occasionally result in the incumbent party being turned out of office.

A particular electoral problem in developing countries is the mobilization of people who have had little or no electoral experience and retain strong traditional ties. Electoral mobilization sometimes inflames existing social cleavages. Most of the countries of Africa and Asia are multilinguistic, multiethnic, and multireligious. If one seeks to mobilize supporters through elections or other means, the most obvious identifications and groups to which to appeal are the primary ethnic,

---

[24]See, for example, Julius Nyerere's article "African Democracy," in Frank Tachau, ed., *The Developing Nations: What Path to Modernization?* (New York: Dodd, Mead, 1972), pp. 173–180.

linguistic, and religious groups. Self-rule actually may lead, at times, to increased splintering, self-awareness, and suspicion of others, based on traditional ties and obligations. Latent primordial hostilities can be aroused that will lead to bloody and cruel confrontations. Elections may provide a mechanism by which to channel some of these emotions, or they may provide an opportunity to arouse these attachments. Consequently, elections may be rejected or manipulated so as to give the voter no opportunity to identify with and be stimulated by disruptive forces.

SUMMARY

Elections, voting, and representation are extremely important political inputs but are not the only means of political participation. As we saw in the two previous chapters, people also participate through interest groups, political parties, and campaigns. Nevertheless, elections and voting provide the most common form of mass participation.

Electoral systems never represent equitably every element in the community. Neither are they as revealing of specific popular feeling as reformers in the nineteenth century had hoped. Despite these qualifications, competitive elections are one means for the largest number of persons to influence government. Popularly chosen legislatures provide a place for the widest range of groups to have a voice and for interaction with, and accountability to, the public. Whether voting, elections, and representation have a major impact on political outcomes varies from country to country. Where they do, these channels provide one of the most effective means for people to influence decision making.

RECOMMENDED READINGS

Barnes, Samuel H. *Representation in Italy: Institutional Tradition and Electoral Choice.* Chicago: University of Chicago Press, 1977. This is an in-depth analysis of voting behavior in Italy.

Butler, David E., Howard R. Penniman, and Austin Ranney, eds. *Democracy at the Polls: A Comparative Study of Competitive National Elections.* Washington, D.C.: American Enterprise Institute, 1981. The book features a cross-national study of electoral systems, campaigns, and elections in 28 democracies and near-democracies.

Butler, David E., and Donald Stokes. *Political Change in Britain: Forces Shaping Electoral Choice.* New York: St. Martin's Press, 1976. This comprehensive study of British voting behavior focuses on some of the factors causing fluctuations and changes in party support.

Cain, Bruce E. *The Reapportionment Puzzle.* Berkeley, Calif.: University of California Press, 1984. This insightful account of the realities of redistricting is written by a reapportionment consultant.

Crewe, Ivor, and David Denver, eds. *Electoral Change in Western Democracies: Patterns and Sources of Electoral Volatility.* New York: St. Martin's Press, 1985. The authors present an analysis of electoral volatility in 12 democratic societies.

Flanigan, William H., and Nancy H. Zingale. *Political Behavior of the American Electorate,* 6th ed. Newton, Mass.: Allyn & Bacon, 1987. This is a very comprehensive analysis of the electorate in the United States.

Grofman, Bernard, et al., eds. *Representation and Redistricting Issues.* Lexington, Mass.: Lexington Books, 1982. An informative collection of articles discusses various aspects of representation. See especially the essays by Dixon, Lijphart, and Wahlke on "fair representation."

Lakeman, Enid. *How Democracies Vote: A Study of Majority and Proportional Electoral Systems,* 3rd ed. London: Faber & Faber, Ltd., 1970. This is a detailed and informative analysis of the electoral systems of the European democracies.

Lijphart, Arend, and Bernard Grofman, eds. *Choosing an Electoral System: Issues and Alternatives.* New York: Praeger, 1984. Several experts present the advantages and disadvantages of the various electoral systems.

Pennock, J. Roland, and John W. Chapman, eds. *Representation.* New York: Atherton Press, 1968. A collection of informative articles examines the most important aspects of the concept of representation.

Pitkin, Hanna F. *The Concept of Representation.* Berkeley, Calif.: University of California Press, 1967. This is a conceptual analysis of the evolution of representative government.

Rose, Richard, ed. *Electoral Participation: A Comparative Analysis.* Beverly Hills, Calif.: Sage Publications, 1980. A compendium of articles examines, on a comparative basis, voting behavior in the democratic societies.

Output Agencies

Chapter
8

The Legislative Process

Legislatures are regarded as less important today than 90 years ago. The earlier "golden age" of legislatures probably was exaggerated, and "real" legislative power rarely resided in a congress or parliament. Democratic legislatures today as in the past do not initiate legislation as much as they scrutinize, modify, reject, or approve executive proposals.

The increasingly active role of the state in the twentieth century means that power has tilted toward executive leadership and the bureaucracy. Managing the economy, conducting foreign policy, and implementing the welfare state resulted in the work and influence of the executive branch increasing faster than that of the legislative branch, but the latter also has grown. Legislatures in most pluralistic systems are doing more. Legislators, like presidents or prime ministers who run immense bureaucratic organizations responsible to them, may find they are doing more, but controlling outcome or subordinates less. Focused leadership, enunciation of policy, and an appearance of positive cohesion (when it exists in a political system) are generally identified with the chief executive or his or her spokesperson. An example of a deliberately weakened legislature is parliament under the constitution of the French Fifth Republic (1958 to date). One reason for the Fifth Republic was the belief there had been too much legislative power in the Fourth Republic, poor policy, avoiding major decisions, and minimal leadership.

The case of a truncated French parliament is not the case in every political system (see Box 8.1). Between August 1989, when a Solidarity government took power in Poland, and January 1990, most Communist governments in Eastern Europe fell. Legislatures in these countries will be one of the two or three most important institutions determining whether or not the new governments will succeed. Even in the Soviet Union where the Communist party of the Soviet Union (CPSU) maintains a dominant position, *perestroika* gives new prominence to legislative institutions. Reporting to the Supreme Soviet at the end of 1988, President Gorbachev declared:

> The main lesson of the recent past is that it is impossible to accelerate our emergence from a state of stagnation without the democratization of all our life and without the rebirth of the Soviets as representative bodies of power and of the people's self-government.[1]

Compared to executive leadership, legislatures have less power now than at the beginning of this century. Setting aside this comparison, however, the scope and function of legislative activities has increased substantially this century.

Whenever a society is larger than an extended familial network, many objectives and values can be achieved only through authoritative rules applying to everyone in society. The numerically and geographically larger a society is, the more complex lawmaking and law-enforcing functions become. Legislatures, especially in pluralistic systems, have a key role in the lawmaking process.

During the twentieth century, groups and organizations have turned increasingly to government to solve a problem or oppose a proposed solution. Contem-

---

[1] *The Current Digest of the Soviet Press,* 40:48 (1988), p. 3.

Box 8.1   ## A Truncated Legislature in the Fifth French Republic

Under the Fifth Republic, parliament became just one state institution among others and is prohibited from acting without an explicit grant of constitutional authority. Further, the executive is granted extensive independent powers and no longer requires a grant of authority by the National Assembly. In fact, the area within which parliament is permitted to act was severely circumscribed, and even within this domain, the government is empowered to exercise tight control over parliamentary activity. . . .

Outside the specified area of lawmaking, the constitution created a new category, termed regulation, over which parliament has no power at all. Within this domain, the bureaucracy is granted power to issue rules and decrees.

Within the area in which parliament is competent, the constitution delegates to the government extensive powers to control legislative activity. The government, not parliamentary leaders, establishes the parliamentary agenda; governmental texts are accorded priority over proposals from members of parliament; and the government is empowered to restrict amendments and debate, as well as to suspend the usual procedures by which parliament deliberates. . . .

Parliament has limited control over the budgetary process. Members of parliament are prohibited from introducing amendments to the budget whose effect is to raise expenditures or lower tax revenues. Further, unless parliament approves the budget within seventy days after it is submitted, the government is authorized to enact the budget by ordinance (though this has never occurred within the Fifth Republic).

Source: Mark Kesselman et al., *European Politics in Transition* (Lexington, Mass.: D.C. Heath, 1987), pp. 179–180.

porary political systems are more politicized because of a tendency to regard government as having responsibilities in most areas of human concern (environment, inflation, defense, education, retirement benefits, and so forth). In **participatory political systems** governments devote a majority of their time to negotiating and balancing the claims and counterclaims of diverse ideas and groups. The volume and complexity of political issues and interests continue to expand.

A democratically elected legislature is directly and frequently accountable to the people. Democratic legislatures are the only political institutions providing public deliberation, broad avenues of access, and regular popular accountability. They also are the political body whose members maintain close links with the general population. A legislature, more than any other government institution, includes among its members individuals representing the broadest range of interests. Such legislatures provide a breadth of representation and normally include persons articulating a wide range of viewpoints.

THE EVOLUTION OF THE DEMOCRATIC LEGISLATIVE INSTITUTION

Contemporary representative legislatures trace their origins to the U.S. Congress, American state legislatures, and the British House of Commons, as they developed in the eighteenth and nineteenth centuries.

The Greek *boule* was the first attempt at a popularly chosen, representative legislature. For less than 150 years in the fifth and fourth centuries B.C., Athens had what is generally considered the world's first democracy. It is to Athens that scholars turn for the origin of democracy and representative government.

> . . . The conclusion [is] that the *boule* was so powerful that it can almost be said that Athens for a few years possessed a representative government.[2]

Throughout the Middle Ages the notion of representation and legislative assemblies was nurtured in Europe, but in practice the resemblance to modern legislatures was slight. Nevertheless, a strain of thought persisted among medieval theorists that the king should be limited in his power, although usually it was not clear how this was to be implemented.

The concept of groups of people consulting and limiting the rulers or monarch never disappeared in Europe, but it was many centuries before effective institutions emerged. Nobility and, later, commoners were called first for consultation to approve new taxes. Subsequently, those called together would submit a list of grievances that the monarch often was compelled to acknowledge before taxes were voted. These assemblies did not originate as a method of popular control but were called into being as a means of strengthening the central government by raising money. The various groups and classes required to attend these meetings, however, gained political information and skills that ultimately undermined the monarchy.[3]

There was ebb and flow in the influence these councils or assemblies had on monarchs. By the fourteenth century the Commons (referring to knights and burgesses from communities, rather than commoners) and the Lords were groupings the English monarch felt compelled to deal with, and the maturation of the **Mother of Parliaments** was beginning. The English Parliament was the visible embodiment of the English people, but it was not an elected or popularly accountable legislature. Nevertheless, toward the end of the centralizing and often

---

[2]J. A. O. Larsen, *Representative Government in Greek and Roman History* (Berkeley: University of California Press, 1966), p. 18. *Boule* means council or plan and is also associated with the verbs *to wish* and *to desire.*

[3]Charles A. Beard and John D. Lewis, "Representative Government in Evolution," *American Political Science Review*, 26:2 (1932), pp. 238–239.

authoritarian period of the Tudor dynasty, an English historian could write about Parliament in 1583 that "every Englishman" was regarded as represented and the consent of Parliament was regarded "to be every man's consent."[4]

The turning point came with the expulsion of the Stuart dynasty in the Glorious Revolution of 1688. It affirmed the ascendancy of Parliament over the monarchy, although the monarchy remained an important institution in the decision-making process until the middle of the nineteenth century. The 1689 Bill of Rights required that Parliament meet regularly and that parliamentary consent was necessary for all laws involving taxation. Twelve years later, the Act of Settlement limited the monarchy to Protestants. It was no longer possible for even a strong monarch to reject a law passed by both houses of Parliament. During the next 100 years constitutional practice (not law) established that the prime minister and cabinet should have the confidence of the House of Commons. The last effort of a king to appoint a prime minister who did not have majority support in Parliament occurred in 1834 when William IV dismissed Melbourne and appointed Peel to form a cabinet. Peel's repeated rebuffs by Commons ultimately forced the king to withdraw the appointment. The "golden age" of parliamentary primacy in the British political system had begun.

Overlapping the emergence of **parliamentary supremacy** was the movement to democratize Parliament by expanding the suffrage. The great British electoral reform bills were those of 1832, 1867, and 1884. Prior to these the number of voters was small and sometimes almost nonexistent in a district and the support of a handful of voters was sometimes bought. Occasionally a member of Parliament (an M.P. is actually a member of the House of Commons) took what we today would regard as a very corrupt view of his legislative role and responsibilities. The following excerpt is from an M.P.'s letter in the eighteenth century, in which he refused a constituent petition:

> You know, and I know, that I bought this constituency. You know, and I know, that I am now determined to sell it, and you know what you think I don't know, that you are now looking for another buyer, and I know, what you certainly don't know, that I have now found another constituency to buy.
>
> About what you said about the excise [tax]: may God's curse light upon you all, and may it make your homes as open and free to the excise officers as your wives and daughters have always been to me while I have represented your rascally constituency.[5]

Parliamentary supremacy preceded democratization, but by the end of the nineteenth century universal male suffrage was established in Britain. The Commons, the dominant house, was elected and accountable to the popular will.

---

[4]Sir Thomas Smith, quoted ibid., p. 225. Westminster Abbey was begun as the monastery for the western part of London. It became the monarch's palace in the tenth and eleventh centuries, and the monastery was maintained as well. Parliament was called to Westminster Abbey to consult with the king. By 1550 St. Stephen's Chapel in the Westminster Abbey had become the permanent home of the House of Commons.

[5]P. G. Richards, *Honorable Members*, 2nd ed. (New York: Praeger, 1964), p. 157.

Representative government was secure, and the most corrupt practices were eliminated through introduction of the secret ballot.

American legislative experience is brief, except to the degree that our representative institutions are an offshoot of the British experience. Pre–Revolutionary War events in America had made the colonists distrustful of a strong executive. The Articles of Confederation (1781–1789) declared Congress supreme at the national level, although actual power was held by the states, through their legislatures. Each of the 13 states had one vote in Congress, but a state could have several members in a congressional delegation. States could withdraw delegates from Congress at any time. All important measures required nine votes, and amendments to the articles required unanimity. In the states, legislatures held dominant power, with governors often elected for only one year at a time with minimal powers. Legislatures were the dominant government institutions in the United States during the nineteenth century, and the right of Americans to participate in elections expanded rapidly in that century.[6]

In summary, limitations on the power of the monarchs and the existence of councils and assemblies in some manner representative have a tradition dating back to classical Greece. The first modern elected legislatures were the English Parliament and American legislative institutions as they evolved in the eighteenth century. The oft-described Anglo-American political tradition has a representative, democratically elected legislature as one of its principal features.

BICAMERAL AND UNICAMERAL LEGISLATURES

Bicameral Legislatures

In many countries the division of legislatures into two houses (bicameral) is a result of historical precedent. Bicameral or even tricameral (the three estates under the ancient regime in France) legislatures were first organized by estates or principal classes in the country. As democratic choice and representative government evolved, the lower chamber—for example, the House of Representatives or the British House of Commons— was based on adult suffrage and popular representation, whereas the "upper" chamber usually was appointed or indirectly elected. The upper chamber was supposed to be a moderating, conservative influence that would check a potentially tyrannical popular majority. It also might represent certain groups in the community that a government, yielding before the claims of mass participation in the lower chamber, hoped would retain a special voice in the political process.

The British House of Lords in the nineteenth century was nearly equal with the Commons, although the selection of a prime minister rested exclusively with the Commons. Today, the House of Lords (about 800 hereditary peers or peeresses

---

[6]Suffrage, except for slaves and women, expanded more rapidly in the U.S. than in England, and property tax qualifications were abolished by all but one state (Massachusetts) before the Civil War. See Figure 2.1 in Robert E. Lane, *Political Life* (Glencoe, Ill.: Free Press, 1959), p. 10.

and 400 life peers or peeresses) has only slight power. The Lords have no budgetary powers. They do have a suspensive veto, rarely implemented, that permits them to reject a bill, which the Commons then must repass in a subsequent session.[7] The most important function of the Lords is that of discussion and revision. Technical errors and other flaws, substantive or minor, can be ironed out during the debate in the House of Lords. Broad questions of public policy and new solutions or approaches can be initiated in the House of Lords, especially since life peers (who are in office only for the lifetime of the individual, as instituted in 1958) are distinguished persons, such as journalists, lawyers, trade unionists, academics, and scientists. Under a parliamentary government, where the principal executive officers are chosen by the popularly elected lower chamber, it is inevitable that the cabinet and the elective house dominate.

Second chambers also are sometimes devised to provide for a different type of representation, even though selection may be by popular vote. Japan's House of Councillors exemplifies this principle. The House of Councillors has 252 members who serve six-year terms. Half are elected every three years. Seventy-six are chosen from prefectural districts (Japan has prefectures rather than provinces or states) every three years, and 50 are chosen from the nation at large. The voter has two votes, one for the prefectural level and one for the national level. The House of Councillors was to combine territorial representation with the selection of 50 distinguished persons who had achieved eminence in their chosen careers. The latter hope was not realized. Beginning with the 1983 elections, national constituency votes are cast for the party, not the individual, increasing the power of the parties. Each party wins national seats in proportion to the popular vote. Thus, if a party received 40 percent of the vote in the national constituency race it would win the first 20 seats ($0.40 \times 50 = 20$) on its list of candidates.

The House of Councillors or the upper house has less power than the 512-member House of Representatives. Budget decisions and treaty ratification remain with the House of Representatives. In other matters, if the two houses pass different bills, the House of Representatives' decision prevails if it passes the bill a second time by a two-thirds majority. The political position of the councillors could increase somewhat because the Liberal Democratic party (LDP) lost control of the House of Councillors in the July 1989 elections. Japan has a parliamentary system, and if the two houses disagree on the selection of a prime minister, Article 67 of the Constitution provides that the decision of the House of Representatives shall prevail (see Figure 8.1).

A frequent reason for a bicameral legislature is a federal political system in which power is distributed through a written constitution between the national government and the states or provinces. The upper house, representing territorial units, is organized differently from the lower house. The territorial chamber may represent a different balance of interests, assuming the federal units have special

---

[7]The Parliament Act of 1911 prohibited the House of Lords from rejecting any financial bill and reduced the power of delay the Lords could exercise over other bills passed by the House of Commons. The act of 1949 states a bill could become law over the House of Lords' opposition if the Commons passed the bill in two consecutive sessions and a year had elapsed between the first reading and final passage.

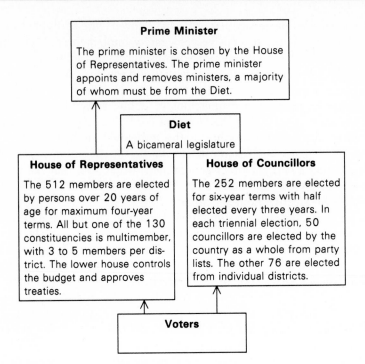

Figure 8.1 The Japanese legislative/executive system.

interests or concerns that are a minority at the national level (such as the French-speaking culture of Quebec).

The upper house in Germany, the *Bundesrat,* or federal council, is made up of delegations from the fifteen states and Berlin. Each state has three to six representatives, depending on the size of its population. Members of the *Bundesrat* are selected by the state governments. Each state delegation must vote as a unit. Constitutional amendments must be approved by a two-thirds vote in both the *Bundesrat* and the lower chamber, the *Bundestag* (federal parliament). Approximately half of the legislation enacted annually involves what the German constitution describes as "consent" law, requiring approval by the *Bundesrat.* The *Bundesrat* has many political interests: first is to represent the special needs and interests of the state government and maintain the position of the states under German federalism. The *Bundesrat*'s special concern with sustaining state government interests, and its indirect representative character, give it a significant political role but has failed to attract much public interest.

The upper house under American federalism is the Senate. It is organized along state lines, two senators per state elected for six-year terms (one-third of the Senate comes up for reelection every two years). Since the Seventeenth Amendment (1913) all senators have been elected by popular vote (before 1913 Senators were chosen for six-year terms by the state legislatures). The Senate shares most powers with the House of Representatives. The Senate alone, however, confirms presidential appointments (majority vote) and ratifies treaties (two-thirds majority). Because the Senate has only 100 members, the individual senator has more visibility than the typical representative. The Senate generally is regarded as the more prestigious and august body.

Unicameral Legislatures

Countries such as Denmark, Finland, Israel, and Sweden have adopted **unicameral** legislatures because they believe one chamber to be more efficient or because they believe bicameralism is less democratic when the upper house is indirectly chosen or election is not based on one person, one vote. In some cases there are no compelling reasons for bicameralism: no historical precedents, such as the House of Lords, need be continued; no special interests require representation; or there is no federal system.[8]

Unicameral legislatures did not appear for the most part until the twentieth century. Moves to abolish second chambers or not to include them in new constitutions were primarily motivated by democratic arguments. Second chambers, however they were selected, too often served as a brake on the democratically elected lower house, it was argued. Furthermore, responsibility for legislative actions could be shifted between the two chambers instead of being precisely identified with a single house. A second chamber was not appropriate to check popular tendencies or impede efficient decision making. Municipal governments in the United States are predominantly unicameral, but most state legislatures are not. (Nebraska adopted unicameralism in 1937, but no other U.S. state has followed suit.) There is minimal evidence concerning the consequences of abolishing second chambers. Those countries with second chambers, for whatever reason, have tended to retain them.

LEGISLATURES IN PARLIAMENTARY AND PRESIDENTIAL SYSTEMS

Parliamentary Government

Under a parliamentary system, sometimes called *cabinet government,* a popularly chosen legislature selects the prime minister, who then chooses the cabinet. The prime minister and cabinet head the executive branch of government. The legislature controls the government through debate, discussion, and voting on government proposals and can force the government to resign if the cabinet loses the confidence of the legislature through a **vote of no confidence.** Generally, parliaments have a maximum constitutional life of four or five years, although new elections may be called at any time by the prime minister or the ruling party. Usually parliaments are dissolved by the government before the term of office is

---

[8]J. Blondel reports that in the early 1970s there were 52 bicameral legislatures out of 108 countries having legislatures in *Comparative Legislatures* (Englewood Cliffs, N.J.: Prentice-Hall, 1973), p. 32.

up, at an auspicious moment when the majority party or parties believe they will enjoy maximum popularity in a forthcoming election. As our subsequent discussion of France indicates, it is unusual for a coalition government to dissolve a legislature simply because it loses a vote of confidence and must resign.

Under a parliamentary system the executive leadership—prime minister and cabinet—are, with few exceptions, members of the legislature. In contrast to separation of powers under a presidential system, formal supreme political authority resides with the legislature, and the cabinet depends on continuing legislative support. Usually, a parliamentary legislator does not play as active a role in the legislative process as does his or her American counterpart.

Parliament in Great Britain   The prototype of parliamentary systems is the bicameral British Parliament, with power in the popularly elected House of Commons, and the House of Lords exercising minimal influence. One becomes prime minister by being the leader of the victorious party in the House of Commons. Because of the close relationship between the British Parliament and the cabinet, it is not surprising that prime ministers have considerable legislative experience. Since World War II, prime ministers have averaged 32 years in parliament before entering 10 Downing Street. The crucial and penultimate step to becoming prime minister is to be the elected party leader of the winning party. By contrast, 10 of the 17 men who became president of the United States in this century never served in Congress.

A distinguishing feature of the British Parliament is the highly disciplined two-party system in the House of Commons. Policy innovation, formation, and implementation emanate from the cabinet, not the legislature. Historically, it is the executive branch that has dominated policy-making. Disciplined party voting in the Commons means that once a prime minister and cabinet are chosen and are committed to a particular policy, there is little likelihood that the members of Parliament will break ranks and defeat the government.

Parliament rarely makes or breaks governments. Under a disciplined two-party system such as the British, party leadership (i.e., the prime minister and his or her cabinet) dominates. The cabinet, not the legislature, generally is the center of power (see Figure 8.2).

Formal voting is not the only way to bring about changes in government personnel or policy, and ruling parties have in the past selected new leaders in critical political circumstances. Events in 1940, for example, demonstrate that a prime minister will resign if a policy erodes the confidence of his party colleagues. In May 1940, Prime Minister Neville Chamberlain was sharply attacked for his previous diplomatic compromises with Nazi Germany (Munich, 1938) and the deteriorating war situation, signaled by Norway falling to the Germans. When the division bells rang and the vote of confidence was taken, Chamberlain's normal majority of 200 slipped to 81. Sixty Conservative M.P.'s abstained and 33 supported the opposition. Within the week Chamberlain had resigned and the House of Commons elected Winston Churchill, a Conservative, to lead a national government.

There is a mix of discipline and deference in the House of Commons: "Once

Queen Elizabeth opening the annual session of the British Parliament.

the Conservatives have chosen their Leader he can stay in office . . . until he himself decides to retire or, as has happened on at least three occasions in this century, he is forced from office by a revolt among his followers."[9] The Chamberlain case reveals there are limits to political government policy failures a British ruling party will tolerate. In such cases, the ruling party selects a new party leader, who then becomes prime minister. This was demonstrated again in November 1990. Conservative Prime Minister Margaret Thatcher won a narrow first-round vote of confidence from Conservative M.P.s, 204 to 152 with 16 abstentions. Support among Conservative M.P.s was dropping because they saw that Mrs. Thatcher's policies were increasingly unpopular with British voters. Her closest advisors convinced her that support within her party was continuing to slip away. The party leader who had served eleven and a half years as prime minister resigned and was replaced by John Major. John Major became prime minister and the Conservative Party remained in power.

The size of the executive also has increased, and it has been charged that patronage inherent in this expansion further reduces M.P. independence and influence.

> With over a hundred members of the ruling party holding ministerial positions, Mr. Wilson [Labour prime minister between 1964 and 1970, and 1974 and 1976] has assuredly dispensed patronage with a liberality which even George III or Lord North

[9]R. T. McKenzie, *British Political Parties*, 2nd ed. (New York: Praeger, 1964), p. 579.

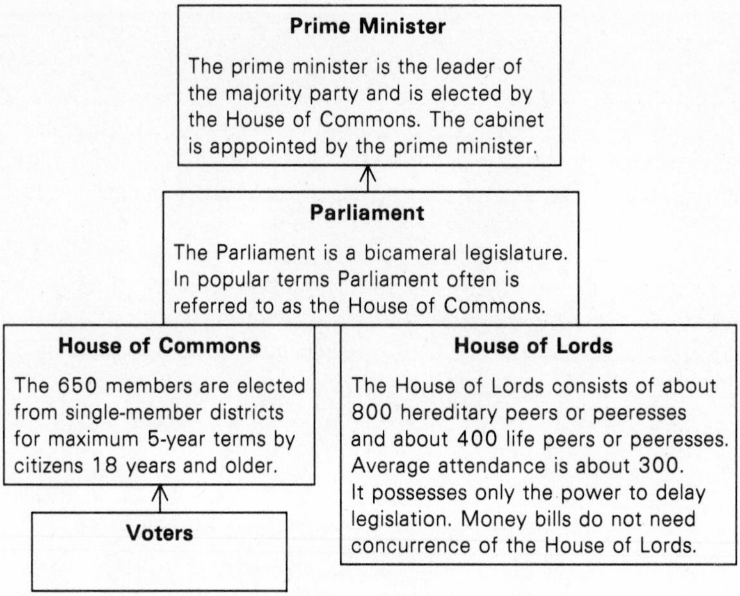

Prime Minister

The prime minister is the leader of the majority party and is elected by the House of Commons. The cabinet is apppointed by the prime minister.

Parliament

The Parliament is a bicameral legislature. In popular terms Parliament often is referred to as the House of Commons.

House of Commons

The 650 members are elected from single-member districts for maximum 5-year terms by citizens 18 years and older.

House of Lords

The House of Lords consists of about 800 hereditary peers or peeresses and about 400 life peers or peeresses. Average attendance is about 300. It possesses only the power to delay legislation. Money bills do not need concurrence of the House of Lords.

Voters

Figure 8.2 The British legislative/executive system.

might have blushed at. Patronage and party discipline have eroded the independence of the members of the legislature . . .[10]

The House of Commons has 650 members; there are 20 or 21 ministries in the cabinet. If one takes into account noncabinet senior ministers and junior ministers (usually with the title parliamentary secretary), there are approximately 100 ministerial appointments to be filled by a government. Thus, 25 to 30 percent of a majority party can anticipate receiving an executive appointment. Appointments balance and mend differences within the party, but appointments are also reward, control, and are "patronage" instruments.

In a constitutional monarchy such as Great Britain, the cabinet does not exercise unlimited power. One limitation is the requirement of consultation and negotiation, so party leaders may maintain the confidence of their fellow M.P.s and present a favorable image to the electorate. British parties are not monoliths, and the spirit of compromise and negotiation generally characterize the party organizations as well as the entire political system.

One example is the *1922 Committee* composed of Conservative backbenchers (the less prominent M.P.s, not holding any ministerial posts). The chair of the committee has access to cabinet ministers, to whom he or she conveys backbenchers' opinions. This committee meets weekly. Its influence is discreet, veiled, and substantial. While formulating policy, British parties are guided by the principle of anticipated response. Policy is drafted and discussed in a manner that takes into account the views of M.P.s not holding ministerial positions.

---

[10]Richard Middleton, "The Problems and Consequences of Parliamentary Government: A Historical Review," *Parliamentary Affairs*, 23:1 (1969), p. 57.

The monarch's role in Britain's constitutional monarchy generally is to do what the prime minister and the cabinet decide. Queen Elizabeth makes the speeches; she signs all laws Parliament passes. The monarch is more visible than influential and takes no side publicly in a political controversy. Many public causes are furthered by a visit or a statement by the monarch or other members of the Royal Family, whether it be an appearance before a well-known charitable group or speaking out for environmental protection.

The monarch's political influence has been informal since the early part of the century. A king or queen's reign normally extends over several governments and prime ministers. The experience and knowledge accumulated by the monarch may be used to advise and even warn the prime minister on government policy during their frequent meetings. Only a handful of people know, however, what part if any a monarch has played in government decision making until many years after monarch and prime minister are out of public life.

Parliament in France   Since the beginning of the French Revolution in 1789 and the execution of Louis XVI in 1793, France has experienced eight political regimes, including two empires, one constitutional monarchy, and five republics. Each time one constitution was replaced with another, a distinct name was given to that regime. For example, the Fourth Republic, which the legislature dominated, was created at the end of World War II and lasted until 1958. Unable to deal with crucial public policy issues, including the insurgency in Algeria, the Fourth Republic was replaced by the Fifth. The new constitution provided for a stronger executive and was intended to establish a proactive, solution-oriented political system. These intentions were effectively represented by Charles de Gaulle, the first president under the Fifth Republic.

Parliament during the French Fourth Republic (1946–1958) had several features missing in Great Britain's system, but not uncommon in parliamentary systems. The National Assembly, the popularly elected lower house, was a multiparty chamber, with no party ever controlling more than 29 percent of the seats (Table 8.1). Except for the Communists, the parties were loosely disciplined, and it was common for a party to have some deputies supporting a bill and others opposing it. The assembly, not the cabinet, was the dominant body.

Governing parties in the Fourth Republic did not include the Communists or Gaullists, who controlled approximately 33 percent of the assembly seats. Coalition governments were a necessity, but the range of potential partners was limited. As a result, a process known as *replâtrage* ("replastering") became common. *Replâtrage* meant continuity of personalities and parties in the cabinet, with political leaders simply occupying different ministries in successive governments. There was stability of a sort, at least among ministers. Between January 1946 and December 1952 16 ministries were held by 66 persons in France (this period includes six cabinets that lasted less than six weeks). During the same period in Great Britain, the 16 counterpart ministries were occupied by 58 persons.[11]

---

[11]Philip Williams, *Politics in Post-War France* (London: Longmans, Green, 1954), p. 375.

Table 8.1   **REPRESENTATION IN THE FRENCH NATIONAL ASSEMBLY (FOURTH REPUBLIC)**

	1946		1951		1956	
	Deputies	Percentage	Deputies	Percentage	Deputies	Percentage
Communists	182	29.4	101	16.1	150	25.2
Socialists	102	16.5	107	17.1	100	16.8
MRP	166	26.9	97	15.5	83	14.1
Radicals and RGR	71	11.5	91	14.5	94	15.8
Conservatives	67	10.8	98	15.7	121[a]	20.3
RPF (Gaullists)			120	19.1		
Poujadists		4.9			42	7.0
Miscellaneous and unaffiliated	30		13	2.1	6	1.0
Total	618		627		596[b]	

[a]Troubled conditions in Algeria made it impossible to hold elections for the 30 representatives from that area in 1956.

[b]The Conservatives in 1956 included the remnants of the RPF, the Social Republicans.

Source: Walter H. Mallory, ed., *Political Handbook of the World* (New York: Harper & Brothers, for the Council on Foreign Relations), 1947, p. 61; 1952, p. 68; 1957, p. 69.

A coalition government is established in a parliamentary system when two or more minority parties combine their votes to form a majority. Ministerial posts are then usually divided among those parties making up the coalition.

Coalition governments such as in the Fourth Republic are the European norm. Among Western Europe's 21 democracies in 1988, only six were single-party governments with a parliamentary majority, the rest being coalition governments. Some governments, such as in Israel and Italy, still must deal with the problem of coalition government instability similar to that faced in the French Fourth Republic.

A principal difference between parliamentarianism in Great Britain and France is that the British system is premised on the need to make and execute policy. Until recently, an enduring theme in French political culture was the politics of defense—parliament restrains government to protect individual or group interests. A French political essayist in the last decade of the Third Republic (1875–1940) expressed an attitude also characteristic of the Fourth Republic when she declared that "the executive is inherently monarchic" and that democracy is "a perpetual struggle by the ruled against the abuses of power."[12]

The constitution of the Fifth Republic (adopted in 1958) includes several changes that increase the executive's authority. The Fifth Republic is a parliamentary/presidential hybrid. The president is popularly elected for a seven-year term; he or she symbolizes national popular choice and, depending on the election issues, carries some type of policy mandate (see Figure 8.3). The president nominates the

[12]Suzanne Berger, "The French Political System," in Samuel H. Beer and Adam B. Ulam, eds., *Patterns of Government*, 3rd ed. (New York: Random House, 1973), p. 361.

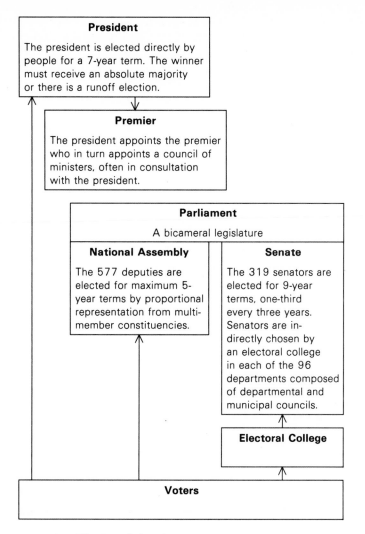

Figure 8.3 The French legislative/executive system.

premier without formal vote of the assembly. The premier cannot be forced to resign unless he or she loses a vote of confidence in the assembly. France has had four strong presidents under the Fifth Republic: Charles de Gaulle (1958–1969), Georges Pompidou (1969–1974), Giscard d'Estaing (1974–1981), and François Mitterand (1981 to date). The president has exerted great influence on the premier. Resignations were issues between the president and premier and did not result from a no-confidence vote in the assembly.

The *ministrable* phenomenon, which under the Fourth Republic led some ambitious deputies to bring about a change in government in the hopes of a ministerial appointment, has diminished. A legislator now must resign his or her seat if he or she accepts a ministerial appointment. In addition, the government (president, premier, and cabinet) has control of the parliamentary agenda, which was not true in the Fourth Republic. The government decides which bills will be considered and in what order and determines which, if any, committee amendments will be debated and voted on by parliament. Thus, the government need not compromise on technicalities or amendments. Should the executive wish to push a bill, the premier can invoke Article 49(3) of the constitution. This obliges the opposition to muster a majority of the *total* membership of the National Assembly—289 votes. An absolute majority in this circumstance is necessary to defeat a government-sponsored bill. The Senate has limited authority, though it has a suspensive veto. The Assembly can override this veto by approving the bill again on a second reading.

The Legislature in a Presidential System

The distinctive feature of a presidential system is **separation of powers:** The chief executive and the legislature are elected independently of one another; each holds office for a definite period of time, which ordinarily cannot be altered by the other; and both the legislature and the executive are not readily controlled by the other (see Figure 8.4).

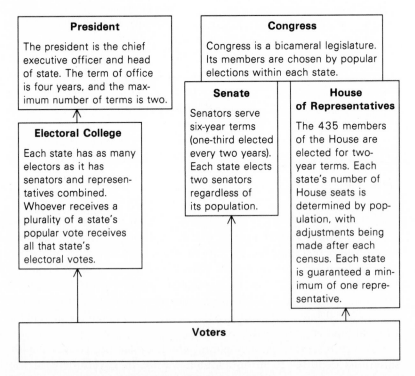

Figure 8.4 The U.S. legislative/executive system.

The American national government is the prototype of **presidential government.** The president is elected for a four-year term by national popular vote via the electoral college and can be removed legally by one of two methods, both of which involve Congress. He may be impeached by majority vote in the House of Representatives, followed by conviction by a two-thirds vote in the Senate. (One president, Andrew Johnson [1865–1869], was impeached; he was adjudged not guilty by one vote in the Senate.) The Twenty-Fifth Amendment also provides that if the vice president and a majority of the cabinet inform Congress that the president cannot discharge his duties, the vice president will become acting president. If the president subsequently declares no inability exists, Congress must decide the issue within 21 days. Other than these two unique circumstances, the presidential term of office is not controlled by the legislature. Periodically, however, the majority in either the House of Representatives or the Senate does not represent the same party as the president. The House of Representatives has been controlled by the opposition party (not the president's party) 26 of the years between the Eightieth Congress, elected in 1946, and the One Hundred First Congress, elected in 1988. The opposition has controlled the Senate for 20 of those years. Even when the opposition party controls one or both houses of the legislature, the president completes his term.

Both the legislative and executive branches share broad spheres of power; policy is a compromise between the two branches. The separation of powers associated with presidential government is actually a system of checks and balances. Powers held by one branch are shared in selected but decisive ways with another branch. Congress has the law-enacting responsibility, but the president holds the veto power, which requires a two-thirds majority of those present and voting in both houses to override. Between 1789 and 1986, for example, only 100 of 2,448 vetoes were overriden by Congress.[13] If Congress is at a disadvantage vis-à-vis a presidential veto, it possesses considerable control through the authority of the Senate to confirm—"advise and consent to"—major presidential appointments. A majority of appointees serve in the executive branch, but a number also involve the judiciary, the third branch of the government. The president nominates, but the Senate confirms. Headlines are made when the Senate rejects a nomination. For example, the nomination of Robert Bork to the Supreme Court by President Reagan was rejected in 1987, after a bitter Senate fight, on the grounds Bork was out of the mainstream of judicial thought. Generally, a continuing dialogue is maintained to avoid an embarrassing rejection. A government acquaintance told one of the authors how the names of "six persons were run by" the Armed Services Committee recently before a nomination to the Department of Defense was submitted. One of the important bargaining tools held by Congress, through the Senate, is the power to confirm or reject executive nominations. In a similar vein, the power of the purse, the power to raise taxes and appropriate money, is a restriction the executive branch cannot readily overcome.

---

[13]Louis Fisher, *The Politics of Shared Power: Congress and the Executive,* 2nd ed. (Washington, D.C.: CQ Press, 1987), p. 30. Pocket vetos were 1,039 of the total. A *pocket veto* occurs when Congress adjourns during the 10-day period the president may sign or veto a bill. Should the president withhold his signature, it is a pocket veto.

President Bush about to deliver his first State of the Union speech in 1989.

A major point at issue, as in parliamentary government, concerns whether or not the legislature is equal with, or overshadowed by, the executive branch. The president, through public messages (State of the Union, Budget Message, and so forth) and through bills drafted by the administration, has the principal role in recommending and innovating policy. The bulk of the expertise resides in the

"The Small Society" by Brickman © Washington Star Syndicate, permission granted by King Features Syndicate, 1978.

executive branch. Congress in recent years has attempted to increase its pool of expertise, but is still overshadowed by the executive and his bureaucracy. Between 1957 and 1983, the personal and committee staff tripled from 4,489 in 1957 to 19,000 in 1983. Each committee has a professional staff, including secretarial support as well as those who do research, write reports, prepare agendas for public hearings, and so forth. Members of Congress have their own personal staff aides paid out of their office budgets. Congress has the largest professional staff of any legislature in the world. As a point of comparison, the British House of Commons has a professional staff of about 800 and both houses of the French Parliament have a staff of 1800.[14]

The period from proposal to law in a presidential system requires negotiation, trade-offs, and compromise. An important contribution to policy-making by Congress is sometimes overlooked. This influence does not always take the form of an amendment or a competing draft bill. Daily contacts between members of Congress and congressional staff and administration officials, frequent conferences and briefings, and visits and inspection tours all contribute to an exchange of views. This continual interaction constrains executive actions and reveals on a day-to-day basis legislation that can reasonably be expected to originate in Congress or be accepted by Congress. Many committee staffs and members of Congress hold office much longer than any presidential appointee in the executive branch (cabinet officers, department heads, undersecretaries) can hope to, and this longevity and network of contacts is a legislative advantage.

Presidential versus Parliamentary Systems

Countries with presidential systems occasionally see advantages to a parliamentary system; for example, when the Republicans won control of both houses of Congress in 1946, Senator J. William Fulbright (D, Arkansas) suggested President Harry

---

[14]Figures quoted in Randall B. Ripley, *Congress: Process and Policy*, 4th ed. (New York: W.W. Norton, 1988), p. 240.

Truman resign and be replaced by a Republican chosen by Congress. Not surprisingly, President Truman vehemently rejected the suggestion. Reversing the coin, frustrated legislators in a parliamentary system sometimes envy the greater autonomy and power of members of the U.S. Congress.

Using the U.S. presidential system as an example, many presidents have discovered their legislative proposals barely recognizable after Congress passed them into law. This has happened even when a president's party controlled both houses of Congress. Senators and representatives know that their first priority is to keep constituents happy. Presidential influence is minimal if it conflicts with constituency interests. The latter is often parochial rather than with broader public interest. Articulation of multiple and specialized concerns by representatives is more prominent under a presidential system. Criticism can turn into obstructionism and no policy. Or, a mushy and compromise policy, minimally satisfying most concerned groups, often provides no long-term solution, for example, the U.S. budget deficit ($3 trillion in 1990); the annual U.S. trade deficit ($120–$150 billion); and the annual trade deficit with Japan ($50 billion).

The British parliamentary model is attractive to many because it is associated with disciplined parties and meaningful party labels, and the campaign pledges of the winning party become public policy. In Great Britain voters expect M.P.'s to follow the party line. Voters do not vote for prime minister, and their power to determine who becomes prime minister is through voting for the M.P. The individual M.P. has less autonomy and input into what becomes public policy than his or her U.S. counterpart. A coalition, parliamentary government is one additional step removed from popular control. The makeup of a ruling coalition and policy compromises are reached after the election. These accommodations and arrangements may not have been anticipated by voters at the previous election. A limitation on coalition builders and the ensuing government is a reading of anticipated voter response at the next election, but this is imprecise at best. Parties that do not maintain voting discipline whether in a two- or multiparty legislature allow more autonomy and input from individual legislators.

Government in a presidential system sometimes seems slow to act. Many elected officials in Congress, and also the president, must approve if policy is to be enacted. The U.S. Constitution gave the House of Representatives, the Senate, and the president fixed but different terms of office (two, six, and four years, respectively). The heart of the system under these conditions is continuous bargaining, accommodation, and compromise; and, despite its label, the role of the legislature remains important in a presidential system.

FUNCTIONS OF LEGISLATURES

Legislative functions involve interaction between legislators and other political actors, such as constituents, lobbyists, political leaders, presidential representatives, and bureaucrats. Democratic legislatures are legitimate, because of their representative quality, links with the people, and willingness to interact with many interests. Figure 8.5 shows the legislative system, which includes the legislature and the interaction process.

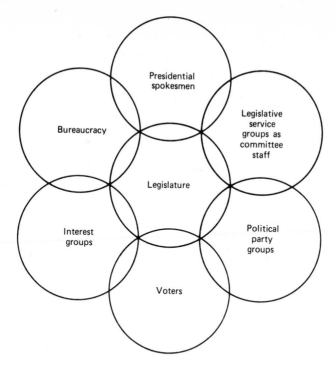

Figure 8.5 A legislative system. *Source:* Adapted from Malcolm E. Jewell and Samuel C. Patterson, *The Legislative Process in the United States,* p. 6. Copyright © 1966 by Random House. Adapted by permission of the publisher.

The functions listed below are not exhaustive, but they give us an awareness of the multifunctional character of legislatures in pluralistic political systems or those moving toward more open and liberal politics.

1. Legislatures share with other institutions and groups the power to initiate, enact, and modify policy through lawmaking and other means. The individual legislator's role in this area is often informal and not open to public view, yet the role is very real. In the British Parliament, for example, disciplined party voting and the cabinet's preeminence suggest that the average M.P. contributes little to policymaking. In practice, though, the M.P. has leverage with ministers, through the party committee in Commons. Legislative whips in Britain officially are given the duty of "whipping" M.P.s into line on a vote but, as in many legislatures, spend more of their time apprising the government of M.P.s' opinions than "whipping" the legislative party. A classic work on the British Parliament explains: "Control means influence, not direct power; advice, not command; criticism not obstruction; scrutiny, not initiation; and publicity, not secrecy."[15]

A democratic legislature's policy-making functions conflict with management

---

[15]Bernard Crick, *The Reform of Parliament* (Garden City, N.Y.: Anchor Books, 1965), p. 80.

principles of quick, decisive action. The legislature provides the arena where competing demands can struggle, negotiate, compromise, and, it is hoped, be at least minimally accommodated. Compromise and, often, delay are institutionalized in the legislative process in a democratic system, and legislative negotiation often provides a stability or balance otherwise difficult to achieve. Speaking about the American system, one study recognized that the demands of some interests might not be met even partially, but that legislatures "can grant these interests a hearing—perhaps not obtainable elsewhere—and this hearing can be an important factor in the management of conflict."[16] An interest group may sway a vote or present a viewpoint generally ignored up to that time. The hearing also can act as a "safety valve," a way of letting off steam by articulating a view, even while recognizing little may change immediately.

En masse, legislators have a range of knowledge and experience in terms of class, ethnic, religious, and geographic origin and an awareness of constituent views that make them exceptionally sensitive to public opinion and demands and most able to judge the acceptability and feasibility of policy. Underlying most legislative functions is the presumption the representative will promote those interests his or her constituency has a strong interest in, for example, retaining a military base, an urban transit subsidy, agricultural price supports, and civil rights.

2. Legislatures usually influence the composition of the chief executive officers. Under a parliamentary system the prime minister and the cabinet are responsible legally to the legislature. British practice provides that the prime minister invariably is the leader of the party that won the election. Even in Great Britain, though, the composition of the cabinet is decided by negotiation and bargaining with various elements of the majority party. The House of Commons no longer makes and unmakes governments during a parliamentary term, but it can make or cripple reputations. A minister must be a "good House of Commons person" and be able to hold his or her own in parliamentary debate, else he or she would falter and feel compelled to resign. One Conservative minister, in describing his first months in office, observed "the remorseless interest of the House of Commons in seeing a man brought down."[17] The Commons provides a setting in which ministers must regularly justify their actions and show competence.

When choosing his or her cabinet and making appointments, a president of the United States must give consideration to the temper and anticipated reaction of the Senate. The Senate does not make a habit of rejecting presidential nominees, but the occasional refusal to confirm an appointment makes it clear that the president should consult with senators prior to announcing a key appointment. Formal approval is provided through the advice and consent power in Article 2, Section 2, of the Constitution. Major presidential appointments must be approved by a majority of senators present and voting.

---

[16]Malcolm E. Jewell and Samuel C. Patterson, *The Legislative Process in the United States,* 2nd ed. (New York: Random House, 1971), p. 12.

[17]*Economist* (February 27, 1971), p. 17, quoted in Beer and Ulam, eds., *Patterns of Government,* p. 238.

The U.S. Senate Budget Committee in session. Prominently featured are senators Domenici, Armstrong, and Grassley.

3. While performing a lawmaking function, committee hearings may perform a valuable role in discovering and/or making public new information. The United States has the most developed legislative committee system in the world.

The 1973–1974 Watergate hearings conducted by the Senate Select Committee on Presidential Campaign Activities brought together and organized information in a situation when most if not all participants themselves had knowledge that was restricted to only small segments of the affair. Committee hearings serve many purposes, including preparation of legislation and supervision of other branches of government. In doing so, they make public and organize information that might not be revealed in any other circumstances.

4. Legislatures legitimize government actions and in turn serve to legitimize the political system. In following accepted procedures, legislatures reassure the public of the rightness and propriety of the policy process. The legitimizing functions include outputs as well as procedures followed. Legitimacy, however, is determined principally by the output and the success in responding to the most pressing demands and accommodating a diverse range of interests.

Transitional political systems that are moving from authoritarianism to a limited pluralism focus on procedures. At the beginning of the transitional stage, the legislature gradually becomes involved in formulating laws and policy as in the case of the Soviet Union discussed later. In unchanging authoritarian regimes, legislatures have minimal influence on the stability or policies of such regimes. The policies and durability of authoritarian systems depend on sources little related to any legislative activities.

5. Democratic legislatures should oversee other branches of government and thereby uphold freedom to criticize and evaluate programs and officials. In the

United States a majority of the supervisory functions occur in committee hearings. It would be hard to find an American high school or college student who is unaware of at least one congressional investigation that has turned the glare of publicity on some government agency or official, whether it be Watergate, military sales to Iran, or improper practices in the Department of Housing and Urban Development.

In Great Britain the most telling public overview takes place during the Question Time, which occurs on the first four days each week when the House of Commons convenes at 2:30. Ministers must respond to questions (written and then followed up orally) submitted by an M.P. Individual responsibility and explanation are rigorously and regularly enforced during the Question Hour. Many ambitions have been lofted or deflated during this grilling period.

6. Educating and informing the public are functions best performed by democratic legislatures. This is a corollary to the previously cited functions, but is of sufficient importance to be included in a separate category. The educative/informational function occurs in legislative debates, committee hearings, and elections, and during the period between elections when legislators attempt to maintain ties with constituents by interpreting major issues in newsletters, in television and radio talks, and through back-home visits.

7. Legislatures can be a bulwark of democracy. Some also function as a transitional institution to a more open society. Legislatures can be a forum for promoting diverse viewpoints not always in harmony with the government of the moment, such as in Mexico and the Republic of China (Taiwan). Where there is an effort to expand the boundaries of political expression, the legislatures will be among the first arenas in which political discussion and criticism are allowed, first during the elections and then in the legislative sessions.

8. Legislatures function as electioneering forums, particularly during the period between elections. The publicity and controversies generated are relevant to the winning and losing of popular support. This is true of both developed and developing political systems. In one sense, governing is a protracted election campaign. The British Parliament has been described as "the agreed arena in which most of the campaign is fought." The parliamentary sessions are the place where the political parties "obtain something like equal access to the ear of the electorate in the long formative period between official campaigns."[18] In many ways, the next election begins the first day the new legislature meets.

9. Individual service to constituents looms increasingly large as a function of legislators in postindustrial society. This is particularly true in the United States but also is a trend in other democracies. Voters often evaluate legislators on the basis of service to constituents and the district, rather than on policy positions. For example, a 1978 survey of American newspapers revealed that legislators in their campaign speeches tended to separate themselves and the job they were doing from Congress and its performance. There is a growing distrust of such political institutions as legislatures, but thus far this has not spilled over into high distrust of

---

[18]Crick, *The Reform of Parliament*, pp. 25–26.

" ....AND THIS IS WHERE CONGRESS MEETS! AS WE STUDIED IN CLASS, CONGRESS REPRESENTS
THE PEOPLE ....THE AUTOMOTIVE INDUSTRY PEOPLE .... THE NATIONAL RIFLE ASSOCIATION
PEOPLE..........THE BIG OIL PEOPLE........ THE AFL-CIO PEOPLE.........THE CONSUMER LOBBY PEOPLE........... "

Drawing by Jim Borgman, the *Cincinnati Enquirer.*

individual legislators. One survey discovered a mere 20 percent said Congress is doing a "good job," while 65 percent gave their own representative in Congress "high ratings."[19] Thus, the legislator emphasizes serving the district but is critical of the job the legislature as a whole is doing.

In most democracies the problems have persisted—inflation, energy sources, budget deficits, heavy defense spending, and so forth. Elections often have not produced changes, and voters are beginning to change their expectation that politicians can deliver on their promises. Many legislators have assumed an increasing service function because they can emphasize this role in contrast to a negative and even cynical attitude people have toward legislatures as formulators of policy. One observer concluded that, in this era of increased government activity, representatives and senators are overloaded with "case work." This refers to activities in legislative offices directed toward coping with problems of individual constituents. Frequently the case results from administration of a federal program or regulation. It often is resolved by a congressional staff member and sometimes even a senator or representative going to an agency to get favorable action such as speeding up approval of a grant application.

10. The nine functions discussed thus far characterize democratic legislatures, or those where the political system is moving toward a more open and competitive situation. Legislatures in authoritarian systems fulfill functions in much the same way as one-party elections (discussed earlier in Chapter 7). Authoritarian legislatures serve as a recruiting device to reward the upwardly mobile party faithful or, in some cases, to take a closer look at an ambitious individual. The Supreme Soviet

---

[19]*Institute for Social Research Newsletter* (Autumn 1979), p. 4.

is careful to represent major vocational and national groups. The legislative overseeing function is minimal to date.

LEGISLATIVE DYNAMICS

Legislative activities and policy-making are important subjects, but space limitations prevent a detailed discussion here. We will, however, provide you with some
appreciation of the influences that affect the workings and output of a legislature.
Often the legislative process is complicated even to the insider. Former German
Chancellor Otto von Bismarck observed there are two things one should not watch
being made—laws and sausage.

The U.S. Congress

The American system disperses influence and activity. Congress has been described
as a conglomerate of little legislatures—the **congressional committees** (22
standing committees in the House, 16 in the Senate). Once a bill is introduced into
either the House of Representatives or the Senate, it is referred to a committee; to
which committee it goes sometimes can be extremely important. Civil rights bills
in the Senate have been sent to either the Judiciary Committee or the Commerce
Committee. The membership of the latter is more liberal and more likely to result
in a favorable vote for the bill. The most common way to kill a bill is to table it
or simply not bring it up for consideration. If a bill is reported out (positive vote)
in the House of Representatives, it must then go to the Rules Committee, which
decides when or if it shall appear on the House agenda, the nature and extent of
debate that will be allowed, and whether or not amendments can be offered.

We might note that proliferation of subcommittees designed to encourage
congressional specialization has also further decentralized power and opened up
even more input opportunities for interest groups of all hues and persuasions. The
flow of legislation, consequently, often is hindered. The House of Representatives
has over 140 subcommittees and the Senate has more than 90. The House has had
up to eight committees and subcommittees dealing with energy. This means that
innumerable interest groups have a wide choice of access points at which to push
their particular proposal.

Over 9,000 bills are introduced in Congress annually (see Figure 8.6). Without
a division of labor, these bills would never be reviewed even superficially. The
political system would be buried under a landslide of legislation if the reviewing,
sifting, and culling process did not, as it does now, eliminate 80 percent of the bills
introduced. After a bill has cleared subcommittees and each chamber, there usually
are differences between the bills approved in the House and Senate. This requires
a Conference Committee composed of members from both houses. The Conference
Committee usually can work out a compromise bill, but in the event that the
committee cannot or Congress adjourns, the bill is dead and must be reintroduced
and go through the entire procedure again. Congress has been called an obstacle
course: "For sheer difficulty the way of a serious legislative proposal through

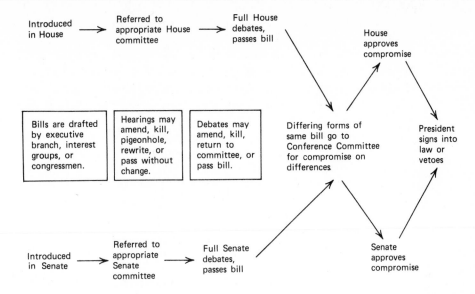

Figure 8.6 How a bill becomes law in the United States.

Congress is equalled only by that of a camel through the eye of a needle or a rich man into the Kingdom of God.''[20] As a result of all of the legislative activity, about 1,000 bills become law during the two-year life of a Congress.

The committee system, reinforced by the service orientation of representatives discussed earlier, has further dispersed power in the American Congress and weakened the role of party leaders. The best-known Speaker of the House this century, Sam Rayburn of Texas, enforced the rule, to get along you have to go along with the leadership. The Democratic House Majority Leader, in effect second in command, complained in 1983: "Nowadays, being speaker gives you nothing more than a hunting license to try to persuade. These Democrats, they elect a leader, and then ignore his advice."[21]

The committee system is a key to the American congressional process. Legislative committees are the only way a large and great country can handle the many issues and proposals that must be considered. The need for specialization often means that pockets of power are controlled by a few persons.

Specialization and legislative dispersal of lawmaking and oversight through the committee/subcommittee system have facilitated "intervention" politics, whereby legislators intervene with bureaucrats on behalf of a constituent. Such case work intervention is quite common, but only rarely becomes public despite the politics of ethics that intermittently prevailed in the late 1980s.

A costly example is Lincoln Savings and Loan, a California-based savings and

---

[20]Robert Bendiner, *Obstacle Course on Capitol Hill* (New York: McGraw-Hill, 1964), p. 15.

[21]T.R. Reid, "Tip O'Neill: Don't Shoot—I'm Your Leader," *Washington Post National Weekly Edition*, 1:3 (November 21, 1983), p. 7.

loan (S&L) institution, which in 1989 set the record for a financial rescue by the Federal Savings and Loan Insurance Corporation—$2.5 billion! Before the Lincoln S&L was placed in conservatorship, its owner, Charles Keating, Jr., complained to several senators that the Federal Home Loan Bank Board had been too heavy-handed in trying to regulate Lincoln's speculative lending and investment policies. Two Washington columnists reported an April 1987 meeting where Senators Alan Cranston (D, California) and John Glenn (D, Ohio) among others "browbeat federal thrift regulators who were perceived as being too tough on a [Lincoln] savings and loan."[22] Other news stories reported Senator Glenn received $200,000 in undisclosed corporate donations for his political action committee. Senator Cranston admitted he solicited $850,000 from Keating for three voter-education projects, including one initiated by Cranston's son.[23] Keating's donations were made through his American Continental Corporation, located in Phoenix, Arizona.

Intervention politics, which links legislators with constituents or supporters, is not always or even usually improper case work. However, service or case work is especially important in the U.S. Congress where each representative must build his or her electoral arrangements, and party support and discipline are weak.

The British Parliament

While 1,000 bills may become law during a two-year U.S. congressional term, the British Parliament enacts about 200 annually. Bills originate in the ministries in discussions involving ministers, the civil service, and, oftentimes, interest groups. The Future Legislation Committee of the cabinet reduces the proposals to a manageable number, and these become the basis for the government's program. Individual M.P.'s cannot introduce bills involving taxation or expenditure. A "private" bill involves primarily minor subjects with a narrow focus, and if it is to be enacted the government must be sympathetic or at least neutral. (Private bills are included in the 200 figure.) Backbenchers have some influence as do the arguments of the opposition. Because a legislative proposal is highly developed before the government introduces it, much of the discussion and compromise occur before the bill is introduced (see Figure 8.7).

There are only six **standing committees** in the House of Commons: A, B, C, D, E, and the Scottish Committee. All except the last consider bills without regard to subject. Committees have from 20 to 50 members, they do not call in outside experts, and as soon as they have reported on one bill they receive another, in order of consideration, not according to subject matter. Following a "second reading," one of the first five committees considers the bill. The bill cannot be tabled, because the cabinet ultimately determines the order of business before the House. The standing committee goes through the bill line by line, noting any

[22]Jack Anderson and Dole Van Atta, "Merry-Go-Round: More Wimps Are Needed," *Express-News* (July 23, 1989), p. 5M.

[23]Washington Post Service, "Donations from S&L Chief to Glenn under Scrutiny," *Express-News* (July 22, 1989), p. 2A.

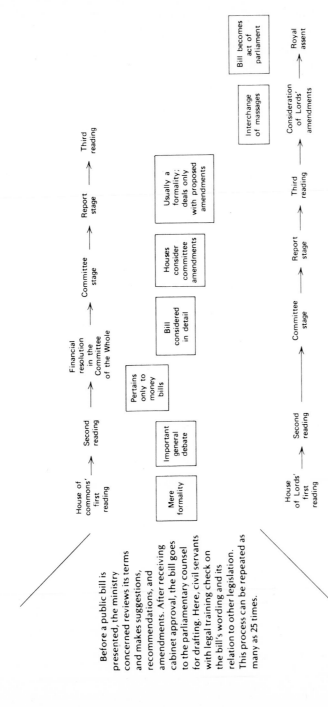

Before a public bill is presented, the ministry concerned reviews its terms and makes suggestions, recommendations, and amendments. After receiving cabinet approval, the bill goes to the parliamentary counsel for drafting. Here, civil servants with legal training check on the bill's wording and its relation to other legislation. This process can be repeated as many as 25 times.

House of commons' first reading → Second reading → Financial resolution in the Committee of the Whole → Committee stage → Report stage → Third reading

Mere formality

Important general debate

Pertains only to money bills

Bill considered in detail

Houses consider committee amendments

Usually a formality; deals only with proposed amendments

Bill becomes act of parliament

Interchange of massages

Royal assent

House of Lords' first reading → Second reading → Committee stage → Report stage → Third reading → Consideration of Lords' amendments

Figure 8.7 How a public government-sponsored bill becomes law in the British Parliament. British bills are categorized as either public or private. Public bills are almost always government sponsored and affect the entire nation. Private members' bills are introduced by individual members and have a personal or local application only. A private bill, distinguished from a private member's bill, usually deals with minor questions, but on rare occasions involves controversial issues that a party does not wish to sponsor.

discrepancies or ambiguities. The government usually accepts only technical amendments at this stage.[24]

Congressional committees in the United States and some legislative committees in continental Europe have much broader policy authority than do committees of the House of Commons, which do not have the power to table a proposal or substantially amend bills. The principles of accommodation and negotiation undergird British politics, although this varies according to the personality of the prime minister. Margaret Thatcher was the most senior chief executive among Western political leaders and is the longest-serving British prime minister in this century. Friends and foes agree that she was a forceful and assertive leader. One result is less accommodation and compromise as compared to most of her predecessors. In authoritarian systems with a weak or nonexistent committee system, legislators find they have negligible influence on policy formation.

Despite centuries of evolution that have strengthened Parliament, in recent years it appears the Mother of Parliaments is losing ground. One reason is the difficulty a typical backbencher M.P. has in functioning as a representative. For starters, there is not enough office space for each M.P. to have his or own office. A backbench M.P. receives less than $15,000 for all staff, including $3,000 for a researcher. The British civil service, as do many bureaucracies, has experience and resources, but this is combined with a strong tradition of secrecy and the sense of obligation to ministers but not to M.P.s. The average M.P. often is overwhelmed in terms of inadequate resources and information.

The sitting time for Parliament is from 2:30 P.M. frequently to as late as midnight, Monday through Thursday, and on Friday mornings. Some argue too many votes are taken late at night by exhausted members. Moreover, despite the emphasis on compromise in British politics, a strong prime minister can still get his or her way. Ultimately the M.P. must vote the party line, not his or her conscience. Hugh Dykes, a Conservative M.P., has called for changes to improve the declining circumstances of M.P.'s as well as to upgrade the legislative process:

> A lot of modern MPs are exhausted, underpaid, understaffed, and overworked. Parliament simply cannot cope with the executive branch any more. Paradoxically, the House of Commons, which likes to think of itself as the strongest chamber of its kind in the world, is in danger of becoming one of the weakest.[25]

The Japanese Diet

In Japan's bicameral Diet, the House of Representatives overshadows the House of Councillors. The July 1989 elections for the councillors that placed the LDP in a minority (111 seats out of 252) for the first time since 1955 may mean that the

---

[24]The first reading is a formality; only the title is read. The bill is printed subsequently and within three weeks, at the second reading, general policy is affirmed by a vote after the bill is debated by the government party and opposition.

[25]Quoted in David K. Willis, "Losing Ground?" *Today,* 6:1 (September 9, 1983), p. 11.

Banzai cheers in the Japanese House of Representatives: The House is dissolved before general elections.

House of Councillors will have more influence in the future. Institutional change can occur even in more stable systems such as Japan.

Legislative dynamics do not always follow an organizational diagram, and this is the case in the Japanese House of Representatives. Personalism is an important element in Japanese politics and reinforces the factional nature of party activity, especially the LDP.[26] Personalism stresses face-to-face relationships and supports a hierarchically ordered authority system. It is not surprising then that in Japanese legislative politics there is a high degree of personalism. Contemporary policy-making in the Diet has been labeled the rise of *zoku,* or tribal politics, where leaders protect their group interests against outsiders. Policy is divided and controlled by a handful of political bosses.

The most important legislative institution is outside the Diet. It is PARC, or the Policy Affairs Research Council of the LDP. This is the focal point where bureaucrats and interest groups make claims on and negotiate with appropriate LDP leaders. PARC's 17 subdivisions are organized to parallel the Diet's standing committees. Each PARC division is dominated by one or two leaders, and these persons are the definitive arbitrators of policy in their respective area. Any change in agricultural policy, for example, must receive the consent of Michio Watanabee and Koichi Kato, well-known defenders of agricultural interests who

---

[26]This section is based on Akira Nakamura, "Party Politics in Japan," *Brookings Review,* 6:2 (Spring 1988), pp. 33–34, and interviews one author had in Tokyo several years ago.

traditionally have favored subsidies for farmers and limits on the import of food-stuffs.

Tribal legislative politics means policy decision making is fragmented and often is slow (as when the United States constantly demands fairer Japanese trade practices). Decision making also is collegial in the sense that various faction or tribal leaders have predominant say in specified policy areas (agriculture, defense, transportation, industry, etc.) and do not generally interfere in one another's jurisdictions. This process means limited pluralism, which favors claims by business/producer interest groups and their bureaucratic supporters.

The Soviet Congress and Supreme Soviet

Since 1917 the Soviet system has operated on the premise that all government institutions are answerable to the Communist party, never the reverse. *Glasnost* and political reform initiated by party General Secretary Gorbachev, including the March 1989 elections to the Congress of People's Deputies (see Figure 8.8), raise the possibility that the party is unable to keep pace with and control the reforms. As the party's prestige plummets, the possibility of losing monopoly control increases.

The Congress of People's Deputies was designed to be an expressive institution, scheduled to meet only a few days each year. However, under the influence of Gorbachev's reform pressures, the Congress took on some of the characteristics of a real democratic legislature. The respected British weekly, *The Economist*, described the May 1989 meeting of the Congress as a "parliamentary free-for-all shown live on Soviet television."[27] There were many speeches made against the party, against specific government policies, and even criticism of Soviet troop behavior in Afghanistan. Individual party Politburo members were criticized by name, and deputies debated how to remove them from control of policy. One deputy urged that the Congress appoint the head of the KGB and review the KGB budget annually.

Congress is constitutionally now the highest political body in the land, but will this transition be halted, or will the now-ruling party Politburo become answerable to the Congress? Creating a Congress through which a stodgy bureaucracy and cautious, sometimes reactionary, party leaders will have to defend themselves publicly, the pervasive rule of status quo conservatives ultimately may be broken through the legislative process. Technically, the Soviet Union has features of both a presidential and a parliamentary system, although direction still comes from the top (President as well as General Secretary Gorbachev) down.

The Supreme Soviet is to have greater power than the former legislature, confusingly also called the Supreme Soviet. The new Supreme Soviet, or parliament, will meet twice annually, each session three to four months long. Its predecessor met for two six-day sessions per year, generally rubber-stamping Communist party decisions. The parliament will draft, amend, and pass legislation (under the

---

[27]"The Show Will Go On," *Economist* (June 3, 1989), p. 48.

President

The president is elected by secret ballot of the Congress and is supposedly accountable to it. He has broad authority to shape foreign and domestic policy, defense, and other major programs.

Council of Ministers

The council is selected by the president and headed by a prime minister. It is the cabinet.

Presidium of the Supreme Soviet

The presidium is the executive council and coordinating body. It is composed of a senior vice president, 15 vice presidents, one from each republic, and chairpersons of Supreme Soviet committees.

Supreme Soviet

The 542 members are chosen by the Congress each year from among Congress deputies. It is a bicameral legislature composed of a Council of the Union and a Council of Nationalities and has full legislative and administrative powers.

Congress of People's Deputies

This newly created government body elects the Supreme Soviet and the president. The 2,250 member, unicameral legislature is the highest state body. One-third of the members are elected from the 15 republics and local districts regardless of population, one-third from territorial constituencies according to population, and one-third from the Communist party and other official organizations.

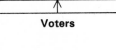

Voters

Figure 8.8 The Soviet legislative/executive system.

close scrutiny of Gorbachev and his supporters) as well as supervise selectively the implementation of government policies. The Supreme Soviet may also function to circumvent and warn bureaucratic opposition, prod party conservatives, and win popular support for reforms as long as General Secretary Gorbachev remains in control.

Initially, the Supreme Soviet, as well as the Congress, was televised. Viewing was so popular, however, that productivity reportedly declined 20 percent during broadcast hours, so live television coverage was discontinued. When debate became too challenging, it was reported that Mr. Gorbachev turned off the microphone. The Supreme Soviet met first in mid 1989, and its role clearly is being shaped and is evolving. Some party members believed the major issue was the role of the Communist party of the Soviet Union (CPSU) itself and believed that the CPSU as any other political-social organization should be subordinate to the constitution, the Congress, and the Supreme Soviet.[28] Premier Nikolai Ryzhkov, after seeing several of his nominees for key government posts rejected by the Supreme Soviet, wondered if the party was not in danger of losing its predominant influence over government institutions.

The gradual liberalization of Soviet society that began in the mid 1980s is most publicly being worked out in the legislative system including legislative elections. This is further facilitated by rapidly diminishing press censorship and the appearance of independent newspapers and journals. If political and economic reform is to take hold in the Soviet Union, possibly the best and most observable place to measure and judge events will be in the Soviet legislative system. Reforms that are orderly and institutionalized will pass through the Soviet legislature. Political regression toward old authoritarian ways, should it occur, would quickly be seen in the roles of Congress and parliament. At the least, any progressive transition will take five to ten years or even more.

INSTITUTIONAL BEHAVIOR AND RULES OF THE GAME

The formal structure of a legislature such as the committee system can be critical in the policy process. The rules of behavior discussed in this section are not written down, but they are understood generally within the institution itself and illustrate another key aspect of legislative policy-making.

Legislative role requirements shape a legislator's actions by virtue of membership in a specific institutional context. Role defines what should be done and what cannot be tolerated. Depending on the length of time the role has existed, the specific behavior patterns that have evolved, and the flexibility and adaptability that have developed during the evolution. A role can be specific down to the most minute behavioral and ceremonial detail, or it can simply define behavior limits in broad and general terms. Role requirements in modern legislatures tend toward broad guidelines, rather than specific details. In a modernizing, democratic context roles adapt and change and allow more variation in behavior patterns as compared to an authoritarian system, which requires highly structured behavior patterns covering nearly all aspects of behavior.

Legislators must relate to their colleagues in an acceptable way or they will not achieve maximum influence. Unwritten rules, customs, rules of the game, or

---

[28]See the ''Inside View of the Soviet Congress,'' by People's Deputy Yuri Vaslov in *Christian Science Monitor* (June 26, 1989), p. 18.

folkways may tolerate several behavior patterns, but the institutional setting determines the limits of appropriate behavior. Our case example is from the United States.

A perceptive analysis of legislative role behavior was done by Donald R. Matthews in his study of U.S. senators in the 1950s.[29] Senate norms at that time discouraged verbosity in an institution that seldom formally limits debate. Specialization and expertise were encouraged and a senator was discouraged from publicly debating each issue of the moment. Tolerance, mutual respect, and friendship guided personal relations. Senators were encouraged to be "compromisers and bargainers" and to use their powers in a restrained and careful manner.

The most generally accepted rule was apprenticeship. For two years, and even more, first-term senators were discouraged from speaking frequently, if at all, on the Senate floor. Respect for senior members bordering on deference makes a senator acceptable to many of his or her colleagues. As one new senator explained: " 'Keep on asking for advice, boy,' the committee chairman told me. 'That's the way to get ahead around here.' "[30]

Courtesy fosters the civility that 100 important people must have if they are daily expected to function as a decision-making body on controversial issues—issues that often are the center of intense popular feelings. Conflicts inevitably exist, but debate usually is restrained by the underlying courtesy rule. A colleague's motives are never questioned, nor are other states criticized. Less personal address formalizes debate and reduces personal emphasis; for example, Senator X is not referred to by name on the Senate floor, but as the "Senator from State Y." Customs, however, are never absolutely binding. Over the nearly 200-year history of Congress, there have been more than occasional outbursts of temper and even physical assaults.

By the 1970s, the Senate folkways were changing. Specialization remained important, but now first-term senators vigorously establish their expertise, such as William Bradley (D, New Jersey) on taxes and Phillip Gramm (R, Texas) on the budget. Assertiveness is more common than apprenticeship and deference. One student of Congress ruefully concluded that the Senate, a quietly productive club that generally followed the rules of the game in the past, has dramatically changed.

> Within our lifetimes, I believe, we have witnessed a transformation of the Senate from an inward-looking, intensely parochial men's club to a publicity-seeking hothouse of policy initiation and senatorial promotion.[31]

Trading support on various issues or mutual logrolling remains prevalent, however. Senator Sam Ervin (D, North Carolina) described his relationship

---

[29]Donald R. Matthews, *U.S. Senators and Their World* (Chapel Hill, N.C.: The University of North Carolina Press, 1960), see especially Chapter 5. The information on senatorial rules of the game is drawn from this book.

[30]Ibid., p. 93.

[31]Nelson Polsby, *Congress and the Presidency*, 4th ed. (Englewood Cliffs, N.J.: Prentice-Hall, 1986), p. IX.

with Senator Milton Young (R, North Dakota) to a North Dakota audience in 1976.

> I got to know Milt Young very well. And I told Milt, "Milt, I would just like you to tell me how to vote about wheat and sugar beets and things like that, if you just help me out on tobacco and things like that."[32]

In the House of Representatives during the past 25 years we have witnessed the decline of party control, the individualizing of decisions and hence fragmentation of power, and the decline in deferential commitment to House mores. These all run contrary to House practices before the 1960s.

Changes occurred partly because of the expanding constituent service role of representatives. Constituent service case work contributed greatly to the fact that 98 percent of incumbent members of Congress seeking reelection in 1986 and 1988 were returned to the House of Representatives. Reelection requires

1. Constant service to individual constituents and nurturing a web of contacts throughout the congressional district.
2. Responsiveness to the most powerful interest groups in the district and state.
3. Ability to raise campaign funds to discourage opposition or be far ahead financially of any challenger.[33]

Most members of Congress have learned these requirements well.

The lessons for electoral survival and the importance of money to accomplish this goal have led to some improprieties and ethical pressures. One member of Congress pinpointed the pressures.

> Elected officials are the only human beings in the world who are supposed to take large sums of money on a regular basis, from absolute strangers, without it having any effect on our behavior.[34]

A study of congressional behavior concluded, "more time is spent [by members of Congress] raising money than legislating."[35]

Unwritten rules, by their very nature, do not specify penalties; but diminished status in the institution may be one result. Rules of the game socialize new members into the institution, but as we have seen continue to change, even in an institution as old as the U.S. Congress.

---

[32]Quoted in Ripley, *Congress: Process and Policy*, p. 116.

[33]Further discussion of these points is found in Jewell and Patterson, *The Legislative Process in the United States*, p. 272. For a readable case study of a new congressman who learned these lessons quickly and adjusted his behavior accordingly, see Fred Barnes, "The Unbearable Lightness of Being a Congressman," *New Republic* (February 15, 1988), pp. 18–22.

[34]Gene R. LaRocque, "Get Congress Off the Defense Gravy Train," *Christian Science Monitor* (February 28, 1989), p. 16.

[35]Norman Ornstein, resident fellow at the American Enterprise Institute, quoted in *Christian Science Monitor* (March 6, 1990), p. 6.

SUMMARY

The diminished role or status of legislatures remains a debated question. Clearly, during the last few decades in even pluralist systems, the executive and the courts have initiated policy and engaged in rule making.

Complex crises also seem to work against the importance of the legislative process. Extended consideration, negotiation, and compromise, which characterize democratic legislatures, sometimes suggest a sluggish response to issues that require quick decisions. Those who stress the necessity of clear-cut and speedy decision making because they honor rationality, efficiency, and an immediate response as supreme virtues, or who identify themselves as strict majoritarians, find the legislative process cumbersome and sometimes in violation of the general interest.

Nevertheless, legislatures are the single institution that can give public voice to the widest range of claims and groups in the rule-making process. Democratic legislatures provide the maximum breadth of representation in society and are also regularly accountable through elections. No other institution has this type of representativeness or accountability. In authoritarian systems that are becoming more pluralistic, it is often in the legislature that the pluralism first appears and is nurtured mostly effectively. Participation in the rule-making process is only one of several valuable functions performed by legislatures. Others include overseeing executive actions, providing a public educational forum, and legitimating government actions. Rule executing, discussed in the next chapter, is an executive administrative function, but the executive branch also performs several other functions.

RECOMMENDED READINGS

Blondel, J. *Comparative Legislatures.* Englewood Cliffs, N.J.: Prentice-Hall, 1973. Legislatures for too brief a period in the late 1960s and 1970s attracted the attention of political scientists. As a focus of political change, legislature may once again attract the attention deserved. This short work is an excellent starting point for future studies.

Goehlert, Robert U., and Fenton S. Martin. *Congress and Law-Making: Researching the Legislative Process,* 2nd ed. Santa Barbara, Calif.: ABC-CLIO, 1989. This is a basic introduction on sources of information on the U.S. Congress and how to use these sources. It includes tables, figures, and a subject index.

Inter-Parliamentary Union. *Parliaments of the World: A Comparative Reference Compendium,* 2 vols, 2nd ed. New York: Facts on File Publications, 1986. These volumes provide in one location basic data on most legislatures in the world. This is a good reference for comparative purposes as well as securing information on a specific legislature.

Loewenberg, Gerhard, and Samuel C. Patterson. *Comparing Legislatures.* Boston: Little, Brown, 1979. The authors provide broad-ranging reviews of legislatures with case examples from Germany, Kenya, Great Britain, and the United States. Emphasis is on history, organizations, and functions. Numerous tables and figures as well as an extended bibliography are provided.

Loewenberg, Gerhard, Samuel C. Patterson, and Malcolm E. Jewell, eds. *Handbook of Legislative Research.* Cambridge, Mass.: Harvard University Press, 1985. Leading figures in comparative legislative systems have contributed substantial essays. This is a useful inventory of topics including the Third World, history, and functions.

Norton, Philip, ed. *Parliament in the 1980s.* New York: Basil Blackwell Ltd., 1985. These excellent essays discuss changes in both the House of Commons and the House of Lords. Backbencher independence, constituency pressures, and the Select Committees are considered as well as the growing professionalism of the House of Lords.

Polsby, Nelson W. *Congress and the Presidency,* 4th ed. Englewood Cliffs, N.J.: Prentice-Hall, 1986. Polsby provides a well-written introduction to Congress. The major organizational characteristics are described effectively as well as policy-making and interaction with the presidency.

Radice, Lisanne, Elizabeth Vallance, and Virginia Willis. *Member of Parliament: The Job of a Backbencher.* New York: St. Martin's Press, 1988. The authors have written a nontechnical, sympathetic, and largely jargon-free description of the work of British backbenchers. It makes extensive use of a 1983 questionnaire and numerous interviews with M.P.s.

Sager, Samuel. *The Parliamentary System of Israel.* Syracuse, N.Y.: Syracuse University Press, 1985. The author served in staff positions in the Knesset for 20 years. This key institution in the Israeli political system is studied from organizational and functional viewpoints. It is a useful prototype for subsequent institutional studies in other countries.

Wheare, K.C. *Legislatures,* 2nd ed. New York: Oxford University Press, 1967. This classic introduction to the role and importance of democratic legislatures provides a balanced discussion of the decline of legislatures.

Chapter 9

Executive Leadership and Administrative Organization

When we think of our country's government, the first person that comes usually to our mind is the president, the highest public official in the United States. He presides over the **executive branch,** which provides the overall leadership in and for the country. A large part of the executive is made up by the bureaucracy that is responsible for implementing the policies of the national government throughout the country. Including the military, some 4 million people are employed in the executive branch of the U.S. government. In this chapter we shall discuss the nature, role, and types of the executive branch in contemporary political systems, starting with its early development.

THE EVOLUTION OF THE MODERN EXECUTIVE

All political units (villages, towns, cities, states, and countries) have had and have some form of central leadership in the form of one person or a small group of people. This central leadership has become known as the executive. Prior to the establishment of viable legislative and judicial institutions, the executive constituted virtually the entire government, and even in recent decades its role often has gone substantially beyond that of simply executing policy. Throughout most of history, executive leadership has been in the form of hereditary kingship, with such brief exceptions as Athenian democracy in ancient Greece and the governments of the Roman Republic. Feudal kings ruled in Europe from the Dark Ages until the Reformation. Modern nation-states developed in Western Europe during the sixteenth and seventeenth centuries, and these were ruled by absolute monarchs. Today, Saudi Arabia is one of the few remaining societies subject to this type of rule.

England was the first country to move toward a constitutional monarchy when Parliament in 1689 placed specific constitutional limitations on the crown, a step that became known as the "Glorious Revolution." The next important development occurred again in England when in the early eighteenth century Sir Robert Walpole established himself as the first prime minister, thereby giving rise to the dual executive consisting of a **chief of state** (the ruling king or queen) and a **chief executive** (the prime minister). The founders of the United States provided for a president, that is, a nonhereditary "king," as chief of state and chief executive, thus establishing the system of a single nonhereditary executive.

In the nineteenth century in some countries the role of the strong king was taken over by strong prime ministers, such as Metternich in Austria, Bismarck in Prussia and, after 1871, in the German Empire.

During the first few decades of the twentieth century, some Western legislatures gained enough power to challenge effectively their executive counterparts. In the United States, for example, in early 1920 Congress defeated President Wilson's quest for U.S. membership in the League of Nations. In 1937 Congress defeated President Roosevelt's "Court-packing" proposal, a plan designed to shift the Supreme Court's viewpoint. More specifically, President Roosevelt had introduced legislation that would permit him to appoint additional Supreme Court justices equal in number to those incumbents who had reached the age of 70. The president hoped that this new Court would rule more favorably on the items of his New Deal legislation. A short-lived ascendancy of parliamentary power can be noticed in continental Western Europe during the 1920s, too.

A number of strong leaders came to office during World War II and the subsequent decade. Is it a historical accident that Churchill became British prime minister after Dunkirk or that de Gaulle took over the leadership of the Free French forces after Pétain's surrender in 1940? Tito emerged as the leader of the Yugoslav partisans during his country's occupation. After World War II, De Gasperi became prime minister of Italy and Adenauer became chancellor of the new Federal Republic of Germany. Did Gandhi and Mao Zedong rise to leadership by sheer chance? According to Max Lerner,

> Often the great leaders have arisen after great catastrophes, to meet the crisis of spirit that follows. . . . The qualities of greatness must be there in the man before he can rise to his stature. But the demands of the occasion and the need and receptiveness of the people are what bring the qualities out.[1]

The steady growth in the real role and power of the chief executive has continued worldwide. Reasons for this development can be found in the growing complexity of economic issues and the political and military crises throughout the world. The tremendous technological advances of recent decades, especially in the areas of armaments, communications, and transportation, have produced a setting that often requires quick and knowledgeable governmental decisions. Many of these need to come from the executive because it is the central collection and evaluation source of important information. It can act much more speedily than legislative bodies, which are by nature deliberative.

The Watergate incident of 1972 and the Iran-Contra scandal, however, clearly illustrate the growth of distrust of executive leaders. Although this noticeable lack of trust may have arisen first in the United States in conjunction with our military involvement in Southeast Asia and with Watergate, it has spread to other nation-states, too. It seems that the people of these countries have become rather ambivalent toward their executive leadership. On the one hand, they distrust strong leadership. On the other hand, however, they do look to the president (or prime minister, premier, or chancellor) to come forth with speedy answers to the problems that confront their societies.

The political executives of today have many different titles, and their range of duties differ from country to country. In most parliamentary systems the chief of state serves as a symbolic ruler, having very little political power, and the actual decision-making process is directed by the chief executive, who may carry the title of prime minister (in English-speaking countries), premier (in French-speaking countries), or chancellor (in German-speaking countries).

An important point to note is that the political structure of a given society has considerable bearing on the scope of power a chief executive may wield. For

---

[1]Max Lerner, "Where Is Strong Leadership in the World Now That We Need It Most?" the *Providence Journal* (January 1, 1975).

Four eminent West European statesmen who were most influential in shaping the post–World War II setting of their countries: Winston Churchill (United Kingdom), Alcide De Gasperi (Italy), Konrad Adenauer (West Germany), and Charles de Gaulle (France).

example, presidents and prime ministers in the countries of the postindustrialized Atlantic community are subject to substantially more restrictions than many of the leaders in developing countries.

A PROFILE OF EXECUTIVE LEADERS

James MacGregor Burns, in his seminal work, *Leadership*, defines the concept as follows:

> Leadership is the reciprocal process of mobilizing, by persons with certain motives and values, various economic, political, and other resources, in a context of competition and conflict, in order to realize goals independently or mutually held by both leaders and followers.[2]

Similarly, William A. Walsh speaks of leadership as "the ability to mobilize human resources in pursuit of specific goals."[3]

Who are the people who, as chief executives of their countries, provide this leadership? They are people who possess, as Robert A. Dahl points out, considerable resources in the form of charisma, desire for power, influence, motivation, skill, and wealth.[4]

In terms of their socioeconomic background, most of the leaders of democratic countries have come from middle- or upper-class families. The "log cabin" heritage has been the exception to the rule. British prime ministers have been usually graduates of Cambridge or Oxford University. We do find a difference, however, when we look at the Communist countries. Lenin came from an upper middle-class family and graduated from law school before becoming a professional revolutionary. Stalin, the son of a cobbler, attended a theological seminary. Khrushchev, in contrast, was an illiterate coal miner during his late teens. He received all his formal education under party auspices. Several other European Communist leaders have made their way from blue-collar ranks to the top leadership office in their respective countries.

Leaders of the developing countries in Africa, Asia, and Latin America have come from a variety of socioeconomic backgrounds. One group, the remaining hereditary monarchs, such as in Jordan, Morocco, and Saudi Arabia, have come from affluent families. A second group, encompassing a number of the presidents and prime ministers of non-Communist African and Asian countries, has come from the upper middle or upper class of the respective society. An example of this would be Indira Gandhi, prime minister of India. A third group of leaders in the developing part of the world is made up of people who have worked their way up from a very lowly socioeconomic childhood setting to the top leadership of their

---

[2]James MacGregor Burns, *Leadership* (New York: Harper & Row, 1978), p. 425.

[3]William A. Walsh, *Leaders and Elites* (New York: Holt, Rinehart and Winston, 1979), p. 18.

[4]See Robert A. Dahl, *Modern Political Analysis*, 4th ed. (Englewood Cliffs, N.J.: Prentice-Hall, 1984), pp. 103–111.

countries. This applies to some of the sub-Saharan African leaders. For example, Jomo Kenyatta, the first president of Kenya, was born and raised in a tribesman's family. He received his early formal education in a Christian missionary school—a feature common among a number of black African leaders.

Among the leaders of Communist-ruled developing societies one can discern some difference in terms of background, too. For example, Ho Chi Minh, the first president of Vietnam, came from a middle-class family. His father was a civil servant. Mao Zedong, the long-time leader of Chinese communism, was the son of a peasant of moderate wealth. Fidel Castro was born to illiterate Spanish immigrant laborers on a Cuban sugar plantation. He received his formal education at Catholic primary and secondary schools and obtained a law degree from the University of Havana. These examples show that the socioeconomic background of Third World leaders is far more diverse than that of the politicians of postindustrial societies.

Looking at the leaders' professional training, we find that a considerable number of them, especially in the developing countries, have come from the military. This group includes President Mobutu of Zaire, Colonel Qaddafi of Libya, and a number of others. In the United States, we may recall, some military officers ascended to the presidency—Washington, Grant, and Eisenhower, for example. Many of the top leaders in the advanced countries are professional politicians. British prime ministers usually have spent between 15 and 25 years in the House of Commons before gaining the office of chief executive. All chancellors of the Federal Republic of Germany (Adenauer, Erhard, Kiesinger, Brandt, Schmidt, and Kohl) have been full-time politicians before becoming chief executives. All the top political leaders in the Communist countries were full-time party officials and/or administrators in their earlier career years. A few top political leaders in the advanced countries have had extensive training in business before moving into politics and ultimately gaining the top office. One example in this category would be Georges Pompidou, second President of the Fifth French Republic.

In terms of their effectiveness, rulers have differed widely. Political historians in this country have ranked American presidents, according to their performance, as "great presidents" (George Washington, Thomas Jefferson, Andrew Jackson, Abraham Lincoln, Theodore Roosevelt, Woodrow Wilson, and Franklin D. Roosevelt); near-great presidents (Harry Truman); average presidents (Dwight D. Eisenhower); and weak presidents (James Polk and Warren G. Harding). A good comparison of leadership stature among British prime ministers would be the contrast between the soft-spoken Neville Chamberlain, who let himself be "hoodwinked" by Hitler at the Munich Conference (1938), and his successor, Winston Churchill, who led Britain successfully through World War II. Churchill undoubtedly would be ranked as one of Britain's great prime ministers. In recent French political history, the charismatic and strong performance of President Charles de Gaulle differs starkly from the weak leadership rendered by his predecessors of the Fourth Republic.

In a broader sense, history depicts many different kinds of rulers. Some have exercised strong leadership, others have been weak, and many others have been moderate in their role as leaders. The reigns of some have been more beneficial to the masses than the reigns of others. Some rulers have been outright cruel to their subjects, indicating clear mental deficiencies. Hitler and Stalin fall into this category of "sick personalities." The world would have been much better off without them. It is imperative that in this age of nuclear weaponry "sick personalities" be kept from obtaining high political or military office.

In summary, we find that the top political executives throughout the world have certain attributes and traits, and it is on the basis of these attributes and traits that these leaders have arrived at the top positions. But we should note that not all leaders exhibit the same traits, and that each particular crisis calls for leaders with traits appealing to the people facing that situation.[5]

The study of leadership is one of the more recent areas of academic inquiry. Much needs still to be learned about the factors and variables that are responsible for elevating a person to a leadership position.

MAJOR VARIETIES OF EXECUTIVE GOVERNMENT

The two major kinds of the executive are the presidential and the parliamentary forms. The only exception to these two major forms are the military regimes, such as presently found in Libya and Ethiopia. As we shall see, the parliamentary and presidential executives exist in many different varieties. Any executive branch, as well as the other parts of the government, will reflect the political culture and heritage of a society, including its democratic, authoritarian, or totalitarian tradition. Let us examine the presidential and parliamentary types of the executive and the functions each performs.

The Presidential Executive

Some 50 countries have presidential executives. Among them are the United States, most Latin American countries, and some in Africa and Asia. A basic characteristic of the presidential type of executive is that the offices of chief of state and chief executive are held by the same person. A president serves as the ceremonial and symbolic leader of a nation-state, but also has to attend to the day-by-day issues of governmental business. Thus, he or she often will become involved in party politics, unlike the chief of state in a parliamentary system.

In some ways the president is the modern counterpart to the king of ancient days: the central point of power in a society. How does a president arrive at this highest political position a country has to offer? Some are popularly elected for a specific term of office, such as the president of the United States.In countries where democratic elections are less established or less meaningful, presidential hopefuls often obtain the presidency through a coup d'état and stay in the office until they are overthrown. This practice is still widespread in Latin America and the developing countries of Africa and Asia.

---

[5]For a discussion and comparison of the "traits theory" and the "situationist theory" of leadership see Robert S. Lorch, *Public Administration* (St. Paul, Minn.: West Publishing Co., 1978), p. 203ff.

"The Small Society" by Brickman. © Washington Star Syndicate, permission granted by King Features Syndicate.

Presidents in democratic societies are subject to greater limitations and restraints than their counterparts in more authoritarian countries in Latin America, Africa, and Asia. The president of the United States, for example, may make treaties only with the advice and consent of the U.S. Senate. Although the president may nominate candidates for high federal positions in the executive and judiciary, the final appointment of these persons, again, requires Senate approval. Moreover, public opinion and the mass media have become important watchdogs of the actions of U.S. executives. Most presidents of developing countries face substantially less internal restraint.

Presidential Functions   The functions and powers of a president perhaps can be explained best by examining the responsibilities of the president in the United States. The presidential system in this country has served as a model for many other nation-states.

1. President Bush serves as *chief of state,* a symbolic and ceremonial function. In this capacity he is expected to exhibit and symbolize the glory, greatness, and values of the United States. He will receive and entertain leading officials from other countries and award medals and other tokens of recognition. The citizenry expects him to be above reproach in his manners and personal life. It is this expectation that, among other things, Mr. Nixon violated during the episode that became known as the "Watergate crisis."

2. The president is the *chief executive* of the country. He carries final decision-making power and ultimate responsibility. President Truman had the famous "THE BUCK STOPS HERE" sign on his desk. President Kennedy went on nationwide television to take full responsibility for the abortive Bay of Pigs invasion in 1961. The president provides leadership for the cabinet and directs the bureaucracy. Finally, he needs to maintain open channels of communication with the people and inform them of major steps taken by the government. Franklin D. Roosevelt used his radio broadcast "fireside chats" for this purpose; more recent presidents have addressed the people via television during prime-time hours.

3. President Bush serves as the *chief legislator* of the country. He will keep pressure on Congress to have it perform according to the charge contained in his State of the Union address. He must cajole and persuade congressional leaders and other influential people to do the things he believes need to be done in the interest of the country. As President Truman put it:

> I sit here all day trying to persuade people to do the things they ought to have sense enough to do without my persuading them. . . . That's all the powers of the President amount to.[6]

The point is that the assertion of presidential leadership in legislative matters is very important; however, the president must lead in a positive and constructive fashion so as not to annoy those whose action and support he seeks. Since legislative assemblies are still in a formative stage in many of the developing countries, their presidents have considerably more leeway in dictating terms than does a president of the United States.

4. The president is the *commander in chief* of the country's armed forces. The philosophy underlying this role is that of civilian control of the military. Presidential command of the armed forces, coupled with congressional fiscal control of military expenses, was intended by the founders of the United States to forestall military coups d'état. However, not all countries that have a presidential executive also provide for civilian control of the military. In Africa, Asia, and Latin America, presidents often have been brought to power by the military and they may wish or are forced to retain the military as their main arm of support, thereby creating "a state within the state."

5. The president serves as the *chief diplomat* of the country. The U.S. Constitution stipulates presidential leadership in foreign relations by stating that the president "shall have the power, by and with the Advice and Consent of the Senate, to make Treaties, provided two-thirds of the Senators present concur," and "he shall nominate, and by and with the Advice and Consent of the Senate, shall appoint Ambassadors." The president can bypass the consent of the Senate provision by concluding an **executive agreement,** instead of a treaty, with the leader of another country. A famous example of this is the agreement concluded between President Roosevelt and Prime Minister Churchill in 1940, whereby the British received 50 outmoded American destroyers in return for leases on British territories along the east coast of the American continent, for the purpose of constructing air bases on some of these islands. An increasing number of executive agreements have been concluded since World War II. Some U.S. presidents have been more active in the making and execution of foreign policy than others. Some have delegated most of the duties in this area to the secretary of state, as, for example, President Eisenhower did with John Foster Dulles. The increasing use of summit meetings since World War II has enhanced further the role of the U.S. president and other chief executives in foreign relations.

These five are the major constitutional duties a president of the United States performs. Since 1789, his roles have expanded to include three others, as follows.

6. With the rise of political parties in this country, the president has become the *leader of his party.* In this capacity President Bush is expected to play an active

---

[6]Quoted in Richard E. Neustadt, *Presidential Power: The Politics of Leadership from FDR to Carter* (New York: John Wiley, 1980), p. 9.

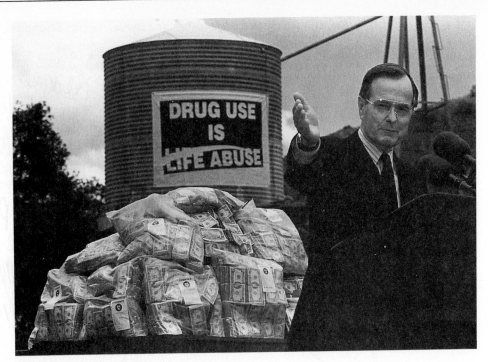

President Bush, in a speech in San Juan Capistrano, California, urges movie stars to join his crusade against narcotics. Four million dollars of seized drug money are displayed behind him.

role in directing the overall affairs of the party and to speak at party gatherings. The president's role as party leader is a difficult one. As president of the United States he is the spokesperson of all people in this country, but on partisan issues his role as leader of his party may limit his capacity to perform his spokesperson role in full. According to Louis W. Koenig:

> The President's uneasy party role is aggravated by the continual tension between his responsibilities to his office and the claims of his party. The office, and therefore its duties and problems, presumably exceed any obligation the party can impose. The President is a politician who must also be a statesman. Yet the party often insistently violates this assumption.[7]

7. Starting with the Great Depression of the late 1920s and early 1930s, the president of this country has played an increasing role in economic affairs as *manager of prosperity*. Examples of this function are found in the New Deal programs of President Roosevelt; in President Truman's efforts to convert the country's economy from a wartime setting to a peacetime economy in the late 1940s; in the policies developed by Presidents Ford and Carter to deal with the

---

[7]Louis W. Koenig, *The Chief Executive*, 5th ed. (New York: Harcourt Brace Jovanovich, 1986), p. 117.

President Bush at a fundraiser for Rudolph Giuliani, the 1989 Republican candidate for mayor of New York City.

energy problem; and the efforts of President Reagan to reduce high rates of inflation and unemployment. The importance that people assign today to presidential leadership in the economic realm can be seen readily in opinion polls judging presidential performance. Increases in the price of gasoline, a rise in the rate of inflation and/or unemployment will automatically trigger a decline in presidential popularity as shown by the polls.

8. A final role performed uniquely by the president of the United States, one that is mentioned rarely and perhaps conceived of less by the people of this country than by people abroad, is that he serves informally as the *leader of the democracies.* This role was placed on the shoulders of the president of the United States in 1945, when this country emerged from World War II as the most powerful nation-state. Certainly there have been changes in the power relationships of countries since 1945, but even today the president of the United States is looked upon by people and governments of many countries to provide the foremost leadership in dealing

Prime Minister Begin, President Carter, and President Sadat at the press conference following the signing of the peace treaty between Egypt and Israel in March 1979 on the White House lawn in Washington.

with the crucial issues of our time. U.S. citizens are often made aware of this expectation during their travels abroad. It is not an easy leadership function, but it is one that neither our president nor the people of this country can abrogate.[8]

The roles performed by chief executives in other countries with presidential systems are more limited. There exist, of course, a number of variations. In some of the developing countries, for example, the single dominant political party has been created by the incumbent president, and his or her role as party leader still is integrated more closely with his or her larger role as chief executive than would be the case in the United States. An example of this has been the relationship between former President Nyerere, the TANU movement, and Tanzanian socialism in Tanzania. The more autocratic a society, the more all-embracing the real powers of a president will be. Post–World War II examples of extreme dictatorial presidential rule are the cases of François ("Papa Doc") Duvalier of Haiti and Idi Amin of Uganda.

---

[8]For a more detailed discussion of the functions of the U.S. president see Koenig, ibid.; Neustadt, *Presidential Power;* and Thomas E. Cronin, *The State of the Presidency,* 2nd ed. (Glenview, Ill.: Scott, Foresman/Little, Brown, 1980).

The Parliamentary Executive

The parliamentary system, characterized by its fusion of power of the executive and legislative branches, has one person holding the office of chief of state and another that of chief executive. The former may be a hereditary ruler (as, for example, in Belgium, Morocco, Thailand, and the United Kingdom) or an elected president (such as in Austria, France, Italy, Israel, and Germany). The latter is usually the leader of the country's majority party or of a coalition government and may carry the title of prime minister, premier, or chancellor. The power of the chief of state has declined considerably in most countries during the past century. A leading exception is France. The writers of the Constitution of the Fifth Republic (adopted in 1958) shifted sizable powers from the office of the premier to that of the president.

With a few exceptions, the chief of state performs primarily symbolic and ceremonial functions. He or she personifies the nation-state and, by taking care of the official ceremonial functions, relieves the chief executive of many time-consuming duties. The political influence wielded by the British queen or president of Germany, to cite two examples, depends to a large extent on the political circumstances as well as the ability, intelligence, personality, and wisdom of the incumbent; however, the presence of the office adds stability to the parliamentary system. Many of the chiefs of state in the democracies have made it a point to stand above domestic politics. Queen Elizabeth has no clear association with any of the political parties in Britain, neither do the monarchs of the Benelux or Scandinavian countries. President Heuss, the first president of the Federal Republic of Germany, resigned his membership in the Free Democratic party when he was elected to his office in 1949. He thought that party membership was incompatible with holding the office of president. Even Charles de Gaulle, after becoming president in 1958, declined to partake in the party work and leadership of the "Gaullists," a political movement he had helped to establish in 1947. He felt that his office required him to stand "above" the squabbles of French party politics.

The prime minister (premier or chancellor), as found in the democratic countries, directs governmental affairs on a day-by-day basis. He or she is usually a person of considerable political experience, having served for a number of years as party official, legislator, and as a minister in a previous administration.

How are prime ministers chosen? In Britain, the prime minister is selected by the sovereign after a national election has taken place. In practice, however, there is little choice in this selection. If, as usually happens in British elections, one political party has obtained a majority in the House of Commons, the leader of the victorious party will be asked by the sovereign to take over the office of prime minister and to form a new government. The British model applies, with some variations, to most of the other parliamentary democracies, too. A major exception is France, which has a hybrid presidential-parliamentary system. Here the premier is appointed directly by the president of France.

The prime minister's duties differ somewhat from those of the president of the United States, who makes ultimate decisions and carries final responsibility. We

Margaret Thatcher, former British prime minister.

would like to explain the functions of a prime minister by using its prototype, the British example.

The Prime Minister's Functions   The main statutory responsibilities of the British prime minister are as follows:

1. The prime minister serves as the *chief executive* of the country. He or she recommends (to the monarch) the appointment and dismissal of all ministers. The prime minister directs the day-to-day work of the government. He or she presides over the cabinet, the inner policy-making and policy-directing body of the government. The prime minister of yesteryear used to be labeled a *primus inter pares* ("first among equals") within the cabinet. Major decisions were made collectively by that body, with the prime minister serving as the chair of the meetings. However, most students of British politics maintain that the contemporary prime minister is substantially more powerful than the Latin phrase indicates. According to Humphry Berkeley,

> The Prime Minister is not, and has not been for a long time, primus inter pares. . . . If the Cabinet discusses anything it is the Prime Minister who decides what the collective view of the Cabinet is. A Minister's job is to save the Prime Minister all the work he can. But no Minister could make a really important move without consulting the Prime Minister, and if the Prime Minister wants to take a certain step the Cabinet Minister would either have to agree, to argue it out in Cabinet, or resign.[9]

Despite the growth of the prime minister's power, the ultimate responsibility for major governmental decisions rests with the whole cabinet, rather than with the prime minister alone.

2. The prime minister is the *chief legislator.* He or she provides leadership in the House of Commons. The prime minister is the chief government spokesperson and leader of the majority party in the House. With the exception of the budget debate, during which the opposition is statutorily in control, the prime minister directs all business in the House of Commons.

3. The prime minister is the *leader of his or her political party.* He or she directs the overall affairs of the party, plans strategy, and chooses the date of an election. When either one of the two major political parties in Britain chooses a new party leader, it, in fact, chooses potentially a future prime minister.

4. The prime minister serves as the *link between the government and the sovereign.* The prime minister informs the monarch weekly of the proceedings in the cabinet and in Parliament, as well as on major national and international developments. Queen Elizabeth is kept, by tradition, informed about major governmental decisions.

5. The prime minister functions as the *chief diplomat.* The only exception to this is in France, where the president performs this role. International relations in the nuclear age often call for speedy decisions, which must be made by the person at the helm of the government. Further, a good deal of diplomacy since the end of World War II has been conducted in summit meetings. The prime minister serves as the country's leading representative at these important meetings.

6. Finally, the prime minister serves as the country's *manager of prosperity.* Recent British prime ministers have taken a special interest and have played an active part in treasury and budget policy-making. The state of the economy has great bearing on the popularity or unpopularity of the prime minister and his or her government.[10]

---

[9]Humphry Berkeley, *The Power of the Prime Minister* (London: George Allen & Unwin, 1968), pp. 23–24.

[10]For a more detailed examination of the duties and powers of the British prime minister see Berkeley, *Power of the Prime Minister,* and Anthony King, *The British Prime Minister,* 2nd ed. (London, Macmillan, 1985).

The Presidential and Parliamentary Executives Compared

A brief comparison of the real powers of the U.S. president and those of the British prime minister shows a mixed bag of similarities and dissimilarities. Both have extensive powers of **patronage,** although major appointments in the United States are subject to Senate confirmation. Both are leaders of their party, but the British prime minister is in a stronger position vis-à-vis the party than the president in the United States. The president serves a fixed term of office, while the prime minister's tenure is not constitutionally set but depends on retention of majority support in the House of Commons. More generally speaking, the president of the United States has substantially broader constitutional powers than does the British prime minister. Lastly, because the president is chief of state as well as chief executive, his or her office portrays the incumbent as a person of greater prestige than the British prime minister.

The power relationship between the president and the chancellor in Germany is in many ways similar to that of the British monarch and prime minister. The president performs largely ceremonial functions and the chancellor serves as the political leader of the country. Similar statements can be made about the relationship between the chief of state and the chief executive in most other democracies having a parliamentary system, with the exception of France because of its strong president and the appointed (rather than elected) prime minister in the Fifth Republic.

Advantages and Disadvantages of the Parliamentary and the Presidential Executives   The parliamentary system, in order to function satisfactorily, requires a well-developed and well-functioning political party system—a level of political sophistication found presently only in the democracies.

The fusion of executive and legislative powers under the parliamentary system provides for a much closer and smoother working relationship between these two branches of government than does the prevailing practice under the presidential system. In turn, one of the advantages of the presidential form lies in the fixed term of office of the incumbent. The prime minister, in order to stay in office, must retain majority support in the lower chamber of the legislature. Does either system provide for better executive leadership? The answer, we think, depends very much on the circumstances. One could argue that the presidential stature and prestige of Lincoln, Wilson, and Roosevelt increased their eminence as wartime leaders. To achieve a similar effect, Churchill, when appointed prime minister in the early days of World War II, broadened the coalition government established by his predecessor Chamberlain, to include all parties represented in the British Parliament. This move created a base of united support for him at home, made him a kind of "super prime minister," and put him on a more equal footing with the president of the United States.

In turn, however, the Watergate dilemma showed that the president and the office of the presidency can suffer inordinate loss of popular respect if the incumbent involves her- or himself—or gets drawn into—the kind of nefarious activities that Mr. Nixon did. The parliamentary system offers a better setting for handling crises of this nature. If a prime minister loses his or her credibility, he or she can resign or be forced to resign. When a prime minister resigns, the presence of the chief of state lends continuing stability to the system, a kind of stability that was not present in the United States during the later phases of the Watergate crisis.

Let us cite an example to illustrate this theory. The Federal Republic of Germany experienced a major crisis in May 1974 that involved the rather popular Chancellor Willy Brandt. Intelligence sources had discovered that a member of the chancellor's immediate staff, Guenther Guillaume, was a spy in the pay of the Communist German Democratic Republic. Mr. Brandt reacted quickly and resigned from his office. With speedy help from the president, a new chancellor was elected within ten days, and the transition was very smooth. The office of chancellor suffered little loss of prestige because of the crisis. The important point is that the presence of a chief of state provided some stability to the West German government during the crucial days because the executive was not completely void of leadership. It must be added, however, that Mr. Brandt's quick resignation—in contrast to Mr. Nixon's drawn-out struggle—also helped to keep the problem within manageable limits.

Both systems, the presidential and the parliamentary executive, may be perverted. Hitler and Mussolini rose from parliamentary settings, while many of today's semideveloped and developing countries are ruled by autocratic or dictatorial presidents.

A last item that deserves mention has to do with the workload of the incumbents. Observers of the presidency of the United States have found that, especially in more recent years, the president's obligation to perform both ceremonial and executive functions places an ever-increasing burden on the shoulders of the incumbent. In this setting political analysts have raised the question of whether the duties of the presidency have become too large to be performed by one person. The split responsibilities of the British dual executive certainly reduce the performance demands a prime minister must face in that country, possibly contributing to better executive performance.

PUBLIC ADMINISTRATION AND NATIONAL BUREAUCRACIES

Modern governments provide a large number of services and regulate a variety of activities. Many of these either did not exist in decades past or were left to the individual or the free market economy. Furthermore, rapid advancements in technology call for more and more expert knowledge at governmental levels. The implementation of public policy is handled by the bureaucracy, a part of the executive branch of government that goes back to antiquity, but has taken on in recent years an increasingly significant role in the governing process of many countries.

The terms "administration" and "bureaucracy" as well as "administrator" and "bureaucrat" are used interchangeably. We shall do likewise. People speak of the national bureaucracy when referring to the administrative part of our federal government. The classic description of bureaucracies, one that still is accepted widely today, comes from the German social scientist Max Weber. He defined bureaucracies as

> Organizations with a pyramidal structure of authority, which utilize the enforcement of universal and impersonal rules to maintain that structure of authority, and which emphasize the non-discretionary aspects of administration.[11]

Obviously, some public agencies are more loosely organized than others, and Weber's definition may apply more directly to some than to others. He developed an intellectual framework of bureaucracies which, in his opinion, contained the major elements common to all of them. Because of the importance that contemporary scholars in public administration assign to this model, we would like to present its major points. According to Weber, a genuine bureaucratic structure includes the following elements:

> Each member of the staff occupies an office with a specific delineation of powers and a sharp segregation of the sphere of office from his private affairs. Remuneration is . . . in the form of a fixed salary. . . . The different offices are organized in terms of a stringent hierarchy of higher and lower levels of authority in such a way that each lower level is subject to control and supervision by the one immediately above it. This control and supervision above all includes the power of appointment, promotion, demotion, and dismissal over the incumbents of lower offices. Fitness for an office is typically determined by technical competence, which in turn may be tested by such rational procedures as examination and very generally involves a long period of formalized training as a condition of eligibility.[12]

This type of bureaucracy, according to Weber, is the most efficient device for large-scale administration in the modern era. With the Weberian formula in mind, let us examine present-day public administration. Before turning to a discussion of its scope and the actors, one important question must be asked: Can public administration be carried on in a politically neutral setting, or do bureaucrats become involved in policy-making and in politics? A famous political scientist and president of the United States, Woodrow Wilson, stated in 1887: "Administration lies outside the sphere of politics . . . it is a part of political life only as machinery is part of the manufactured product."[13] Today Woodrow Wilson's account is looked upon as wishful thinking. It is widely recognized these days that public administrators are involved in policy-making and are drawn into political struggles. According to B. Guy Peters:

> Administration and policy, instead of being discrete phenomena, are actually interrelated. In both an objective and a subjective manner the nature of the administrative system can influence the policy outputs of the political system. Administration does

---

[11]Quoted in B. Guy Peters, *The Politics of Bureaucracy*, 2nd ed. (New York: Longman, 1984), p. 3.

[12]Max Weber, *The Theory of Social and Economic Organization*, introduction by Talcott Parsons, ed., A. M. Henderson and Talcott Parsons, trans. (New York: Free Press, 1947), p. 58. See also pp. 333–334.

[13]Quoted in William L. Morrow, *Public Administration: Politics and the Political System* (New York: Random House, 1975), p. 4.

make policy, although these policies are not always written and promulgated in the same manner as the rules made by the legislatures and executives.[14]

Bureaucrats become involved in policy-making in at least two areas: (1) in the budgetary process the administrator's input will help to build the foundation for future policy outputs and (2) most statutes, as promulgated by legislatures, are general prescriptions and often need to be interpreted by administrators before they can be applied to specific situations; this interpretation may add new substance to a law and thus constitute a kind of policy-making. In turn, members of the bureaucracy may initiate new legislation by way of reporting difficulties they have encountered in the process of implementing existing laws. A number of complaints regarding a particular rule will lead legislators to enact improved legislation.

National bureaucracies in all countries have a tendency to grow in size and complexity. They range from a few hundred national employees in the smallest countries to a number of millions in the largest countries. The People's Republic of China and the Soviet Union have by far the largest and most complex national bureaucracies.

The Scope of Public Administration

Public administration takes place at all levels of government—international, national, state, and local. Our discussion will focus primarily on the national aspects of public administration.

A good deal of the public administration process is carried out by the executive departments or ministries; however, the growing need for specialization in recent decades has led, in many countries, to the creation of regulatory boards, commissions, and other agencies. These bodies have the authority to issue rules within their sphere of jurisdiction, to supervise the implementation of these rules, and to settle disputes originating from the implementation of the rules. Examples of U.S. regulatory agencies as shown on Table 9.1, are the Federal Trade Commission, the Interstate Commerce Commission, and the National Labor Relations Board. British governmental agencies include the British Broadcasting Corporation, the London Passenger Transport Board, and the corporate boards in charge of the nationalized parts of British industry. The Soviet Union has a large number of state committees overseeing areas as diverse as cinematography and the utilization of atomic energy.

Public administration covers a wide range of activities in all societies. It ranges from the delivery of mail to the negotiation of a treaty and includes the many governmental activities in areas such as conservation, health, public works, and welfare. In every country administrative agencies are deeply involved in the preparation of the national budget, but more so in the developed countries than in the developing societies. In Britain, for example, about 80 percent of the national budget is prepared by members of the civil service.[15] However, there are stark

---

[14]Peters, *The Politics of Bureaucracy*, p. 12.

[15]See Hugh Heclo and Aaron Wildavsky, *The Private Government of Public Money: Community and Policy in British Political Administration* (Berkeley, Calif.: University of California Press, 1974).

Table 9.1   **NATIONAL ADMINISTRATIVE AGENCIES IN THE UNITED STATES AND THE SOVIET UNION: A COMPARISON**

United States

Executive departments

Agriculture

Commerce

Defense

Education

Energy

Health and Human Services

Housing and Urban Development

Interior

Justice

Labor

State

Transportation

Treasury

Veterans Affairs

Regulatory agencies, governmental corporations, commissions, and independent agencies

American Battle Monuments Commission

Board for International Broadcasting

Central Intelligence Agency

Commission of Fine Arts

Commodity Futures Trading Commission

Consumer Product Safety Commission

Environmental Protection Agency

Equal Employment Opportunity Commission

Export-Import Bank of the United States

Farm Credit Administration

Federal Communications Commission

Federal Deposit Insurance Corporation

Federal Election Commission

Federal Emergency Management Agency

Federal Home Loan Bank Board

Federal Labor Relations Authority

Federal Maritime Commission

Federal Mine Safety and Health Commission

Federal Reserve System

Federal Trade Commission

General Services Administration

International Development Cooperation Agency

Interstate Commerce Commission

National Aeronautics and Space Administration

National Capital Planning Commission

National Credit Union Administration

National Foundation of the Arts and the Humanities

National Labor Relations Board

National Science Foundation

National Transportation Safety Board

Nuclear Regulatory Commission

Occupational Safety and Health Review Commission

Office of Personnel Management

Overseas Private Investment Corporation

Panama Canal Commission

Peace Corps

Postal Rate Commission

Railroad Retirement Board

Securities and Exchange Commission

Selective Service System

Small Business Administration

Tennessee Valley Authority

U.S. Arms Control and Disarmament Agency

U.S. Commission on Civil Rights

U.S. Information Agency

U.S. International Trade Commission

U.S. Postal Service

Table 9.1 (*Continued*)

Soviet Union

All-Union Ministries

Automotive Industry
Aviation Industry
Chemical Industry
Chemical and Petroleum Machine
  Building
Civil Aviation
Communications Equipment Industry
Construction in the Far East and
  Trans-Baikal Region
Construction of Petroleum and Gas
  Industry Enterprises
Defense
Defense Industry
Electrical Equipment Industry
Electronics Industry
Foreign Trade
Gas Industry
General Machine Building
Heavy and Transport Engineering
Instrument-Making, Automation
  Equipment, and Control Systems

Machine Building
Machine Building for Animal Husbandry
  and Fodder Production
Machine Building for Construction, Road
  Building for Construction, Road
  Building, and Municipal Services
Machine Building for the Light and Food
  Industries and Household Appliances
Machine Tool and Instrument-Making
  Industry
Medical and Microbiological Industry
Medium Machine Building
Merchant Marine
Petroleum Industry
Power Machine Building
Radio Industry
Railways
Shipbuilding Industry
Tractor and Agricultural Machinery
  Industry
Transport Construction

Union-Republic Ministries

Coal Industry
Communications
Construction
Construction of Heavy Industry
  Enterprises
Construction Materials
  Industry
Culture
Education
Ferrous Metallurgy
Finance
Fish Industry
Foreign Affairs
Geology
Grain Products
Health
Higher and Secondary Specialized

Education
Industrial Construction
Installation and Special Construction
  Work
Internal Affairs
Justice
Land Reclamation and Water
  Resources
Light Industry
Mineral Fertilizer Production
Nonferrous Metallurgy
Petroleum-Refining and Petrochemical
  Industry
Power and Electrification
Timber, Pulp, and Paper and Wood
  Processing Industry
Trade

Table 9.1 *(Continued)*

State committees

Agroindustrial	Material Reserves
Cinematography	Material and Technical Supply
Civil Construction and Architecture	Physical Culture and Sports
Computer Technology and Information Science	Planning
	Prices
Construction Affairs	Publishing Houses, Printing Plants, and Book Trade
Foreign Economic Relations	
Foreign Tourism	Safety in the Atomic Industry
Forestry	Standards
Hydrometeorology and Environmental Control	State Security
	Supply of Petroleum Products
Industrial Safety and Supervision of Mines	Television and Radio Broadcasting
	Utilization of Atomic Energy
Inventions and Discoveries	Vocational and Technical Education
Labor and Social Affairs	

Other agencies

Administration of Affairs	Central Statistical Administration
Administrative Board of the USSR State Bank	People's Control Committee
	State Board of Arbitration
Bureau for Machine Building	

Note: All-Union Ministries are in complete charge of their sphere of administration throughout the Soviet Union. Union-Republic Ministries, in contrast, have a central ministry in Moscow and corresponding ministries in the republics.

Sources: U.S. Senate, *Organization of Federal Executive Departments and Agencies* (January, 1990), and Philip G. Roeder, *Soviet Political Dynamics: Development of the First Leninist Polity* (New York: Harper & Row, 1988), p. 189.

differences in the scope of these activities between the democracies that have a mixed-market economy and the Communist societies, as well as those developing countries that have a command economy, nearly all the aspects of which are controlled by the government.

The governments of democratic societies exercise only a limited amount of control over their economies, with most of it being in private hands. Thus, their public sector is considerably smaller than that of command economy countries. Among some 20 democracies, the United States has the smallest public sector, because all the other democracies, in addition to the public administration activities in the United States, have nationalized health systems, and their governments exercise control over airlines, railroads, radio and television systems, some aspects of banking, and selected industries. In the category of democratic countries, Finland has the largest public sector, with state-owned industries accounting for approximately 10 percent of that country's gross national product, followed by France, Britain, Sweden, and Norway, who are in the 7 to 9 percent range.

Public administration in the command industry countries covers a much larger sector, because their governments control practically the whole sector of the economy.[16] For example, the government of the Soviet Union, as stated cogently by D. Richard Little, has managed, prior to the reforms initiated in the early 1990s,

> every factory and farm in the country, every restaurant, gasoline station, and barbershop, every newspaper and magazine, every sports team, youth organization, social club, and vacation resort. Virtually every citizen is employed by the state, shops in state-owned stores, and is born, married, and buried in state-owned facilities.[17]

To make the difference in the administrative scope of command economy countries and those with a mixed-market economy still more visible, Table 9.1 lists the national administrative agencies of the United States and those of the Soviet Union as they stood in October 1990. (Efforts by Mikhail Gorbachev to decentralize his country's economy may result in many of the Soviet agencies becoming obsolete.)

What we may find in years to come is that, assuming that Mr. Gorbachev succeeds in implementing parts of his idea of *perestroika,* the public sector in the Soviet Union will slowly decline, while it will continue to grow in the United States and some other democracies because here people look increasingly to the national government for help of one kind or another, especially in the areas of health and social welfare.

Public Administration Personnel

Members of the bureaucracy fall into one of the following three categories: (1) political appointees, (2) civil servants, and (3) non–civil service career officials. The personnel in the first group is appointed to office by political officials for one of many reasons, ranging from particular qualifications to nepotism.

The civil service, initiated in the United States with the passage of the Pendleton Act in 1883, is the successor to the patronage or *spoils system,* an arrangement that too often gave rise to "bossism" and corruption. Civil servants are recruited through a system of open competition organized by the Civil Service Commission of a given country. The basic concept of the civil service system is that people employed under its auspices are politically neutral and will carry out faithfully the policy instructions of their superiors, disregarding which democratic party is in office. Civil service jobs are tenured in contrast to those of political appointees, who come and go with a particular government.

Non–civil service career officials, mainly faithful party members in the one-party countries, staff the bureaucracy in those polities that do not have a standard-

---

[16]The command economy system is not exactly the same in all Communist countries. In the People's Republic of China the post–Mao Zedong government has leased land to the farmers, but farmers are required to sell a certain amount of their produce to the state.

[17]D. Richard Little, *Governing the Soviet Union* (New York: Longman, 1989), p. 129.

ized civil service system, such as the Communist societies and some of the developing countries.

In order to have an effective administrative process, the chief executives of democratic societies need to select and place in the upper range of the bureaucracy a number of political appointees. Their job is to exercise control over the civil servants in the respective departments. How many political appointees are required for this process? Their respective number differs from country to country. The United States, as compared with the parliamentary democracies, has a very large number of political appointees in the White House staff, the 14 executive departments, and the regulatory agencies. In this country, some 4,500 political appointees oversee approximately 2.8 million civil servants, who are either under the General Schedule (GS) system, which ranges from grade GS 1 to grade GS 18, or are members of the Crafts, Protective, and Custodial (CPC) system, which encompasses all the blue-collar jobs. Because of the large number of political appointees in the United States, each change in administration produces a substantial amount of turnover in the upper administrative echelon.

This situation is in sharp contrast to the staffing of the British bureaucracy, where political appointments do not number more than 150. Thus, the British civil service reaches much higher in the top-level administration than its counterpart in the United States. The highest-ranking British civil servant, the permanent secretary, would equal an assistant secretary (a political appointee) in the United States. Founded in the 1780s, the British civil service is the oldest in the Western world, and it has served as a model for the civil services in a number of the other democracies as well as some of the developing countries.

The smallest number of political appointees is found in Germany numbering not more than 70. These are the ministers and one or two officials in each ministry, analogous to that of an undersecretary in the United States or parliamentary secretary in Britain.

In contrast to Britain and Germany, where the political appointees come from the House of Commons or the Bundestag respectively, political appointees in the United States come from more diverse sources, such as business, law, and the universities. Most of them stay with the federal government only a short time, an average of not more than two years. In most instances they have little prior knowledge of the specifics of the agency they are to administer. They are people who have been successful in their career and are selected largely because they agree with the policy preferences of the incumbent president.

Which administration, the one with a small number of political appointees or the one with a large number, provides for more effective government? There are advantages and disadvantages in both types of systems. In terms of advantages, one finds that the high-reaching civil service, as exemplified by Britain and Germany, provides for a strong continuum in governing, whereas the United States example provides for a greater inflow of new ideas. Among the disadvantages, it could be argued, is that high-ranking civil servants can at times become "an administration within an administration," as was the case with the administrative class in Britain prior to the implementation of the recommendations of the Fulton Committee. In turn, an administration with a large number of political appointees can suffer from administrative instability if the turnover rate is too large. Also, the higher the civil service reaches into the upper echelon of the administration, the more high-ranking civil servants will become involved in the policy-making process.

The concept of an effective civil service system is associated customarily with democratic societies. How democratic are the leading civil service systems in terms of recruitment and advancement? A study of the administrations of the major democracies will show that, in terms of the given criteria, the civil service systems of most European democracies and that of Japan are substantially more elitist than that of the United States. In our country at least half of the officials who are now members of the Senior Executive Service (GS 16–18) started their career at the GS 5–7 level after graduating from one of the more than 2,000 colleges and universities in the United States. No group of colleges or universities has a monopoly in graduating the future high-ranking civil servants.

In contrast, substantially more elitism prevails in Europe and in Japan. In Britain, despite the various efforts to implement the major thrust of the Fulton Committee recommendations to democratize the British civil service,[18] nearly all of the highest-ranking civil servants (especially the permanent secretaries) are still people who graduated with honors from Cambridge or Oxford. France has a four-tier civil service system, and inside promotion is rather rare. The top jobs are held by the graduates of the Ecole Nationale d'Administration, perhaps the finest civil service–type college in the world. As in France, there are four categories in Germany with little movement in between, and the members of the highest category *(Höherer Dienst)* come from the elite universities. In the case of Japan, the civil service elite consist largely, but not exclusively, of graduates of Tokyo University, who have done well on the highly competitive examination for entering the senior level. Similar examples could be cited from other democracies. Although in recent years some efforts have been made to democratize the recruitment and advancement procedures and possibilities in some of these countries, their systems are still substantially more elitist than that of the United States.[19]

Our previous analysis has focused largely on the administration in the democratic societies, thus we would like to add some discussion of the bureaucracy of the Soviet Union and that of the developing countries.

Administration in the Soviet Union

The Soviet bureaucracy differs substantially from its counterparts in the democratic societies. The scope and responsibility of the Soviet administration is still

---

[18]The Fulton Committee was appointed in 1966 to examine the effectiveness of the British civil service. Its final report included a number of recommendations aimed toward modernizing the country's civil service. The most important of these called for the abolition of the strict quadripartite division (the administrative, executive, senior clerical, and clerical categories, each with its own entrance route) and suggested a single hierarchical structure, similar to that of the civil service in the United States.

[19]An excellent source comparing the bureaucracies of democratic societies is Donald C. Rowat, ed., *Public Administration in Developed Democracies: A Comparative Study* (New York: Marcel Dekker, 1988).

vast as of 1990. It directs and supervises nearly all areas of societal endeavors: the traditional areas of public responsibility such as foreign affairs, defense, finance, and justice, as well as agriculture, civil aviation, communication, culture, education, all industries, public health, and transportation.

The head of the Soviet executive and administration is the president, holding an office that has been endowed with vast powers by the Congress of People's Deputies in March 1990. Under the president's supervision the Council of Ministers directs the administrative structure and the implementation of policies. In its present composition the Council of Ministers consists of the chair (prime minister), one first vice chair, 12 vice chairs (the above 14 form the presidium and serve as a kind of cabinet), and approximately 90 other members, including ministers of functional departments, chairs of state committees, and the 15 chairs of the Republic Councils of Ministers. The components of the Council of Ministers have been subject to frequent change. All members of the Council of Ministers are appointed by the Supreme Soviet (the national legislature).

The primary function of the Council of Ministers is to supervise the huge administrative apparatus (see Table 9.1) and to implement all the party decisions that pertain to the vast area of executive/administrative jurisdiction in the Soviet Union, including the allocation of resources in the economic realm, the overall direction of economic and social affairs, and the execution of defense and foreign policies.

The Soviet bureaucracy employs a large number of people at the national, state, and local levels. Estimates of their number range from 15 to 25 million. There is no Western-type civil service in the Soviet Union; however, most bureaucratic officials are career people. These employees can be classified loosely into three categories:

1. Party officials whose job it is to see that party policies are properly administered in the administrative realm.
2. Administrators who put into practice the government program (as distinguished from party policies).
3. Specialists, such as architects, artists, biologists, chemists, dentists, educators, physicians, physicists, and so forth.

Recruitment to positions in the bureaucracy and promotion within the ranks has been supervised by the party and is based on capability, performance, and political loyalty.

Perhaps the greatest shortcoming in the Soviet bureaucracy is that its complexity—resulting from its size and duplications caused by the existence of concurrent party and government agencies in nearly all areas of administrative endeavors—has given rise to an inordinate amount of red tape. Accounts in Soviet newspapers abound with complaints about the prevalent apathy and inefficiency in the bureaucracy. While the Soviet leadership, under the heading of *perestroika*, has tried to remedy the most flagrant abuses and shortcomings, it has made little headway in its attempts to make the bureaucracy more efficient. The monstrous size of the Soviet bureaucracy makes any kind of reform difficult. However, some changes may be in the making. In February and March of 1990 the Supreme Soviet passed two major bills that foreshadow the development of a limited private sector in the Soviet Union. The first of these bills permits agricultural workers to lease land from the state and farm it privately. This lease may even be extended to their children. A second bill, passed a few weeks later, gives citizens the right to establish and own small-scale factories and other businesses for the first time since the 1920s. At this time we do not know how many people will avail themselves of these new opportunities.

Administration in the Developing Countries

More than 100 countries are labeled by social scientists as "developing countries" or the "Third World."[20] These are the nation-states in Latin America, Africa, the Middle East, and Asia, excluding, of course, Japan. A number of these developing countries are still in the agrarian stage of development. With a few exceptions, the per capita income of the Third World countries is much lower than that of the developed societies found in Europe and North America, as well as those of Japan, Australia, and New Zealand.

Although most of the Latin American countries have been independent for a long time, nearly all the countries of Africa and Asia have become independent since the late 1940s. Many of the developing countries have established a Western-type bureaucracy, whereas some others have followed the Communist model.

Looking more specifically at the countries that became independent since World War II, we find that most of them had, at the time they became independent, fairly well-established administrative systems, but little in terms of other political institutions. A resulting problem has been described by Fred Riggs, one of the foremost scholars on the bureaucracies of the developing countries.

> A phenomenon of the utmost significance in transitional societies is the lack of balance between political policy-making institutions and bureaucratic policy-implementing structures. The relative weakness of political organs means that the political function tends to be appropriated, in considerable measure, by bureaucrats. Intrabureaucratic struggles become a primary form of politics. But when the political arena is shifted to bureaucracies—a shift marked by the growing power of military officers in conflict with civilian officials—the consequences are usually ominous for political stability, economic growth, administrative effectiveness, and democratic values.[21]

The major point made by Riggs is that in many of the countries that became independent during the past four decades the bureaucracies were far more developed than any other political institution and played, therefore, a leading role in the policy-making process, challenged only by the military.

The replacement of foreign (i.e., colonial) administrators, who had occupied

---

[20]Specialists divide the Third World into a Third, Fourth, and Fifth World, depending on the countries' per capita income. Using this categorization, Bangladesh, mentioned later, would be a Fifth World country and Singapore, also mentioned later, would be an advanced Third World country.

[21]Fred W. Riggs, "Bureaucracy," in Frank Tachau, ed., *The Developing Nations: What Path to Modernization?* (New York: Dodd, Mead, 1972), p. 115.

the high-level positions, with indigenous bureaucrats went ahead more rapidly in ex-British colonies than in ex-French colonies, because Francophone Africa had substantially fewer indigenous administrators at the time of independence than Anglophone Africa and Asia. Further, as stated so candidly by a Nigerian official,

> The decision was taken by our leaders that the British officials should be replaced, not because they hated or distrusted them, but because they felt that political independence was a sham unless you had also a great measure of administrative independence. You could not be politically independent and remain administratively dependent, over a long period of time, without misunderstanding and tensions arising between administrator and his indigenous political master.[22]

It is of interest to note that with the departure of the foreign administrators, the indigenous bureaucrats—in their demeanor, working patterns, and even in the organizations of their offices—mirrored in large part the characteristics of the former colonial administrators. Some of the Francophone African governments have retained French civilian advisors and military units until the 1980s. A good example is the Republic of Chad.

Generally speaking, the major current features of the bureaucracies in the developing countries are the following.

1. The administrative structure and its endeavors are imitative rather than indigenous, in that they are modeled, at least in part, after those of democratic or Communist (Soviet or Chinese) countries. As mentioned earlier, the imitation is especially close in the former British or French colonies.
2. The bureaucracies in most of the developing countries are short on highly trained administrators with the management skills and up-to-date technical competence necessary for rapid politicoeconomic development.
3. In most of the developing countries the bureaucracy has a large measure of operational autonomy, a system that dates back to colonial days. It has a near monopoly of technical expertise and benefits from the prestige accordingly. There is little in terms of legislatures and/or grass-root interest groups to act as watch dogs over the administration.
4. The absence of public control lends itself to a high degree of corruption, ranging from payments to low-rank officials to bribes of considerable dimension at the higher level. The corruption problem has been brought to our attention at various occasions by students from developing countries.[23]

Of course, these are broad generalizations. The nature of the bureaucracy differs from country to country. For example, a South Asian scholar describes the bureaucracy of Bangladesh (one of the most poverty-stricken countries in the world) with these words:

---

[22]S. O. Adebo, "Public Administration in Newly Independent Countries," in Burton A. Baker, ed., *Public Administration: A Key to Development* (Washington, D.C.: Graduate School, U.S. Department of Agriculture, 1964), p. 28. Quoted in Ferrel Heady, *Public Administration: A Comparative Perspective*, 3rd ed. (New York: Marcel Dekker, 1984).

[23]For a more detailed discussion of these points see Heady, *Public Administration: A Comparative Perspective*, pp. 281–285.

The bureaucratic machinery is top heavy, elitist, decadent, inefficient, and expensive. It can no longer justify its existence in its present form except on the selfish ground of self-preservation. . . . It is difficult to perceive any end to this bureaucratic rot and the consequent citizens' nightmare unless there is radical reform in the socio-political and economic spheres in the country.[24]

In stark contrast to this, another Asian scholar portrays the bureaucracy of Singapore (one of the most advanced developing countries) as remarkably effective in carrying out the country's developmental goals, in a manner that includes only a minimal amount of corruption: "The public bureaucracy plays an important and effective role in national development in Singapore."[25] Among other factors, the state of politicoeconomic development has a great deal of bearing on the kind of bureaucracy and bureaucratic effectiveness present in a developing country.

BUREAUCRACIES: SOME CONCLUDING COMMENTS

A primary constitutional function of the democratic executive is to implement policy. It does so with the help of an administrative organization that is responsible to the elected political leadership. How much of a bureaucracy is needed? Enough to do the required work well. How to find this proper equilibrium is a more difficult question. How often have people gotten angry when, after a snowstorm, it took the local public works department a day or more to plow their street? Yet there will be complaints when the town government proposes to raise taxes in order to buy more snow-removing equipment and enlarge the staff of the public works department.

The size of the public sector has a bearing on the size of the administration, but it is not the only determinant. A study published by the International Monetary Fund shows that, among the democracies, Sweden has the largest public sector employment (16.31 percent of the population) and Japan, the smallest (4.44 percent). The United States ranks in the middle with 8.07 percent, having a larger percentage of public employees than Italy and the Netherlands, both of which have larger public sectors than the United States.[26] Like each town or city, each state and each country must find an equilibrium that enables its government to perform the needed services without taxing its citizens unduly.

One other point should be mentioned. Various students of public administration have expressed concern that bureaucracies may deviate from their role of implementor (instrumental role) and may become the actual wielders of power in

---

[24]Mohammad Mohabbat Khan and Habib Mohammad Zafarullah, "Public Bureaucracy in Bangladesh," in Krishna K. Tummala, ed., *Administrative Systems Abroad*, rev. ed. (Lanham, Md.: University of America Press, 1982), p. 181.

[25]Jon S. T. Quah, "The Public Bureaucracy and National Development in Singapore," in Tummala, ed., *Administrative Systems Abroad*, p. 63.

[26]Peter S. Heller and A. A. Tait, *Government Employment and Pay: Some International Comparisons* (Washington, D.C.: International Monetary Fund, 1983), p. 41.

the polity.[27] To prevent this, as Max Weber cautioned a number of decades ago, the elected political leadership must exercise firm control over the administration.[28] There is little evidence, however, that the administrations at large have usurped their powers in post–World War II democracies. In some instances the bureaucracy has performed a stabilizing role in keeping the country going in the presence of governmental instability. This applies especially to Italy, which has just inaugurated its forty-ninth post–World War II government, and the government of France from 1946 to 1958.

What has happened, however, is that individuals or branches within the administration have at times exercised power far beyond their proper roles. J. Edgar Hoover, the first director of the Federal Bureau of Investigation, was a person who wielded enormous influence in the U.S. government. Further, questions have been raised at one time or another in a number of democracies about the proper role of their internal and external intelligence organizations. It is of some interest to note that similar questions are being raised these days in the rapidly changing political climate of some of the Communist societies. For example, in early July 1989 the newly elected Supreme Soviet questioned the director of the Committee for State Security (KGB) in a more critical and exhaustive fashion than most presidential nominees are quizzed by the respective U.S. Senate committees. Members of the Supreme Soviet made it very clear to the director of the KGB that from now on they would exercise close control of the KGB, something unheard of in Soviet history.

Finally, whatever our views of our local, state, and national administrations may be, we have to accept the fact that we cannot do without them. We need the services they render. However, further thoughts need to be given on how to make the bureaucracy more efficient, more cost-effective, and more accountable to the taxpayers while retaining flexibility and discretion to accomplish its objectives.

RECOMMENDED READINGS

Aberbach, Joel D., Robert D. Putman, and Bert A. Rockman. *Bureaucrats and Politicians in Western Democracies.* Cambridge, Mass.: Harvard University Press, 1981. A comparison of senior civil servants and politicians is made in terms of their similarities and differences in seven democracies.

Barber, James D. *The Presidential Character: Predicting Performance in the White House,* 3rd ed. Englewood Cliffs, N.J.: Prentice-Hall, 1985. The author presents a comprehensive evaluation of twentieth-century U.S. presidents with special emphasis on their personality traits.

Burns, James MacGregor. *Leadership.* New York: Harper & Row, 1978. This is an excellent study of leadership with focus on personality traits and the styles and types of leadership.

---

[27]An informative discussion of this issue is found in Heady, *Public Administration: A Comparative Perspective,* pp. 408–427.

[28]Weber, *The Theory of Social and Economic Organization,* p. 386ff.

Gorbachev, Mikhail. *Perestroika: New Thinking for Our Country and the World.* New York: Harper & Row, 1987. Gorbachev presents his plans for restructuring Soviet society politically, administratively, and economically.

Jenkins, Peter. *Mrs. Thatcher's Revolution: The Ending of a Socialist Era.* Cambridge, Mass.: Harvard University Press, 1988. Jenkins presents a detailed study of Mrs. Thatcher's leadership and the changes that her administration has produced.

King, Anthony. *The British Prime Minister,* 2nd ed. London: Macmillan, 1985. King provides the most comprehensive and up-to-date study of the office and the duties of the prime minister in Britain.

Koenig, Louis W. *The Chief Executive,* 5th ed. New York: Harcourt Brace Jovanovich, 1986. This is a prominent text dealing with the creation of the U.S. presidency, the selection process, and the duties of the incumbent.

Neustadt, Richard E. *Presidential Power: The Politics of Leadership from FDR to Carter.* New York: John Wiley, 1980. Neustadt's book is the classic study of presidential performance.

Nigro, Felix A., and Lloyd G. Nigro. *Modern Public Administration,* 7th ed. New York: Harper & Row, 1989. This is a leading text in public administration: comprehensive, readable, and up to date. It contains a number of interesting case studies.

Ola, R. O. *Public Administration in Nigeria.* London: Routledge Chapman & Hall, 1984. Ola provides an in-depth study of the structure, processes, and shortcomings of public administration in one of the leading developing countries.

Rosenbach, William E., and Robert L. Taylor, eds. *Contemporary Issues in Leadership,* 2nd ed. Boulder, Colo.: Westview Press, 1989. A good selection of articles focuses on effective leadership.

Rowat, Donald C., ed. *Public Administration in Developed Democracies: A Comparative Study.* New York: Marcel Dekker, 1988. This is an excellent comparative study of public administration in 20 democratic societies.

Chapter 10

The Judicial Process: Law and the Courts

LAW AND JUSTICE

The judicial branch constitutes the third governmental output agency. It entails law, judges, and courts. These forces play a role in all political systems. It is difficult to think of the state without law, because when people live in close proximity, they require rules and regulations to define their respective rights and obligations as members of society.

Law generally is regarded as one of the greatest achievements of civilization. Law properly should be concerned with basic rules of conduct that reflect to some degree the concept of **justice.** These rules concern the relationships of the individual with government and with other people. Justice is a common standard for judging the legal and moral relationships of people. It is often subjective, and many believe it has eternal and metaphysical validity. Impartiality, fairness, and equal treatment are terms often associated with justice in democratic political systems. Law in many political systems is, unfortunately, simply a tool of the state.

An ideal of justice frequently expressed is that government should be a government of laws and not of men. Whether this goal can be achieved is questionable, as laws are made and administered by men. In practice this ideal generally is interpreted to mean a legal system that treats everyone equally and is not subject to change through the arbitrary acts of a dictator, or even the whim of transient majorities.

There are many kinds of law, and no single definition of the term is possible, as scholars are not in agreement on the nature of law. The rules of law are based on custom or legislation and court decisions, but the language of the law is technical and not easily understood, and the proceedings through which the courts function are frequently complex.

Positive Law and Natural Law

Positive law is associated with the nineteenth-century English utilitarian philosopher, John Austin, who defined law as consisting of well-defined rules of human conduct, enforceable by appropriate sanctions of government.[1] Law, in this sense, is man-made and is essentially a relationship between ruler and ruled.

To many there is another type of law, one traditionally called **natural law,** more basic than man-made law and one based on fundamental principles of justice. A human law that conflits with natural law is void. The idea of natural law was developed first by the Greek and Roman Stoic philosophers. The Roman jurist Cicero (106–43 B.C.) defined the law of nature as "right reason" implanted in nature, which is the basis of measuring justice and injustice. This concept was adopted by the Christian church and incorporated into the philosophy of the great medieval thinker Thomas Aquinas. In more modern times it became part of the philosophy of John Locke, the seventeenth-century English philosopher who derived the idea of natural rights from the concept of natural law. When Thomas

---

[1] See John Austin, *Lectures on Jurisprudence,* vol. 1, 3rd ed. (London: J. Murray, 1869), pp. 182–183.

Jefferson spoke of "life, liberty, and the pursuit of happiness" in the Declaration of Independence, he was stating in new language Locke's ideas of natural rights.[2]

Civil and Criminal Law

Civil law, in its most widely used sense, is concerned with the relations between individuals and their legal rights. A typical civil suit would be for breach of contract, a divorce action, or tort action (an injury to one's person or property) such as a suit growing out of an automobile accident. Usually civil actions are between private individuals, but it is possible for the government to be party to a civil suit. For example, the U.S. government might sue a corporation for breach of contract.

All crimes are offenses against society, and the state as the representative of society charges the individual or corporation with a violation of law. A penalty for such violation usually is provided by statute. Crimes may be serious, such as murder or arson, or petty, such as violation of a traffic law. Punishment ranges from death or imprisonment to a fine.

Constitutional, Administrative, and Statutory Law

A constitution is the fundamental law of a country. It may be unwritten in the sense that it is not limited to a single document. The British constitution, for example, consists of historic documents such as the Magna Carta (Great Charter) of 1215, which the English barons forced King John to sign at Runnymede; acts of Parliament of extraordinary importance such as the Reform Act of 1832, which enfranchised much of the middle class; important judicial decisions; and custom and tradition. Even the United States with its written Constitution, has a supplementary "unwritten Constitution" growing out of judicial decisions, important acts of Congress and executive orders of the president, and custom and tradition. American political parties, for example, had their origin in custom and tradition and are not mentioned in the written Constitution.

Constitutional law consists of interpretations of a nation's constitution by the courts. In the United States, for example, the Supreme Court may decide the meaning of congressional power over interstate commerce or state power over abortion.

Somewhat similar to constitutional law is **administrative law,** which is concerned with the legal accountability of government officials in carrying out government policy as expressed in statutes. This branch of law also consists of the rules and regulations written by bureaucrats after Congress delegates this authority to them. In the United States, for example, Congress has delegated to administrators extensive rule-making authority. The federal courts may review the rules and regulations of the Federal Trade Commission concerning "unfair and deceptive"

---

[2]See George H. Sabine and Thomas L. Thorson, *A History of Political Theory,* 4th ed. (Hinsdale, Ill.: Dryden Press, 1973). Chapters 9, 14, and 27.

trade practices to determine whether the administrators have acted within the scope of the law.

Legislatures inevitably must state the rules embodied in statutes in general terms, for they cannot anticipate all the problems that will arise over specific provisions. Law created by acts of the legislature is **statutory law.** Related to this are court interpretations of statutes, which help determine the meaning of statutory law. An important standard the courts employ in this respect is *legislative intent.*

CIVIL LIBERTIES AND CIVIL RIGHTS

The courts frequently play a leading role in the preservation of **civil liberties.** The U.S. Supreme Court, under Chief Justice Warren (1953–1969), lent support to the "civil rights revolution" through its interpretation of the "equal protection" clause of the Fourteenth Amendment as a prohibition of segregation laws.

Often the terms "civil liberties" and "civil rights" are used interchangeably, but this is incorrect. Civil liberties are usually stated outright in a bill of rights or a constitution. Civil liberties provide the individual protection against unfair or arbitrary government actions. For example, the First Amendment of the Constitution, among other things, protects the individual's freedom of speech. Civil rights provide the individual protection against unfair or arbitrary actions by other individuals or groups. A law or statute that provides protection from racial or sexual discrimination in employment is an example of a civil right.

In general, the U.S. Supreme Court has furthered the cause of civil liberties by **nationalizing civil rights.** Since the 1920s, the Court has held that the First Amendment freedoms (speech, press, assembly, and religion) are incorporated into the "due process" clause of the Fourteenth Amendment, which restricts the states from abridging the rights of citizens. In recent years more and more of the **Bill of Rights** has been incorporated into the Fourteenth Amendment by judicial interpretation. Since the Bill of Rights restricts Congress, the result of the nationalizing of civil rights has been to make much of the Bill of Rights indirectly binding on the states through the Fourteenth Amendment. Today the result is that the Supreme Court not only protects the First Amendment freedoms from violation at the state level, but also extends the application of procedural rights, such as the right to counsel and protection against self-incrimination, to the state level. In *Escobedo v. Illinois* **(1964),** the Court held in a five-to-four vote that in criminal prosecutions the right to representation by counsel extended back to the time a suspect is subjected to questioning.[3] Two years later, in another five-to-four decision, the Court ruled in *Miranda v. Arizona* **(1966)** that in order for a conviction to stand—if obtained by evidence introduced at the trial as a result of *custodial interrogation*—it would be necessary to show that the suspect had been told he or she could remain silent, informed that any information volunteered

---

[3]378 U.S. 478 (1964).

could be used against him or her, told that he or she may have an attorney present during interrogation, informed that an attorney would be furnished if the suspect could not afford one, and, lastly, allowed to end police interrogation at any time.[4]

The purpose of these rules is to protect the prisoner against self-incrimination and preserve his or her right to counsel. Not only is the Supreme Court divided on the wisdom of extending procedural safeguards this far, but so is public opinion. Critics claim that the Court is discouraging the use of voluntary confessions and making the conviction of criminals difficult. Defenders of the Court point to the unquestioned fact that in the past the procedural rights of suspects frequently have been violated, especially on the state level. Probably an important factor dividing opinion on this issue is that the Court has acted at a time when the public is understandably concerned about the rising tide of crime in our cities.

In Great Britain the primary responsibility for the preservation of civil liberties rests upon alert public opinion. It is part of the "unwritten constitution" of that country that Parliament shall pass no law infringing upon the traditional civil liberties of the realm. Nevertheless, as we have seen, while the courts cannot hold an act of Parliament unconstitutional, judges in Great Britain do have the authority to restrain executive officials from depriving people of their rights. Any invasion of civil rights usually is raised in Parliament. Any British citizen who believes his or her rights have been violated usually can find a member of Parliament to cross-examine an appropriate member of the ministry to get all the facts. Evidence of a violation of basic rights may lead to extended debate in Parliament. Even without the power of judicial review, the courts are effective in protecting civil rights. They make certain that the executive branch, in carrying out its functions, adheres to the rules of procedure laid down by law. Through judicial interpretation, the courts also have construed seditious conspiracy narrowly. Although violence may not be used to change the constitution or the laws, any type of agitation that does not include violence may be used.[5]

The preservation of civil liberties is of particular importance in Germany today. The Nazi regime (1933–1945) not only destroyed the independence of the judiciary but also established special courts not bound by any law. Fortunately, the new German regime has shown an awareness of the importance of civil liberty. The constitution restored the principle that punishment must be inflicted only according to law after a fair trial. Furthermore, the establishment of extraordinary courts is forbidden and double jeopardy (more than one prosecution for the same offense) is prohibited. The Constitutional Court of Germany is authorized to hear all complaints by individuals against any violation of their constitutional rights. The Court's record is generally considered progressive.[6]

---

[4]384 U.S. 436 (1966).

[5]See Sydney D. Bailey, *British Parliamentary Democracy*, 2nd ed. (Cambridge, Mass.: Houghton Mifflin/The Riverside Press, 1966), pp. 97–100; and Gwendolyn M. Carter and John H. Herz, *Major Foreign Powers*, 5th ed. (New York: Harcourt, Brace & World, 1967), pp. 52–53.

[6]See Arnold V. Heidenheimer, *The Governments of Germany*, 3rd ed. (New York: Thomas Y. Crowell, 1971), Chapter 7, for a discussion of the constitutional court.

Before the mid 1980s and the onset of *glasnost* there were no civil liberties, in the Western sense, in the Soviet Union. Changes are now occurring slowly and the end results are yet to be determined. Although the constitution of 1977 contains a bill of rights, the emphasis is on social and economic rights, such as the right to work and the right to a free education, rather than freedom from interference by the government. The social and economic rights are merely declarations of intention, not enforceable by the courts. Until recently, even such political guarantees as freedom of association and the press are only for those who support the regime.

Neither procedural rights, such as **habeas corpus,** nor bail traditionally are allowed in the Soviet Union.[7] A Soviet citizen who is arrested can be detained in jail for nine months while the charges against him are investigated. He or she cannot have an attorney until the day before the trial.[8]

Many African constitutions provide for substantive civil liberties, such as freedoms of the press, speech, and religion. In these countries, however, there is less emphasis on procedural rights, such as right to counsel and jury trial. In Nigeria during what was known as the Action Group crisis of 1962, which grew out of a split in the leadership in the western region of that country, the governor removed the prime minister and a struggle developed over control of the office. The leader of the opposition party and others were charged with treason, felony, and conspiracy against the government. The defendants were not allowed to use counsel brought from England in their defense. When the late Tom Mboya was minister of justice in Kenya, he indicated jury trial was foreign to Africans. On issues of evidence, some African courts have ruled that they would make a presumption in favor of the government.[9]

What are the future trends likely to be? Professor L. C. B. Gower of Lagos University believes that it is likely that if African courts apply provisions of bills of rights frequently, civil rights will either be abolished completely, whittled away, or the bench will be packed with judges who will do the government's bidding.[10]

In the United States considerable progress has been made in advancing civil rights, especially through court decisions outlawing segregation and imposing the procedural guarantees of the Bill of Rights of the U.S. Constitution on state as well as federal courts. In Great Britain civil rights continue to be protected, despite the absence of judicial review. Communist nations reject the Western conception of civil rights. On the other hand, progress has occurred at least in a formal sense in Japan and many of the developing nations, which have included bills of rights in their new constitutions.

---

[7]In the United States, a person who claims to have been imprisoned unjustly may apply to a federal court for a writ of *habeas corpus.* If the court finds that the imprisonment is contrary to some provision of the Constitution or laws of the United States, the writ will be issued and the person released.

[8]Ellsworth Raymond, *The Soviet State* (New York: Macmillan, 1968), pp. 211–212 and 240.

[9]Dorothy Dodge, *African Politics in Perspective* (Toronto: D. Van Nostrand, 1968), pp. 138–140.

[10]L. C. B. Gower, *Independent Africa: The Challenge to the Legal Profession* (Cambridge, Mass.: Harvard University Press, 1967), pp. 82–83.

Civil liberties in the People's Republic of China (PRC) have been tolerated more when power has been decentralized such as 1986–1988. When factional struggles intensify, civil rights conditions worsen, as in 1989. There has been an ebb and flow in tolerance toward dissent. Deng Xiaoping, the dominant political figure in the PRC since 1978, has, however, intermittently condemned student and intellectual criticisms of the government and party for undermining the social order. On several occasions he has advocated that such dissent should be dealt with severely. Renewed repression was initiated again on June 3 and 4, 1989, when about 3,000 students, workers, and bystanders died as the People's Liberation Army brutally cleared student protestors from Tiananmen Square in Beijing. Since then, there have been numerous arrests and executions of government opponents.

The 1982 constitution grants citizens many civil liberties, but there have been few laws to protect these rights and even less implementation. For example, when traveling, Chinese citizens still must have a letter of introduction from their employing institution in order to secure hotel accommodations. If they stay with relatives, they must register with the local police. The government only permits one to move to another locality to accommodate an employment change, if the workplace agrees. Compared to the Mao Zedong political era (1949–1976), there are fewer political prisoners. The PRC contends it has no political prisoners today; it imprisons only criminals and "counterrevolutionaries."[11]

ANGLO-AMERICAN LAW

The Common Law and Equity

The basis for the legal system of Great Britain, the United States, and most of the English-speaking countries is the common law. The common law is judge-made law. Its roots go back to the twelfth century in England when the king sent itinerant justices throughout the realm to settle local disputes on the basis of general customs. Gradually a body of legal precedents was developed from the various decisions of the royal judges.

In hearing disputes, the judges consider previously decided cases. In determining the relevance of a previous decision, they reason by analogy to reach a decision. They determine whether an earlier case of a similar nature is sufficiently comparable to the case at hand to constitute a binding precedent. If so, it becomes the basis for deciding the case. This process of following earlier precedents is known as **stare decisis.** On the other hand, judges may distinguish the controversies before them from an earlier precedent. This is no simple, mechanical process, however, as no two cases are exactly alike and judges ordinarily have considerable latitude in reaching their decisions. Stare decisis leads to both stability and flexibil-

---

[11]The material on the PRC is drawn from Hungdah Chiu, "China's Changing Criminal Justice System," *Current History,* 87 (September 1988), pp. 265–272, and Ta-Ling Lee and John F. Copper, *Reform in Reverse: Human Rights in the People's Republic of China: 1986/1987* (Baltimore, Md.: Occasional Papers/Reprints Series in Contemporary Asian Studies, No. 6-1987, passim.

ity in the law. It also permits judges to modify old law to meet new social conditions. Regulations of public utilities, for example, grew out of old common-law doctrines regulating innkeepers.

The common law was carried to British colonies in various parts of the world. When many of these countries became independent, they continued to apply the common law. In the United States, the states generally apply the common law in varying degrees but, as in Great Britain, it has been modified considerably by statute. Common-law marriages, for example, are not usually recognized by statute.

Another source of Anglo-American law is **equity,** which developed because the early common-law courts did not always ensure justice. These courts, for example, usually allowed only monetary damages as a remedy in most civil cases. Litigants who could not get justice in the regular courts appealed to the chancellor, the king's legal adviser, who frequently provided relief on the basis of general principles of justice. Eventually, a complementary system of law was developed by a new court known as a Court of Chancery. The primary difference between the justice administered by the two systems of law was in the remedy. Under the common law a person whose property rights were threatened could take no action until the injury occurred, in which case he or she could sue for damages. However, Equity Courts could issue an injunction to prevent irreparable harm to property. An injunction prohibits a person or persons in general from committing acts that would result in injury to the property. For violations of an injunction, the judge may summarily punish by fine or even imprisonment in some instances. Injunctions frequently have been used in labor disputes. Another difference between common law and equity is that juries are not used in equity cases.

Equity, like the common law, was carried overseas into new English-speaking settlements, but in Britain and most of the American states today the same courts administer both common law and equity. The American federal courts have jurisdiction in all cases in law and equity involving the Constitution, laws, and treaties.

Judicial Review and Judicial Interpretation

Judicial review is the process by which courts determine whether the legislative and executive branches, especially the former, have exceeded their power. Judicial review is most likely to exist in a federal system such as the United States and in countries with written constitutions. In a federal system, with power divided between the central government and the member states, the courts are the logical branch of government to determine the power boundaries between the two levels of government.

Although judicial review exists in a number of countries, its scope is broadest in the United States. In countries where judicial review exists, the judiciary usually plays a more significant role in the governmental process than in countries where the courts do not exercise this power. In the United States both federal and state courts have held federal and state laws invalid under the federal Constitution. The U.S. Supreme Court has the last word on the constitutionality of a federal or state law. Judicial review is important not only because of its use, but also because of the threat of the judicial veto. Congress and the president, in making policy, always must consider the possible unconstitutionality of their acts.[12]

Judicial review is not granted specifically in the Constitution, but it has been exercised since 1803 with respect to acts of Congress.[13] Many more state laws have been held unconstitutional, however, than acts of Congress or the president. Since 1789, about 80 congressional laws have been held unconstitutional. The instances where executive acts have been held beyond the power of the president are relatively few. One of the more recent examples occurred in 1952, during the Korean War, when the Supreme Court held that President Truman did not have authority to seize the steel industry to avert a strike. In 1974, the Supreme Court in a unanimous decision, forced President Nixon to turn over the Watergate tapes to Congress.[14] Although originally the subject of controversy, judicial review is accepted today.

In 1803 the Supreme Court first ruled on the constitutionality of a federal law in ***Marbury v. Madison* (1803),** thus establishing the power of judicial review for federal courts. The right was established for the Supreme Court and lower federal courts to ultimately decide on the constitutionality of state and federal laws and executive acts if they were legally challenged.

After *Marbury v. Madison,* no act of Congress was held unconstitutional until 1857, more than 50 years later. It was in the period from about 1890 to 1937 that the Supreme Court acquired the reputation of being a "super legislature" by striking down many federal and state laws. Because the Supreme Court during this period generally reflected conservative economic and political values, many of the laws held unconstitutional were regulations of property rights. Following the "constitutional crisis" of 1937, provoked by President Franklin D. Roosevelt's unsuccessful attempt to enlarge the Supreme Court's membership to make the liberal minority of judges a majority, the Supreme Court generally has deferred to the judgment of Congress and the states with reference to laws regulating property rights. This shift in the Court's position is explainable in that two of the "middle-of-the-road" judges joined the liberal minority after 1937 to constitute a new majority and in the replacement of the conservative members of the Court following their retirement or death. Since the mid 1950s the Court has used judicial review actively to promote civil rights. This trend is discussed in the sections Civil Liberties and Civil Rights and The American Judicial Process.

Judicial review exists in some European countries, but in no country has it existed as long as in the United States, nor does the judiciary in these countries play a role comparable to the U.S. courts.

In France, under the Fifth Republic, the constitutional council is a body con-

---

[12]See Loren P. Beth, *Politics, the Constitution, and the Supreme Court* (Evanston, Ill.: Row Peterson, 1962), pp. 58–61, for a succinct discussion of judicial review.

[13]*Marbury v. Madison,* 1 Cranch 137 (1803). The opinions of the Supreme Court are now published by the U.S. government. Until 1875 the reports were cited according to the name of the reporter, in this instance Cranch. The first number refers to the volume and the second to the page.

[14]*Youngstown Sheet and Tube Co. v. Sawyer,* 343 U.S. 579 (1952).

sisting of all ex-presidents of France and nine other appointed individuals. The council, which is not part of the regular judicial system, may hold unconstitutional certain laws if they are referred to it by the president of the republic, the premier, or the presidents of both houses of the legislature. This is very limited judicial review, for no individual can challenge the constitutionality of a law. The weakness of the council is illustrated by its refusal to rule on President de Gaulle's referendum on direct election of the president of France in 1962, despite the fact that the French constitution did not authorize such action.[15]

Germany has a special constitutional court, which may decide the validity of any federal or land (state) law and which protects the fundamental rights of citizens. This court assumed a role of importance in the previous West German governmental system. Among its important decisions were two that declared both the Communist party and neo-Nazi party to be unconstitutional as organizations detrimental to a democratic state.[16]

The postwar Japanese constitution, as a result of the American occupation and influence, allows the review of all laws, ordinances, administrative regulations, and official acts of government. The final authority rests with the Japanese Supreme Court. In practice, however, the Japanese court has not exercised this power to any great extent. The Supreme Court has been charged with being too timid and hesitant to exercise judicial review, particularly because judicial review did not exist in pre-World War II Japan. The Court has been slightly more assertive in recent years. It ruled in 1976 that the apportionment of seats among the 130 House of Representatives' districts was unconstitutional, because it did not reflect the heavy urbanization of Japan after 1945. This indicates that the Supreme Court may gradually begin to act more forcefully in exercising judicial review. This certainly would be closer to the intent of the framers, many of whom were American, who drafted the present constitution during the Occupation.

Judicial review is also common in Latin America, due to the influence of Anglo-American law. Mexico has a unique form of judicial review in the form of the writ of *amparo,* which permits a citizen to apply to a federal court for redress if a law or act of a government official impairs any right guaranteed by the constitution of Mexico. This writ, however, is less than real judicial review, because the judges do not grant relief to each petitioner who files a complaint.[17]

Interpretation of statutes by the courts, as well as judicial review, is important in analyzing the role of the courts in making national policy. In the United States, the country where judicial review is most important, statutory interpretation and development of doctrines growing out of the common law substantially enhance the power of the courts. Many acts of Congress are complex and their meaning is not always clear. Ultimately, a federal statute means what the U.S. Supreme Court says it means.

---

[15]Henry J. Abraham, *The Judicial Process,* 5th ed. (New York: Oxford University Press, 1986), pp. 296–299.

[16]Ibid., pp. 311–312.

[17]See Alexander T. Edelmann, *Latin American Government,* rev. ed. (Homewood, Ill.: Dorsey Press, 1969), pp. 483–484.

For example, Congress in 1940 enacted the *Smith Act,* which made teaching and advocacy of the overthrow of the government by force a criminal offense. What is the meaning of this provision? It presumably would not prevent the teaching of the revolutionary doctrines of Marx and Lenin in a college class; but on the other hand, is there a distinction between abstract advocacy of violent overthrow of the government and incitement to violence now or as soon as practical? In **Yates v. U.S. (1957),** Justice Harlan, speaking for the U.S. Supreme Court, gave the Smith Act a narrow interpretation by holding that to convict under the act the government would have to prove advocacy of violent action now or in the future. Mere belief in the desirability of violent overthrow of the government as an abstract doctrine is not enough to convict.[18]

What is true of the United States also would be true in other countries where the courts play an important role in judicial interpretation.

The British Judicial System

The lord chancellor, chosen by the prime minister, is the head of the British judicial hierarchy. The lord chancellor presides over the House of Lords and advises on all judicial appointments. The legal section of the House of Lords consists of nine highly skilled and distinguished judicial experts, the Lords of Appeal in Ordinary, plus the lord chancellor. Together (often called the 9 plus 1) they are the final avenue of appeal for both civil and criminal matters in the British system. The British courts are known for the outstanding legal qualifications of their judges.

The legal profession in Great Britain is divided into two categories—*solicitors* and *barristers.* Solicitors are office lawyers who handle legal problems before the trial stage. Unlike barristers, solicitors are not required to have university training. They become members of the Law Society by passing special examinations. The barristers, who have greater prestige, are exclusively trial lawyers who are trained in one of the four famous Inns of Court, which are both law schools and guild associations and enforce very high standards on their members. Judges are chosen from the more outstanding barristers.[19]

Unlike the United States, Britain maintains a separate system of civil and criminal courts except at the highest level, the House of Lords, which serves as an appellate court hearing cases on appeal from lower courts. The appellate jurisdiction of the House of Lords is limited to civil and criminal cases involving important points of law. Permission to hear the case must be given either by the Courts of Appeal or the House of Lords. Since 1876, the judicial functions of the House of Lords have been carried out by specialists—either specially appointed life peers or peers who have held high judicial office. There is no judicial review in the sense of declaring a parliamentary act unconstitutional.

---

[18]355 U.S. 66 (1957).

[19]See William Martin Geldart et al., *Elements of English Law* (London: Oxford University Press, 1975), for an excellent introduction to English law.

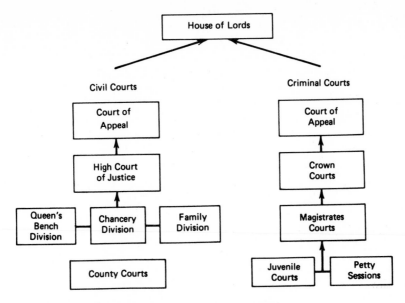

Figure 10.1 The court system of England and Wales.

The highest civil court is the Court of Appeal, which hears appeals from the High Court of Justice and county courts. There are three divisions of the High Court of Justice, as shown in Figure 10.1. The Queen's Bench includes commercial and admiralty matters. This division often has original jurisdiction in civil matters, for example, if a case involves an amount of money that exceeds the county court limit. The Chancery Court deals with trusts, land, taxation, and bankruptcy. The Family Court handles domestic issues such as divorce, child custody, and adoption.[20]

The highest criminal court is the Court of Criminal Appeal. The trial courts for all criminal cases except those of a petty nature are a group of courts known as the Crown Courts. At the bottom of the judicial structure are the Magistrate Courts, for juvenile offenses and minor crimes.

The American Judicial System

The essence of a federal system is a fundamental distribution of powers between the central government and the member states. Our governmental system is federal in nature because the constitution divides power between the national government and the states. The national government possesses only these powers that are delegated or may be implied from the delegated powers. However, the national government is supreme within the scope of its powers. This supremacy is guaran-

---

[20]For a detailed discussion of the British court system see Max Beloff and Gillian Peele, *The Government of the UK*, 2nd ed. (New York: W.W. Norton, 1985), Chapter 12.

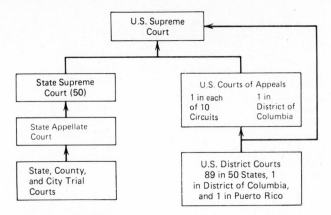

Figure 10.2 The United States court system (with special and legislative courts omitted).

teed by Article VI, Section 2, which provides that the Constitution and laws and treaties made under the authority of the United States, are the supreme law of the land and the judges of every state are bound thereby. The national government may exercise its powers over every square foot of this country and may act directly on the citizens. Article VI, Section 2, is the arch that supports the entire constitutional structure.[21]

Because the American governmental system is federal in nature, this country possesses a dual court system of federal and state courts (see Figure 10.2). Although there are variations among the state court systems, typically the lowest courts are police magistrates or **justices of the peace**. Usually there are general trial courts based on a county or combination of counties, which are courts of general jurisdiction; as such they hear a variety of cases. These courts also hear appeals from police magistrates and justices of the peace. Above the general trial courts, appellate courts are common. Usually each appellate court hears appeals from general trial courts within its district. At the top, every state has a court of appeals with statewide jurisdiction, usually called the supreme court.

Very few cases originate in the U.S. Supreme Court, which is primarily a court of appeals. The two primary procedures for reaching the U.S. Supreme Court for review are appeal and the writ of **certiorari.** Examples of the right of appeal are where a lower federal court or a state court holds an act of Congress unconstitutional.

The writ of certiorari is used more frequently, and the issuance of the writ is up to the discretion of the Court. Technically, certiorari is a writ issued by a higher court, such as the U.S. Supreme Court, calling up the record of a lower court for

---

[21]See *McCulloch v. Maryland,* 4 Wheaton 316 (819), for an excellent interpretation of the doctrine of implied powers. This doctrine is the basis for much of the increase of congressional power over the years.

The U.S. Supreme Court building.

review. The writ is limited to cases of constitutional importance involving actions of government officials, such as the denial of a fair trial or the denial of a constitutional right such as trial by jury.

State courts are not inferior to federal courts, despite a common opinion to the contrary. State courts have exclusive jurisdiction of all cases not within the constitutional grant of power to the national government. Only in certain limited areas may the U.S. Supreme Court review state court decisions.

State judges are chosen by a variety of methods.[22] Until recently, election for a term of years, commonly on a party basis, was the prevailing method. In five states the legislature selects judges with considerable gubernatorial and party influence. In a few states the governor appoints judges.

Election of state judges has been subject to considerable criticism on the ground that the quality of the state judiciary has suffered. The most frequent criticism is directed at police magistrates and justices of the peace, who frequently are nonprofessionals with little knowledge of the law. Municipal-court judges or other local judges frequently are indebted to a local political machine. State supreme court judges rarely are appointed to the U.S. Supreme Court. Notable exceptions

---

[22]See Henry Robert Glick and Kenneth N. Vines, *State Court Systems* (Englewood Cliffs, N.J.: Prentice-Hall, 1973), pp. 39–47, for a good discussion of methods of electing judges.

were Oliver Wendell Holmes and Benjamin N. Cardozo, both of whom were not only distinguished jurists, but also well known as philosophers of the law.

A new trend toward a mixed elective-appointive system divorced from parties or politics began in Missouri and California in the 1930s. In these states, judges go before the voters at the end of their terms or after a fixed number of years to determine whether or not they should be retained in office for another term. The essence of this plan is that judicial vacancies are filled by the governor from a list of nominees submitted by a nonpartisan commission.[23]

Today, 25 states have adopted some variation of the Missouri and California plans. In these states there are nonpartisan elections and little party influence in the selection of judges.

The only court required by the Constitution is the U.S. Supreme Court. Since 1789, however, Congress has provided for a system of lower federal courts. Today, there are 91 district courts within the 50 states and territories. Although each state has at least one district court with at least one judge, some districts have more than 20 judges and many states have more than one district court. These are courts of general jurisdiction, where most lawsuits originate.

Above the district courts are the 11 judicial circuits, each one of which has a court of appeals. Most cases never get beyond the court of appeals. The minority of cases that reach the U.S. Supreme Court usually do so through the writ of certiorari, which may be granted at the discretion of at least four judges of the U.S. Supreme Court from the highest state court if a federal question is raised.

All federal judges are appointed by the president, subject to confirmation by the Senate. Most judicial appointments are of the same political party as the president. U.S. Supreme Court appointees are usually people who reflect the same philosophy of government as the president, even when they are chosen from the opposite party. Other judicial appointments, especially district court judges, are subject to "senatorial courtesy." This means that the president, in filling appointments for judicial vacancies, must consult with the state's senator or senators if they are of his own party. Senatorial courtesy is a custom that permits a senator of the president's party to block the confirmation of an objectionable appointee from his or her own state. In effect, the president does not have a free hand. Where there is no senator from the president's party in a given state, his range of choice is greater.

The Judicial Process in America

When attorneys are appointed to the judiciary, they carry with them their social and political philosophies. Most judges seek to be objective in deciding a case and to avoid prejudices, but all judges possess basic attitudes that are outgrowths of social background, legal training, professional experience as lawyers, and political

---

[23]See Charles Aiken, "A New Method of Selecting Judges in California," *American Political Science Review*, 29 (June 1935), pp. 412–414; and Thomas E. McDonald, "Missouri's Ideal Judicial Selection Law," *Journal of American Judicial Society*, 24 (April 1947), pp. 194–199.

affiliation. Attitudes toward what are commonly called "liberalism" or "conservatism" frequently will be reflected in judicial opinions, especially where questions of social policy are involved. As we have seen, American presidents, when they appoint judges, usually are influenced by what they consider to be a judge's social philosophy. President Nixon, in appointing Chief Justice Warren Burger (1969–1986), sought someone who would follow *judicial restraint* and be less of a *judicial activist* than his predecessor, Chief Justice Earl Warren. President Reagan appointed Sandra Day O'Connor (keeping a campaign pledge to appoint a woman to the Supreme Court), Antonin Scalia, and Anthony Kennedy partly because they were perceived as supportive of judicial restraint rather than judicial activism.

A judicially restrained Supreme Court would not impose its views on the on the federal or state governments unless there is a clear violation of the Constitution. An example that represents both points of view is the 1962 reapportionment case, *Baker v. Carr,* which decided that citizens in legislative districts with large populations were denied equal rights.[24] The decision said that since the Constitution guaranteed equality under the law, inequalities in the population size of legislative districts was unconstitutional. However, then Justice Felix Frankfurter, the Court's foremost advocate of judicial restraint this century, argued that the Supreme Court should stay out of apportionment issues because it involved "political entanglements." He argued, unsuccessfully, that the Supreme Court should uphold its 1946 decision that declared the number of constituents represented by a legislator was a political question to be settled by the state legislature.

A judicially active Court seeks to shape government policy through its powers of judicial review. An example of judicial activism was the unanimous decision in **Brown v. Board of Education (1954)** by the Warren Court.[25] The precedent-breaking decision, buttressed by sociological and psychological arguments and reasoning, declared that state-mandated racial segregation in the public schools violated the equal protection guarantees of the Fourteenth Amendment. Segregation by race was unconstitutional.

In deciding cases, judges make law. Obviously, they do not do so in the sense that a member of the legislature does, but they do make policy. Today the traditional idea that judges "discover" the law generally has been discarded. This "slot machine" idea of the law assumed that judges arrived at their decisions by applying the correct rule or principle to the case at hand. If the case involved the constitutionality of an act of Congress, the U.S. Supreme Court supposedly would merely lay the law alongside the Constitution to see if there was a conflict. If Congress, for example, passed a law making income-tax rates higher in Illinois than elsewhere, its invalidity would be obvious, for the Constitution provides that national taxes shall be uniform throughout the United States. The type of controversy that comes before the Supreme Court is far more complex and cannot be resolved by such a simple test.

To state that American courts do not decide cases by a process of logical

---

[24]369 U.S. 186 (1962).

[25]347 U.S. 483 (1954).

deduction is not to suggest that they act in an arbitrary manner. Courts generally take precedents seriously, but frequently there are competing judicial doctrines available with respect to open-ended clauses of the Constitution, such as interstate commerce. Precedents are not always consistent and can be interpreted narrowly or broadly, as the decision demands. At times the Court specifically will overrule an earlier precedent, but most judges usually try to decide cases on the basis of sound legal reasoning and to provide some continuity to the law.

The Supreme Court decision in **_Oregon v. Mitchell_ (1970)** illustrates the operation of the judicial process.[26] In 1970, voters in four states approved extending the suffrage to 18-year-olds. For many years Congress had refused to pass a constitutional amendment lowering the voting age from 21 to 18. Public pressure during this Vietnam War period ("if you're old enough to be drafted and sent to Vietnam, you're old enough to vote") became so strong that Congress did, however, pass legislation lowering the voting age to 18 in all elections. Congress did not propose a constitutional amendment at that time. In this case the Court, by a five-to-four opinion, held that, by statute, Congress could reduce the voting age to 18 in federal elections but that Congress lacked the power to reduce the voting age to 18 in state and local elections.

Contrary to popular belief of recent years, there is no specific provision of the Constitution granting Congress the power to fix voting qualifications. In fact, the determination of who shall vote has been considered a state function. Article I, Section 2 of the Constitution states that the electors for the House of Representatives "shall have the qualifications requisite for electors of the most numerous branch of the state legislature." The Seventeenth Amendment, providing for direct elections of senators, has identical qualifications for voters. Article II provides that presidential electors shall be chosen in the manner the state legislature directs. The two suffrage amendments, however, require that in fixing qualifications, the states cannot discriminate on account of race or sex. (The Fifteenth and Nineteenth Amendments are worded in the negative.) Article I, Section 4, grants to state legislatures the power to determine the "times, places and manner of holding elections" for Congress, subject to such alterations as Congress may make.

The primary constitutional argument advanced on behalf of the law was that Congress, in exercising its enforcement powers under the Fourteenth Amendment, could determine that the denial of suffrage to 18-year-olds was a denial of "equal protection."

Actually, the Court in _Oregon v. Mitchell_ (1970) was even more deeply divided than the five-to-four decision might indicate. Justice Black, who wrote the official opinion, held that Congress, on the basis of Article I, Sections 2 and 4, had general supervisory power over congressional and presidential elections but not state or local elections; however, no other member of the Court agreed with his reasoning or conclusions. Four of his colleagues—Douglas, Brennan, Marshall, and White—believed the equal protection clause gave Congress power

---

[26]400 U.S. 112 (1970).

to determine age limits for voting in all elections, in the interests of equal protection. On the other hand, Justices Stewart, Blackmun, Harlan, and Chief Justice Burger held that the states had exclusive authority over age limits for voting. Justice Stewart contended that the "manner" of holding elections does not include the qualifications of voters, as Section 2 of Article I spells out what these qualifications are. The issue, according to Justice Stewart, was not whether it was good policy for 18-year-olds to vote, but whether Congress had the power to decide the issue in this way, rather than through the slower and more complex process of a constitutional amendment.[27]

In *Oregon v. Mitchell,* the U.S. Supreme Court made important public policy by upholding part of a controversial act of Congress. Sometimes the Court breaks new ground by dealing with a problem that Congress refuses to act on for political reasons. For many years, segregated public schools were common in the South and parts of the North. The Court, in the case of **Plessy v. Ferguson (1896),** had set forth the "separate but equal" doctrine, which allowed segregation in public facilities as long as facilities were "equal."[28] By holding that southern segregation laws did not violate the equal protection clause of the Fourteenth Amendment, the justices encouraged segregation as a policy.

By the 1930s and 1940s there was growing criticism of this policy by blacks and many whites. At first the U.S. Supreme Court responded by "tightening up" the requirement of equal facilities for blacks. The best solution would have been for Congress to outlaw state segregation by passing a law under its enforcement powers set out in the Fourteenth Amendment. This was politically impossible due to southern opposition and the possibility of a filibuster in the Senate. Finally, in 1954, as we have seen, the Court repudiated segregated education in *Brown v. Board of Education,* by holding it a form of "invidious discrimination."[29] This was followed by cases holding other forms of segregation unconstitutional. This policy gave a boost to the "black revolution" and ultimately (despite southern opposition) contributed to the creation of a climate of opinion that forced Congress to act by passing the various civil rights laws between 1957 and 1968.

More recently the Court has had to deal with the problem of **affirmative action** programs. These programs are designed to aid members of minority groups who have suffered past discrimination in employment and education. As this is an area where public opinion is deeply divided, the Court is proceeding with caution. By affirmative action we mean programs that seek to correct past discrimination or current inequities in terms of the percentage of minorities or women. Positive action programs occur in such areas as employment, allocations of contracts, composition of students in a school, and so forth. In 1986, for example, the Supreme Court affirmed in three separate affirmative action cases that minority plans with

---

[27]Since this decision, the Twenty-Sixth Amendment has been added to the Constitution. This grants suffrage to those 18 years old and over, in both federal and state elections.

[28]163 U.S. 537 (1896).

[29]347 U.S. 483 (1954).

timetables and numerical goals, even if jumping over more qualified or more senior whites, were constitutional. The same year, the Court also held that affirmative action layoffs or dismissals that would force innocent white employees to lose their jobs were not constitutional.

The activism of the Warren Court in ending school segregation and the granting of civil rights to black people has won general approval over the years, but other aspects of the Court's activism have been more controversial, as will be recalled from our discussion of civil liberties earlier in this chapter.

The appointment of four "conservative" judges by President Nixon led to the expectation that the judicial trend would be reversed. However, except for some changes in criminal procedure in a conservative direction, the Burger Court was as activist as the Court under Warren.

The problem of the constitutionality of state laws regulating abortion is an area where the Burger Court has broken new ground. The court found in ***Roe v. Wade (1973),*** that the right to privacy included a woman's right to have an abortion.[30] However, the right to an abortion was not absolute, but subject to regulation where the state has a "compelling interest," as in public health.

Intense opposition to the Court's decision has existed for the past 18 years on philosophical and religious grounds. A national consensus on this question is as far away as ever despite the defeat by the Senate of a proposed amendment banning all abortions. Few issues in our history have divided the country as deeply as the abortion question, as a clash of strongly held values are involved.

Roe v. Wade was modified by the *Webster v. Reproductive Health Services* opinion delivered on the last day (July 3) of the 1988–1989 Supreme Court term. The five-to-four decision opened up the possibility of further restrictions on abortion by sending the issue back to the state legislatures, where it has become a political "hot potato." The Missouri law that the Supreme Court upheld prohibits the use of public employees or facilities to assist in abortions unless necessary to save the mother's life. Public funds cannot be expended on abortion counseling. The most contentious aspect of the Court decision is the requirement that a doctor must perform appropriate medical tests to determine whether "the unborn child is viable" if the physician has reason to believe the woman is 20 or more weeks pregnant. Changes in Supreme Court membership and changing circumstance, as in this instance, reveal that the Court can modify previous decisions in important ways. Recent public opinion polls show, for example, that while a majority of Americans support abortion or freedom of choice, they do not support late pregnancy abortion, repeated abortions instead of birth control, or abortion used to select the sex of a child.

Yet, despite criticism, especially in law-enforcement circles, of such cases as *Miranda* and *Escobedo,* and criticism of the abortion decisions by many religious groups and some scholars, the Court has not become the subject of political controversy comparable to that of the 1930s, when it ruled on the constitutionality of

---

[30]*Roe v. Wade* 410 U.S. 110 (1973).

the New Deal. Up to now at least, the Court has avoided the great danger of allowing judicial activism to get ahead of public opinion and of making decisions that are not enforceable.[31]

However, considerable criticism has focused on two important developments of the past 20 years: First, an increase in the number of practicing lawyers in the United States went from 300,000 to nearly 600,000 in the two decades between 1960 and 1980. The United States has one lawyer per 400 persons (compared to one doctor for every 500), three times the lawyers per capita as in Great Britain and 20 times the Japanese ratio. Former Chief Justice Warren Burger observed: "We may well be on our way to being overrun by hordes of lawyers, hungry as tourists, and brigades of judges in numbers never before contemplated." Second, there has been a dramatic increase in the number of civil cases and a severe case backload. Derek Bok, former president of Harvard University and past dean of its law school, stated that the increase in the number of lawyers is the principal cause of the increase in lawsuits. One legal scholar complained, "Of late the itch to litigate has approached the absurd" in the United States.[32] Between 1960 and 1980, the number of civil cases brought to federal district courts each year climbed from 59,000 to over 168,000—a 185 percent increase. During the same period, civil cases taken to appellate courts accelerated from 3,899 to 23,200—a surge of 495 percent.

The increase in litigation may be due in part to the civil rights movement of the 1950s and 1960s, which turned to federal courts as the branch of government most sympathetic to its aims. Also, the movement has probably served as a catalyst for the use of courts to solve social problems. More people are aware today to use the law in order to defend their constitutional rights. Many scholars believe that this trend has in many ways led to a fairer and more equitable society.

However, there is also an influential group that believes that the courts are going too far, by playing an ever-larger part in administering schools, mental hospitals, and other such institutions. A related criticism is that the states and Congress, respectively, have failed to address many social problems, with the result that more and more individuals and groups of people turn to the courts to fill the gap by increasing their jurisdiction.[33]

Civil and Criminal Procedure

Courts generally will take jurisdiction over a civil question only if there is a real controversy of a legal nature between two or more parties and not simply an abstract question of law to be decided. Thus, in a *civil case* a typical justiciable issue would be a suit by party *A* against party *B*, alleging that *A* was injured by

---

[31]Nathan Glazer, "Toward an Imperial Judiciary," *Public Interest,* 41 (Fall 1975), pp. 104–123.

[32]Former Chief Justice Warren Burger's quote and data taken from A. E. Dick Howard, "A Litigation Society?" *Wilson Quarterly* (Summer 1981), p. 99.

[33]Nathan Glazer, "Should Judges Administer Social Services?" *Public Interest,* 50 (Winter 1978), pp. 64–80.

B who, while negligently driving his automobile, ran into *A*, who was crossing the street. *A*'s attorney would file a complaint alleging the above facts. *B* would respond with an answer. If *B* in his answer denied any negligence, the issue before the court would be whether *A*'s injury was due to *B*'s negligence.

Criminal procedure begins with the law-enforcement process. Six steps are involved in this process: arrest of law violators, preliminary hearing, preferring of charges, **arraignment,** trial, and punishment of convicted persons.

On the local level, law enforcement is primarily the function of the police or, in rural areas, the sheriff. Persons arrested for violating the law are brought before a minor magistrate for a preliminary hearing, the purpose of which is to decide whether the evidence against the accused is sufficient to hold him or her for action by the prosecutor or **grand jury.** If the accused is held for further action, the magistrate would set bail unless the offense is a nonbailable crime punishable by death. Traditionally, the next step is action by the grand jury, a body of 5 to 23 persons summoned by the prosecutor to determine whether the evidence against the accused justifies returning an **indictment,** a simple statement describing the essential ingredients of the crime. The local prosecutor is usually an elected county official, whereas in the federal courts there is a district attorney, appointed by the president with the consent of the Senate, for each district court.

In Great Britain there is no official comparable to either the U.S. federal or state district attorney. There is a director of public prosecutions, who may direct the prosecution in such serious criminal cases as murder. In England and Wales the police initiate and conduct most prosecutions. This arrangement is possible only because of the lower crime rate in Great Britain.

Great Britain also has abolished use of the grand jury. Some American states virtually have discontinued use of the grand jury. A majority of our states permits some use of an alternative procedure known as prosecution by information for lesser crimes. This differs from the traditional indictment only in that it is filed by the prosecutor without a grand jury. After the charges are filed, the accused is arraigned before the trial court where a plea of "guilty" or "not guilty" is entered.

The Anglo-American court system is based on the **adversary system.** Each side in a lawsuit, whether civil or criminal, presents evidence to support its case. The trial jury, if one is used, is traditionally a body of 12 competent citizens who must render a unanimous verdict on the basis of the facts and the law. Today, some states in civil cases and trials for lesser crimes have relaxed the unanimity rule and provided for juries of less than 12 members. It is assumed that the jury can arrive at the truth from the testimony presented by each side. The role of the judge is essentially that of an impartial referee, who is responsible for observance of the rules of evidence and procedural safeguards. If there is no jury, the judge performs the function of the jury. In a criminal action the state must prove its case beyond a reasonable doubt, whereas in a civil case the plaintiff, the party who institutes the suit, need only present a preponderance of the evidence in his or her behalf.

If a verdict of guilty has been returned by the trial jury in a criminal case, the court pronounces the sentence.

"You have a pretty good case, Mr. Pitkin. How
much justice can you afford?"

Drawing by Handelsman; © 1973 The New Yorker
Magazine, Inc.

CONTINENTAL EUROPEAN SYSTEMS OF LAW

In countries of continental Western Europe the law is based on Roman law and
generally tends to be codified in contrast to common law. Its origins go back to the
code prepared for the Roman Emperor Justinian in 533 A.D. During the Middle Ages
the Roman Catholic church based its canon law on Roman law. In the French and
Italian universities of the twelfth and thirteenth centuries, Roman law was redis-
covered. It had great appeal to the educated and rising mercantile classes and to
many European monarchs who in particular liked its authoritarian features. In
more modern times the law codes of Napoleon I have been of great importance.
They have influenced not only the legal systems of European countries and Latin
America, but the Canadian province of Quebec and the state of Louisiana as well.

The codes assume that the fundamentals of the country's law can be stated in
comprehensive statutes. The codes, of course, require interpretation and elaboration. This task is more the responsibility of law teachers than of the judges. Typical
subjects of a code are civil and criminal procedures, property, commercial law, and
the like.

The differences between code and common law should not be overstated. The
code law is more the work of the legislature than the courts. Although the judges
tend to see the law as written reason in code-law countries, common-law systems
also rely on statutes and have legal commentaries and some codification, but to a
lesser degree. Even in interpreting a statute, Anglo-American judges refer to prior

relevant decisions. Under the code law judges are supposed to follow the code alone.

Another difference between the two systems of law is found in criminal procedure.[34] In a typical code-law country such as France the first step in a criminal case is a preliminary examination of the accused and chief witnesses by an investigating judge, who determines whether the accused should be tried formally. The trial itself repeats this "inquisitorial" procedure to get at the truth. The role of the judge is that of an active participant in the procedure and there is little emphasis on procedural safeguards for the defendant. The French system, however, gives the judge complete control of the trial and permits him or her and the prosecutor to develop the case against the accused on the basis of the dossier resulting from the preliminary examination.

By the time a suspect has undergone this thorough preliminary examination and is standing trial, the general assumption is that he or she is probably guilty. This is unlike the Anglo-American law, which, through its many safeguards for the defendant, seeks to minimize the possibility of an innocent person being found guilty. French code law lays more stress on preventing a guilty person from escaping punishment.

In France, the jury system plays only a minor role. There is nothing comparable to the grand jury, and the trial jury is used only in cases of serious crimes tried by the local trial courts. When used, the jury consists of nine local citizens who sit with one or more judges. No unanimity is required. In France, the jury frequently is regarded as an instrument for confusing the issues in a case.[35]

The French legal system seeks to provide justice economically and to make it readily available to the French people. Although the French have a separate system of civil and criminal courts, the separation is in many respects more apparent than real. First, the two highest courts, the Court of Cassation (supreme court of appeal) and the Appeal Court, review both civil and criminal cases. Second, civil and criminal courts on the lower level have the same judges and use the same buildings (see Figure 10.3). The Court of Cassation limits its jurisdiction to interpretations of law in civil and criminal cases.

The French court system was streamlined under President Charles de Gaulle in 1958. The highest civil courts are the 172 courts of Grand Instance, which have unlimited civil jurisdiction and appellate jurisdiction over the courts of First Instance, which are limited to minor civil cases. The assize courts have jurisdiction over most serious crimes, whereas the criminal courts decide lesser offenses. For minor offenses there are local police courts. Certain special courts are not shown in Figure 10.3.

An important feature of the French judicial system, as well as those of most continental European democracies, is that judges and prosecutors are part of the

---

[34]See Henry J. Abraham, *The Judicial Process*, pp. 98–103, for a comparison of the Anglo-American adversary system with the accusatorial practice of code countries.

[35]Ibid., pp. 110–114.

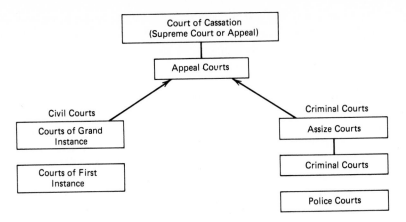

Figure 10.3 The regular court system of France.

same public service. Prosecutors are under the ministry of justice, but judges have security of tenure and are not subject to government discipline by the ministry. Another difference is that in France an individual decides at the beginning of his or her career whether to become a lawyer or a member of the judiciary.

Another important feature of French law is the separate system of administrative law, which utilizes special administrative courts. There are no comparable courts in Britain and the United States. These tribunals hear complaints and lawsuits against the state itself and afford the citizen protection against arbitrary decisions of government officials. The function of the administrative courts is the annulment of rulings where officials have exceeded their power. The highest administrative court is the Council of State, which has an excellent reputation both in France and abroad. The council frequently has awarded generous damages to individuals injured by the government. It also has protected civil servants wrongfully dismissed by the government.

In Anglo-American countries the state may not be sued without its consent for the actions of government employees committed in the discharge of their duties. In the United States and Great Britain the public official personally is charged with dereliction, not the state, and is sued in the regular courts. Other code-law countries follow the French practice in having a separate system of administrative law.

The German judicial system is similar to the French in many ways. First of all, it is based on code law in judicial procedure. The judge dominates the proceedings and juries are used only to a limited extent.

Although Germany is federal in nature, it does not have a dual system of courts, like the United States does. Instead of a separate state and federal court system, there is one integrated system. The top-level courts are national and the three lower-level courts are state and local courts. Virtually all cases originate on the state level. Uniformity in the law results from the national codes that regulate both legal and substantive law.

There are local and provincial courts that exercise both original and appellate jurisdiction and hear both criminal and civil cases. Above these are the superior courts, which have two sections, civil and criminal. At the top of the judicial structure is the Federal High Court.

Since the early nineteenth century, judges in Germany have all been possessors of a higher degree. Like other members of the higher civil service, they are well educated and also traditionally conservative. Today, the minister of justice makes appointments to the judiciary with the assistance of nominating committees on both the national and state levels. He or she also supervises the courts.

To avoid a repetition of the loss of basic rights under the Nazis, the first section of the Constitution declares the dignity of people "inviolable" and the duty of all governmental authority to protect it. It goes on to prohibit extraordinary courts and double jeopardy. It also guarantees basic rights such as habeas corpus.

The Constitution also sought to prevent a repetition of the acts of the Nazis and Communists in the last days of the Weimar Republic in the early 1930s. Neither of these groups believed in democracy, but abused democratic rights to gain power legally and then establish a dictatorship. In this struggle, only the Nazis were able to obtain complete power. The Constitution seeks to prevent abuse of freedom by outlawing groups whose aims are to pursue violent actions against the government.

Thus, the Germans have tried to strike a balance between liberty and justice.

COMMUNIST LAW AND LEGAL SYSTEMS

The Marxist Conception of Law

The Marxist (Communist) conception of law is fundamentally different from that of Western democratic countries. The latter assume that law is binding upon the governors and governed alike and that individuals should be guaranteed certain rights that protect them against state action.

Marx and Engels assumed that law is a tool of the state and that the state in turn is the instrument of the ruling class. Judges in capitalist countries, according to Marx, because of their training and background, would favor the interests of property in their decisions. He felt that even guarantees of equality before the law were of little value to the poor because they could not afford the best lawyers and the high cost of legal proceedings.

In his views of a Communist country, Marx was utopian. He believed that coercion ultimately would become unnecessary and the power of public opinion would be sufficient to maintain an orderly and peaceful society. Marx, however, recognized that there would be a short period of transition between the Communist revolution and the attainment of this ideal state. During this interim period it would be necessary to revise bourgeois law so that it no longer would protect property rights against justice for the masses. The selection of judges sympathetic to communism also would be necessary.

The Soviet Judicial System

Needless to say, the Soviet Union, although it came into existence in 1917, has not attained the condition of pure communism where law is unnecessary. In fact, law is very much a part of the Soviet system; however, Soviet law assumes that, as the Soviet state is the product of the type of revolution Marx and Lenin predicted, it embraces all the interests of its citizens. Thus, according to this assumption, there can be no conflict between the interests of the state and the rights of the individual. Because the Soviet Union is a state presumably based on the welfare of the proletariat, or working class, its law and court decisions always reflect the interests of the working class in theory.

In practice, law plays a greater role in the Soviet system than in Western democratic countries because all spheres of life are subject to government control. For example, there are commercial courts that have jurisdiction over state enterprises and organizations that buy or sell from each other.

Whenever the interests of the regime are affected, law is simply an instrument of state policy. This explains the lack of procedural safeguards in criminal procedure and the fact that the bill of rights in the Soviet Constitution of 1977 is a mere declaration of intention, of no legal significance, and not enforceable in the courts. The law codes assert that the state is supreme over the individual and that the conduct of a criminal trial reflects this fact. The defense attorney, who is a state employee, is chosen from a lawyers' collegium that is subsidized by the state. Neither the defense attorney nor the defendant is shown the state evidence until the day before the trial. The judge, as in countries with code law, questions the defendant and witnesses. Furthermore, the defendant must prove his or her innocence, and cases may be reopened by a higher court after acquittal in a trial court.

The structure of the Soviet courts is in many respects like that of Western European countries (see Figure 10.4). At the bottom of the regular court system are regional courts, with a supreme court in each of the union republics. At the top of the pyramid is a supreme court of the union, which is primarily an appellate court. There are also peoples' courts, which are quite informal. These are organized in neighborhoods and places of work and are administered by nonprofessionals. Minor cases, such as drunkenness and petty theft, are tried in these courts, which

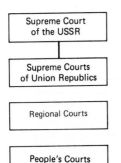

Figure 10.4 The court system of the Soviet Union.

consist of one lay judge and two lay assessors. Their jurisdiction is limited to the simplest of disputes. Judges are elected, but candidates always are politically reliable.

To the citizens of the Soviet Union, a basic principle of their legal system is Soviet legality. This concept stresses the necessity of strict observance of and adherence to all laws and agencies of the state.

The Soviets also lay great stress on the educational function of the law. This emphasizes the process of lifelong legal socialization, including the development of law-abiding behavior. The Soviets rely on the educational role of the law as a deterrent to illegal behavior. For example, at least one-fifth of Soviet trials are held in places of work or residence, rather than in courtrooms. Not only are those being tried "reeducated," but so are their families and coworkers as well.[36]

The formal court structure of the Soviet Union reflects the theoretical federalism of that country. The Supreme Court of the USSR has jurisdiction over serious political crimes and disputes between republics, as well as limited appellate jurisdiction. Judges and lay assessors of the courts are chosen by the Soviets (legislative bodies) of their respective areas, except in the people's courts, in which they are popularly elected. Courts outside of the regular system are not shown in Figure 10.4.

During the Khrushchev era (1953–1964) the government issued new and less harsh rules of both civil and criminal law. For example, in criminal law, punishment by analogy was abolished. Under this doctrine, in force since the revolution, an act that was not a crime but similar to a criminal act could be made punishable as a crime by a judge. Nevertheless, Soviet criminal law is still harsher than that of Western democratic countries. Political crimes usually are still tried in military courts, which exist in every military district. The trials are conducted in secret. Civilians convicted of treason, espionage, and assassination of a public official abroad, to name some of the more serious crimes, can be sentenced to death.

An important post in the Soviet legal system is that of the *procurator general* of the Soviet Union. There are also procurators in each of the republics and districts as well. The procurator's duties extend to the organization of the courts and execution of the rules of law in use, as well as the traditional duties as prosecutor for the state. The procurator general of the Soviet Union is one of the most important officials in the country and is always a high-ranking member of the Communist party.[37] All procurators are appointed for five-year terms by the immediately superior procurator.

Both General Secretary Gorbachev and Soviet Vice President Antoly Lukyanov graduated in law from Moscow State University in the mid 1950s. They are the first high-ranking Soviet leaders with law degrees, although Lenin studied law but

---

[36]See Donald D. Barry and Carol Barner-Barry, *Contemporary Soviet Politics: An Introduction*, 3rd ed. (Englewood, N.J.: Prentice-Hall, 1987), Chapter 8.

[37]For excellent studies of Soviet law see the following: George Feifer, *Justice in Moscow* (New York: Dell Publishing, 1964); Eugene Karneuba, "The Soviet View of Law," *Problems of Communism* (March–April 1965), pp. 8–16; John A. Hazard, "Soviet Law and Justice," in John W. Strong, ed., *The Soviet Union under Brezhnev and Kosygin* (New York: Van Nostrand, 1971); Alfred C. Meyer, *The Soviet Political System: An Interpretation* (New York: Random House, 1965), pp. 300–355.

did not graduate. In 1988, reports began circulating that Gorbachev was verbally supporting a theory of rule under law that would imply an independent judiciary, government, and party officials subordinate to the law, and the emergence of citizen rights rather than emphasis on citizen obligations to the state. One lawyer told the government paper *Izvestia:* "For the last seven decades, the highest power has been in the hands of the state—the Communist Party, or rather its apparatus." Another Soviet lawyer declared the concept of state too often has been confused with raw power.[38]

Creating a more independent judiciary could take a long time. There are signs, however, that the Soviet judicial process, which places the needs of the state and state security first, is being questioned at the highest levels of government. The Soviet Union could be at a stage where an independent judiciary may begin to evolve.

Law in the People's Republic of China

The PRC is both a developing country and a Communist political system. Law, when it is regarded as useful, is to bring order and predictability to the economic, social, and political system as well as maintain the dominance of the Communist party.

When **Maoism** (Mao Zedong ruled 1949–1976) dominated the PRC, everything was to be subordinated to policy. The Communist revolution was not subject to legal regulations according to Maoist ideology. Some scholars conclude Mao not only did not find a legal system useful, but held it in contempt. The driving force as well as the cement of society was to be Communist ideology. There would be rapid, often violent change as the Communist system established itself. Revolutionary justice and political expediency became pillars of the system.

Deng Xiaoping (ruled 1978 to date) has replaced politics in command with a Socialist legal system. Deng had bitter personal experiences during the anarchic, revolutionary justice period of the Cultural Revolution (1965–1969) when he was purged and nearly executed. Deng's son fell from a third-story window, ecsaping Mao's rampaging, school-age Red Guard and today is a paraplegic. A Socialist legal system would be authoritarian, but it would provide unity, order, and predictability. A secure political order would supposedly reduce violent conflict and help build a modern, Socialist country. Conflicts will be decided through the judicial system and even party members are subject to the law. A working legal system is necessary if the PRC is to develop economically, aggressively seek out foreign investment, and actively participate in international trade.[39]

---

[38]Paul Quinn-Judge, "Rule of Law in USSR: A 180 Degree Turn?" *Christian Science Monitor* (January 18, 1989), p. 2.

[39]For an analysis of contradictory Communist perspectives on law and the legal system in the PRC see Carlos Wing-hung Lo, *The Legal System and Criminal Responsibility of Intellectuals in the People's Republic of China: 1949–82* (Baltimore, Md.: Occasional Papers/Reprints Series in Contemporary Asian Studies, 1985), No. 2-1985 (67), especially Chapter 1. This excellent series in contemporary Asian studies includes one or more publications on some aspect of PRC law each year.

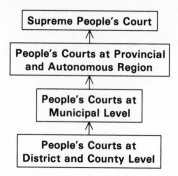

Figure 10.5 The court system of the People's Republic of China.

The 1982 Constitution was to establish firmly the legal basis of Chinese Communist society. A legal order does not, as we noted earlier, presume that there shall be any significant degree of civil liberties.[40] The court system (Figure 10.5) is simple.

The Supreme People's Court (SPC) is responsible to the Standing Committee of the National People's Congress. The Standing Committee's function is to interpret and supervise implementation of the 1982 Constitution. Because the Standing Committee decides if any law violates the constitution, in practice there is no judicial review.

The Supreme People's Court is responsible for supervising the administration of justice in the approximately 3,500 people's courts, at the district/county level, the municipal level, and the provincial/autonomous region level. At the district/county level each court has separate judges for a criminal and a civil division. Appeals can be made to the next higher level court.

Parallel to the court system is the procurator system. The procurators are responsible for authorizing the arrest of criminals and counterrevolutionaries. The procurator examines the charges and evidence brought by the public security bureau (police) and determines if a case should go to trial. Often during a trial the procurator serves as a public defender.

The Chinese Communist party (CCP) ultimately determines who will serve as judges and procurators. Signs of judicial independence quickly lead to reassignment.[41] The inclusion of counterrevolutionary activity in the criminal code suggests strong ideological overtones.

There are a little over 20,000 lawyers in a country of 1.1 billion people. Lawyers cannot work privately, but are employed by state legal advisory services that assign

---

[40]For a recent analysis of the latest PRC constitution, see Hungdah Chiu, *The 1982 Chinese Constitution and the Rule of Law* (Baltimore, Md.: Occasional Papers/Reprints Series in Contemporary Asian Studies, 1985), No. 4-1985 (69), pp. 1–18.

[41]For an excellent overview of the PRC judicial system see James C. F. Wang, *Contemporary Chinese Politics*, 3rd ed. (Englewood Cliffs, N.J.: Prentice-Hall, 1989), pp. 133–143.

them cases. In criminal cases, the lawyer's first obligation is to defend state interests and principally advise the person charged on the law as it applies to that case. Courts usually assume any person brought to trial is guilty. "In practice, most Chinese trials are sentencing hearings at which defense lawyers or representatives plead for leniency for their clients."[42]

Historically, China, as most Asian societies, has not been litigious. The informal method of mediation was institutionalized in 1980. Today there are over 1 million neighborhood mediation committees. Mediators are elected at the basic level and are to mediate by persuasion and education on a voluntary basis. One source estimated that up to 90 percent of minor criminal and civil cases are handled by mediation committees.[43]

A rule by law system is emerging in the PRC. The mainland remains, however, an authoritarian system with law to establish predictability, stability, and continuing control through a party elite.

LAW IN DEVELOPING COUNTRIES

The term "developing countries" is used to refer to those nation-states that differ from modern Western societies in a number of ways, including a low rate of literacy, low per capita income, a basically rural economy, and little technological development. Some of these countries have primitive economies with no food reserves, a limited cultural and artistic life, and limited political development. The newly independent countries of Africa and Asia are typical of this Third World, but the older political societies of Latin America also share many of the characteristics of developing nation-states.

Western legal systems generally were introduced in the developing countries of Africa and Asia prior to independence, but the impact of Western law was negligible, since colonial rulers generally permitted much of customary law and practice to remain in force on the village level. One of the important problems facing the newly independent governments has been to reconcile Western legal standards with existing customary practices.

The new governments of the developing countries frequently have looked upon Western law as an obstacle to desirable new programs. This often has resulted in disregarding established legal procedures. In some instances ruling ethnic or racial groups have used established law to dominate minorities. The result has been that the role of law continues to be in a state of flux.

In Africa, many changes have been made in the legal systems imposed by former colonial rulers, because the new leaders believed the inherited system did not reflect contemporary needs and aspirations. Customary law based on tradition also has been modified in many ways. For example, in some African countries, the

---

[42]Hungdah Chiu, "China's Changing Criminal Justice System," p. 267.

[43]Quoted in James C.F. Wang, *Contemporary Chinese Politics*, p. 139.

Jacobo Timmerman, an Argentine journalist, visits the detention center where he had been held by the previous Argentine regime.

giving of gifts at a time of marriage or a feast at baptism is limited to minimize the impoverishment of African families, and marriage has been secularized and arranged marriage forbidden.

As to the new legal codes, Marxist influence appears to be minimal. The French governmental structure is retained in the former French colonies. Although the old courts administering customary laws are abolished, specialists in the old law are advisers in the new courts.[44]

The civil law of Spain and Portugal was carried over to the New World and became firmly established throughout Latin America. Since countries achieved independence, the civil law of other European countries has had considerable influence, but the influence of the United States has not been absent. The writ of habeas corpus, for example, has had widespread adoption in Latin America.

Judicial procedure in Latin American is quite unlike that of the United States and Great Britain. In Argentina procedures are fairly typical of Latin America. A trial of a civil action is usually a private hearing in which a secretary presides over the proceedings and keeps a detailed record of everything that takes place. The

---

[44]See John H. Hazard, "Law and Social Change in Marxist Africa," *American Behavioral Scientist,* 13:4 (1970), pp. 575–584.

judge usually does not bother to attend the hearing. Instead, his or her decision is based on the written record.

Argentine criminal procedure offers the defendant fewer safeguards than Anglo-American practices. A person arrested and charged with a criminal offense is brought before a judge who combines the functions of a committing magistrate and grand jury. He or she decides whether the accused will be held for trial and in what circumstances, if any, he or she will be released on bail. Pending trial, the accused may be held incommunicado for a number of days. During this time the police attempt to obtain criminal evidence. When the trial takes place, it is held without a jury and usually behind closed doors. The trial judge frequently is absent during part of the proceedings. Sometimes his or her judgment is based to a large extent on written evidence prepared by a secretary. It is said that justice often depends on the accuracy of a secretary's notes. Another variation from Anglo-American practices is that the public prosecutor, as well as the accused, may appeal the verdict. This makes it possible for a person found innocent in a lower court to be adjudged guilty in a court of appeals.[45]

SUMMARY

There are a variety of legal systems in the world. The two systems generally associated with democratic regimes, the Anglo-American common-law system and the code law of continental Western Europe, differ in numerous ways. The former is based to a greater degree on judge-made laws and stresses procedural safeguards for defendants in criminal cases, limiting the role of the judge to that of an impartial referee in the conduct of a trial. Judicial review, so important in the American legal system, is not found in the British system, but is provided for in some code-law countries.

The Communist legal system reflects to varying degrees the authoritarian nature of the Communist governmental systems. Japan and the developing countries are influenced by both the Western legal systems and indigenous factors.

It is clear that courts make policy. In a sense in the United States, the Constitution is what the judges say it means. In the short run, there may be a conflict between the ways in which a majority of the U.S. Supreme Court justices interpret the Constitution and the manner in which the majority of the people desire the Constitution to be interpreted; however, in the long run, the Supreme Court is likely to interpret the Constitution in the way the majority desires. This is because presidents are likely to appoint judges who reflect dominant policy values. Also, failure on the part of the Court to reflect such values over a period of time is likely to undermine its prestige.

In Communist countries and many developing countries, it is generally difficult for judges to exercise independence from political pressures and to maintain objectivity. It is likely that there is some relationship between the relative indepen-

---

[45]Alexander T. Edelmann, *Latin American Government and Politics*, pp. 480–482.

dence of the courts and the countries whose judicial system is based on the common law. Perhaps, as Theodore L. Becker has suggested, "Where judges can rely, in a common law system, on norms *they* produce, they need rely less on other norm-producing structures, that is, the legislature, the administrative agencies, etc."[46]

RECOMMENDED READINGS

Abraham, Henry J. *The Judicial Process: An Introductory Analysis of the Courts of the United States, England and France,* 5th ed. New York: Oxford University Press, 1986. This book is considered the standard introduction to the U.S., British, and French judicial systems. It is a thorough work which considered such topics as judicial review and staffing the courts.

Cappelletti, Mauro. *The Judicial Process in Comparative Perspective.* New York: Oxford University Press, 1989. This is a more advanced study of comparative judicial processes. Recent and useful, this book was written by a scholar who has published for many years in this area.

Holmes, Oliver Wendell, Jr. *The Common Law.* Boston: Little, Brown, 1951. First published in 1881, this has become a classic of the common law. It was written by one of the most distinguished justices of the Supreme Court.

Katz, Alan N., ed. *Legal Traditions and Systems: An International Handbook.* New York: Greenwood Press, 1986. This collection covers most areas of the world including Southeast Asia and the Soviet Union. The authors focus on historical development, organization of the respective legal systems, and the recruitment and training of law personnel.

Leng, Shao-chuan and Hungdah Chiu. *Criminal Justice in Post-Mao China.* Albany: State University of New York Press, 1985. Mao's China stressed party domination, mass line tactics, and class justice. Since 1977, with the political reemergence of Deng Xiaoping, mainland China has worked toward a Socialist legal system with Chinese characteristics. As the book demonstrates, legal regularity is closely tied in with efforts to achieve the four modernizations.

Merryman, John Henry. *The Civil Law Tradition: An Introduction to the Legal Systems of Western Europe and Latin America,* 2nd ed. Stanford, Calif.: Stanford University Press, 1985. This short book is written for the nonspecialists. It discusses the commonalities of European and Latin American legal systems and how they are set apart from the Anglo-American systems.

Pritchett, C. Herman. *The American Constitution,* 3rd ed. New York: McGraw-Hill, 1977. This is a somewhat dated but superb analysis of what the U.S. Constitution means. The author begins with the Constitutional Convention and its background and then presents analytical summaries of leading Supreme Court cases under topical headings.

Upham, Frank K. *Law and Social Change in Postwar Japan.* Cambridge, Mass.: Harvard University Press, 1987. The Japanese emphasize political consensus. The author looks

---

[46]Theodore L. Becker, *Comparative Judicial Politics: The Political Functioning of Courts* (Chicago: Rand McNally, 1970), p. 161.

at various social conflicts and how some groups use the legal system to induce change. Also considered is the elite's effort to control change via the law.

White, Robin C. A. *The Administration of Justice.* New York: Basil Blackwell, 1985. This book provides a comprehensive critique of the British legal system. It discusses the civil and criminal courts and the legal profession.

Wu, Yuan-li et al. *Human Rights in the People's Republic of China.* Boulder, Colo.: Westview Press, 1988. This study analyzes the political control and limitations on human rights in the People's Republic of China since 1949. Why human rights are violated and the special groups targeted, including religious minorities, are discussed.

FOUR

Political Change and International Politics

Chapter 11

Dynamics of Political Change and the Developing World

The developing world, or Third World, includes Africa, Asia, Latin America, and the Middle East. This is in contrast to the postindustrial democratic countries of Western Europe, the United States, Canada, Australia, New Zealand, and Japan, often called the *First World;* and the *Second World,* the Communist countries of Europe. The People's Republic of China (PRC), with a population of approximately 1.1 billion, generally is identified as a Third World country. The developing world accounted for 71 percent of the world's population in 1975 and at current growth rates will contain 80 percent of the world's population in the year 2000. It is a majority of the world we *cannot* ignore (see Figure 11.1).

The Third World includes Latin America. In several ways, however, Latin American is unique. Almost all of the Latin American countries achieved their independence by 1824. For the rest of the developing world, independence came generally after World War II. Latin America also has a shared inheritance, which many developing countries, even those that border one another, do not have. Most of Latin America was a Spanish or Portuguese colony. The countries' social, political, and economic backgrounds are similar. These countries shared common reli-

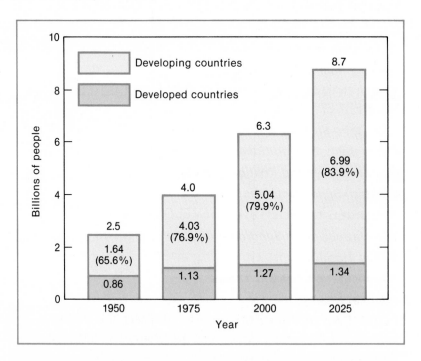

Figure 11.1 World population growth and distribution, 1950–2025. Projected growth for developing world is 2.1 percent annually and 0.6 percent annually for the developed world. Percentages show the developed world's share of total world population. *Source:* Based on data from *Concise Report on the World Population Situation in 1977* (New York: United Nations, 1979), p. 8; and *1989 World Population Data Sheet* (Washington, D.C.: Population Reference Bureau, 1989).

gious, political, and economic structures for many years before and after independence. When you look at other continents, one sees contiguous countries where one colony was ruled by Great Britain and neighboring colonies by France, Belgium, Portugal, or the Netherlands. The colonial heritages and traditions are much more diverse in Asia, Africa, and the Middle East than in Latin America.

There are some 170 sovereign nation-states in the world today. Over half of these have come into existence since World War II (1945). These new countries are commonly referred to as *developing countries,* or *developing political systems.* U.S. government publications refer to these countries as *Less Developed Countries* (LDCs). We do not use that term in this book because it suggests that countries labeled LDC have an inferior status.

These new developing political systems share certain characteristics:

1. Their formal independence is relatively recent. Most are less than forty years old.

2. The government and constitutional structures are new and still evolving, as are the organization and responsibilities of the executive branch; the organization, training, and functioning of the administrative service; and the organization and functioning of legislative and judicial institutions. These structures are just beginning to institutionalize, and their organization and duties are often subjects of intense political disputes.

3. Many political organizations, such as political parties, are unsure of their objectives (whether to participate in government or overturn the political system).

4. There are few autonomous interest groups, such as trade unions and business organizations, that have a history of making independent claims on government.

5. There is a tradition of avoidance politics, where the village head, village council, or religious or clan leaders seek to minimize the impact of government. The masses had no opportunity to influence policy-making, but they were concerned with avoiding or mitigating more arbitrary or demanding government requirements, such as taxes, conscription, or "voluntary" labor.

6. Governments are often oppressive, and their functions are usually limited to providing security, transportation, facilities, and occasionally irrigation and flood-control projects. Governments require taxes, military conscripts, and the corvée (unpaid contributed labor for public works projects).

7. A number of quantifiable socioeconomic characteristics are present, such as low per capita income; limited distribution of technology; a predominantly rural society, with often as high as 80 to 85 percent of the population living in rural areas; a small percentage of the population working in manufacturing; lower levels of caloric consumption; limited medical and health facilities, with fewer doctors or nurses per 1,000 population; limited educational opportunities and high unemployment for those who do earn a college degree; relatively low literacy, often below 50 percent; high birth rate; limited social mobility; and so on.

8. Exports are largely primary products such as bauxite, copper, oil, rubber, wood, rice, copra, spices, coffee, tea, and other agricultural products. It has been estimated that 80 percent of the developing world's foreign earnings come from such sales. There is little local processing of these goods, and it is the processing and manufacturing that provides more jobs, profits, and tax revenue. The processing and distribution of the final product often occurs in the developed, industrialized countries.

CATEGORIES OF THIRD WORLD COUNTRIES

Each of the more than 120 developing countries will not have all of the traits listed. The Third World can be divided into various categories. One of the simpler ways to categorize is to group countries by economic traits.

1. The first group is the most advanced developing countries, often called **NICs,** or **newly industrializing countries.** These include Brazil and the four tigers of Asia—Hong Kong, Singapore, South Korea, and the Republic of China (Taiwan). Mexico and Thailand are moving toward this category. The NICs, especially the four tigers, base their success on manufacturing and worldwide sales of manufactured items such as textiles, shoes, ships, steel, appliances, electronic goods, and so on. Average real per capita annual income growth was above 4 percent between 1960 and 1980 in these countries.

2. The oil-exporting countries of the Middle East plus Brunei in Southeast Asia make up the second group. They have extremely high per capita incomes and small populations and are blessed with an abundance of oil. Some would say these countries have too much money and not enough places to put it.

3. The intermediate or third group continues to depend extensively on exports of commodities (such as coffee, sugar, tin, rubber, palm oil, cocoa, and some petroleum) whose prices have persistently fallen. Several of these countries include oil among their exports, and most are promoting the development of manufacturing and an export market. This group averaged annual per capita real growth rates of 2.3 percent between 1960 and 1980. Countries in this category include India, Mexico, Thailand, the Philippines, Egypt, Honduras, Nigeria, and the PRC (mainland China). When the bottom fell out of the oil market, those countries with substantial oil exports and large populations (such as Mexico and Nigeria) faced considerable adjustment and then restructuring. For example, Nigeria's unrestrained spending and massive corruption led to replacing an elected civilian government by a military coup in 1983. Falling oil prices have contributed to Nigeria's problems since 1981 and are one example of the rapid changes faced by several countries in this category. A Yale-educated Nigerian economist explained:

> We used to charge up to $40 a barrel; we're down to $10. . . . In 1981–82 we earned $24 billion from oil. This year [1988] we are lucky if we earn $5 billion from oil—and $6 billion total in exports.[1]

4. The poorest group of developing countries had annual per capita growth rates of 1 percent or under between 1960 and 1980. These countries include Bangladesh, Burma, Haiti, much of black Africa, and Vietnam.

---

[1]E. A. Wayne, "Nigeria Charts Path of Major Reform," *Christian Science Monitor* (October 26, 1988), p. 5.

Superimposed over these four categories are such things as geographic variation, racial cleavages, religious divisions, and so forth. The interests and claims of
these countries on the world stage often are a welter of conflicting demands and
proposals.

MAJOR PROBLEMS IN DEVELOPING COUNTRIES

Problems facing the developing countries are numerous and sometimes seem overwhelming. In many ways they seem even greater when compared to the situations
new countries were facing 100 years ago. A simple listing gives one some indication
of the unprecedented demands that are being made on these countries and particularly on the governments, which are regarded as responsible for responding to most
of the challenges.

Improving the Standard of Living

1. Rapid migration to urban centers often takes place because there are no jobs
in the countryside, there is rural violence, or both. Generally, though, the increase
in a city's population is not matched by an increase in urban employment opportunities. The result is millions living in squatter slums. Mexico City, the fastest
growing urban area in the world, is but one of numerous examples. In 1975 it had
12 million residents; in 1989, 18 million; and in 2000 it is projected that Mexico
City will be the largest city in the world with 31 million people. Too many people
jammed together in miserable conditions can lead to increasing levels of material
and psychological frustration.

2. There is a popular revolution of rising expectations with regard to the
material standard of living. The communications revolution, which brings to the
masses an awareness of the fruits of modern society, stimulates consumer appetites
and can lead to growing popular frustration. This is particularly true if income and
consumer spending are very inequitable and dominated by a wealthy elite, and
these inequities are highly visible in the political system.

3. Encouraging economic development, with an effort to improve productivity
in the rural areas and facilitate industrialization in the urban areas, is critical for
providing jobs and offsetting dependence on the agricultural sector. Between the
years 1980 and 2000 estimates are that the work force in the postindustrial countries will increase 10 percent; in Asia the work force will increase 55 percent; while
in Africa and Latin America the work force increase will skyrocket 80 percent or
more.[2]

4. A high population growth rate that can reach over 3.5 percent annually as
in Nicaragua in 1989 is not uncommon. An annual population growth rate (APGR)
of 3.5 percent, for example, means a country will double its population in 20 years.
The APGR figure is divided into 72 to determine the number of years it will take

---

[2]John Naisbitt, *Megatrends* (New York: Warner Books, 1982), p. 62.

Large-scale population movements from rural to urban areas have greatly increased slum areas in many developing countries. Pictured here, Mexico City.

for a country's population to double if a given rate continues. A high APGR is not insurmountable, but it requires active government policy both in terms of family planning and absorbing people into the work force. Latin America, for example, must create 115 million new jobs in the two decades beginning in 1985, a number equal to the entire U.S. work force in 1985.[3]

Current data suggest that the growth rate for all of Africa rose from 2.5 percent in 1960 to 3.2 percent today.[4] Nigeria is the eighth most populous country in Africa and just recently launched a comprehensive family planning program. Should its growth rate continue at the 1989 rate of 2.9 percent annually (45 percent of its population was under 15 years of age in 1988), Nigeria's population would double to 224 million persons in 24 years.

5. The effects of social mobilization will be discussed at length later in the chapter.

Population growth, a young population, hunger, inflation, and unemployment are interlocking problems that often seem to continue without end.

---

[3]Correspondence to Thomas J. Bellows from James W. Brackett, director, Public Policy Analysis of the Population Institute, Washington, D.C., June 2, 1986.

[4]*POPLINE: World Population News Service* (Washington, D.C.), 11 (March–April 1989), p. 1.

One country that illustrates many of these problems is Mexico. Mexico is an oil-exporting country and has confronted major economic crises for more than a decade. Part of the problem is overdependence on petroleum sales, compounded by an often corrupt and mismanaged government (at least until 1982) and inequitable distribution of economic benefits. In the late 1970s, Mexico's **gross national product** (GNP) grew at 8 percent annually in real economic terms. For two years, Mexico was the fastest growing economy in the world. From 1977 to 1981 Mexico was exporting $16 billion of petroleum each year. However, the drop in oil price in mid 1981 and again in 1986 reduced oil exports to $8 billion annually, and 40 percent of the national revenue disappeared. The initial drop in oil prices in 1981 led to few changes in government policy, because the drop was believed to be temporary. The public lost faith, symbolized by the plummeting value of the peso (see Table 11.1). In July 1982, alone, $9 billion was transferred by Mexican citizens from domestic banks to overseas deposits where the currency was more stable. By mid 1982, government inaction and corruption had led to a pervasive loss of confidence and pessimism.

Government austerity measures were initiated by former President de la Madrid who assumed office in 1983. These measures were designed to curb inflation, which escalated to 200 percent annually in the mid 1980s. The economy gradually began to correct itself. However, the austerity measures also caused living standards for the average Mexican citizen to fall 50 percent between 1983 and 1988. Unemployment and underemployment climbed above 40 percent as the policy of reduced expectations was implemented. Half the massive international debt with foreign countries and international banks was renegotiated in 1989. Mexico's foreign debt topped $107 billion, at that time, the second highest international debt in the world. Repaying principal and interest consumed up to 70 percent of the Mexican national government's spending per year.

Some positive signals appeared in late 1989, reflecting international concern as well as more effective government action. President Salinas's record low electoral victory with under 52 percent of the popular vote in 1988 brought to the forefront the better-educated of the ruling Institutional Revolutionary party (PRI). They favor dialogue and accommodation and are not as committed to monopolizing power. For example, since the 1988 national elections, opposition parties control 48 percent of the seats in the House of Representatives. There are opposition members in the Senate for the first time in six decades. The first opposition

Table 11.1   **MEXICAN PESOS PER U.S. DOLLAR
AT THE END OF EACH YEAR**

Year	Pesos Per U.S. Dollar
1980	24
1982	160
1985	465
1989	2,560

Table 11.2   **DECLINING INFANT MORTALITY: A SELECTED COMPARISON**

Country[a]	1960–1965	1982
Nigeria	177	134
South Africia	129	95
Mexico	86	55
USSR	32	23
Costa Rica	81	19
United States	25	11
Japan	24	7

[a]Although in each case numbers declined, the country order remains the same except for the USSR and Costa Rica.

Source: UN Department of International, Economic, and Social Affairs, *Population Studies,* No. 78 (1982), p. 7. Copyright 1982 by the United Nations. Reprinted with permission.

candidate for governor in 60 years won and assumed office in the state of Baja Norte in 1989. A supporter of political reform, newly elected PRI Senator Blanca Ruth Esponda summarized it well, "We cannot keep being attached to the traditional way of governing—that is, imposing, controlling."[5]

The austere economic restructuring by Harvard-trained President Salinas and his Harvard-trained predecessor, Miguel de la Madrid, has facilitated a gradual economic upturn. Many factories are hiring again, and the GNP is expected to grow between 2.2 and 2.4 percent in 1989. Mexico has experienced a decade of hardship, massive foreign debt, a 50 percent drop in living standards, triple-digit inflation, and even years of negative growth. Cynicism and despair are slowly declining, however, because of the renewed possibility of a viable future.

There are other developments in the Third World suggesting at least incremental progress is taking place. During the 1970s, one-half of all the deaths in the developing world were children under age 5. Most of these deaths were caused by a combination of infection and malnutrition. Each year there were 200 million cases of malaria, a similar number of snail fever cases, and 40 million cases of river blindness. The World Bank estimated more than 1 billion people were permanently malnourished. Hunger and starvation were tragic problems for many children.[6]

The more recent decline in the infant mortality rate (IMR) allows for some optimism (see Table 11.2). IMR is a statistic that represents the number of infants out of every 1,000 live births who die before their first birthday. One expert explained:

---

[5]Rushworth M. Kiddler, "Fresh Breezes Blow in Mexico," *Christian Science Monitor* (August 2, 1989), p. 12.

[6]A basic summary of the dramatic statistics is in "The Growing Crisis," *War on Hunger: A Report from the Agency on International Development,* 2 (September 1975), pp. 1–9.

No cold statistic expresses more eloquently the differences between a society of sufficiency and a society of deprivation than the infant mortality rate. . . . The number of children who die before they are one year old is closely related to the overall well being in a country or a region. . . .[7]

Despite shortfalls in adequate medical and health care, conditions are better than they were at the beginning of this century. The percentage of people killed in local wars in the developing world is reduced as compared to the eighteenth century. One consequence is that the birth rate, survival rate, and life expectancy have increased to the point that today the population growth rate (birth minus death rate) for the developing world is more than three times that of the developed world. For example, at present high growth rates, Egypt, Nigeria, the Philippines, and Mexico will double their populations in 29 years or less. It will take the United States and Canada 110 years to double their populations and Western Europe 365 years!

The number of people increases, and, surprisingly, there has been a corresponding growth in food production. During the 1960s there occurred what is popularly known as the *Green Revolution,* making available "miracle rice" and "miracle wheat" hybrid strains. Production jumped in the late 1960s (for example, from 105 million tons of food grain in South Asia in 1966 to 148 million tons in 1970), but this increase leveled off in the 1970s. There were many problems. The wealthier, middle-sized, and large farmers had the money and the larger-sized farms to buy and effectively use fertilizer and farm equipment. The wealthier farmers could build and maintain the necessary irrigation and drainage systems. The small farmers did not have the surplus to invest and in too many cases lost their land as their production and profits fell behind. In some ways, what was to be a humanitarian breakthrough created more economic inequality.

On a positive note, between 1960 and 1986, the amount of land worldwide dedicated to grain production increased by 11 percent. Improved crops and planting practices allowed grain harvests to more than double during this period. Food production in developing countries is increasing at 4.4 percent annually, nearly twice the average APGR for all developing countries.[8] Nevertheless, malnutrition and starvation continue to exist. One study concluded that in 1980 340 to 730 million people in the Third World (excluding China) had incomes too low to provide adequate nutrition: 340 million represents serious health risks and growth-stunted children; 730 million includes those with a chronically deficient diet that restricts an active working life.[9]

Inadequate income, inequitable income distribution, food distribution problems, misguided government policies, and natural catastrophes such as drought or

[7]Kathleen Newland of Worldwatch Institute, Washington, D.C., quoted in *The Decline in Hunger-Related Deaths* (San Francisco: The Hunger Project, 1984), p. 4.

[8]Data from Dieth Schneider, "Scientific Advances Lead to Era of Food Surplus Around World," *New York Times* (September 9, 1986), p. 19.

[9]Shlomo Reutlinger, "Food Security and Poverty in LDCs," *Finance and Development,* 22:4 (December 1985), p. 7.

Table 11.3   COMMODITY PRICES PER POUND IN U.S. DOLLARS[a]

Year	Copper	Nickel	Tin	Sugar
1975	$ 0.642	$ 2.20	$ 3.40	$ 0.25
1980	1.01	2.85	8.46	0.22
1986	0.661	1.86	3.83	0.16

[a]The given prices are in constant dollars and do not account for inflation, which means even lower dollar values.

Sources: U.S. Department of Commerce, Bureau of the Census, *Statistical Abstract of the U.S., 1989* (Washington, D.C., U.S. Government Printing Office, 1989), Table 764, and ibid., 1980, p. 484.

flooding still leave tens of millions on the edge of starvation or starving. Per capita income for sub-Saharan Africa actually dropped in constant dollars (controlled for inflation) from $610 in 1977 to $460 in 1987.[10] Third World countries dependent on commodity exports that continue to decline in price have been hardest hit.

Many countries or population segments still confront severe economic hardship. A majority of Third World countries continue to depend principally on commodity exports (rather than manufactured goods or processed agricultural products) to earn the necessary hard currency to import items not locally manufactured. Table 11.3 illustrates the gradual decline in value of raw material exports, which in turn often means the national earning power of many countries has declined. Copper prices, for example, when accounting for inflation, fell 60 percent between 1980 and 1986. By early 1986, raw material or commodity prices were at their lowest level in this century relative to the prices of manufactured goods. A Washington-based economic consultant warned: "The future is bleak for those who produce everything that comes from the ground."[11] Because of the increasing use of man-made materials, there is a reduced need for raw materials by manufacturers in the industrial countries. Combined with advancing technology (robotics, etc.), this means the future of those countries depending on labor intensive industries and commodity exports will become more difficult.

The economic difficulties of Third World countries are increased by their need to import vital energy supplies for industrial and agricultural modernization. An example is oil. Acting as a unit, the **Organization of Petroleum Exporting Countries (OPEC)** quadrupled the price of oil during the last three months of 1973.[12] The cost of this price increase to the developing world was approximately $10 billion in 1974, an amount equal to almost all forms of development assistance the developing countries received from industrialized, donor coun-

---

[10]Robert M. Press, "Sagging Incomes Keep Africans Hungry," *Christian Science Monitor* (February 10, 1989), p. 2.

[11]Bruce Stokes, "Revolution in the Making," *National Journal* (September 27, 1986), p. 2309.

[12]A readable and still useful analysis of petroflation and its consequences is the Committee for Economic Development, *International Economic Consequences of High-Priced Energy* (New York: CED, 1975).

tries. By the early 1980s, oil was selling at a high of $40 per barrel, an increase of over 1,000 percent since early 1973. This was an intolerable burden on most Third World countries that did not produce oil. The non-oil-producing Third World needs oil not only as fuel but for many other products as well, such as commercial fertilizer, most of which is petrochemical in origin. Over half the population in the Third World has an average annual per capita income of under $500. These countries with the least money were hurt most by skyrocketing oil prices, which then leads to price increases on almost all other imported items.

As discussed earlier, the exports of most developing countries are primary products. As the price of manufactured goods inflate, the prices received by developing countries for other primary products drops. The peoples of the developing world often seem caught in a vicious cycle just to survive economically. Medical and health improvements, although limited, have contributed to high population growth. Many of these countries do not have the hard cash earned through exports to purchase the necessary items to increase agricultural and industrial production. A difficult situation is complicated by increased oil prices, which penalized the developing world most.

Paradoxically, even as oil prices stabilized and began to fall in the early 1980s, we were faced with a new set of problems. Several oil-producing countries (Mexico and Nigeria) had borrowed heavily from Western banks and international lending agencies. Now they are unable to meet their heavy repayment schedule, which in turn has caused serious economic dislocation. Moreover, it is not only oil-producing countries that borrowed heavily. Many Western banks, booming because of petrodollar deposits from OPEC, loaned more than they should have to Third World countries. By 1990, the total foreign debt of all borrowing countries was $1.3 trillion, what some refer to as the *debt bomb.* This aftermath of petroflation in the 1970s continues to disrupt the world financial system linking postindustrial, developing, and OPEC countries. One consequence is that the middle class and wealthy in many developing countries immigrate financially. The capital flight means money is not in the home country to invest and build the economy or to tax in order to pay off the debts or sustain government programs. Seeking out safe countries and financial havens further weakens developing economies. Morgan Guaranty Trust Company estimates, for example, Mexicans have deposited or invested $84 billion overseas; Venezuelans, $58 billion; and Argentinians, $46 billion.[13]

Two other general categories of problems that confront the Third World (as well as the First and Second Worlds) are control of the environment and political integration.

Controlling the Environment

Control over and efficient use of the environment refers to the physical, economic, and social aspects of the environment. This has been one approach used to summa-

---

[13]David R. Francis, "Needed Cash Flees Debtor Nations," *Christian Science Monitor* (February 13, 1989), p. 9.

rize the principal tasks of governments in the developing countries. Often the emphasis is on the technological, but of course technology has important implications for social and political control of human resources. Historian Karl Wittfogel has shown that in China the development of complex hydraulic (irrigation and flood control) systems along the Yellow River and other major Chinese rivers resulted in a highly organized, hierarchical, and authoritarian society. In order to maintain the hydraulic system for hundreds of miles, it was necessary to regulate the populations and to create a complex bureaucratic system to supervise and administer the geographic and human environment. Traditional Oriental government was semimanagerial. It possessed total political power, but it exerted only limited social and intellectual control over its subjects. The result was, in Wittfogel's terminology, "Oriental despotism."[14]

The development of a public policy to meet the essential economic and political needs of a country may result in a population so organized and regimented that it will lose most political liberties. Society may be harnessed to achieve what government officials believe should be the maximum use of the environment. The latest in technological development does not necessarily increase personal freedom.

One common denominator of **political development** (or **political modernization**) is the weakening of traditional political systems. Progress is uneven. Urbanization and industrialization may occur, industrialization may lead to a larger GNP, and the Green Revolution in agriculture may increase total agricultural output. Literacy and the exposure to newspapers and radio spreads. Social and political inequalities can, however, be intensified as a few wealthy business people and officials reap the benefits of economic change. Economic production figures of the country may climb as the result of industrialization policy and new technology in the rural areas, but the urban worker may suffer for many years while new industries are established. The small farmer may be unable to take advantage of the latest technology and expensive fertilizers, resulting in the loss of land to the more affluent landowner who has access to credit and can adopt the new agricultural technology. Even though some progress may be occurring in the economic system and there may be pockets of economic and social change, positive political and social changes may be restricted to a small middle class. The poorer parts of society may become even poorer as in mainland China, where the living standards for new college graduates and university instructors plummetted 50 percent in the 1980s.

It is obvious that one aspect of development or modernization is to allow more rational and effective exploitation of the natural resources these new countries possess. Will the development of these resources lead to further social and economic inequity in society? How much investment of resources and management skills is required and who will bear the burden of this investment? Only a relatively small percentage of the population—10 to 20 percent—may benefit for many years,

---

[14]See Karl J. Wittfogel, *Oriental Despotism* (New Haven, Conn.: Yale University Press, 1957); and "The Historical Position of Communist China: Doctrine and Reality," *Review of Politics,* 16:1 (January 1954), pp. 463–474.

Famine in the Sahel: People collect and eat animal fodder dropped by French military planes for livestock.

while the majority may find that conditions are worse for several decades. European experiences are not encouraging. The British industrial revolution began in 1760 and continued for over a century. The average British citizen actually was worse off as industrial development took place than in the preindustrial period. Charles Booth's *Life and Labor of the People of London* shows that 30 percent of London was at or beneath the level of base subsistence at the end of the nineteenth century.[15]

Inequitable distribution of income is a depressing fact in many Third World countries. Too often the poor seem to get few of the economic benefits the wealthiest 20 percent of the population obtains. Table 11.4 reveals how little of the country's spendable income the poorest 40 percent of the population receive annually in selected developing countries. In all the countries listed, the wealthiest 5 percent receive 40 to 50 percent of the national income annually!

Economic inequity has many explanations. Three of the more common include:

1. A ruling **oligarchy** makes policy that will direct most economic surplus to the ruling elite and its close supporters through such things as awarding government contracts or allowing private monopolies.
2. Limited resources (such as land and oil) historically have been controlled

---

[15]See O. F. Christie, *The Transition to Democracy: 1867–1914* (London: George Rutledge, 1934), p. 287.

Table 11.4　**PERCENTAGE OF HOUSEHOLD INCOME RECEIVED BY POOREST 40 PERCENT OF THE POPULATION**[a]

Iraq	8.0
Mexico	9.9
Nigeria	14.0
Peru	7.0
South Africa	6.1

[a] Data as shown are difficult to acquire and are for the 1960s and 1970s.

Sources: Irma Adelman and Cynthia Taft Morris, *Economic Growth and Social Equity in Developing Countries* (Stanford, Calif.: Stanford University Press, 1973), p. 152; and The World Bank, *World Development Report* (London: Oxford University Press, 1988), pp. 272–273.

by a few, and a principal function of government is to maintain the status quo.

3. Some countries invest in highly technological industries that employ few people at high investment costs of $200,000 per job or more.

The use of older equipment, smaller enterprises, and labor-intensive industries is frequently rejected. Those who are employed benefit, but there are far too few jobs necessary to employ all those needing work; moreover, as we discussed earlier in this chapter, the Green Revolution and mechanization of agriculture often have benefitted only the wealthy landowner and further impoverished the small farmer.

Coordination of resources as well as the determination by a few to retain a monopoly on power, control economic resources, and determine economic policy can lead quickly to authoritarian and arbitrary government policies.

Forging Political Integration

Some form of **political integration** is necessary if a country is to survive. This is true if only to prevent the twin problems of **separatism,** where a segment of the community, usually geographically concentrated, wishes to break away as an independent country; and **irredentism,** where a segment of the community again usually geographically concentrated, wishes to become part of a neighboring political system and separate from the country it is currently a part of, such as some Irish Catholics in Northern Ireland and Palestinian Arabs in Israel.

Political integration is a subjective feeling of community among often diverse groups within the same country. There are social, economic, psychological, and political ties existing that give the population a feeling of identity, self-awareness, exclusiveness, and a sense of belonging to a common nation or political system. Political integration occurs when government contributes to the material and psychological cohesion of the political system. A sense of interdependence and cooperation grows. Citizens come to believe that their personal well-being depends in part on citizenship in the country, and, at least in some ways, personal well-being can be advanced by government policies. A minimum requirement is that government provide the individual with an acceptable degree of security while political integration is occurring. One shared experience that is potentially positive and provides shared distinctiveness is living under the same government. If political integration is taking place, the bulk of the population will not be inclined to respond to irredentist or separatist appeals. There will be little popular support for rapid, drastic, and violent changes in the political system.

The colonial experience often complicates political integration. The political boundaries of many of the new countries were decided in the nineteenth century by the European colonial powers. The African country of Gambia, a former British colony that became independent in 1965, is a rather extreme example of a national boundary that has scant relationship to previous identities. Gambia "defies all principles of boundary making. There are no geographical features or other lines of demarcation, whether economic, cultural, or racial, separating it from the country surrounding it."[16]

Most Third World countries must slowly nurture political integration. Even in Europe it was, and in some instances still is, an arduous process. Two observers of European problems before World War II noted somewhat satirically that a country was "a society united by a common error as to its origins and a common aversion to its neighbors."[17] A single language and culture are absent as often as they are present. In only half the world's countries do 75 percent of the population speak the same language. The PRC, or mainland China, for example, with 4,000 years of continuous history has over 100 million minority peoples who occupy half the territory. The struggle for independence by Tibetans is a clear-cut example of an intense, often bloody struggle for autonomy.

The Dalai Lama, exiled Buddhist religious and political leader of Tibet, received the 1989 Nobel Peace Prize in recognition of 40 years of nonviolent struggle to end Chinese domination of Tibet. In 1951, the PRC invaded Tibet and took power from the Dalai Lama. A Tibetan uprising was crushed by Chinese troops in 1959, and the Dalai Lama and 100,000 refugees fled to India. The issue today often concerns the preservation of Tibetan culture. Tibetans assert over 5,000 temples have been looted and destroyed by the Chinese since the 1959 rebellion. There have been over 20 proindependence protests since September 1987, and as a result **martial law** was proclaimed in early 1989 (see Box 11.1). The PRC foreign

---

[16]E. W. Evans, *Britannia Overseas* (London: Thomas Nelson, 1946), pp. 55–56.

[17]Julian Huxley and Alfred Court Haddon, *We Europeans: A Survey of Racial Problems* (London: Jonathan Cape, 1935), p. 16, quoted in Robert J. Jackson, Doreen Jackson, and Nicolas Baxter-Moore, *Politics in Canada* (Scarborough, Ontario: Prentice-Hall Canada, 1986), p. 16.

Box 11.1 **Separation versus Consolidation**

Under martial law, China has jailed hundreds of Tibetans who took part in some of the biggest proindependence demonstrations in Lhasa since Chinese troops annexed the region in 1951.

Many imprisoned Tibetans, including Bhuddist monks and nuns, were tortured by local authorities during a severe crackdown on dissent, according to international human rights groups.

Thousands of troops stationed in and around Lhasa are maintaining a tense calm in the Tibetan capital, which remains closed to foreign journalists, diplomats, and travelers—including Tibetan emigres—with the exception of those escorted on official tours.

Source: Ann Scott Tyson, "Nobel Prize for Dalai Lama Puts China on Defensive," *Christian Science Monitor* (October 10, 1989), p. 6. Reprinted by permission of the *Christian Science Monitor.* © 1989 by the Christian Science Publishing Society. All rights reserved.

ministry harshly criticized the decision of the Nobel Peace Committee for encouraging separatists who sought to weaken national unity and split China.

Economic development, industrialization, and urbanization have not always brought the political integration expected, even in Communist states where a classless society was to submerge ethnic, religious, linguistic, and regional differences. The Soviet Union manifests the type of problems faced by Third World countries where **primordial** groups are sometimes treated differently and even demand independence (see Box 11.2). The year 1989 saw both peaceful and violent demonstrations in Estonia, Lithuania, and Latvia (the Baltic States), Georgia (Stalin's home state), the Ukraine, Adzerbaijan, and Armenia demanding concessions from Moscow and in some cases independence. General Secretary Gorbachev warned the "nationalist card" was, ironically, being used by enemies of *perestroika* to prevent change and return to authoritarianism, one-party rule.

Summaries of a series of studies of the Soviet Army show in a very understandable way how difficult political integration can be when there is not a dominant culture and social cleavages remain deep.

Reforms that allow more autonomy and freedom of expression may in the short run lead to an explosion of primordial sentiments. These may be difficult to channel into an orderly dialogue stressing accommodation within the existing political boundaries. Self-expression emerging from years of authoritarian suppression can lead to demands for independence.

A government, then, must promote policies that will foster social, economic, and psychological interdependence and will begin the process of political integration. This may be difficult to do. Political integration does not assume that tensions, conflicts, and policy disagreements will cease. It suggests, however, that most of the public issues be handled within a broad framework of rules of the game so that

Box 11.2 **Primordial Cleavages versus Political Integration**

The most important demographic development is the dramatic slowdown of the population growth of Russians and other Slavs in the Soviet Union from 1959 to the present, coupled with the considerably higher growth rate of the non-Slavic population, particularly the Muslim-Turkic peoples of Central Asia and the Caucasus. The Russian share of the Soviet population fell from 54.6 percent in 1959 to 52.4 percent in 1979, whereas that of the Muslim-Turkic peoples rose from 12.6 percent to 17.4 percent in the same period. . . .

As one former Soviet serviceman explained, "In my company there was a kind of subdivision into ethnic groups. Ukrainians were friendly only among themselves, like a separate group; they defended one another—a kind of fraternity. . . . The same can be said about Georgians, Armenians and so on."

. . . The picture drawn from former servicemen (many of them now emigres to the United States and elsewhere) is of a military establishment in which segregation by race is a pervasive influence on conscripts and in which racial discrimination is accepted and routinized.

Soviet forces have long depended most heavily on the Slavic and Baltic populations to man positions of authority and technological sophistication. Balts are regarded by military people as the best educated and skilled servicemen, followed at some distance by Slavs (Russians, Ukrainians, and Byelorussians), Georgians, and Armenians.

Consequently, in branches of the military where advanced technology plays a large role, such as the air force, navy, or strategic rocket forces, ethnic clashes are least prevalent because of the relatively small number of non-Slavs.

Combat units are staffed by a clear majority of Slavic soldiers, who account for about 80 percent of the corps. Non-Slavs, especially Central Asians, serving in these units are often relegated to kitchen duties or warehouse work.

On the other hand, construction battalions and other noncombat units, for reasons that include language deficiencies, low educational achievement, and perceived disloyalty to the regime, are staffed by non-Slav majorities with a strong Central Asian overrepresentation. . . .

A former commander of a stroibat [construction] company described the division of labor in his unit: "The Russians usually handled the most sophisticated equipment; Ukrainians and other Europeans would be laying cable inside the building, while the 'churkas' (an epithet applied to Central Asians meaning literally 'wood chip') would be outside digging ditches or whatever other hard work needed to be done."

Internal security units, used primarily for guard duty in prisons and labor camps and for general policing tasks, are heavily staffed with Central Asians and Caucasians, perhaps as high as 50 to 60 percent of the entire force. Those interviewed who served in these units indicated that this imbalance may be part of a well-thought-out policy of exploiting ethnic antagonisms for the regime's purposes.

According to one of the study's respondents, "They (Central Asians) do an

> excellent job in their guard duties and are considered the most reliable guards for prisons and camps. They are also very tough and cruel, having no sympathy for the prisoners and displaying great hostility toward the Russian inmates."
>
> **Source:** Excerpted from "Racial Problems in the Red Army," *Rand Checklist,* No. 320 (June 1984), pp. 3–5.

the fundamental existence of a particular political system is not challenged as conflicting inputs are handled.

TRADITIONAL AND TRANSITIONAL SOCIETIES: SOME MISPERCEPTIONS

The study of developing political systems frequently is complicated by wrong assumptions. Four examples are discussed so that you will be aware of some of the pitfalls to avoid.

The Static-Stability Error

Traditional societies often are described as stable and experiencing slight or no change in social and political patterns. Traditional societies are usually farming, hunting, fishing, gathering, and sometimes nomadic. There are few inventions, technological changes, or innovations. Trade is minimal and often by barter. There is little economic specialization and most of the labor force is in primary (agricultural or fishing) production. Loyalty is to the family, clan, tribe, or village. Rule is usually by one person or a few (oligarchy). The masses do not participate, and their freedom of action usually is limited because society is hierarchical, with a ruling and a subject class, the latter far more numerous. Landowning is often the single source of wealth and power. Custom dominates most of day-to-day living, with limited need to respond to new circumstances. An article written by the sociologist F. X. Sutton in the 1950s contrasted "intensive agricultural" (traditional) and "industrial" (modern) societies.[18] A distinguishing feature of traditional society is stability with regard to work patterns and rewards within the village. People are familiar with and committed to the locality and the status quo. Change is minimal.

Traditional, non-Western, or historically older societies do undergo fundamental changes, though. When British colonial officials began to assert control over northern Burma, they encountered a group of hill people known as the Kachin, who lived adjacent to the Chinese border and near the Assam area in India. E. R. Leach, a British anthropologist who has studied the Kachin in detail (300,000

---

[18]F. X. Sutton, "Representation and the Nature of Political Systems," *Comparative Studies in Society and History,* 2 (October 1959), pp. 1–10.

people in an area of 50,000 square miles), describes a revolutionary political transformation occurring as late as 1870, shortly before the British arrived (see Figure 11.2 on page 340).[19]

Typically, Kachin villagers had to cultivate the hereditary leader's land without compensation and were required to pay various taxes to him. During the latter part of the nineteenth century a series of village "revolutions" occurred. Many leaders were killed and were replaced by popularly responsible leaders.

The revolutionary villages were called "rebel villages." At one point Leach speaks of the "spontaneous" emergence of the rebel villages. It is clear that among the Kachin, at that time little affected by Western, British contacts, fundamental changes occurred in the political system. The spread of rebel villages either was the result of new settlements (three or more "original" houses of equal status that intermarry) or of political revolt.

> There is a tradition of revolution in which the former gumsa chiefs were either driven out or reduced to the status of lineage headman having no special rights.[20]

Interestingly, British officials, who might be said to represent modernization, opposed the republicanism of the rebel villages. It was much easier to deal with a hereditary leader-owned village where the leader was friendly and could control his subjects. The newly emergent "representative" village government developed by the Kachin was inconvenient in the eyes of British officials. Revolution took place in this "traditional" society, but not as a consequence of Western colonial contacts. British colonial officials eventually succeeded in reversing the trend toward "representative" village government among the Kachins and actually discouraged change.

Adaptability of Traditional Institutions

Sometimes traditional institutions are treated as hindering political change. It is assumed they either contradict efforts to establish a national identity and loyalty, or they impede the growth of more open, participatory political processes. This is not always so.

One example of a traditional institution that assumed a new democratic function is the Indian caste association. Over the centuries the Indian caste system was an indispensable feature of India's repressive and stratified social system.

> Membership in a caste is completely ascriptive: once born into a caste, a man has no way to change social identity insofar as the social structure and cultural norms recognize caste. Caste norms prescribed the ritual, occupational, commensal, marital and social relationships of members, and caste organization and authority enforce these norms. . . . The unit of action and location of caste has been, until recently, the sub-caste in the village or group of villages.[21]

---

[19]E. R. Leach, *Political Systems of Highland Burma* (Atlantic Highlands, N.J.: Humanities Press, 1977; first published in London, 1954). Material for this section was taken principally from pp. 197–207.

[20]Ibid., pp. 206–207.

[21]Lloyd I. Rudolph and Susanne Hoeber Rudolph, "The Political Role of India's Caste Association," *Pacific Affairs*, 33:1 (1960), p. 6.

Adapted from Robert P. Clark, *Power and Policy in the Third World*, 2nd ed. (John Wiley and Sons, 1982), pp. 30–31.

Today, caste associations are more influential at the state level in the Indian federal system, rather than at the national level. Caste organizations with specific objectives emerged in the nineteenth century with the spread of communications, transportation, and a market economy during the British colonial period. At first the lower caste associations concentrated on upgrading their position in society by encouraging members to adopt the behavior of the higher castes: for example,

World

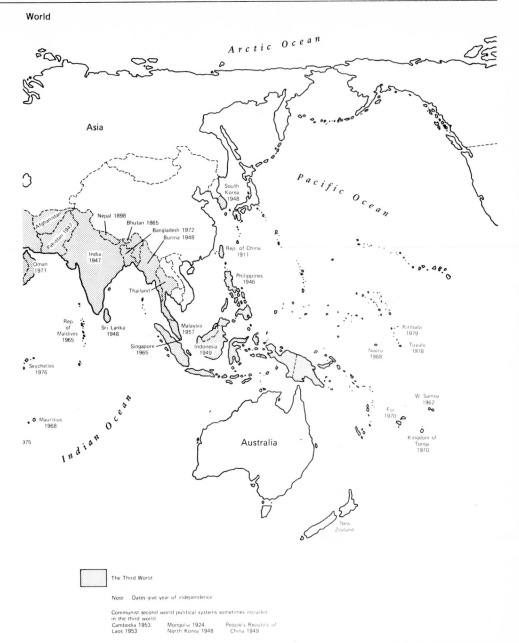

The Third World

Note   Dates give year of independence

Communist second world political systems sometimes included
in the third world
Cambodia 1953   Mongolia 1924   People's Republic of
Laos 1953   North Korea 1948   China 1949

vegetarianism, abstention from liquor, preventing widows from remarrying, and demanding more university scholarships from the colonial rulers. After independence, the local associations supported members for elective office, either through existing parties or by forming new parties. The intention of the caste associations is to maximize caste influence and representation in governing bodies at the state and local level. The associations have been praised for their capacity "to organize

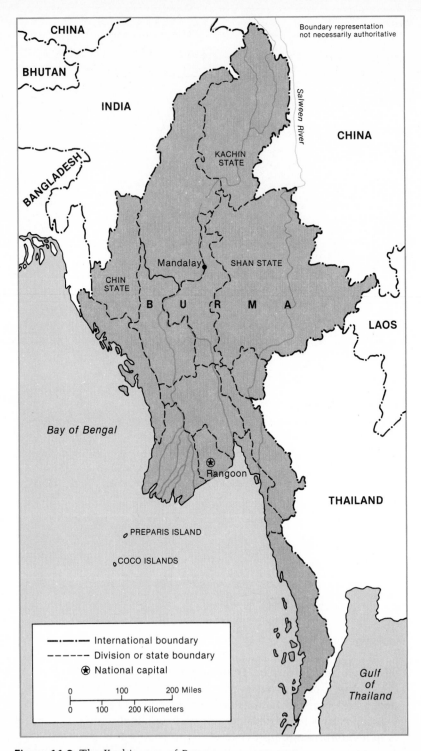

Figure 11.2 The Kachin area of Burma.

the politically illiterate mass electorate, thus making possible in some measure the realization of its aspirations and educating large sections of it in the methods and values of political democracy."[22] Castes have facilitated India's political development process.

Modernization and Political Development

Modernization and *political development* are terms often used interchangeably. This section questions the assumption that modernization is usually an integrated process moving all elements of a society in a single harmonious direction. Daniel Lerner's study of Middle Eastern societies concludes that "urbanization, industrialization, secularization, democratization, education, and media participation do not occur in a haphazard and unrelated fashion." They seem to be "highly associated" and "went together so regularly because, in some historical sense, they *had* to go together."[23]

We have discovered, however, that some parts of society may change while others remain isolated and unaffected by the changes. Iran dramatically illustrates these tensions. Since the late Shah was forced into exile in early 1979, Iran has become a theocratic regime ruled until June 1989 by a religious leader, the late Ayatollah Khomeini. The three-decade-long modernization process begun in the 1950s was confined principally to the urban centers and one-quarter of the population. The Iranian "revolution" is a rejection of what are regarded as the least attractive features of Western-style modernization: alcohol, movies, materialism or conspicuous consumption, relaxing of dress codes, disinterest in religious life, and so forth. To a majority of Iranians, Ayatollah Khomeini was a man of God, a miracle worker with special appeal to a country where 60 percent of the population cannot read. The Koran (Muslim holy book) and the mosques are their sources of education. Islam makes no distinction between religion and government, and in its struggle to reassert itself the Iranian sword of Islam is attacking what it sees as atheistic Western influences.

A perceptive study of Sicily, one of the more traditional regions in Europe, further illustrates compartmentalized change.[24] The Sicilian case shows that modernization and development are not identical concepts. Change can affect some groups in the population but not others. The case study of Sicily defines modernization as imported change: attitudes, behavior patterns, institutions, commodities, expectations, and the like, which are stimulated by contact with postindustrialized countries. The example of Sicily suggests that as a modernizing region becomes

---

[22]Ibid., p. 5.

[23]Daniel Lerner, *The Passing of Traditional Society: Modernizing the Middle East* (Glencoe, Ill.: Free Press, 1958), p. 438. Samuel Huntington has listed nine characteristics that various writers on modernization assign to this concept. See "The Change to Change," *Comparative Politics*, 33:3 (1971), pp. 288–290.

[24]The Sicilian data are taken from Peter Schneider, Jane Schneider, and Edward Hansen, "Modernization and Development: The Role of Regional Elites and Noncorporate groups in the European Mediterranean," *Comparative Studies in Society and History*, 14 (June 1972), pp. 328–329.

Reflections of turmoil in Khomeini-ruled Iran.

dependent on urban-industrial centers, it imports indiscriminately those items that are easier to acquire and that have more appeal. Development is defined as being more difficult—a region's efforts "to acquire an autonomous and diversified industrial economy on its own."[25] During modernization, some incomes may rise, fewer people will be employed in agriculture, urbanization and mass communications will expand, but the changes will occur primarily in a few urban areas that have economic linkages with distant, developed societies (in Sicily's case, Western Europe). Some changes take place because of foreign investment, although these often are isolated pockets of economic change that do not spill over on the rest of society. Frequently workers leave the region for employment in distant, prosperous areas, such as Germany, Switzerland, and France, and remit portions of their salaries to their home, increasing purchasing power and consumption. Between 1950 and 1961, more than 400,000 men left Sicily for employment in Western Europe. A third source of funds changing life-styles is tourism. In one town near the Sicilian coast, the local youth quickly equated the behavior and possessions of the American, British, French, and Scandinavian youth with the "desirable and modern."

> Coca-Cola and Scotch became prestigious drinks, juke boxes in glossy new bars blared hard rock music, and sexual standards of local maidens were threatened by comparison with the reported conduct of foreign girls on the coast. This too is modernization.[26]

[25]Ibid., p. 341.

[26]Ibid., p. 343.

China discovers Coca-Cola.

Modernization may bring change that does not develop and benefit society equally. In some cases, of course, modernization has set in motion fundamental, interrelated, and far-reaching changes, as Karl Deutsch suggested would happen in his theory of social mobilization. The Republic of China (Taiwan) and Singapore are two examples. However, Sicily and Iran are examples of instances where modernization has not brought about such changes. A middle class emerges, but it invests for short-range profit. It does not invest in industrial or agrarian enterprises, which require a slower profit return. The principal investments of the Sicilian middle class

> include real estate speculation, commerce appropriate to the new consumer markets which modernization engenders, and perhaps agricultural or light industrial production, cautiously capitalized because of its vulnerability to fluctuations on world markets. . . . If anything, modernization implies either the fragmentation and dispersal of money, or its waste.[27]

We would add that modernization implies a third option regarding money: placing profits and income in foreign banks, rather than investing it in the local economy.

Modernization and development are not two different words to describe the same phenomena. One means of distinguishing between development and modernization is to regard development as an evolutionary process in which local institutions adapt and control change and are not simply caught up in imitating and reacting to outside forces. Modernization often is contemporary, imported, and creates a dependency on the technologically advanced urban/industrial centers, without helping local political and social institutions to grow and adapt. Development means that a system has some ability to be selective in the type and pace of

---

[27]Ibid., p. 344.

changes and does not haphazardly import what is appealing and affordable to the local affluent consumer, whether it be high-priced liquor, unnecessary computers, or blue jeans.

Modernization is not a "consistent whole," where all good things go together. Modernization is not always associated with general social improvement that benefits most of the population. Modernization may sometimes be only the most current in personal lifestyles. Often its impact on society is haphazard, limited to a wealthy elite in the urban areas. The modernization process can lead to the introduction of serious tensions rather than laying the groundwork for a series of changes moving toward a transforming and prosperous society.

Western-Style Democracy

A fourth misconception of developing political systems assumes that unless a political system has freewheeling, competitive, national elections, with one or more major opposition parties, it is not "politically developed."

The movement toward individual freedom need not necessarily be symbolized, or guaranteed, by a competitive party system at the national level. An anthropologist, Clifford Geertz, has argued persuasively that competitive elections in some of the newly independent societies may have negative consequences. Part of the reason for this is that many people in these new, heterogeneous countries believe that their individual identities and basic values are tied to primordial attachments, such as kinship, race, ethnic group, religion, language, and region of birth.[28] These attachments are combined with a growing awareness that government can protect and enhance these values for some groups. Competitive politics may arouse and organize these primordial attachments as the surest and easiest way to attract popular support and in so doing deepen and intensify social cleavages.

The Congress party (CP) of India dominated the politics of that country since its independence in 1948 until 1989. The CP championed a united India of Hindus, Muslims, Sikhs, and Christians and avoided primordial, more popularly called communal, appeals. As the political ground shifted in 1983, the late Prime Minister Indira Gandhi, who headed the CP, began making appeals to Hindu nationalism. Hindus constitute 73 percent of India's some 700 million population, and special appeals to Hindus was considered a way to rejuvenate fortunes. Mrs. Gandhi was accused of playing communal politics and a leading opponent said the CP power overnight has become the defender of Hindu rights, reversing previous policy. Mrs. Gandhi was assassinated on October 31, 1984, by two of her Sikh bodyguards.

A growing rule of law, with protection of civil liberties, and the increasing freedom of individuals and groups in society may often be a more effective approach to nurturing political pluralism in a developing country. The opportunity for individuals to involve themselves in those choices that most directly affect

---

[28]For an overview of primordial attachments and some political implications, see Clifford Geertz, "The Integration Revolution: Primordial Sentiments and Civic Politics in the New States," in Clifford Geertz, ed., *Old Societies and New States: The Quest for Modernity in Asia and Africa* (Glencoe, Ill.: Free Press, 1963), pp. 105–157.

them might provide a better strategy than instant national elections. The latter can intensify social divisions and are often abolished or become transformed into one-choice plebiscites to ratify government policies. One example that is working is the Republic of China (Taiwan).

There are 22 county farmers' associations and 324 township farmers' associations in Taiwan.[29] The effective level of operation of the farmers' association is at the township. Each association has an elected board, which is the policy-making instrument of the local organization. This board selects the administrative staff, somewhat analogous to our county agents, as well as budget officers, managers of the cooperative store, and so forth. Approximately 6 percent of the regular members of the farmers' association hold elected positions in the association. Another 3 percent are members of village extension committees, while other villagers hold office in the local government, irrigation associations, farmer tenancy committees, credit unions, and the like. The elections and decision making by local farmers at this level are not controlled by the central government except in terms of such general policies as encouraging greater use of fertilizer and encouraging sugar-cane production.

The farmers' associations were developed in conjunction with a far-reaching land-reform campaign in Taiwan in the 1950s. The associations have been effective in increasing production and making available marketing arrangements for the rural economy. The various office-holding opportunities opened up by the development of the associations have created a large number of new leadership positions in society, beyond the number of traditional, village elder leadership positions that existed in pre–World War II, Japanese-occupied Taiwan. Two foreign-aid specialists who have studied Taiwan and a number of other developing countries concluded that new leadership positions

> are a way of subjecting traditional leaders to competition. But most important of all, the application of this principle confronts the traditional leaders with a choice. Either they must become leaders of development or run the risk of losing their positions.[30]

The new local institutions have not been taken over by the traditional elites or officials from Taipei, the capital. The central government insists that farmers' associations prepare annual work programs and budgets, assisting them and making sure that these programs are carried out. They also assist the associations in obtaining budgeting information, financial aid, and general information about production and marketing. In such a way, the potential abuse and power at the local level by traditional elites or the more wealthy farmers is controlled. Individual villagers not only are concerned with carrying out decisions affecting their personal livelihood but also have the opportunity to have a voice in making these decisions. Represent-

---

[29]For a historical analysis of Taiwan's changing rural society, see Martin C. Yang, *Socio-Economic Results of Land Reform in Taiwan* (Honolulu: East-West Center Press, 1970). For a superb comparison of Taiwan with land reform in seven other countries see Hung-chao Tai, *Land Reform and Politics: A Comparative Analysis* (Berkeley, Calif.: University of California Press, 1974).

[30]Edgar Owens and Robert Shaw, *Development Reconsidered* (Lexington, Mass.: D.C. Health, 1972), pp. 27–28.

ative politics is emerging at the grassroots level in Taiwan. The local cooperatives involve the farmers in participating in rural change and using the most efficient agricultural techniques. They also provide an opportunity for independent decision making that has been carried forward to local township government councils, where there is growing freedom of political choice in electing members.

The importance of self-conscious participation and a growing feeling of being effective and of identification with the political system are affirmed in *The Civic Culture*, a book that studies the political cultures of five countries, West Germany, Great Britain, Italy, Mexico, and the United States:

> Organizations in which there is some opportunity for the individual to take an active part may be as significant for the development of democratic citizenship as are voluntary organizations in general. . . . Democracy depends upon citizen participation, and it is clear that organization membership is directly related to such participation. . . . Membership in a politically oriented organization appears to lead to greater political competence than does membership in a nonpolitical organization, and active membership in an organization has a greater impact on political competence than does passive membership.[31]

Participation is a crucial aspect of political development. Participation may be initiated more effectively at the local level than at the top in national elections. Habits and skills of participation often do not percolate downward very rapidly, if at all, but the introduction of local participation can contribute to building a more open political society.

THEORIES OF POLITICAL DEVELOPMENT

There is no universally accepted theory of political development. Many of the definitions various authors have drawn up overlap and share several features. Three representative theories discussed are the development syndrome and those of Karl Deutsch and Samuel P. Huntington. Each has substantial elements of truth, but none of them always and comprehensively explains political development.

The Development Syndrome and the Five Crises

One of the first and still widely used terms, "development syndrome," suggests a movement whose ultimate objective seems to be a pattern similar to what has been achieved in the Western world.[32] The result is the emergence of a "world culture":

---

[31]Gabriel A. Almond and Sidney Verba, *The Civic Culture: Political Attitudes and Democracy in Five Nations* (Boston: Little, Brown, 1965), pp. 262–263.

[32]This definition represented the thinking of the Committee on Comparative Politics of the Social Sciences Research Council and was set forth in Lucian W. Pye, *Aspects of Political Development* (Boston: Little, Brown, 1966).

But at an ever-accelerating rate the direction and volume of cross-cultural influences has become nearly a uniform pattern of the Western industrial world imposing its practices, standards, techniques, and values upon the non-Western World.[33]

The development syndrome (a syndrome is a pattern of interrelated traits) included three characteristics. The first was *equality,* which anticipated universal adult electoral participation with popular interest and involvement. Equality also meant a general system of laws that would apply to all citizens equally. Opportunity for social mobility was an aspect of equality, particularly as related to political office or the public service. Achievement standards were introduced rather than a spoils system or a system that emphasized ascriptive or inherited status qualities, such as ethnic group, religion, kinship, nobility over commoner, or region of the country. Demonstrated merit was the principle for hiring and advancement.

A second feature of the development syndrome was the *capacity* of a political system in terms of the types and range of activities government undertook and its effectiveness in making and implementing public policy. A high-capacity government would achieve high professional standards including such things as professional training, technical skills, rational approaches to policy, and results (such as land reform in Taiwan or industrialization in Japan).

The third characteristic was *differentiation* and *specialization.* We assume that as society and government become more complex and specialized, political pluralism will emerge. Specialization, or expertise, is considered important. Each agency will perform specialized and limited functions; therefore, it can be more responsive and capable in its activities. Unfortunately, there has been little thought given to the coordination of the various specialized government departments. A hundred subdepartments approaching a problem from multiple angles can, as we have learned, impede effective and responsive public policy.

The development syndrome recognized that there would be inherent tensions between various groups, some making demands for equality, others emphasizing capacity or a strong government, and still others stressing technological innovation. The particular mix of these demands and the way the political system reacted would result in patterns of development. Advocates of the development syndrome also emphasized five "crises" that every developing political system confronts and deals with if it is to evolve as a developed state.[34] The crises listed will not be followed in sequence by every country although it is obvious that the order in which they are presented is based on British experience:

1. The *identity crisis* is surmounted when a people within a given territory feel a sense of group identity, recognizing that this is their national territory. It can be described as a sense of togetherness and the absence of significant separatist or irredentist pressures. It is similar in many respects to political integration, discussed earlier.

---

[33]Ibid., p. 9.

[34]The seventh volume of the Committee on Comparative Politics, which discusses these crises in detail, is Leonard Binder et al., *Crises and Sequences in Political Development* (Princeton, N.J.: Princeton University Press, 1971), parts of which are used in this discussion.

2. The *legitimacy crisis* refers to popular acceptance of the constitutional nature of the political system or the commonly accepted rules of the game. Legitimacy also is related to the responsibilities or functions of a government and the popular feeling about whether government is effectively doing what it should be doing, that is, taking care of internal security, land reforms, new jobs, and health care.

3. The *penetration crisis* concerns the ability of government to influence basic policies and decisions throughout the country. A government that is restricted to the major towns and a few of the main roads during the daylight hours will not be able to carry out its work and develop feelings of confidence and rapport between government officials and citizens.

4. The *participation crisis* is the small number of people participating in the political system, the range of alternatives that can be publicly discussed/debated, and the lack of opportunity to select between competing candidates in elections. The participation crisis is worked out through the evolution of organized interest groups, a political party system, and competitive elections. In most developing countries if universal suffrage is bestowed almost immediately after independence, there is formal participation. We might question, however, if this participation is really effective in solving issues and note that voting is sometimes merely a controlled election with no true choice.

5. The *distribution crisis* occurs as government attempts to encourage the distribution of goods and services throughout society, eliminating the more flagrant inequalities, and making more equitable the benefits received by the population. Such policies as unemployment legislation, social welfare, minimum wage, and public parks tend to reduce gaps between the wealthy and the poor. Government may be active in providing opportunities for groups that previously had been at a disadvantage, such as through job quotas or scholarships. An industrialization program that provides help, even modestly, for the under- and unemployed is a form of distribution response.

These five crises were based on the British experience. In the British case each crisis took decades, if not centuries, to solve. The appearance of these crises occurred in the order discussed. Frequently, several generations of people were involved in dealing with a particular crisis.

Many developing countries confront several crises simultaneously. An unbearable strain may be placed on government. An insurgency, which generally is a legitimacy crisis, can make it impossible for a reform-minded government to deal with other crises, such as penetration, participation, and distribution. The inability of the government to deal with other pressing issues in turn makes its legitimacy even more suspect and unstable. An administrative apparatus, systematically subjected to a war of attrition, cannot perform even the minimal output functions necessary to build legitimacy. A tragic example is the former country of South Vietnam, where data reveal thousands of deliberate political assassinations between 1957 and 1963.

> The common characteristic of this activity against individuals is that it was directed at the village leader, usually the natural leader—that individual who, because of his

age, sagacity, or strength of character, is the one to whom people turn for advice and leadership. Many were religious figures, schoolteachers, or simply people of integrity and honor. Since they were superior individuals these persons were more likely to stand up to the insurgents when they came to the village and thus most likely to be the first victims. The assassination rate declined steadily from 1960 to 1965 for the simple reason that there was only a finite number of persons to be assassinated. Many villages by 1966 were virtually depopulated of their natural leaders, who are the single most important element in society.[35]

Political systems cannot survive this systematic terrorism against a government over a period of many years. Legitimacy in the developing countries requires young governments to win popular support by delivering outputs. Without an administrative service, no government can do more than survive for a few years. Public policies cannot be developed and implemented because of the day-to-day need for physical survival. Too many developing countries face a brutal and extended internal war, which is an intolerable drain on already limited resources and makes it difficult to solve any of the five crises.

Social Mobilization

Political development also has been analyzed as sets of **dependent variables.** These are political responses to changes that occur in society and that in turn require reactions by government if the political system, those particular political leaders, and the existing rules of the game are to survive. Implicit is the notion that many of the social changes that occur are not directed or inspired by government policies, but evolve as the society responds and adapts to complex pressures. Karl Deutsch set forth a widely quoted approach known as **social mobilization.**[36]

Deutsch maintained that social mobilization increases the probability of political tensions and demands in society and brings about fundamental changes in the nature of the political system because of the "changing range of human needs that impinge upon politics." People expect their governments to do more. Social mobilization occurs as more people move to the cities and as more people are exposed to political events through newspapers and radios, both in the cities and in the rural areas. People come to believe that there are needs the villages no longer meet, either because they have new concerns for better schools, better water supplies, the introduction of a partial cash economy, and so forth or they have left the village and moved to a new location usually to seek jobs and economic survival. One consequence is that more people take part in political discussions, possibly in demonstrations or riots, strikes, insurgencies, and various organizations that speak to government officials, demanding more services and benefits.

The traits or variables Deutsch identifies as part of social mobilization are empirically measurable, and most are available in various statistical data books

---

[35]Douglas Pike, *Viet Cong* (Cambridge, Mass.: The M.I.T. Press, 1966), p. 248.

[36]Karl Deutsch, "Social Mobilization and Political Development," *American Political Science Review,* 55 (September 1961), p. 495.

published annually.[37] Social mobilization politicizes individuals who previously did not play an active role in the political process. The number of claims on government increases in scope and intensity. Government is held responsible for the changes and their effects on society, or it is regarded as the only institution capable of responding to the new and diverse challenges. Sometimes people believe the existing government must be overthrown if any positive changes are to occur. Some of the characteristics or measures of social mobilization are

1. Decreasing percentage of labor force in agriculture and an increasing percentage in manufacturing.
2. Increasing percentage of population in cities with 100,000 or more inhabitants.
3. Growing percentage of population over age 15 that is literate.
4. Increasing number of radios and television sets and newspaper circulation per 1,000.
5. Population growth (the lower the rate, the better).
6. Increasing voting participants as percentage of adult population.
7. Increasing number of persons who have changed residence or locality since birth.

Social mobilization exposes people to "modernity" and makes them want change. It encourages or makes it possible for them to change their residence, occupations, communication patterns, reading habits, peer groups, aspirations, political outlooks, levels of political information, general attitudes toward the political system, and expectations about what the political system should do. People expect government to do more and do it better.

It is implicit that the final outcome in terms of literacy, birth rate, life expectancy, exposure to mass communication, and so forth will approach contemporary Western standards. A "world culture" bias is apparent in social mobilization analysis. Also apparent is the belief of a general "forward" movement in society, which affects most groups more or less equally. Changes in the political system are more a result than a cause of the social mobilization process. We believe there is a certain weakness in an approach that overlooks the fact that political actors and institutions usually influence the social system more than any other single cause, including the seven just listed.

The Institutionalization Thesis

Samuel P. Huntington has written on political development and political change for many years.[38] He is a political scientist who has changed his perspectives over

---

[37]For example, Charles L. Taylor and David A. Jodice, eds., *World Handbook of Political and Social Indicators*, 3rd ed. (New Haven, Conn.: Yale University Press, 1983); *The Economist, The World in Figures* (Boston: G.K. Hall & Co., 1987); and The World Bank, *World Tables, 1987*, 4th ed. (Washington, D.C.: The World Bank, 1988); as well as various UN publications.

[38]A superior overview of the political development literature, including summaries of his own works, is found in Huntington, *The Change to Change*, pp. 283–322. Most of the references to Huntington are taken from this article. Huntington documents his previous political development writings in this essay.

the years and acknowledges this change in his own writings. He was one of the first to point out that we cannot assume that all political systems will be moving together in a progressive development pattern. Some political systems will regress or "decay," at least for a time.

Huntington believes that one should distinguish between *political development* and *political modernization.* To use the terms interchangeably restricts one's focus. It would be very difficult to analyze modernization in the time of the Roman Empire or the Middle Ages because these periods are not modern by our standards. Political development, on the other hand, has occurred over the centuries and is not a term that should be applied only to recent events.

In *Political Order in a Changing Society,* Huntington presents his institutionalization thesis, which continues to have considerable usefulness. Here he is concerned with interaction between the demands of political participation and the necessity of political institutionalization in order for day-to-day governing to occur. The pressure for political participation is present throughout most of the contemporary world and can be set into motion by a multitude of historical experiences. Political institutionalization is regarded as a means by which societies respond to this striving for some form of political participation. Traditional or colonial political systems that have experienced a high level of institutionalism (for example, a bureaucracy, a governing council, or a partly elected legislature) will be more capable of responding to pressures for political participation and inputs. Huntington also suggests that certain leadership groups drawn from the traditional aristocracy, the military, or a revolutionary leadership might be able either to adapt or create new institutions that would allow a political system to respond to or control pressures in an orderly fashion. Stability and the ability to survive by responding to the most intense demands will be achieved through working political institutions in the society. One difficulty is that a highly institutionalized political system, such as the Soviet Union, could be classified as politically developed. This would be true in terms of institutionalization, but not true in terms of personal and group freedoms and some freedom of political choice. A second difficulty is that by stressing political participation as a catalyst, the focus remains on the modern or contemporary. This was an orientation Huntington had previously criticized.

Huntington later expanded his thesis and argued that two modifications should be made: There were factors other than political participation that should be taken into consideration, and political development more properly should be called political change. It takes place in the First and Second worlds, as well as the Third World. There should be an effort to relate changes in one part of the system to changes in another part to begin to establish some cause-and-effect relationships. Political scientists should concentrate on the institutions and processes in the political system that seem to be dominant. Institutions remain crucial. Those countries that can adapt existing institutions or build new, effective institutions are more likely to experience orderly and progressive change.

Political Change

Every political system experiences change. Analysis need not be restricted to a specific time period. A single political system can be studied over a period of time such as the French Fourth and Fifth Republics, or two or more political systems during a given period of history can be compared. Our concern is back to the political, where it should be for political scientists. Political institutions and political leaders are factors that shape the natural and social environment, generally more than they are shaped by the environment. Social and economic changes often are more a result of political decisions than many writers have acknowledged. Industrial parks, the commitment of resources to hydroelectric or nuclear power plants, defense expenditures, increasing literacy through more schools, the availability of basic medical facilities, birth control programs, government-nurtured foreign export programs—all influence the intensity and scope of demands made on governments, as well as government capacity. A focus on change recognizes the crucial role of political decisions and their consequences for the country. Political change is key to studying political development.

POLITICAL DEVELOPMENT: AN OUTMODED TERM?

In recent years we have witnessed a shift in emphasis away from the term "political development." Many believe it implies the ultimate objective is some type of Anglo-American democracy based on a two-party system, underpinned by a popular political consensus. Early writings on political development went so far as to divide the world's political systems into Western and non-Western and to speak of a unique non-Western political process. One political scientist drew up a "generalized model" of 17 traits that were "dominant and distinctive characteristics of a non-Western political process."[39] Non-Western countries were fundamentally different. These differences would affect the way these societies moved toward a more rational, prosperous, and Western-style political system.

Almost immediately a lucid rejoinder by another political scientist appeared. The rejoinder said the distinction between a Western and a non-Western or Third World political process was not valid. The problems of rapid change and the efforts to industrialize rapidly are not new. Western Europe in the nineteenth century experienced similar political, social, and economic problems as it sought to deal with the French revolution, the industrial revolution, capitalism, and the revolutionary claims of Karl Marx.[40]

Almond and Coleman's *The Politics of Developing Areas,* published in 1960, argued convincingly that all political systems were "mixed."[41] Every political system is in some degree of transition, and each has a mixture of modern and traditional elements. Almond illustrated this "mixed" character of modern political systems with an American example.

[39]Lucian Pye, "The Non-Western Political Process," *Journal of Politics,* 20 (August 1958), pp. 468–486.

[40]Alfred Diamant, "Is There a Non-Western Political Process?" *Journal of Politics,* 21 (February 1959), pp. 123–124.

[41]Gabriel A. Almond and James S. Coleman, eds., *The Politics of Developing Areas* (Princeton, N.J.: Princeton University Press, 1960), p. 23.

Several early studies of the impact of mass communications (radio, newspapers, and movies) in the United States suggested a situation whereby the electorate was composed of "atomized individuals" linked "to a system of mass media which were assumed to monopolize the communication process." Further research revealed this model of political communications was inaccurate. Newer studies indicated media information was filtered to individuals through opinion leaders. The opinion leader was commonly "a trusted individual whose political influence was often a diffuse consequence of other roles," who might be listened to and respected by virtue of being the landlord, a well-liked and respected friend in the peer group, a religious leader in the village or parish, or a vigorous and extroverted personality. There was a "mixed" (modern/traditional) two-step communication process. The informal opinion leader was often the intermediary who made others aware of significant political information and interpreted this information. The opinion leader in turn was influenced more by other people than the mass media. The opinion leader was considered traditional when compared with "modern" political parties:

> The modern, mass, bureaucratically organized, political party has not supplanted the informal coteries of notables which preceded it, but combines with this "more primitive" type of structure [local organization leaders] in what amounts to a mixed system.[42]

This recognition that political systems in all parts of the world share fundamental features led some to reject the notion of political development as artificially dividing Western and non-Western systems. Actually, development was a process North America and Europe went through and, as our earlier discussion of postindustrial societies in Chapter 2 illustrated, are still experiencing. A specialist on European development offers an interesting example of forced changes that were imposed on pre-1917 Russia, as it strove to develop:

> When Russia faced a serious food shortage, the potato was introduced, and then the peasants refused to eat them. They were ordered to plant potatoes, but they dug them out at night. So the Russian Tsar sent soldiers to guard the potatoes at night. Eventually, the peasants found the potatoes edible. There are many oligarchical or authoritarian features in European history during the modernization phases. It is not a speciality of non-Western countries.[43]

Despite parallels between the industrial/postindustrial world and the Third World, the concept of political development still applies principally to non-Western countries. This underlying theme, often present in political development literature, presumes a movement toward a "Western" objective and does not consider seriously the possibility of regression. If a military junta or a Communist-led insurgent group takes over a country, it frequently is seen as an unpleasant necessity on the road to rationality, efficiency, and maximum use of

---

[42]Ibid., pp. 20–21.

[43]Karl W. Deutsch quoted in *Free China Review* (Taipei) (November 1983), p. 51.

national resources rather than a new leadership that may mismanage worse than its predecessors.

Political change is not limited to particular parts of the world or to specific periods in history. Nevertheless, this recognition of change and transition as the essential focus for political science should not discourage us from studying something called political development. Political change with special reference to the problems of the developing or emerging countries is an appropriate focus; in fact, the term "political development" is now so widespread that it is used even by Third World officials to describe the deliberate construction of a more open political system. The individual who became president of Korea after the 1979 assassination of the autocratic President Park spoke of a historic mission and promised his country: "I will be the cornerstone in achieving political development amid stability and Constitutional order."[44]

The study of developing countries does not rule out study and appreciation of the Western experience. The recognition that political change is universal, there are stages of development or regression in political systems, and all political systems are mixed in nature allows for comparisons that draw on Western examples to comprehend better underlying changes, crises, and contemporary government responses in developing countries. Many of the same problems and development stages occurred in the West decades or even centuries ago.

Political development as an area of inquiry has shed its non-Western exclusiveness. In the future, political development will refer to challenge, response, and change, with a bias toward stable, nonrevolutionary, and non-violent adjustments. Political development does not necessarily have an Anglo-American democratic model as its objective. Its essence is innovative responses by political leaders that make possible orderly adjustments. It is committed to the optimum degree of social, economic, and political freedoms, recognizing that each country has unique qualities. Therefore, no single pattern will emerge.

Political development also presumes that new political institutions will emerge or there will be substantial modifications in existing institutions. Problems of village parochialism; primordial sentiments such as first loyalty to religion, language group, region, and so on; and the need to create employment and reduce the population growth rate are juxtaposed against government leadership with only limited resources. There is an inadequate tax base, a shortage of motivated and skilled labor, and, all too frequently, an externally supported insurgency that may force a government to concentrate on military and physical survival, passing over important social and economic problems. At this moment in time the burdens and capacities of the developing countries differ in important ways from those of the Western countries. A central problem is to distinguish between threats to the security of the country and threats to the security of the ruling group. Ruling elites tend to define all challenges as threats to national security. The result is that political reform is even more difficult to achieve.

---

[44]"Peaceful Transfer of Rein Mission," quoted in an article in *The Korean Herald* (November 25, 1979), p. 5.

PROBLEMS WITH THE AUTHORITARIAN SOLUTION

The authoritarian solution maintains a naive faith in the unique integrity, capacity, and wisdom of the ruling elite. Pluralism recognizes aggregation and accommodation as critical in effective nation building and assumes policy is not simply rule and administration, but includes a broad range of inputs.

Whenever a society is composed of more than an extended family network, most members believe that certain objectives and values can be achieved only by authoritative rules applicable to everyone in society. As society becomes numerically and geographically larger and more complex and impersonal, citizens regard government as the most promising way of enforcing laws binding on everyone in the social system. Disagreement over who will make the laws, what the laws should be, and how they shall be applied is political conflict. The amount of participation and discussion allowed and the administration of enforcement procedures locate a political system on a scale between authoritarian and pluralistic.

Many assume that a strong, authoritarian government is the most appropriate institution to confront the challenges of the 1980s. This is especially true in the Third World where the demands made on new governments are significantly greater than demands made at similar points in Western political development. In the West problems such as national identity, industrialization, population growth, social mobilization, Communist subversion, elections, and the revolution of rising expectations often were sequential rather than simultaneous.

A government that seeks to control everything through centralized planning, however, runs into serious problems. For example, the Chinese Communist party (CCP) newspaper, *People's Daily,* has discussed overcentralization. It reported that a small, isolated, mountainous county printed over a million pages of documents in 1978. The county's party chief had to study an average of 16 daily reports from superiors, while the 360 county officials spent over one-third of their time traveling to the county seat to attend meetings. The determination to enforce a policy of absolutely following the government/party line has led in the PRC to what is called the "three evils": too many meetings, too many documents, too many inspections.[45] We tend to overlook the inefficiencies of authoritarian government or be shielded from them by censorship.

Even those with a personal liberal philosophy sometimes urge developing countries to adopt authoritarian solutions because it will be easier to bring about orderly change. A sympathetic overview of the emancipation of African and Asian peoples, written nearly 30 years ago by a Harvard scholar, declared:

> For a backward people precariously moving out from under colonialism with all the problems of economic development still ahead of them, it is highly doubtful that the sovereign remedy is a full-scale installment of democracy. . . . [T]he prime require-

---

[45]Reported by Fox Butterfield, "China Posts a New Target: Bureaucratic Ossification," *New York Times* (February 17, 1979), p. 2.

ment is not more freedoms but for discipline and hard work, not for opposition but for a national consolidation of all forces and talents.[46]

Traditional societies may feel uncomfortable with the concepts of individual expression and civil liberties that are core in political pluralism. Put in the best light, this may seem to be a dangerous exaltation of the individual over the political community. In several African languages, for example, the words "opponent" and "enemy" are synonymous. There is no concept of a loyal opposition.

Like it or not, a common theme throughout the world's political history is rule by the few, most commonly for the benefit of the few. The most populous Third World country, the PRC, recently emphasized again its belief in rule by a few.

For a few months in 1978 and 1979, PRC officials permitted political dissent. The most famous example is the two-block-long "democracy wall" in Peking, where people could paste up posters criticizing government policies. This was stopped in 1979.

Student demonstrations in 1986–1987 were suppressed in January 1987. They had been tolerated for a few months, but were considered too disruptive and were forcefully halted, although with a minimum of arrests and loss of life. Students were complaining about study and living conditions, as well as calling for political liberalization. There was division in the PRC leadership over how much political pluralism should be allowed. The more flexible head of the CCP at that time, General Secretary Hu Yaobang, favored dialogue with the students. He was removed from his post in February 1987. Deng Xiaoping, the de facto, supreme leader of the PRC and a majority of others on the CCP Politburo reaffirmed the need for party monopoly of political power and minimal political pluralism.

On April 15, 1989, Hu Yaobang died. Students at universities in Beijing put up posters praising Hu and his more tolerant approach. By the end of April, thousands of students marched and camped out in Tiananmen Square. Subsequent demonstrations and marches in the capital involving up to 1 million people included students from around the country, workers, and civil servants. Students took over and filled Tiananmen Square, and prodemocracy demands grew in intensity. Political deterioration and social unrest were everywhere, and it appeared the government was losing control of Beijing.

Again, there were divisions in the top leadership. Zhao Ziyang, who replaced Mr. Hu as CCP general secretary, favored negotiations with the students. Conservative hardliners urged an end to public demonstrations and restoration of order. Free political expression ended on the night of June 3 and the early hours of June 4 when armed troops cleared the square. Approximately 3,000 unarmed persons were brutally killed (shot or crushed by military vehicles) and thousands more were arrested, tried, and sentenced to prison (10,000 to 25,000). Some were executed. The official CCP line was that the counterrevolution was over. At 7:40 A.M., June 4, a government loudspeaker announced to an empty, bloodstained Tiananmen

---

[46]Rupert Emerson, *From Empire to Nation* (Boston: Beacon Press, 1962), pp. 289–290.

Square: "Rebellion has been suppressed, and the soldiers are now in charge of Tiananmen."[47]

Mr. Zhao was removed as CCP general secretary and placed under house arrest. Political authority is no longer publicly divided. There still are divisions within the Politburo as to how far to recentralize the economy and whether to curtail ten years of gradual, free-enterprise economic reforms. The fact is that economic growth since liberal economic reforms were begun in 1979 has led to double-digit inflation in the urban areas, widespread corruption, and the appearance of a wealthy elite whose economic status came through government connections and special privileges.

There is apparent agreement among the post–June 4 leadership, though, that all of China's resources must be mobilized through an authoritarian, one-party state. Only then is it possible to try to balance centralized, economic state capitalism, private initiative, and economic growth. One of the first steps to reassert government control was intensified Marxist indoctrination. The government's campaign after the June 4 crackdown focused on combating bourgeois liberalization, a principal cause of the counterrevolutionary rebellion of 1989. The one-party state in 1989 mainland China seeks to reassert total control in most parts of society. How much economic initiative will be tolerated is yet to be decided. A return to more centralized economic planning is likely. More certain is the consolidation of all political power in the hands of a few in Beijing, at least for now.

We would like to suggest that the values of national political integration and respect for the autonomy of the individual spirit usually can be achieved better through less authoritarian political arrangements. In part, this is because of our bias against authoritarian regimes. Practically, we believe that better results can be achieved via a more democratic form of politics. Furthermore, revolutionary dogmatism offers as many failures as successes. Those developing countries that are most economically successful have opted for some degree of political pluralism rather than a pervasive authoritarianism or are in the process of gradually liberalizing, such as Chile, Malaysia, the Republic of China, Singapore, South Korea, the Ivory Coast, Nigeria, Brazil, Costa Rica, Venezuela, and others.

Developing countries are usually heterogeneous—multiethnic, multitribal, multilinguistic, multireligious, having valley and hill peoples, and so forth. Authoritarian, or "strong," governments have a disturbing tendency to represent only one community in the country; consequently, other groups become increasingly alienated and grievances give rise to various degrees of insurrection, leading to more authoritarian government responses.

Finally, we must mention the terrible cruelties authoritarian regimes impose upon their citizens in the name of the new utopia or just to retain unchallenged power. Often we ignore these tragedies because they are not in the immediate present, covered by instant television, or because the world press is not interested

---

[47]"Special Report: The Shattered Dream," *Los Angeles Times* (June 25, 1989), Part I-A, p. 1.

or cannot obtain access. The description in Box 11.3 illustrates the terrible, hidden toll of totalitarian governments.

A French social scientist, Emile Durkheim, observed that national integration, or "solidarity," could be achieved "mechanically" or "organically." Under mechanical solidarity, beliefs and values are to be common to all members. Mechanical solidarity and individual choice are opposed. Mechanical solidarity typifies traditional societies or contemporary authoritarian and totalitarian systems, as in Stalin's Soviet Union, where there is little freedom of choice.

Organic solidarity describes a more open, pluralistic society, one that has achieved specialization and a division of labor or is moving in that direction. Durkheim stated that individualism, innovation, and independence increased in society as organic solidarity evolved. Further, he argued that the human potential could be realized only in a society based on organic rather than mechanical solidarity. As individuals' specialized and creative functions are possible only "if each one

---

Box 11.3 **The Cruel Road to Utopia**

It was a debate that can never be settled, yet it will continue to engage historians for many years. It is whether Adolf Hitler or Joseph Stalin was the man responsible for the greatest amount of suffering in human history.

The difficulty in resolving this question lies in the fact that each man's crimes are so similar. Each set out deliberately to murder millions of innocent men, women, and children; showed himself utterly devoid of any touch of kindliness or mercy; and combined unspeakable cruelty with the most revolting hypocrisy. Hitler was portrayed as the unselfed, tireless warden of his people's welfare; Stalin was the kindly, pipe-smoking "Uncle Joe."

Hitler's millionfold murders are well known, not least because of the present German government's readiness to have them publicized. Stalin's equally large sowing of death among Ukrainian peasants and others has received far less publicity, because of the Soviet government's continuing refusal to admit to the horrors of its own past. Nor are these deeds of Stalin without tragic relevance to the present. The enforced collectivization that in the single year of 1932–1933 starved to death 6 million to 8 million individuals still governs a bumbling Soviet agriculture.

. . . The result was not only a land littered with the bodies of millions of dead (that same year the Soviet Union exported 1.5 million tons of grain, more than enough to have saved the lives of all who starved), but the reduction of Russian agricultural production to a level markedly below what had prevailed under the excoriated czars.

Source: Excerpted from a book review of Miron Dolot, *Execution by Hunger: The Hidden Holocaust* (New York: W.W. Norton, 1985), reviewed by Joseph Harrison, "Grim Tale of Starvation during Stalin's 'Hidden Holocaust.'" *Christian Science Monitor* (November 25, 1985), p. 34.

has an individual sphere of action, consequently a personality." Each unit "has its special physiognomy, its autonomy. Yet as the unity of the organism increases the more marked is the individuality of its parts."[48] Political development requires autonomy and creativity, as well as effective government, diversity, and unity.

We do not advocate a return of the night watchperson state, which confined itself to external and internal security and maintaining a communications and transportation network. The numerous crises telescoped into a narrow time span in the developing countries require active, efficient, rational, and honest governments to deal with problems ranging from external subversion to rice shortages caused by drought or flood. Simultaneously, we must realize that the capacity of governments in the developing world is limited. As more demands are made on governments, the demands must be balanced against a rather narrow resource base upon which these governments can draw for taxes, technicians, and so forth. In addition to all their internal problems, there are external forces that impinge on the functioning of developing political systems. Organic solidarity, though, is more appropriate than brutal authoritarianism, both morally and in terms of material results.

INTERNATIONAL FACTORS

Political development is more than forces and decisions operating within the boundaries of a particular country. Many developing countries have a history of being influenced significantly by pressures outside the country, over which they have little or no control. Students also should note, however, that the Western or developed nation-states also are influenced by groups not readily subject to national control. Awareness of the international environment as a source of factors influencing internal stability, development, and decay is useful. We offer two examples of international influence to illustrate the types of problems facing the Third World. One example is political, the other, economic.

Insurgency and International Intervention

The challenge of communism is still present, often as an insurgency movement demanding revolutionary change and reform. The myth of the "great revolution," beginning with the French Revolution in 1789, propagates a false belief that a successful revolution means anything is now possible. Communist-influenced **insurgencies** are much fewer in number today, but still exist in such countries as El Salvador, the Philippines, Peru, and Cambodia. Islamic fundamentalism presents a similar-type problem in the Middle East. The case of the Tho, concentrated in the mountainous Vietnam-China border area, illustrates the chal-

---

[48]These quotes are taken from Book 1, Chapter 3, of Emile Durkheim's *Division of Labor* (Paris: F. Alcan) first published in 1893. For a succinct interpretation of Durkheim's writings, see George Simpson, *Emile Durkheim: Selections from His Work, with Introduction and Commentaries* (New York: Thomas Y. Crowell, 1963).

lenge of communism from both a historical and international perspective.[49] (See Figure 11.3).

When the French took control of various parts of what is now Vietnam in the nineteenth century, it was a time of vigorous territorial expansion for both the French and the Vietnamese. This territorial spreading out of the lowland Vietnamese threatened the non-Vietnamese hill tribes who had been the only inhabitants of the sparsely populated highlands. The French separated uplanders, or Montagnards, from Vietnamese administration and ruled these peoples directly or through local tribal officials whom they appointed. There was general acceptance of this policy by the Montagnards, except in the case of the 400,000 Tho. The Tho had allied with an unsuccessful rebellion by a Vietnamese faction in the sixteenth century against the central government. Determined to avoid future incidents, the victorious Vietnamese emperor sent Vietnamese officials to intermarry with the Tho and to administer them. The descendants of the resulting intermarriages—the Tho-ti—became the ruling elite, were accepted as rulers, and became the political link with the lowland Vietnamese. The Tho-ti were alienated because they were passed over by the French as the French colonial rulers appointed local officials. A major Tho tribe rebellion against the French occurred in 1940. The scattered remnants of the Indochinese Communist party, which had been weakened by an unsuccessful revolt against the French in 1930–1931, now fled from the lowlands and delta to the Tho area. They promised equality and autonomy to the Tho. The Tho mountain area became the first major Communist base, as both groups joined against the common French enemy. When the first Vietnam war, against the French, ended in 1954, 20 percent of the anti-French insurgents (Vietminh) were composed of Tho tribespeople. The international aspects of this Tho-Vietminh alliance is summarized by a political scientist who studied this situation in detail:

> But possession of a base area in the Tho homeland was more important to the Viet Minh for another reason. The Tho homeland provided the all-important supply route to China through which the Viet Minh obtained external assistance—thereby internationalizing the Viet Minh war.[50]

Before the Communists seized mainland China in 1949, the Vietminh and Tho had traded opium for guns. After 1949, political motives were the source of Chinese support for the insurgents. Some analysts suggest that if it were not for the weapons from China, the Vietminh insurgency would have failed.[51]

The results of the protracted Vietnamese Communist insurgency are self-evident. In April and May of 1975, South Vietnam fell to the insurgents, and Saigon

---

[49]See John T. McAlister, Jr., "Mountain Minorities and the Viet Minh: A Key to the Indochina War," in Peter Kunstadter, ed., *Southeast Asian Tribes, Minorities, and Nations*, vol. 2 (Princeton, N.J.: Princeton University Press, 1967), pp. 780–788.

[50]Gary D. Wekkin, "Tribal Politics in Indochina: The Role of Highland Tribes in the Internationalization of Internal Wars," in Mark W. Zacher and Stephen Milne, eds., *Conflict and Stability in Southeast Asia* (Garden City, N.Y.: Anchor Press, 1974), pp. 129–130.

[51]David Feingold, "Opium and Politics in Laos," in Nina S. Adams and Alfred W. McCow, eds., *Laos: War and Revolution* (New York: Harper & Row, 1970), pp. 335–336.

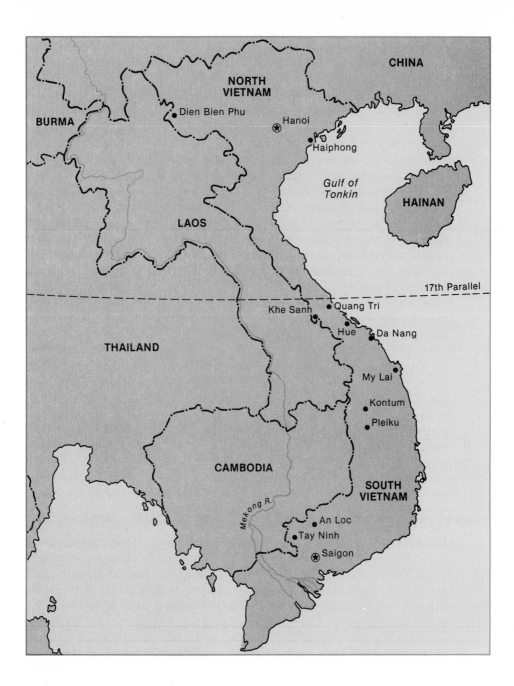

Figure 11.3 Pre-1976 Vietnam.

became Ho Chi Minh City. One factor that influenced the continuation of the Vietnam wars for 29 years (1946–1974) was the outside assistance contributed by the Chinese, the Soviets, the French, and the Americans. The United States alone spent more than $150 billion between 1960 and 1975, in part to defeat a Communist-directed insurgency. This "international aid" was a crucial factor influencing political development and political decay in Vietnam.

Today, we observe a continuation of such involvement in other war-torn countries. Afghanistan is an example of support for anti-Communist insurgents and support for a Communist government. The Soviet invasion of Afghanistan in 1979 to shore up a Communist government torn by factionalism and opposed by non-Communist *mujahedin* (rebels) changed little. By the end of 1987, 115,000 Soviet troops, plus 30,000 to 40,000 additional troops regularly used for special operations from bases inside Soviet Central Asia, had not brought about a political or military solution. The Afghan resistance was getting stronger, supported with material assistance from anti-Communist countries. After considerable debate within the Reagan administration, the surface-to-air missile Stinger was provided to the mujahedin in September 1986. Relatively inexpensive, resistant to jamming, it enhanced the position of the anti-Communist guerrillas immeasurably. Some analysts believe it turned slow defeat into potential victory. Rarely has the introduction of a weapon had such an impact on a war. Certainly the Soviet determination and ability to fight were gradually reduced. During the 20 months after September 1986, 270 Soviet aircraft were shot down, principally by the Stinger missile.

Under General Secretary Gorbachev's reforms and overseas retrenchment, the last Soviet troops left Afghanistan in February 1989; some advisors remained behind. The Soviet Union continues, however, to supply the Communist government whose jurisdiction is limited to the capital, Kabul, and other urban areas. From February through September 1989, the largest Soviet military airlift in history took place. The 3,800 supply flights brought in military equipment valued at more than $1.5 billion.

Revolution and support of insurgents is not confined to Communists and anti-Communists. Iran, discussed earlier in this chapter, also exports its ideology, often violently. The Shi'ites are a major division within the Muslim religion. Shi'ite Muslims form over 90 percent of Iran's population and are the largest Islamic group in Bahrain, Iraq, Lebanon, and eastern Saudi Arabia. The Shi'ites claim they represent the true Muslim inheritance and that the leadership following Muhammad's death should have passed through the Prophet's family. Shi'ite leaders are called *Imans*. There was a permanent breach in the Muslim movement when the prophet's grandson was murdered by the Caliph of the Sunnis, the other major Muslim group. The late Ayatollah Khomeini (died June 1989) claimed to represent the last "hidden Mahdi" who will return on the day of judgment. The Shi'ite resurgence and its call to return to basic Muslim principles and the establishment of theocratic state send tremors through many non-Shi'ite Arab governments. Iran provides verbal, written, and material support to its many adherents, and also military weapons and trained terrorists throughout the Middle East.

The situation of many Third World countries often makes them susceptible to or dependent on outside support and/or influence. External input is not always bad. Korea's leading opposition figure, Kim Dae Jung, spoke about this. Mr. Kim was discussing former President Chun's reluctant acceptance of democratic reforms in 1987. Kim declared:

> The American government's recent attitude—strong support for democracy and firm opposition to military intervention in politics—has given a strong influence on Chun's regime.[52]

Multinational Corporations

The nation-state and the **multinational corporation** (MNC) have been described as the "two dominant institutions in the world in the late twentieth century."[53] One way to show the impact of MNCs is to draw up two lists: a list of countries ranked according to their GNP and a list of corporations ranked according to their gross annual sales, with the countries having the highest GNP at the top of the one list and the companies having the highest gross annual sales at the top of the other list. If these lists then are merged and the 100 names at the top are separated, nearly half the names on the list are MNCs. General Motors' 1988 gross annual sales are higher than the GNPs of Switzerland, Nigeria, and South Africa. Toyota Motor Company's sales are higher than Portugal or Ireland's GNP.

An MNC is a corporation that has access to a common pool of human and financial resources and has operations in several countries. Firms are duplicating their activities or dispersing essential parts of their operation among several different states.[54] One of the first MNCs was Bata, which was founded in Czechoslovakia and later transferred to Canada during World War II. In 1968 Bata was manufacturing shoes in 79 countries and selling them in 89 countries. MNCs have corporate headquarters in a number of countries, but American firms no longer dominate as they did in the 1970s.

Direct private foreign investment has grown rapidly since World War II. The MNCs are principally, but not exclusively, from North America, Europe, and Japan. There are a growing number of Third World MNCs. For example, Formosa Plastics Company committed $1.3 billion to construct an ethane plant in Calhoun County, Texas, in 1988. Venezuela's state-owned Petroleos de Venezuela acquired all of Citgo Petroleum Corporation in 1989. Citgo is pumped primarily at 7-Eleven stores. This is the *first* case of an OPEC member owning all of a large U.S. oil refiner and marketer.

---

[52]Daniel Sneider, "South Korea: What Led to Government Concession?" *Christian Science Monitor* (June 30, 1987), p. 36.

[53]Lester R. Brown, "The Multinationals and the Nation-State," *Vista: The Magazine of the United Nations Association*, 8:6 (1973), p. 15.

[54]For a review tracing the development of the term "multinational corporation," see Howe Martyn, "Development of the Multinational Corporation," in Abdul A. Said and Luiz R. Simmons, eds., *The New Sovereigns: Multinational Corporations as World Powers* (Englewood Cliffs, N.J.: Prentice-Hall, 1975), pp. 30–43.

Accurate figures are difficult to obtain. Based on value at time of investment, U.S. direct investment in overseas plants and equipment at the end of 1988 was $326.9 billion.[55] Interestingly, there was no Third World country among the first eight countries rank-ordered by dollar amount of U.S. investment. These eight countries, five in Western Europe plus Canada, Japan, and Australia accounted for $207.4 billion of U.S. direct business investment abroad. Today, over half of all MNC foreign investment is in manufacturing. Petroleum, mining, services, and agriculture together account for less than half of foreign investment.

An IBM Corporation executive summarized IBM's overseas operations as follows:

1. We operate in 126 countries overseas with some 125,000 employees.
2. We do business in 30 languages, in more than 100 currencies.
3. We have 23 plants in 13 countries.
4. We have 8 developed laboratories in as many countries.
5. And we have a very healthy offshore growth rate, going from $51 million in gross income in 1950 to $5.14 billion in 1973. In fact, since 1970 our overseas business has accounted for more than half the corporation's net income.[56]

Developing countries seek outside investment to provide jobs, to introduce technology, as a source of loans and investment dollars, and to be affiliated with a worldwide marketing network. Economic development requires savings and investment. Many developing countries could not acquire these through their own resources without brutally squeezing already low levels of consumer consumption. Much of the investment in the developing countries comes through multinational corporations. If one looks at the total world product (WP), that portion dominated by the multinational corporations accounts for just under 20 percent of WP, and the percentage increase in MNC sales steadily grows faster than WP. Jobs, economic development, urbanization, unemployment, and equitable or unreasonable distribution of profits and wages often are important factors contributing to the stability of a political system. Some MNC investment may help reduce widespread discontent, it also may provide taxation resources for a new government faced with numerous demands.

Each MNC's global strategy is concerned with such decisions as where to secure raw materials; which components will be manufactured in what factory in which particular country where the assembling of various components will occur; in which countries or with which banks one should seek capital for financing; and where assembly plants, manufacturing plants, employee training, research plants, management offices, and research laboratories should be located most efficiently

---

[55]"Where Does American Business Invest Abroad?" *Christian Science Monitor* (August 2, 1989), p. 9. The true current investment value is not considered because value appreciation is not calculated. The above figure is based on dollar value at time of investment.

[56]Jacques Maisenrouge, "How a Multinational Corporation Appears to Its Managers," in George W. Ball, ed., *Global Companies: The Political Economy of World Business* (Englewood Cliffs, N.J.: Prentice-Hall, 1975), p. 15.

and most cheaply. Most critically, is the potential host Third World country politically stable enough now and in the future to warrant external private investment?

MNC critics say the MNCs are only interested in profits; therefore, they are attracted to developing countries because of low wages, access to cheap raw materials, and lax safety and environmental rules. Those with nationalist sentiments stress the need for national control over the domestic economy and wish to minimize control by foreign companies and money.

Counterarguments include the fact that the level of investment would not occur if it had not been for MNC investment. Dollars, managerial skills, international markets, taxes, and employment all accrue from MNC investment. One study calculated that in Mexico foreign enterprises paid wages 1.7 times higher than domestic enterprises paid in the same sector. For Latin America as a whole,

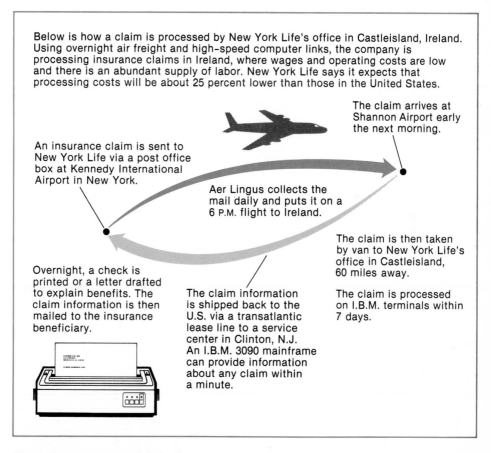

Below is how a claim is processed by New York Life's office in Castleisland, Ireland. Using overnight air freight and high-speed computer links, the company is processing insurance claims in Ireland, where wages and operating costs are low and there is an abundant supply of labor. New York Life says it expects that processing costs will be about 25 percent lower than those in the United States.

The claim arrives at Shannon Airport early the next morning.

An insurance claim is sent to New York Life via a post office box at Kennedy International Airport in New York.

Aer Lingus collects the mail daily and puts it on a 6 P.M. flight to Ireland.

The claim is then taken by van to New York Life's office in Castleisland, 60 miles away.

Overnight, a check is printed or a letter drafted to explain benefits. The claim information is then mailed to the insurance beneficiary.

The claim information is shipped back to the U.S. via a transatlantic lease line to a service center in Clinton, N.J. An I.B.M. 3090 mainframe can provide information about any claim within a minute.

The claim is processed on I.B.M. terminals within 7 days.

Figure 11.4 How one global office system works. *Source: New York Times* (October 10, 1988), p. Y29. Copyright © 1988 by The New York Times Company. Reprinted by permission.

U.S. subsidiaries paid wages between 1.4 and 2.1 times higher than similar domestic enterprises, while in India and Pakistan MNC wage ratios were, respectively, 2.4 and 2.6.[57]

Overseas investment by U.S. investors and the sale of licenses and patents also can mean a loss of jobs and economic suffering for workers in the United States. This is true of other industrial First World countries. U.S. producers of radios, televisions, and videocassette recorders are gone, like the dinosaurs. Offshore manufacturing (plants established in foreign countries) results in half of IBM computer parts being made in Japan and Singapore. It is estimated that in the 1970s between 450,000 to 650,000 U.S. jobs were lost as a result of "runaway shops" (plant sites moved to foreign countries).[58] A 1986 issue of *Time* described a "hollowing out" of many U.S. manufacturing companies that is taking place, that is, they have become assembly plants for foreign-manufactured components. "Even in domestic auto plants, 15% of the parts used (e.g., engines and transmissions) are produced outside the United States."[59] Figure 11.4 illustrates how globalization of service industries is reducing the number of jobs.

MNCs have helped to decentralize the world economy. The impact has been experienced as good and bad by both First World countries and Third World countries.

SUMMARY

Unity, national integration, political development, political modernization, or political change are phenomena that affect most of the world's population, but are of special importance to people living in the developing world. The developing countries include over three-quarters of the world's population and more than 120 political systems. The Third World confronts most of the problems the developed countries face, as well as additional ones, such as substantial and long-term unemployment, low income, high percentage of the population 15 years old and under, insurgencies, and numerous other problems discussed earlier. Unfortunately most of these countries are short of the necessary resources, such as trained personnel and tax revenue, to deal effectively with many of the problems they face. Theories of political development help us to understand better what the major problems are, but they provide no clear solutions, except that with limited resources priorities must be established, and difficult choices must be made.

We believe political and economic improvements are better achieved by accommodation of diverse claims, recognizing that much of the impetus for change,

---

[57]Adeoye A. Akinsanya, *Multinationals in a Changing Environment* (New York: Praeger, 1984), p. 138.

[58]Barry Bluestone and Bennett Harrison, *The Deindustrialization of America* (Chicago: Basic Books, 1982), p. 26.

[59]"Singing the Shutdown Blues," *Time* (June 23, 1986), p. 59, quoted in Carolyn C. Perrucci et al., *Plant Closings: International Context and Social Costs* (New York: Aldine de Gruyter, 1988), p. 2.

evolution, and improvement can be achieved by social and economic decisions and innovations not dictated by government. An evolving political integration is superior to an imposed political uniformity. History shows that authoritarian regimes seldom maintain a spirit of reason, efficiency, and charity. In general, some degree of political and social freedom of choice is the surest way to proceed toward political, economic, and social development. The problems that confront developing systems oftentimes seem insurmountable. Authoritarian solutions are then too frequently adopted for purposes of short-run survival, but do not lead to better decisions efficiently implemented.

RECOMMENDED READINGS

Brown, Lester R., et al. *State of the World, 1990.* Washington, D.C.: Worldwatch Institute, annually. The authors take a careful look at some of the major worldwide policy issues ranging from global warming to demilitarizing the world economy. There are numerous tables and figures, many going back to 1950.

Chang, David Wen-wei. *China under Deng Xiaoping: Political and Economic Reform.* New York: St. Martin's Press, 1988. This is a somewhat optimistic review of economic and political reforms between 1977 and 1987. The author includes a useful biographical analysis and has valuable insights on a broad range of topics.

Dahl, Robert A. *Polyarchy: Participation and Opposition.* New Haven, Conn.: Yale University Press, 1971. Political pluralism is not achieved easily in Third World countries. The author considers, on a worldwide basis, the probability and problems of authoritarian political systems becoming more pluralistic.

Diamond, Larry, Juan J. Linz, and Seymour Martin Lipset, eds. *Democracy in Developing Countries:* vol. 2, *Africa;* vol. 3, *Asia;* vol. 4, *Latin America.* Boulder, Colo.: Lynne Rienner Publishers, 1988 and 1989. These are solid country studies, although not every country in each region is covered. Unfortunately, Africa is the briefest volume. Each volume begins with an analytical overview; data for most countries are through 1986.

Elliot, Jeffrey M. *Annual Editions: Third World.* Guilford, Conn.: The Dushkin Publishing Group, 1989. This eclectic grouping of articles on the Third World covers topics including definitions of Third World leadership and human rights. There is no bibliography, and it is updated annually.

Glass, Charles. *Tribes with Flags: A Dangerous Passage Through the Chaos of the Middle East.* New York: Atlantic Monthly Press, 1989. The author is a former ABC correspondent who was held hostage for nine weeks in Lebanon. This is an excellent introduction with a good historical setting.

Hamerow, Theodore S. *From the Finland Station: The Graying of Revolution in the Twentieth Century.* New York: Basic Books, 1990. The author compares revolutionary development in Cuba, mainland China, the Soviet Union, and Vietnam. He delineates the gulf between promises and vision and empirical achievements, authoritarianism, and elitism.

Randall, Vicky, and Rolin Theobald. *Political Change and Underdevelopment: A Critical Introduction to Third World Politics.* Durham, N.C.: Duke University Press, 1985. This book provides an overview of the major approaches to the study of Third World politics. The analysis of the various approaches is enhanced with extended case examples.

Tai, Hung-chao, ed. *Confucianism and Economic Development: An Oriental Alternative?* Washington D.C.: The Washington Institute Press, 1989. A mixture of Western capitalism and Oriental culture gives East Asian economic and political systems characteristics different from Western market economies. The impact of Confucian culture on Japan, Taiwan, Singapore, South Korea, and Hong Kong is analyzed.

Vogel, Ezra F. *One Step Ahead in China: Guangdong under Reform.* Cambridge, Mass.: Harvard University Press, 1989. This study by a well-known Harvard East Asian specialist analyzes the past decade of the reform movement in Guangdong province. Guangdong is ahead of most provinces in mainland China. Analysis is in the context of other East Asian industralizing economies.

Weiner, Myron, and Samuel P. Huntington, eds. *Understanding Political Development.* Boston: Little, Brown, 1987. This excellent collection assesses contemporary scholarly thinking on development and change in the Third World. Students will find this book full of hypotheses and generalizations to test, refine, support, or challenge.

Zolberg, Aristide R., Astri Suhrke, and Sergio Aguayo. *Escape from Violence: Conflict and Crisis in the Developing World.* New York: Oxford University Press, 1989. The rapid and tragic increase in Third World refugees during the past two decades is traced, and the various causes are analyzed. Case studies from Africa, Asia, and Latin America are included.

Chapter 12

Components of International Politics

International politics refers to the relations between the approximately 170 countries in our present world. These polities range in size from the Soviet Union (8,649,489 square miles) and Canada (3,851,809 square miles) to such minute entities as the Vatican (109 acres) and Monaco (600 acres) and, in terms of population, from China (1,072,200,000 people) and India (748,000,000 people) to Naura (8,042 people) and the Vatican (1,250 people).[1]

Let us reemphasize that we are speaking here about countries, *not nations.* As pointed out in Chapter 1, these labels refer to two quite different entities. The Soviet Union, for example, is a *multinational country,* and the Estonians, Latvians, Lithuanians, Ukrainians, Georgians, Armenians, Kazakhs, Uzbeks, and other ethnic groups constitute *nations* within the Soviet Union. This knowledge is important to our understanding of the present restlessness in these republics and the people's demands for more autonomy from the Soviet government.

Most of us will agree that we need to know more about the world around us, especially because of the rapidly increasing international interaction brought about largely by technological development. Today you can travel around the globe in a matter of some 20 hours in contrast to the three years needed by the adventurer-sailors of the sixteenth century. You can contact people in a number of countries in a few seconds or minutes by telephone. Our supermarkets and department stores feature goods from many countries, while a number of our goods are sold abroad.

The economic interdependence and dependence are growing continuously. Take the example of the most self-sufficient country in the world, the Soviet Union. Just to maintain the present low standard of living in that country, its government must import substantial quantities of goods, such as corn and wheat from North America. Gorbachev's attempts to raise the Soviet standard of living will require increased imports. An even better example is that of the highly technological country of Japan. Lacking domestic energy resources, it imports 99% of its oil, mostly from Indonesia and the Middle East. Should Japan be prevented from purchasing oil abroad for some reason, its domestic reserves would last 149 days, after which major components of the Japanese industry would grind to a halt.

The growing interaction on the international scene has not been accompanied by a commensurate growth in knowledge. How much do we know about the people and their aspirations in other parts of the world? How much do they know about us? If the United States is to remain a major political and economic power in decades to come, it is imperative that we learn more about the other countries. It is important that we improve our knowledge in geography, foreign languages, and the sciences. If we fail to do so, we will become a second-rate power.

The technological discoveries of this century have been far from unilateral blessings. Although some of them have had merits, others have encouraged the

---

[1]These data are from John Paxton, ed., *The Statesman's Year-Book 1988–89* (New York: St. Martin's Press, 1988), and *Political Handbook of the World: 1988* (Binghamton, N.Y.: CSA Publications, 1988).

PROGRESS OF MAN

production of weapons capable of destroying humanity. Today, the United States and the Soviet Union possess enough nuclear weapons to extinguish life on planet Earth. Even the peaceful domestic use of nuclear power can have major harmful international consequences. Just take note of the damage caused by the 1986 Soviet nuclear disaster in Chernobyl. According to present-day estimates, the radiation fallout will cause environmental harm in parts of the Soviet Union, Finland, Sweden, Poland, Czechoslovakia, and Germany for the next 20 years. Will the world community succeed in establishing sufficient social and political counterbalancing forces to nuclear power? We believe that humankind has the ability to control and correct the ecological, economic, military, and social problems of our time.

"The Wizard of Id" by permission of Johnny Hart and Field Enterprises, Inc.

SIMILARITIES AND DIFFERENCES BETWEEN DOMESTIC AND INTERNATIONAL POLITICS

In some respects, international politics is similar to domestic politics. Political actors in both settings try to achieve their desires, and some succeed more than others. The actors on the domestic scene are individuals or groups of people in private or public organizations. In international politics the primary decision makers are the rulers of countries (that is, the leaders of the United States, the Soviet Union, France, Japan, Nigeria, and so on). Moreover, in both spheres the more powerful customarily wield more influence over economic, military, and political processes than those with less power.

The main point of difference between domestic and international politics has to do with the degree of authority and order, in the sense of law, that prevails in each sphere. Domestic governments, by and large, have a preponderance of authority and power in their societies. This means that these governments will have enough military and policy support to make their decisions stick and to squash internal unrest. In addition, a national government is the source of final sanction in the judicial sphere. Should a government lose its preponderance of power, it will be overthrown by coup d'état or revolution. The Russian Revolution (1917), the Spanish Civil War (1936–1939), the Cuban Revolution (1958–1959), and the multitude of coups d'état in the developing countries serve as examples. By and large, however, the domestic scene has been more peaceful than the international scene. According to Quincy Wright, only 70 out of 244 wars in which European countries participated between 1480 and 1941 were civil wars.[2] Since 1945, however, the worldwide number of civil wars has increased to equal the figure of wars among countries. There has been more anarchy on the international than on the domestic scene. The reason is that internationally there is no institution having a preponderance of power. The Security Council and the General Assembly of the United Nations are at best weak facsimiles of domestic governments. War is still the ultimate method of sanction on the international scene, and conflicts among countries often are settled on a "might makes right" principle, rather than on the

---

[2]Quincy Wright, *A Study of War*, 2nd ed. (Chicago: University of Chicago Press, 1965), p. 651.

basis of what is right according to international law. History abounds with examples of an action successfully executed by the stronger party becoming "the just decision" in the minds of the victors and their supporters.

THE ACTORS IN INTERNATIONAL POLITICS

We have said that the leaders of countries are the principal political actors on the international scene, along with international and regional organizations (discussed in the following chapter), multinational corporations (MNCs), and political terrorists.

Countries have certain common characteristics. They are political entities separated from other countries by boundaries that are usually officially recognized. In some instances, however, boundaries of a country, or even the existence of a country, may be disputed by some other countries. The Indian-Pakistani conflict is an example of the former, whereas the Chinese claim to Taiwan exemplifies the latter.

Countries have central governments and maintain diplomatic relations with other countries depending upon their standing in the world community. For instance, the United States, Canada, and Sweden maintain diplomatic relations with many other countries, whereas Taiwan and Albania have diplomatic relations with relatively few countries. Countries are said to be sovereign according to international law. Sovereignty implies equality with other countries and independence from outside interference in the pursuit of domestic and international affairs. In reality, however, no country enjoys absolute sovereignty. The policies and pursuits of one country frequently will have bearing on the actions of others. Powerful countries often will limit the foreign policy range of weaker countries or even interfere directly with their domestic affairs. An example of the first type can be seen in the relationship between the Soviet Union and its European allies between 1945 and 1989. The United States committed actions of direct interference in Guatemala in 1954, in Laos in 1962, in the Dominican Republic in 1965, and in Panama in 1989; the Soviet Union in East Germany in 1953, in Hungary in 1956, in Czechoslovakia in 1948 and 1968, and in Afghanistan in 1980.

Countries differ greatly in terms of power. By power we mean the capability to make one's influence or will prevail over others. Some are labeled superpowers, whereas others are ranked in a second, third, or fourth category. What are the ingredients that help to make one country more powerful than another? The following are some of the major elements that contribute to power.

1. Geographic element (size, climate, location, and terrain). Size lends itself to power in that it provides flexibility for retreat and relocation of labor and industry. The vast size of Russia and its climate presented insurmountable problems to Napoleon and Hitler. In turn, countries like Andorra or Liechtenstein have not become great powers. Certain locations and terrains have constituted advantages in the premissile age. For example, the British Isles have not been invaded by a conquering force since the eleventh century, and the mountains have protected Switzerland in the modern era. In World War II Hitler's High Command refrained from invading either of the two, in part because of logistical considerations.

2. The demographic element (population). A large population will lend power to the country, provided that the people are adequately nourished, well trained in industrial and professional skills, and highly motivated in supporting the aims of the incumbent power elite. Without these ingredients, a large population may be a deterrent to power. For example, the Soviet government found itself greatly weakened during the early 1930s because of the widespread famine leading to substantial starvation in many areas of the country, including the Ukraine—the primary breadbasket of the USSR. Likewise, the government of the People's Republic of China was occupied during the 1950s largely with raising enough food for its many millions of people. India, with the second largest population of any country in the world, still struggles to meet the basic necessities of its people.

3. Natural resources, technology, and transportation. Extensive natural resources readily accessible for exploitation and an adequate plant system to transform the natural resources into commercial and military goods add considerably to the power of a country. Essential to the production process and the maintenance of domestic unity are up-to-date and well-functioning systems of communication and transportation. Keeping in mind the confusion and chaos an occasional brownout, blackout, or strike by airline employees causes, the results of a complete breakdown of communication and/or transportation facilities would be infinitely more chaotic and confusing and could render a postindustrial society helpless. Technological superiority customarily will give a country an advantage over those who are less developed. The perpetuation of the power potential depends on the continuous allocation of resources (labor and money) for further research. A society that calls a halt to scientific and technological developments soon will come to a technological standstill. The arms race between the United States and the Soviet Union since World War II is, among other factors, a sign of the perpetual technological-military competition between the two superpowers. While efforts have been made to curtail this race, both societies will continue their technological-military research in order to protect their **national interests,** by which we mean, as stated comprehensively by Frederick H. Hartmann, "those things that states could or do seek to protect or achieve *vis-à-vis* other states."[3]

4. Military power and preparedness. The presence of a strong and well-trained military establishment equipped with up-to-date weaponry is perhaps the most obvious element of national power. There is some difficulty in calculating actual military power. How many infantry battalions, how many tanks, how many pieces of artillery equal a 5-megaton nuclear bomb? To what extent does the tremendous work force potential in the People's Republic of China equal Soviet nuclear strength? Another question pertains to the speed with which the resources in work force and weaponry can be mobilized.

Whatever system of calculation is used, the United States and the Soviet

---

[3]Frederick H. Hartmann, *The Relations of Nations*, 6th ed. (New York: Macmillan, 1983), p. 7.

Union are substantially ahead of all other countries in military power. Both have vast quantities of nuclear weapons and the delivery systems for short- and long-range missiles. The other members of the "nuclear club" are France, the People's Republic of China, and the United Kingdom. Furthermore, India has tested nuclear devices, and it generally is assumed that Israel and the Republic of South Africa have a nuclear capacity, too. A number of other countries have the capability to produce nuclear weapons, but most have refrained from producing them. An expansion of the **nuclear club** would make international relations more complex and more dangerous.

5. Governmental leadership. Last but not least, the quality of governmental leadership has considerable bearing on the power of a country. The leaders in the national government set the priorities and determine the allocation of resources for the armed forces, foreign aid, and domestic purposes. It is of paramount importance for society that the top leaders in the national government keep fully informed about the happenings at home and abroad. Furthermore, it is extremely important that these leaders make wise decisions, wise in terms of short-term and long-term implications. History abounds with examples of leaders who have fumbled and have led their societies into catastrophes, such as those committed by Napoleon, Mussolini, the Japanese military oligarchy of World War II, and Hitler.

Strength and wisdom in leadership help to produce a stronger country, and it is a rare quality of a society to develop the kind of political system that brings the most able leaders into the top national positions and supports and sustains their decisions.

The five elements just cited are some of the main criteria of national power. Obviously, they are not all-inclusive, and exceptions to the rule as well as special circumstances need to be taken into consideration when examining a particular case.[4]

THE NATURE OF INTERNATIONAL POLITICS

The origin of the modern nation-state system dates back to the sixteenth century. The Italian writer and diplomat Niccolò Machiavelli (1469–1527) provided an early analysis of and justification for leadership and centralized power at the national level in *The Prince.* Since those days the number of existing countries has increased considerably. Many of the 100-plus countries customarily classified as "developing countries" have become independent only since World War II. A large number of countries have been born in a revolutionary or semirevolutionary setting. The people in the United States declared their independence from Britain during their revolutionary war. Other colonies were granted independence under

---

[4]The main points of this discussion are drawn from Vernon Van Dyke, *International Politics,* 3rd ed. (New York: Appleton-Century-Crofts, 1972), pp. 223–242. See also Hartmann, *The Relations of Nations,* pp. 41–67. Hartmann's presentation includes some useful tables comparing the population structure, production of vital materials, and the armed forces of selected countries.

more peaceful settings. An example would be that of Britain granting independence to the Bahamas in 1973.

The community of countries exists in a setting of constant change. While some new countries are being born, others are being swallowed up by more powerful ones. For example, the former Baltic countries of Estonia, Latvia, and Lithuania were annexed by the Soviet Union during World War II. Still other countries have been divided and temporarily swallowed up by adjacent countries. A good example of this would be Poland, which was divided three times during the eighteenth century and again during World War II. Germany and Korea were divided at the end of World War II. Germany was unified in 1990, but Korea is still divided. Because of perpetual shifts in the power relationship among countries, the process of change will exist as long as the country remains the primary unit of the international community.

The Viability of a Country

Which countries are likely to remain in their present geographical form and which will experience losses of territory or division or will disappear completely? The perpetuation of a country in its present geographical makeup is based on external and internal considerations. External factors include the country's power position vis-à-vis its neighboring countries and other potential adversaries, the presence of natural frontiers, and the ubiquity of enlightened leadership. The power of a country (as defined in our earlier discussion) will exercise restraints upon the ambitions of other governments. Natural frontiers, such as the Pyrenees between France and Spain, are unlikely to lead to boundary disputes. Finally, enlightened politicians will try to resolve their disputes with other leaders in amicable rather than belligerent ways, thereby refraining from endangering the existence of their country.[5]

The opposite example would be the story of the Third Reich, where the policies of the superbelligerent and paranoid Hitler regime led to the destruction of Germany and the death of many millions of people.

Internal factors are very important to the viability of a country. For a country to remain viable, there must exist a high degree of national integration, including enough nationalism to bind society together,[6] sufficient ethnic homogeneity, preferably a uniting language, and wise leadership. Nationalism, as related to the viability of a country, refers to the public loyalty put forth by the citizenry. The large majority of citizens must extend their public loyalty in the first instance toward their country, rather than a subunit thereof or a foreign country. Ethnic homogeneity and a unifying language serve as helpful ingredients. Countries such as Iceland, Norway, and Sweden are leading examples of these requirements, and the homogeneity of their societies has reinforced their viability as countries consid-

---

[5]For an extensive treatment of the issues of national integration, see Karl Deutsch, *Nationalism and Its Alternatives* (New York: Alfred A. Knopf, 1969), pp. 3–91.

[6]See Hans Kohn, *The Idea of Nationalism* (New York: Macmillan, 1961).

erably. In contrast, the Austro-Hungarian Empire, which was a conglomerate of national groups and languages, fell apart in 1918 because the individual national groups desired to achieve independence. The people in former East Pakistan, having little in common with the people and government in West Pakistan, fought successfully for independence and established their own country, Bangladesh, in 1971. In contrast, some years earlier, the Ibos fought for independence from Nigeria and lost.

African countries have been especially beset by internal divisions, and boundary changes and further efforts toward tribal independence can be expected in Africa in years and decades to come. The present boundaries, drawn arbitrarily by the colonial powers in the nineteenth century, frequently fail to reflect tribal locations and language considerations. A case in point would be Nigeria, where the population consists of a number of tribes—the largest ones being the Hausa, the Ibo, and the Yoruba. The Hausa are the most populous tribe in Nigeria, but they also overlap into neighboring Niger. The Yoruba, in turn, overlap into the Republic of Benin. Most likely, some of the tribal aspirations will be contained through domestic power struggles (such as the violent conflicts between the Hutu and Tutsi in Burundi and Rwanda) and others through civil wars (as the Ibo case illustrates). Some other ethnic conflicts undoubtedly will lead to boundary changes in the years to come.[7]

An Asian example of geopolitical complexity is India. The country features about a dozen major languages and several hundred dialects. Various efforts to make Hindi, the most widely spoken language, the official language of the country have been opposed by measures that at times included demonstrations, violence, and bloodshed. As a consequence, the Indian government has seen no choice but to retain English as the official language of the country. Only about 30 percent of the Indian people speak Hindi. Would a future imposition of Hindi as the national language lead to separatist movements by the non-Hindi-speaking groups?

The most recent example of separatist activities can be seen in the Soviet Union, where the Lithuanians, Latvians, Estonians, and some other nationalities would like to secede.

Foreign Policy and International Politics

The term "international politics" embraces the sum total of the countries' foreign policies. A country's **foreign policy** consists of its government's relations with other countries. More specifically, these relations are based on considerations of national interest and may involve political, economic, cultural, and military matters. The basic element underlying the foreign policy of all countries is the quest for security, which, depending on the strength and leadership of a given country, may range all the way from the pursuit of status quo policies to blatant imperialism.

Foreign policy involves sets of objectives and strategies, often conceived over

---

[7]A good source for ethnic information and country profiles of sub-Saharan Africa is Donald G. Morrison, ed., *Black Africa: A Comparative Handbook*, 2 vols., 2nd ed. (New York: Irvington, 1988).

a period of time, involving three ingredients—conception, content, and implementation. In the words of Frederick Hartmann:

> Because a foreign policy consists of selected national interests presumably formulated into a logically consistent whole that is then implemented, any foreign policy can be viewed analytically in three phases: conception, content, and implementation. Conception involves the strategic appraisal of what goals are desirable and feasible given the presumed nature of the international system. Content is the result and reflection of that appraisal. Implementation looks to both the coordinating mechanisms within a state and the means by which it conveys its views and wishes to other states. Although inefficiencies and failures can be very costly in any of these three phases, it is apparent that the most critical phase is conception.[8]

Hartmann's three-step formula can be applied to the foreign-policy-making process of all countries. What differs, however, are the goals pursued by the individual countries. These differences have to do with the power capabilities of a country, its needs, location, and so forth. The Soviet Union and the United States, our present-day superpowers, pursue worldwide interests and have these reflected in their foreign policies. Botswana or Paraguay, in contrast, are underdeveloped and landlocked countries with rather limited foreign policy aims and pursuits.

THE CONDUCT OF INTERNATIONAL POLITICS

Channels of Communication

Once foreign policy has been formulated, by what means is it put into effect? How do countries deal with each other? The range of possible relations is wide, stretching from friendly diplomatic acts on the one hand to warfare on the other. **Diplomacy,** according to Nicolson, is

> the management of international relations by means of negotiation; the method by which these relations are adjusted and managed by ambassadors and envoys; the business or art of the diplomatist.[9]

Diplomacy is the means by which governments conduct business among themselves. In order to facilitate the conduct of diplomacy, nation-states customarily establish some degree of diplomatic relations with each other. For example, country *A* may have a trade mission in country *B* and use this trade mission for conducting trade and diplomatic matters. A country may maintain a special office or legation in another country, headed by a chargé d'affaires or minister. For example, the United States was represented in some of the Arab countries by chargés d'affaires after the 1967 war. Some countries maintain only consular relations (i.e., less than full diplomatic relations) with each other. The Republic of South Africa, for example, has only consular relations with Denmark. Although the South African

---

[8]Hartmann, *The Relations of Nations*, p. 68.

[9]Harold Nicolson, *Diplomacy*, 3rd ed. (New York: Oxford University Press, 1963), p. 15.

"Confrontation isn't getting us anywhere. We have to talk."

Drawing by Ross; © 1989 The New Yorker Magazine, Inc.

government would like to maintain full diplomatic relations, the Danish government prefers, for political reasons, to keep relations at a less conspicuous level.

Countries that have full diplomatic relations with each other exchange ambassadors. All diplomats are employed by the state department or foreign ministry of their home country. They enjoy certain privileges, such as diplomatic immunity. Should a diplomat violate the laws of the host country he or she may not be tried there; rather, he or she would be declared persona non grata and asked to return to the home country. Governments customarily adhere to the international rules obliging the host government to protect consulates and embassies, as well as the immunity privileges of foreign diplomats. The 1979 takeover of the U.S. embassy in Tehran by Iranian militants and their further action of holding those diplomats as hostages—steps taken with the approval of the Iranian government—constitute gross violations of international law and were condemned as such by all civilized governments.

How are diplomatic relations established? As a new country comes into being, the governments of other countries will decide whether to establish diplomatic relations or not. Various political considerations are involved in this decision-making process. For example, will our establishment of diplomatic relations with country *X* offend country *Y*, a friend of ours? What will be our economic and political gains in establishing these relations? For instance, when Bangladesh became independent in December of 1971, the U.S. government temporarily held back extending diplomatic recognition to that new country in order not to offend our ally, Pakistan. After a number of other countries had recognized Bangladesh, however, the United States followed suit. The U.S. government did not recognize the government of the Soviet Union until 1933,[10] and some degree of diplomatic relations with the People's Republic of China was established only after President Nixon's 1972 visit to that country.

Disputes between countries will lead at times to a reduction in diplomatic relations or a complete severance. For instance, the U.S. government severed diplomatic relations with some of the Eastern European countries after they had been taken over by Communist regimes at the end of World War II. Following the abortive Hungarian Revolution of 1956, our government reduced its diplomatic representation in Hungary by recalling the ambassador and leaving a chargé d'affaires in control of our embassy. Full restoration of diplomatic relations occurred some years later, after a considerable improvement in United States–Hungarian relations had taken place. The United States and most Latin American countries broke diplomatic relations with Cuba after the Castro takeover, but in recent years a number of them have moved toward reconciliation. At this time, several democracies do not have diplomatic relations with Iran. The point is that diplomatic recognition is used often as an instrument of political expediency and a means of reward or punishment. Generally speaking, however, governments will find it more convenient to maintain diplomatic relations with other countries than not to do so. In the absence of diplomatic relations, other sources have to be found to negotiate existing issues. For example, during the late 1950s and most of the 1960s, our ambassador in Warsaw met on a fairly regular basis with his Communist Chinese counterpart to negotiate matters of interest to both countries.

Before a government appoints a person as ambassador, inquiries will be made regarding whether he or she is acceptable (persona grata) to the host country. If not, a more suitable person will be selected. Diplomats serve two primary functions: They represent the home government in the host country and they keep the home government informed about the cultural, economic, military, and political happenings in the host country in order that the state department or foreign ministry at home can formulate intelligent policies toward the other country. The diplomats stationed abroad attend to the day-to-day items of business. Issues of great concern are more likely to be dealt with by special negotiators appointed to conduct a particular conference, by secretaries of state or foreign ministers, or by the leaders of the countries themselves.

In addition to the embassy, a country may maintain one or more consulates in the host country. The consular staff attends to matters such as issuing visas, assisting citizens traveling abroad, promoting trade, and providing public information.

---

[10]The issues surrounding the late U.S. recognition of the USSR are discussed in detail in Edward M. Bennett, *Recognition of Russia: An American Foreign Policy Dilemma* (Waltham, Mass.: Blaisdell, 1970).

President Bush greets President Gorbachev at the May 1990 summit meeting in Washington, D.C.

Since World War II a number of **summit meetings** have been held between the leaders of the major countries, as well as those who are still in a developing stage. For such meetings to be successful, a great deal of preliminary work needs to be done at the professional diplomatic level. Three important summit meetings took place during and at the end of World War II: Tehran, 1943 (Churchill, Roosevelt, and Stalin); Yalta, 1945 (Churchill, Roosevelt, and Stalin); and Potsdam, 1945 (Churchill, Attlee, Truman, and Stalin). At these three meetings, the Allies' war aims, the fate of the vanquished countries, and the creation of the United Nations were discussed, and important decisions were made on these subjects. In 1955 the leaders of France, the Soviet Union, the United Kingdom, and the United States met in Geneva to sign the Austrian State Treaty and to consider the future of Germany and European security. The meeting between Kennedy and Khrushchev in Vienna in 1961 served as an exchange of United States and Soviet views on confrontation issues in Europe and Southeast Asia. Nixon's 1972 visit to the People's Republic of China, led to the establishment of partial diplomatic relations between the United States and China. His subsequent visit to Moscow led to the signing of SALT I, and the 1979 meeting between Carter and Brezhnev in Vienna culminated in the signing of SALT II. The meetings of Reagan and Gorbachev in Geneva, Reykjavik, Moscow, and Washington, D.C. (where the Intermediate Nuclear Forces [INF] Treaty was signed) and Bush and Gorbachev on Malta and in Washington D.C. are more recent examples of big-power conferences.

Methods for Conducting International Relations

The previous discussion has centered on the *channels* used by countries to conduct their official affairs with each other. The following discussion deals with the *methods* used by governments in the pursuit of their foreign relations. International problems can be solved through amicable political or judicial methods or through nonamicable means, including retortion, reprisal, or even war. The main amicable political instrument is that of **negotiation.** Representatives of two or more countries will meet with the purported purpose of achieving agreement on a given issue. The process of negotiation is based on the assumption that the parties involved have some interest in solving the problem at hand. Fred Charles Iklé classifies the objectives of governments in international negotiations into four types. The first three are: extension or renewal of an existing agreement with perhaps slight changes of the former; the normalization of relations, such as the negotiations that led to U.S. recognition of the Soviet Union in 1933; and a redistribution of territory and/or political power. This latter type of negotiation is conducted between an offensive and a defensive party, with the offensive side trying to acquire something from the other. For example, in 1958, the Icelandic government claimed a 12-mile offshore zone for native fishery exclusively. The British, having fished previously in that area, began to comply with the Icelandic demand in order to forestall future difficulties, which developed anyway. Of greater politicomilitary importance were Khrushchev's repeated demands during the late 1950s for a change in the status of West Berlin. In this instance, the West did not acquiesce. The fourth type of negotiation includes innovation agreements that serve to establish a new relationship between the parties involved. The Contadora agreements and the Arias peace plan (1987), both Latin American diplomatic efforts to establish peace in El Salvador and in Nicaragua, serve as recent examples.[11]

Do leaders always negotiate to achieve agreement on an issue of concern? According to Iklé:

> Side-effects—that is, effects not concerning agreement—may be an important part of the outcome, even if all parties negotiate primarily for the purpose of reaching agreement. They may arise either by accident or by design of one party or all parties involved. When diplomacy produces agreements only rarely—as between East and West—the objective of producing side-effects, in fact, often dominates.[12]

Iklé lists six major points of negotiating for side effects:

1. The purpose of one or both negotiators may be plainly that of maintaining contact with each other to keep open the channels of communication. An example of this would be the negotiations between the Soviet Union and the United States regarding the German question and, more specifically, the status of West Berlin during the 1950s and early 1960s. Although the parties had arrived at a stalemate on these issues, the leaders in Moscow and Washington decided that the negotia-

---

[11]Fred Charles Iklé, *How Nations Negotiate* (New York: Frederick P. Praeger, 1967), pp. 26–42.

[12]Ibid., p. 43.

tions should be continued to prevent a worsening of the situation, which could have had dire consequences for both.

2. Negotiations can serve as a substitute for violent actions. The argument made in support of this thesis is that the process of negotiation can be so pleasing to one's adversary or catalyze in him or her the feeling of obligation to see the negotiations through that he or she will refrain from taking the violent action he or she would have taken otherwise. Iklé goes on to say that the thesis holds true in some instances, while it does not apply to others. For example, contrary to Neville Chamberlain's hopes, the Munich Conference did not keep Hitler from starting World War II; neither did the United States—Japanese negotiations in 1941 forestall Japan's attack on Pearl Harbor.

3. Negotiations may be used to gather intelligence information about the adversary. During the process of negotiation the opponent may reveal some of his or her intentions, long-term aims, or range of negotiability—that is, the minimum and maximum desires. There is some evidence that President Nixon's talks with the Chinese and Soviet leaders in 1972 served in part to get a reading of their views regarding Southeast Asia and that the president developed his subsequent policies accordingly.

4. The major purpose of a particular negotiation may be deception—to deceive the opponent about one's aims. An example of deception took place during the Hungarian Revolution in 1956. During the first four days of the uprising the Soviet ambassador in Budapest, then Yuri Andropov, negotiated with the leaders of the new Hungarian government about their political aims and the withdrawal of the Soviet troops. This period gave the Soviet Politburo enough time to plan its counterattack to overthrow the Nagy government.

5. Negotiations sometimes are used for propaganda purposes. In this setting one or both sides will set forth proposals, knowing that they are unacceptable to the other side. The prime aim is to gain favorable publicity. Important forums, such as summit meetings and the rostrums of the Security Council and the General Assembly of the United Nations, lend themselves well to gaining publicity and prestige. Presidential speeches, here and abroad, are filled with statements favoring peace and the well-being of humankind. While there may be some true intention in these comments, the point is that often one side tries to outdo the other in order to score points with the rest of the world by making the other side look hypocritical. One case in point is the publicity during the disarmament conferences of the past eight decades and, in particular, the Soviet proposals, commencing with Lenin, for complete disarmament.

6. Negotiations may be for the purpose of influencing or intimidating a third country. For example, some governments of developing countries have tried to play Washington against Moscow and vice versa in order to obtain favorable economic deals.[13]

In summary, negotiations often have been used for purposes other than those purported. Nevertheless, negotiations are far preferable to less amicable alterna-

---

[13]For a more detailed discussion, see ibid., pp. 43–58.

tives. In order for negotiations to make sense, there must be a negotiable issue and the parties involved must have some desire for agreement and must show some flexibility, because the outcome of successful negotiations is usually a compromise solution.

Sometimes the process of mediation is employed. Here a third party is called upon to disentangle the problem between two parties and to help to bring about an agreement. Most likely, this third party will be an outside government or an international forum such as the Security Council of the United Nations.

A good example of high-level mediation occurred in 1978, when President Carter invited the leaders of Egypt and Israel, President Sadat and Prime Minister Begin, to Camp David and, in the process of lengthy and difficult discussions, helped considerably to improve the relations between the two countries. President Carter continued his mediation efforts until the Egyptian-Israeli peace treaty was finalized.

While a number of international problems have been settled through negotiations in a fairly amicable fashion, other conflicts have led to nonamicable measures, customarily involving a good deal of coercion. Scholars in international politics speak of four types of nonamicable methods based on the intensity of conflict: retorsion, reprisal, intervention, and war.

Retorsion is a deliberate, unfriendly, but legal act that has a retaliatory purpose. For instance, government *A* may be displeased with an action taken by government *B* and to show its indignation may reduce or sever diplomatic relations with the latter. A less severe step would be a temporary curtailment of trade or trade

Economic summit meeting in Houston, Texas, 1990.

privileges. For example, in December 1979, President Carter expelled 183 Iranian diplomats from the United States, thereby reducing their number in this country to 35. This was one of several actions taken by the U.S. government to show its extreme displeasure concerning the takeover of our embassy in Tehran by Iranian militants.

The term **"reprisal"** refers to a deliberate, unfriendly, and illegal action taken in response to a prior violation of international law by the other country. It usually involves some kind of military action. One case in point is the Gulf of Tonkin incident of 1964. Although even today few facts about this affair are known to the public, the point is that as a consequence of North Vietnamese action as reported to President Johnson, he ordered an all-out air attack on North Vietnamese oil storage facilities and PT boat bases, thereby substantially escalating our military involvement in Southeast Asia.

Intervention means direct interference by one country in the affairs of another. This type of interference is usually of broader scope than an act of reprisal and may result without a provocation by the other country. Intervention is an act committed by governments for one of several purposes. Intervention may involve meddling in the electoral process of another country to ensure the election of a candidate favorable to the intervening country, or it may lead to pressure on the other government to pursue or not to pursue a certain foreign policy. Intervention may involve the sending of troops into another country to force that government and segments of the population "to fall into line." For example, in the early decades of this century the U.S. government sent marines into several Latin American republics. In more recent years, the U.S. intervention in the Dominican Republic in 1965 and in Panama (1989), the Soviet reoccupation of Hungary in 1956, its occupation of Czechoslovakia in 1968 as well as its invasion of Afghanistan, commencing in late 1979, are obvious examples of intervention.

In the absence of an international authority that has a preponderance of power, **war** remains the ultimate means for settling a conflict on the international scene. History abounds with examples of countries having gone to war against each other after they had exhausted the existing political and judicial means for settlement or even before they had tried some or all of them. Thus, war still plays an important function in international politics. It remains the ultimate method for settling a problem. This fact makes it more difficult to reduce or to outlaw war successfully on the international scene.

The previous discussion of methods used in international relations does not include such judicial means as arbitration and adjudication. They will be explained in Chapter 13, under the section International Law. The choice of method used by governments to solve a given problem will depend very much on the circumstances at hand, the objectives pursued, the attitudes of the leaders (reasonable and rational or belligerent and revengeful), the power ratio between the countries involved, the willingness of both sides to compromise, and other factors. Suffice it to say that it is better to talk with each other than to shoot at each other. It is hoped that in the years to come more and more leaders will be able to solve their disputes by amicable means rather than through warfare.

INTERNATIONAL POLITICS IN THE POST–WORLD WAR II ERA

Having examined the elements of international politics and the methods employed by countries in their relations with each other, we would like to scrutinize briefly the major international developments since World War II, by paying special attention to the nuclear arms race between the United States and the Soviet Union.

The Brief Period of Bipolar Development

The United States and the Soviet Union emerged from World War II as the two global powers. Clearly, in 1945 the United States was substantially stronger than the Soviet Union, which had suffered considerably from the effects of the war. However, the immense size of the Soviet army, its presence in most of the Balkan countries, in Poland, in the heart of Germany, in Manchuria, and in the northern part of Korea, plus the strength derived from the dictatorial government of the country, compensated for some of the points of Soviet weakness and gave the Soviet Union an important power position in world affairs.

In comparison to the two giants, other major World War II Allies had become, at best, secondary powers. The United Kingdom emerged economically weakened from the war. Its hold over its vast colonial empire began to crumble, and with the independence of the Indian subcontinent in 1947 a movement was set into motion that led in the next 15 years to the independence of most of the British colonies. France after World War II was economically weak and politically divided. A major general strike in 1948 led the country to near chaos. In addition, domestic political instability and the Indochina crisis, as well as the problem in Algeria, kept France from playing any influential role in foreign affairs until the return to office of de Gaulle in 1958. In the Far East, the end of World War II signaled the resumption of the civil war between the Communists, led by Mao Zedong and the government forces under Chiang Kai-shek. In 1949 the Communists won the war and Chiang Kai-shek fled with the remnants of his forces to Taiwan. These developments and others left the Soviet Union and the United States temporarily uncontested global rulers.

The governments of both powers set out to consolidate their areas of influence and, by doing so, established a **bipolar** order. The major line between these two spheres cut through the center of Europe. As Sir Winston Churchill stated so appropriately in his famous May 5, 1946, speech at Westminster College, Missouri:

> From Stettin in the Baltic to Trieste in the Adriatic, an iron curtain has descended across the Continent. Behind that line lie all the capitals of the ancient states of Central and Eastern Europe. Warsaw, Berlin, Prague, Vienna, Budapest, Belgrade, Bucharest and Sofia, all these famous cities and populations around them lie in what I must call the Soviet sphere, and all are subject in one form or another not only to Soviet influence but to a very high and, in many cases, increasing measure of control from Moscow.[14]

---

[14]Randolph S. Churchill, ed., *The Sinews of Peace: Post-War Speeches by Winston S. Churchill* (London: Cassell, 1948), p. 100.

Churchill's classic statement points at the **Iron Curtain** as the artificial division between the two spheres of interest and alludes to the commencement of the Cold War era, an epoch that continued, with a varying degree of severity, until after the Cuban missile crisis.[15]

The only Western enclave behind the Iron Curtain was West Berlin, the part of the city occupied by British, French, and United States troops since the summer of 1945 and governed by the Western Allies. During the late 1940s and 1950s, the Soviet government made several attempts to eliminate Western presence in Berlin, the more serious ones being the 1948–1949 blockade and Khrushchev's demands in 1958 and 1959 to turn West Berlin into a "free city" after the withdrawal of the Western troops. All these attempts failed. A major change in Soviet foreign policy brought about the opening of the Berlin Wall and the Iron Curtain in December of 1989 and cleared the way for the unification of Germany.

The new types of order established after the end of World War II under the **hegemonic** control of the two superpowers in Eastern and Western Europe differed considerably from each other. In Western Europe, democratic systems were reestablished and soon gained a strong momentum of their own. In contrast, the imposition of Soviet-type communism in the East European countries required considerable force. One feature of this difference can be seen in the large number of people who fled to the West from the countries under Soviet control. There is clear evidence that as early as 1949, in the absence of foreign military intervention, the government in West Germany and its democratic order could have sustained itself quite readily without the presence of British, French, and United States troops in the country. In contrast, evidence shows that during the same time period the Communist regimes in Czechoslovakia, East Germany, Hungary, and Poland were kept in power only with the help and as a result of the presence of Soviet troops. As the Soviets changed their policy in the 1980s, these polities moved toward democracy. Over the years, both major powers have faced difficulties in maintaining hegemony in their respective area. A general assessment of the developments in Europe and Asia shows that the Soviet Union clearly faced the greater difficulties.

The Growth of the Third World

Following World War II the colonial empires remaining in the control of the British, Dutch, and French disintegrated rapidly. After the British had granted independence to the Indian subcontinent, some 70 countries in Africa, Asia, and Latin America achieved independence within the next three decades. The new countries and others that have been independent for some time but are still in the

---

[15]For perceptive analyses of the Cold War, see Lynn Etheridge Davis, *The Cold War Begins: Soviet-American Conflict over Eastern Europe* (Princeton, N.J.: Princeton University Press, 1974); John L. Nogee and John Spanier, *Peace Impossible—War Unlikely: The Cold War Between the United States and the Soviet Union* (Glenview, Ill.: Scott, Foresman/Little, Brown, 1988); Bernard A. Weisberger, *Cold War, Cold Peace: The United States and Russia since 1945* (New York: American Heritage Press, 1985); and Daniel Yergin, *Shattered Peace: The Origins of the Cold War and the National Security State* (Boston: Houghton Mifflin, 1978).

The fall of the Berlin Wall. A view of the remnants of the infamous wall after the collapse of the Communist system in eastern Germany.

developmental state (such as Ethiopia and Liberia) customarily are referred to as the "Third World" to distinguish them from the postindustrial democracies and the Communist countries of Europe.

The countries of the Third World have several important features in common. Most of them are still in an early stage of industrial development and are trying to industrialize their societies as quickly as possible. Their governments are putting forth considerable efforts to build cohesive countries. This applies especially to sub-Saharan Africa, where substantial tribal differences still need to be overcome. Common to almost all these countries is the desire not to be dominated or manipulated by either of the two superpowers. As a consequence, most of the developing countries try to remain as nonaligned and uncommitted as possible.

The developing countries have become an important element for the superpowers. The Third World makes up about two-thirds of the membership of the United Nations. In addition, some of these countries have large resources of oil, minerals, and other materials of great importance to the industrially advanced societies. The governments of the People's Republic of China, the Soviet Union, the United States, and some European powers have put forth considerable efforts to gain and increase their influence in the Third World countries via foreign aid, the Peace Corps, information offices, and other methods. Neither of the great powers or other developed countries has gained, or will gain, a monopoly of influence in the Third World. Rather, the competition for influence will continue in the future.

In recent years the phrase the "north-south split" has become popular among students of international relations. The term refers to great cleavages in the living standards of the postindustrial societies on the one hand and many of the developing countries on the other. The point is that now and in the years to come the developing countries need various kinds of help from the postindustrial societies, but they want it on their own terms, with no strings attached. The desire to remain independent of outside influence is a natural desire, but does not always jibe with the pursuits of the great and near-great powers in their dealings with the developing countries. Although the latter need the help of the former in some areas, the same holds true in reverse; however, as the developing countries become more viable, their leaders will insist still more strongly on receiving equal treatment in the family of nation-states. The governments of the People's Republic of China, the Soviet Union, and the United States, as well as others, will have to adjust their foreign policy dealings with the developing countries accordingly and at all times will have to learn to cope with temporary behavior patterns that are enigmatic at best.

The Nuclear Arms Race: An Important Issue of Our Time

Although the bipolar order has changed to a multipolar system, the Soviet Union and the United States have retained their position as great powers primarily because of their immense military power. The governments of both countries, however, have realized over the years that their countries cannot play the role of world police in perpetuity. In the case of the United States, our large-scale military involvement in Southeast Asia in the 1960s and early 1970s raised a number of questions and led ultimately to a large-scale reappraisal of U.S. foreign policy on a global scale. The beginning of a new approach was enunciated by President Nixon in his Guam speech of July 1969. The policy—known as the Nixon Doctrine—called for a more restrained style of conducting foreign affairs:

> We will attempt, consistent with protection of our own interests, to reduce our official presence and visibility abroad. We will emphasize mutuality and multilateralism. We will encourage others to assume a greater share of the responsibilities for the security and economic development of the area.[16]

Whatever the relations of the United States and the Soviet Union are at a given time, the governments of both countries are basically in agreement on several crucial issues of world politics. The most important of these is an understanding that the governments of both countries must do their utmost to prevent a war between themselves. Both sides are aware of the consequences of such a war. It would mean the annihilation of the Northern Hemisphere and, according to recent

---

[16]From *United States Foreign Policy 1969–1970: A Report of the Secretary of State* (Washington, D.C.: U.S. Government Printing Office, Department of State Publication No. 8575, 1971) p. 36.

scientific studies, could put planet earth in a "deep freeze" imperiling the entire human race.[17] The implicit point is that a war between the Soviet Union and the United States would quickly escalate into an all-out nuclear war.

Furthermore, the governments of the Soviet Union and the United States are in agreement to keep the "nuclear club" (i.e., the number of countries that possess nuclear weapons) as limited as possible. They are fully aware that a proliferation in the number of countries having nuclear weapons would increase the chance of nuclear war, be it by accident or by intent. How to prevent secondary powers from developing such weapons is one of the crucial questions of our time.

One indicator that the United States and the Soviet Union no longer manage most of the world's great issues is that many of these problems are of a worldwide scope. Pollution, famine, energy scarcity, infectious diseases such as acquired immunodeficiency syndrome (AIDS), and terrorism need to be dealt with jointly by the members of the international community. However, one issue of crucial importance to which the two superpowers still hold the key is the arms race.

The arms race between the superpowers has been going on since 1945, and thousands of billions of dollars have been spent in military pursuits. During the early years of the arms race, the United States had a four-year lead over the Soviet Union. For example, the United States had its first operational atomic bomb in 1945 and the hydrogen bomb in 1949. The respective years for the Soviet Union are 1949 and 1953. During the following years, which saw the development of missiles, the sophistication of warheads, and the production and employment of MIRVs (multiple independent reentry vehicles), the Soviet Union succeeded in slowly but surely narrowing the gap. Both sides have continued to upgrade their missile weaponry in recent years and have added new types of weapons and delivery systems to their inventory.

The governments of both superpowers in recent years have come under increasing pressure at home to allocate more resources for domestic improvements and less for military efforts. The disarmament conferences of the 1960s produced the 1963 Nuclear Test Ban Treaty (banning nuclear tests in the atmosphere) and the Nuclear Nonproliferation Treaty of 1968. The Strategic Arms Limitation Talks (SALT) between the Soviet Union and the United States commenced in 1969. SALT I, signed by President Nixon and General Secretary Brezhnev in May 1972, consists of two parts: (1) the ABM Treaty and (2) the Interim Agreement. The ABM Treaty deals with the *defensive* part of the two countries' nuclear weaponry systems. In essence, the treaty limits the Soviet Union and the United States to the construction of two ABM (antiballistic missile) sites only, thus preventing both from building nationwide ABM systems.[18] The number of ABM sites subsequently was reduced to one for each side by the ABM Protocol of 1974. The Interim Agreement set the basis for SALT II.

---

[17]Statements to this effect have been made by U.S. and Soviet scientists. See Carl Sagan, "Nuclear War and Climatic Catastrophe: Some Policy Implications," *Foreign Affairs*, 62 (winter 1983/84), pp. 257–292. For a corresponding view from a leading Soviet physicist, see Sergei Kapitzka, "A Soviet View of Nuclear Winter," *Bulletin of the Atomic Scientists*, 41 (October 1985), pp. 37–39.

[18]The text of the ABM Treaty is published in *The Department of State Bulletin*, 66 (June 1972).

Negotiations for SALT II commenced in 1973 and were completed in 1979. The final agreement stipulated that both countries would reduce the number of their delivery vehicles immediately following the signing of the treaty to 2,400 each and reduce them further to 2,250 each by 1981. Restrictions within this ceiling stipulated that neither country was to have more than 1,320 MIRVed missile launchers and heavy bombers with long-range cruise missiles, that no more than 1,200 of these be MIRVed missile launchers, and no more than 820 within that latter group be MIRVed ICBM (intercontinental ballistic missile) launchers. Another part of the agreement placed certain restraints on the development of cruise missiles and mobile ICBMs.[19] SALT II was signed by President Carter and General Secretary Brezhnev in Vienna in 1979. Preliminary discussions of the treaty took place in the U.S. Senate during the autumn of 1979. On January 3, 1980, however, President Carter urged the Senate to postpone further debates of the treaty because of the invasion of Afghanistan by Soviet military forces. While SALT II has not been ratified by the U.S. Congress, its provisions have been tacitly observed by the governments of the United States and the Soviet Union.

In pursuit of arms control endeavors, the technological revolution has posed substantial problems for the negotiators. New weapons systems have been developed even before control agreements have been achieved on the already existing systems. For example, in the early 1980s the United States and the Soviet Union came forth with operational cruise missiles, a complicated weapons category to achieve a verifiable agreement on. Furthermore, in late 1982, the U.S. Congress approved the MX missile program. The Soviet military actions in Afghanistan and the concurrent anti-Soviet stand taken by the Reagan administration led to a new low in U.S.–Soviet relations, dubbed by some the "New Cold War."

After Mikhail Gorbachev became the leader in the Soviet Union, relations between the two superpowers began to improve and led to a series of summit meetings, as indicated earlier. In the area of arms control negotiation, substantial emphasis was placed now on the intermediate nuclear missile issue. The following gives you some background on the issues underlying the INF negotiations.

Since 1977 the Soviet Union had deployed several hundred MIRVed SS-20 missiles (with three warheads each) in the European theater—as replacements for some, but by far not all, single warhead SS-4s and SS-5s (see Figure 12.1). By the early 1980s, the Soviet Union had achieved a considerable advantage in intermediate missiles in the European theater. To achieve parity, then West German Chancellor Helmut Schmidt proposed that the United States redress the balance by introducing newer intermediate missiles in the European theater, too. Based on the Schmidt proposal, the NATO governments developed a plan for deploying 108 Pershing II (replacing the shorter-range Pershing I missiles) and 464 Cruise missiles in Western Europe (see Figure 12.1).

Upon extensive discussion and consideration of the above proposal, NATO, in December 1979, announced a "two-track" policy. The first track was the decision

---

[19]For the text of the SALT II Treaty, see *The Department of State Bulletin*, 79 (July 1979). It can be found, too, in the appendix of Strobe Talbott, *Endgame: The Inside Story of SALT II* (New York: Harper & Row, 1979).

		Warsaw Pact			Nato	
Missiles range 1000-5500 km		SS-20, 5500 km, total so far 1080 (360 launching systems, each with 3 warheads; 243 systems in Europe) SS-4, SS-5	723 ca. 300		So far none. At most there will be 108 Pershing II (1800 km) 464 Cruise (2500 km)	(572)
	Total		over 1000			(572)
Missiles range 500-1000 km		SS-12 (Scaleboard) to be replaced by SS-22 (900-1000 km) Scud B to be replaced by SS-23 (250-500 km)	100 550		Pershing I. To be reduced by up to 108	180 (72)
	Total		650			180 (72)
Missiles range 80-200 km		Frog 7, to be replaced by SS-21 (80-120 km)	650		Honest John or Lance (110 km)	100
Guns, artillery range 30 km			300		Extent of reduction not yet known	1000
Fighter aircraft land-based		(Badger, Blinder, Fishbed, Fitter, Flogger, Fencer, Brewer)	up to 2500		(F 111, Vulcan, F-4, F-104, Jaguar, Buccaneer)	up to 800

The counts are of warheads, apart from the aircraft. Most of the aircraft carry one. Only the larger carry two or three.
Main source: Nato General Secretariat, 1982.
References "to be replaced by" and bracketed figures mean if and when deployment of Nato missiles, in accordance
FAZ-Grafik Kaiser   with the 1979 double decision, is carried out.   Frankfurter Allgemeine Zeitung/Grafik Kaiser

Figure 12.1 Nuclear weapons systems as they existed in Europe in early 1983. *Source: Frankfurter Allgemeine Zeitung* as translated and printed in the *German Tribune.*

to employ the Pershing II and Cruise missiles mentioned earlier. The second track consisted of the commitment to pursue, at the same time, negotiations with the Soviets to limit nuclear forces in the European theater.

President Reagan reinforced the "two-track decision" in late 1981 by proposing a cancellation of the deployment of the missiles just mentioned, if the Soviet government would dismantle all its SS-4s, SS-5s, and SS-20s. Subsequent proposals made by President Reagan provided more flexibility, calling for less than the dismantling of all Soviet intermediate missiles. However, negotiations on this issue did not bring any acceptable results and, as a consequence, the United States started with the deployment of Pershing II's and Cruise missiles in Western Europe in late 1983. The Soviet reaction was to walk out of START and INF negotiations. However, negotiations resumed at a later date and on December 8, 1987, the INF Treaty was signed by President Reagan and General Secretary Gorbachev.

The INF Treaty stipulates that the United States and the Soviet Union dismantle and destroy all their intermediate-range nuclear missiles within three years of the ratification of the treaty (see Figure 12.2). U.S. inspectors have been stationed in the Soviet Union and Soviet inspectors in the United States to assure compliance with the treaty. A major point of the INF Treaty is that, for the first time ever, a whole category of nuclear weapons, although only amounting to approximately 5 percent of the total nuclear arsenals of the superpowers, will be destroyed and

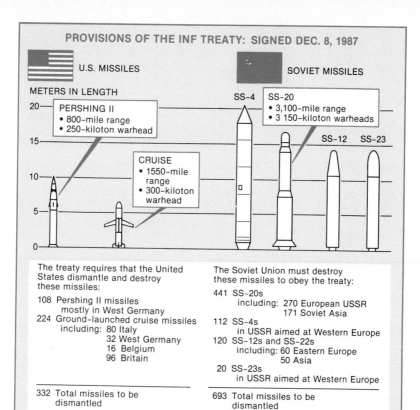

PROVISIONS OF THE INF TREATY: SIGNED DEC. 8, 1987

U.S. MISSILES

SOVIET MISSILES

METERS IN LENGTH

PERSHING II
• 800–mile range
• 250–kiloton warhead

CRUISE
• 1550–mile range
• 300–kiloton warhead

SS–4

SS–20
• 3,100–mile range
• 3 150–kiloton warheads

SS–12   SS–23

The treaty requires that the United States dismantle and destroy these missiles:

108 Pershing II missiles
    mostly in West Germany
224 Ground–launched cruise missiles
    including: 80 Italy
                 32 West Germany
                 16 Belgium
                 96 Britain

332 Total missiles to be dismantled

The Soviet Union must destroy these missiles to obey the treaty:

441 SS–20s
    including: 270 European USSR
                171 Soviet Asia
112 SS–4s
    in USSR aimed at Western Europe
120 SS–12s and SS–22s
    including: 60 Eastern Europe
                50 Asia
 20 SS–23s
    in USSR aimed at Western Europe

693 Total missiles to be dismantled

The superpowers have agreed to what would be an arms control landmark: the first treaty to dismantle existing missiles instead of merely imposing limits on future deployments.

This map shows the location of the missiles that would be dismantled.

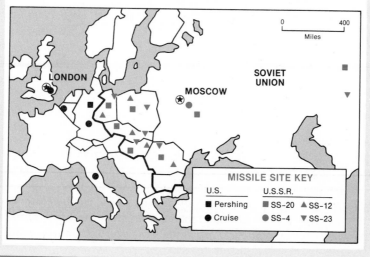

MISSILE SITE KEY

U.S.	U.S.S.R.	
■ Pershing	■ SS–20	▲ SS–12
● Cruise	● SS–4	▼ SS–23

verification teams will check on compliance. This is an important step forward in the nuclear arms control process.

Arms control negotiations have been held in four other areas:

1. Negotiations to cut U.S. and Soviet long-range missiles (those with a range over 3,300 miles) by 50 percent.
2. Talks that are aimed to reduce and ultimately eliminate all short-range missiles in Europe.
3. Discussions regarding conventional forces in Europe. Proposals made in this area suggest a reduction in the number of aircraft, tanks, artillery, armored troop carriers, and military personnel presently employed by the United States and the Soviet Union and to establish equal ceilings for both countries.
4. The last item of negotiations deals with chemical weapons and aims, as enunciated by President Bush in his September 1989 address to the General Assembly of the United Nations to reduce substantially and ultimately eliminate all chemical weapons.

At the June 1990 summit in Washington, D.C., presidents Bush and Gorbachev agreed in principle on a major reduction of ICBMs and chemical weapons by both countries. Specific details are still being worked out at the time of this writing.

According to Ralph Earle, former chief of the U. S. delegation to the Strategic Arms Limitation Talks, our negotiators must keep two points especially in mind: First, *the Soviet leadership is very insecure regarding the West.* Some degree of insecurity has always been present in Russian society, but it has grown considerably in intensity under Soviet rule. Reasons for this insecurity have to do with

1. The geographical location of the country (for example, its navy is subject to "choke points" at all exits).
2. Soviet leaders have not forgotten that, in 1918, Western expeditionary forces intervened on the side of the pro-Czarist forces in the Civil War. Hence, they share the belief that the West is still out to destroy communism.
3. The Soviet government faces a great deal of direct or indirect hostility in surrounding Communist or former Communist countries (especially in China and Poland).

The second point, which is also very important in negotiating with Soviet representatives, is that *they wish to be treated always as equals by their U.S. counterparts.* Anything less may produce a walkout by the Soviet delegation.[20]

Whatever the differences between the governments of the United States and the Soviet Union, their cooperation is imperative for the survival of humankind.

In addition to the five members of the "nuclear club" (United States, Soviet Union, Britain, France, and the People's Republic of China), India, Israel, and the

---

[20]These points were related to coauthor Winter in some detail by Ralph Earle II, our chief negotiator of SALT II.

"THE RUSSIANS ARE GAINING! THE RUSSIANS ARE GAINING!"

"THE AMERICANS ARE GAINING! THE AMERICANS ARE GAINING!"

Paul Conrad, 1977, *Los Angeles Times.* Reprinted with permission.

Republic of South Africa have apparently obtained a nuclear capability. Other governments presently highly motivated to obtain this capacity include Libya, Iran, Iraq, Pakistan, Argentina, and Taiwan. The greater the number of countries possessing nuclear weapons, the greater the possibility of a nuclear war. If further proliferation of nuclear weaponry is to be prevented, the United States and the Soviet Union will need to find ways to collaborate on international controls.

Looking beyond the politicomilitary issues, mention has to be made of the developing countries, populated by about two-thirds of the world's people. Most of these people are poor and illiterate. A "revolution of rising expectations" is sweeping the Third World. Generally speaking, the leaders of the developing countries would like to move their societies into modern age as quickly as possible.

*"I, on the other hand, find it frustrating that we have more missiles
than we know what to do with."*

Drawning by Ross; © 1984 The New Yorker Magazine, Inc.

These countries need aid and advice in many areas. The postindustrial societies
have the means to render help. Ways should be found to reduce more successfully
than in the past the cleavage between the rich and the poor countries.

SUMMARY

"International politics" refers to the relations among countries. Its components
include diplomacy, trade, threats, intervention, and war.

No two countries are alike. Some are large, others are small. Some have large
populations, while others have less than a million people. Some countries have a
high standard of living, while others are very poor. There is a great deal of difference
in the degree of self-sufficiency and power among the countries. Elements that may
contribute to power are size, location, population, natural resources, and the military strength of a society.

Throughout the ages, there has been a substantial degree of hostility among
countries. The post–World War II era has been marked by an immense arms race
between the United States and the Soviet Union, an arms race that has been based
on distrust and fear. It is only in the last few years that this distrust and fear has
decreased by degrees, enabling the governments of the two superpowers to conclude treaties that not only place caps on certain weapon categories, but will lead
to the elimination or drastic reduction of certain weapon categories.

The interdependence of countries has grown rapidly since World War II, and
this phenomenon is likely to continue. We hope that the features of improving
relations and growing interdependence will stimulate a growing number of govern-

ments to join forces to tackle with increasing emphasis the major global problems such as pollution, illicit drugs, poverty, and AIDS.

In this chapter we have examined the nature of international politics, its actors, the characteristics of the international system, the methods used for interaction on the international scene, the major developments in international politics since World War II, and the nuclear arms race. Collective efforts toward peace through collective security, international and regional organizations, as well as through international law, will be the subject of the final chapter.

RECOMMENDED READINGS

Brzezinski, Zbigniew. *The Grand Failure: The Birth and Death of Communism in the Twentieth Century.* New York: Charles Scribner's, 1989. The national security advisor to former President Carter analyzes the progressive decay of communism and forecasts its demise as a force in world politics.

Edelman Spero, Joan. *The Politics of International Economic Relations,* 4th ed. New York: St. Martin's Press, 1990. This book is a comprehensive discussion of contemporary economic relations and their impact on international politics.

Harvard Nuclear Study Group. *Living with Nuclear Weapons.* Cambridge, Mass.: Harvard University Press, 1983. Leading U.S. specialists examine the complexities and problems of the nuclear arms issue.

Jones, Walter S. *The Logic of International Relations,* 6th ed. Glenview, Ill.: Scott, Foresman/Little, Brown, 1988. This is a very readable and comprehensive text on international relations.

Kegley, Charles W., Jr., and Eugene R. Wittkopf, eds. *The Nuclear Reader: Strategy, Weapons, War,* 2nd ed. New York: St. Martin's Press, 1989. A good collection of informative articles deals with various important aspects of the nuclear arms race.

Kennedy, Paul. *The Rise and Fall of the Great Powers.* New York: Vintage Books, 1989. This book has been a national bestseller. Kennedy examines, in a highly readable fashion, the major economic and political changes as well as the military conflicts from the sixteenth century to the present day.

Koehane, Robert O., and Joseph S. Nye. *Power and Interdependence,* 2nd ed. Glenview, Ill.: Scott, Foresman/Little, Brown, 1989. These authors provide a succinct analysis of the political and economic changes in the contemporary world and the growing interdependence among countries.

Nathan, James A., and James K. Oliver. *United States Foreign Policy and World Order,* 4th ed. Glenview, Ill.: Scott, Foresman/Little, Brown, 1989. This is a comprehensive analysis of U.S. foreign policy from World War II through the Reagan administration.

Nogee, Joseph L., and John Spanier. *Peace Impossible—War Unlikely: The Cold War Between the United States and the Soviet Union.* Glenview, Ill.: Scott, Foresman/Little, Brown, 1988. A detailed examination of U.S.–Soviet relations in the post–World War II era is provided in this book.

Olson, William C., ed. *The Theory and Practice of International Relations,* 7th ed. Englewood Cliffs, N. J.: Prentice-Hall, 1987. This excellent collection of articles covers the major aspects of international politics.

Rubinstein, Alvin Z. *Soviet Foreign Policy since World War II: Imperial and Global,* 3rd ed. Glenview, Ill.: Scott, Foresman/Little, Brown, 1989. The author provides a well-written analysis of Soviet foreign policy with special emphasis on its regional dimensions.

Stoessinger, John G. *Why Nations Go to War,* 5th ed. New York: St. Martin's Press, 1990. This is a highly readable case study of the major wars in the twentieth century.

Chapter 13

Collective Means for Cooperation and Integration in the International Community

The roots of international law as well as regional and international organization reach back to antiquity. For many centuries humankind has tried to find mechanisms to solve conflicts by reason rather than by combat, which ignores the question of right and wrong.

Rapidly growing global interdependence, discussed in the previous chapter, has accentuated in recent decades the quest for a greater degree of law and order on the international scene. This movement has aimed to counteract the "might makes right" syndrome. Endeavors in this direction have encountered a number of difficulties, however. Some have to do with the fact that countries come in all different sizes and power capabilities. Further, the countries of our time are in different stages of development. Throughout history, the more powerful countries have "flexed their muscles" more than the weaker countries.

But some progress toward more law and order on the international scene has been made. Violations of established rules of conduct do occur, but they are more strongly condemned these days than decades and centuries ago, as the following example illustrates.

In December 1979, both the Security Council of the United Nations and the International Court of Justice as well as the mass media and public opinion in many countries condemned strongly the Khomeini forces in Iran for taking over the U.S. Embassy in Tehran and holding the U.S. personnel hostage. Although these nearly worldwide condemnations did not produce the immediate release of the hostages, they did ease the way for subsequent negotiations leading to their release.

The outcry shows that there are established rules of behavior on the international scene, and that most people throughout the world expect governments to follow these rules. So there is at least a semblence of international morality in the world.

Critics who argue that the United Nations, regional organizations, and international law are ineffective tend to forget that the effectiveness of these institutions and rules reflects by necessity the degree of order—or disorder—that is present in the world. Whatever their influence is at a given time, it is important to note that these institutions and rules serve also as beacons to show the people on the planet earth directions on how to achieve a greater degree of law and order on the international scene.

This chapter attempts to examine briefly the nature of international law, international and regional organizations, and the role these play in international politics today. International law and organizations are collective in the sense that they are supposed to apply to and serve all countries and all of mankind, rather than one group of people or one country. These forces are means that can and do place limitations on the behavior of countries in their relations with each other. Let us first look at international organizations.

INTERNATIONAL ORGANIZATIONS: THE HISTORICAL PERSPECTIVE

International organization is a response to insecurity in the multicountry system. The **League of Nations** was established after World War I to prevent another worldwide war. In 1945, the **United Nations** was created "to save succeeding generations from the scourge of war."[1] The underlying aim of international organization is to increase cooperation among the countries and to decrease friction and violence on the international scene.

Attempts at international organization date back as far as the League of Greek City-States at the time of Plato and Aristotle. The modern era of international conferences commenced with the Treaty of Westphalia (1648), when hundreds of envoys, representing nearly every European country, met and catalyzed a new era of European relations. A number of plans toward international federation and organization were proposed during the seventeenth and eighteenth centuries. For example, William Penn and Abbe de Saint-Pierre proposed plans for a "Parliament of Europe."

The Congress of Vienna (1815) set the stage for the Quadruple Alliance and its periodic congresses—a system that became known as the "Concert of Europe," which in essence was a system of balance of power—maintained by the four great continental powers of that time. This arrangement succeeded in maintaining a relatively high degree of peace in nineteenth-century Europe.

In 1899 and 1907 two international conferences were held in The Hague, Holland. The professed aim of these meetings was to bring about general disarmament and to develop means for the peaceful settlement of disputes. Although these conferences were far from being successful, they had some importance for the development of international organization because representatives of a number of non-European countries joined their European colleagues at these gatherings, and the principle of one country–one vote (as found in the voting procedure of the General Assembly of the United Nations) was put into operation.

The prevalent political climate at the end of World War I led to the establishment of the first nearly universal organization, the League of Nations. Its permanent headquarters was located in Geneva, Switzerland. The major bodies of the league were the Assembly, in which all member countries were represented, and the Council, which was made up of the great powers. The day-to-day staff work was handled by a permanent secretariat under the direction and supervision of the Assembly and Council. The organizational structure of the league, as well as its practices and experiences, had, as we shall see later on, a considerable influence on the shaping of the United Nations in the 1940s.

Although the existence of the League of Nations lent itself to improved international relations during the 1920s, it did not fulfill the Wilsonian hopes of preventing another world war. By the late 1930s the league, for all practical purposes, had become a defunct organization. Although a number of reasons could be cited for this, the most important one was that the major powers never showed a concurrent, full commitment to support the league and its principles. The United States, whose president had been the prime mover in establishing the league, did not even become a member of the organization. Related to this, the principle of collective security, written in rather loose language into Articles 10 and 11 of the League Covenant, never became operative. The concept of *collective security* denotes a security arrangement wherein all members pledge themselves to common

---

[1]This passage is taken from the preamble to the charter of the United Nations.

retaliatory action in the case of an attack against a member country. In the 1930s, beginning with Japan's invasion of Manchuria in 1931, the league consistently failed to invoke such retaliatory action against aggressors and so lost its credibility as a force for international order.[2]

One of the greatest long-range values of the League of Nations lies perhaps in the fact that the founders of the United Nations were able to learn from the league's experience and, accordingly, write a United Nations Charter that was substantially superior to the League Covenant.

THE UNITED NATIONS

Representatives of 51 countries met in San Francisco in the spring and early summer of 1945 to draft the charter for a new international organization—the United Nations. The final document was signed on June 26, 1945. The name "United Nations" was coined by President Roosevelt and Prime Minister Churchill during their Arcadia Conference in 1941. During the early 1940s the governments of the United Kingdom and the United States spearheaded the drive toward establishing this new international organization.

In contrast to 1919, public opinion in the United States was rather favorably disposed toward a United Nations, and it was a foregone conclusion that the United States would play a leading role in creating the organization and would be one of its major members.

The first meeting of the United Nations was held in London in January 1946. In the next few years a permanent headquarters was built along the East River in New York City and became operative in early 1950.

The Functions of the United Nations

The functions and purposes of the United Nations are stated in Article I of the charter:

1. To maintain international peace and security, and to that end: to take effective collective measures for the prevention and removal of threats to the peace, and for the suppression of acts of aggression or other breaches of the peace, and to bring about by peaceful means, and in conformity with the principles of justice and international law, adjustment or settlement of international disputes or situations which might lead to a breach of peace.
2. To develop friendly relations among nations based on respect for the principle of equal rights and self-determination of peoples, and to take other appropriate measures to strengthen universal peace.
3. To achieve international cooperation in solving international problems of an economic, social, cultural, or humanitarian character, and in promoting

---

[2]See F. P. Walters, *A History of the League of Nations,* 2 vols. (London: Oxford University Press, 1952).

and encouraging respect for human rights and for fundamental freedoms for all without distinctions as to race, sex, language, or religion.

4. To be a center for harmonizing the actions of nations in the attainment of these common ends.[3]

The Structure of the United Nations

Article 7 of the United Nations Charter delineates six principal organs of the organization (see Figure 13.1):

1. The General Assembly.
2. The Security Council.
3. The Economic and Social Council.
4. The Trusteeship Council.
5. The International Court of Justice (located in The Hague and discussed later in this chapter).
6. The Secretariat.

A number of specialized agencies are affiliated directly with the United Nations, and the major ones are shown in Figure 13.1. The following listing gives the date of their establishment and their place of headquarters in parentheses: Universal Postal Union (1875, Berne); International Telecommunications Union (1865, Geneva); International Labor Organization (1919, Geneva); Food and Agriculture Organization (1944, Rome); International Monetary Fund (1944, Washington, D.C.); International Bank for Reconstruction and Development (1944, Washington, D.C.); United Nations Educational, Scientific, and Cultural Organization (1945, Paris); World Health Organization (1946, Geneva); International Civil Aviation Organization (1947, Montreal); World Meteorological Organization (1950, Geneva); International Finance Corporation (1956, Washington, D.C.); Intergovernmental Maritime Consultative Organization (1958, London); and International Development Association (1960, Washington, D.C.).

The General Assembly: An Approximation of a World Forum   The **General Assembly** is the basic forum of the United Nations in that all member countries are represented in it. Voting in the assembly emphasizes the principle of equality, with each member country having one vote in its decisions. The only exception is the Soviet Union, which has three (one for the Soviet Union at large, one for the Ukraine, and one for Byelorussia—a compromise forced by Stalin at the Yalta Conference in 1945). The General Assembly holds annual sessions that start in September and may continue until the early spring of the following year.

The functions and powers of the General Assembly are very broad. According to the charter:

---

[3]The full text of the charter is published in, among other sources, the *Yearbook of the United Nations* (New York: United Nations Office of Public Information, published annually). A helpful and popular source of information about the United Nations and its affiliated agencies is *Everyone's United Nations*, 10th ed. (New York: United Nations Office of Publications, 1986).

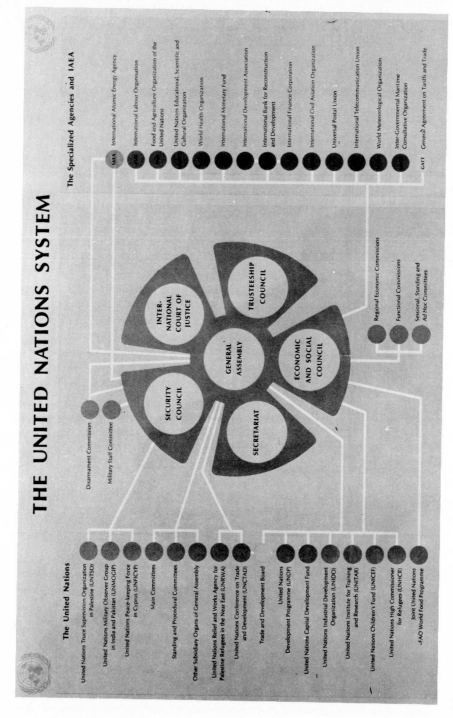

Figure 13.1 The structure of the United Nations.

"The Small Society" by Brickman. © Washington Star Syndicate. Permission granted by King Features Syndicate, 1973.

> The General Assembly may discuss any questions or any matters within the scope of the present Charter or relating to the powers and functions of any organs provided for in the present Charter, and, except as provided in Article 12 [which states that the General Assembly shall not make any recommendations on a dispute while it is being discussed by the Security Council], may make recommendations to the Members of the United Nations or to the Security Council or to both on any such questions or matters.

In size, the General Assembly has grown from its original 51 members to 159 in 1990. It has served as a valuable forum for debate and exchange of views. In the decision-making area, it by and large has left specific actions on security matters and peace-keeping functions to the Security Council. It should be pointed out, however, that in this area the General Assembly has become a backstop of the Security Council with the passage of the Uniting for Peace Resolution in 1950. This resolution grew out of the experience derived from the early part of the Korean conflict—the recognition that a permanent member of the Security Council could block easily a majority-approved UN peacekeeping action. To circumvent this, Article I of the Uniting for Peace Resolution provides that in emergencies, when the Security Council is prevented from acting (on account of a veto or the threat of a veto), the General Assembly is authorized to meet on short notice and to recommend any appropriate collective measures, including the use of armed force. The resolution enabled the General Assembly to deal with several important security problems during times of a deadlock in the Security Council, such as periods of the Korean conflict in 1950 and the Congo crises in 1960.

The rapid increase in membership has given the General Assembly a nearly universal flavor and representation. Over the years, its function as a forum for discussion and debate of regional and worldwide economic, military, political, and social issues has been of considerable value to the world community.

The Security Council: An Approximation of an International Presidium
Underlying the composition and the voting procedure in the Security Council is the concept of big-power control, or "world sheriff." The council, as created in 1945, consisted of 11 members. Five of these were permanent members: China,

The United Nations Security Council in session September 25, 1990. It discussed and voted that day on resolution 670, banning air transport to and from Iraq and occupied Kuwait.

France, the Soviet Union, the United Kingdom, and the United States. The 6 nonpermanent members were to be elected for two-year terms by the General Assembly. In 1963 the number of nonpermanent members was increased to 10, in recognition of the growing membership of the United Nations.

Some mention needs to be made of the voting procedure in the Security Council. Each member country has one vote. Decisions on procedural matters (recommendations that do not include sanctions) require the affirmative vote of any 9 of the 15 members. Substantive decisions, however, require the affirmative votes of 9 members including those of all 5 permanent members. It is here that the veto may occur. The negative vote of a permanent member on a substantive issue constitutes a veto and will block Security Council action.[4]

According to Article 24 of the United Nations Charter, the members of the organization "confer on the Security Council primary responsibility for the mainte-

[4]Both the governments of the Soviet Union and the United States insisted during the preparatory stage that the veto principle be built into the United Nations Charter. For an excellent discussion on the use of the veto, see Sidney D. Bailey, "Veto in the Security Council," *International Conciliation,* No. 566 (January 1968), pp. 5–66.

nance of international peace and security, and agree that in carrying out its duties under this responsibility the Security Council acts on their behalf." The particular powers granted by the charter to the Security Council to discharge its duties are laid down in Chapters VI (Pacific Settlement of Disputes), VII (Action with Respect to Threats to Peace, Breaches of the Peace, and Acts of Aggression), VIII (Regional Arrangements), and XII (International Trusteeship System). In essence, the actions of the Security Council will involve one or several of the following: It may suggest methods of reconciliation; it may offer specific resolutions (this was done, for example, in the Congo crisis); it may order a provisional truce (as on Cyprus in 1964 and 1974); it may invoke nonmilitary sanctions (in 1965 the Security Council invoked economic sanctions against Rhodesia); and finally it may resort to military sanctions, as it did in Korea and in the Congo.

Over the years, the Security Council often has been handicapped by the quarrels among its permanent members and has not been fully able to mobilize the United Nations as intended by the founders. Its best area of success has been and is in disputes where the aggressor is not a permanent member of the Security Council and is not being directly supported by a permanent member. The presence of the veto usually prevents the Security Council from taking action against a permanent member or another country actively supported by a permanent member.

The peacekeeping capability of the United Nations was enhanced in 1956 when the General Assembly passed a resolution creating the United Nations Emergency Force (UNEF), an international military force with the task of supervising armistice arrangements decreed by the United Nations. The members of this military force were to be drawn from member countries, with the exception of the permanent members of the Security Council. Since 1956 UNEF has served in the Congo (where it was known as ONUC) and several times at critical places in the Middle East (in Cyprus, near the Suez Canal, and in the Golan Heights). A number of countries have contributed troops to UNEF; for example, Finland, Sweden,

"We've just been admitted to the United Nations."

"Off the Record" by Ed Reed, reprinted courtesy of *The Register* and Tribune Syndicate.

Canada, Austria, Ireland, India, and several African countries sent troops during the Congo operation. The UNEF is the first step in modern history toward establishing an international military force. The important service rendered by the UN peacekeeping forces was officially recognized by the international community in 1988 when UNEF was awarded the Nobel Peace Prize.

The Secretariat: An Approximation of an International Civil Service

The Secretariat performs the day-to-day administrative tasks of the United Nations. It is directed by the **secretary general,** who is appointed by the General Assembly upon recommendation by the Security Council. The functions of the secretary general are spelled out in Chapter XV of the United Nations Charter:

> He shall be the chief administrative officer of the Organization.
>
> The Secretary-General shall act in that capacity in all meetings of the General Assembly, of the Security Council, of the Economic and Social Council, and of the Trusteeship Council. . . . The Secretary-General shall make an annual report to the General Assembly on the work of the Organization.
>
> The Secretary-General may bring to the attention of the Security Council any matter which in his opinion may threaten the maintenance of international peace and security.

As the highest administrative officer, he or she oversees the work of thousands of international civil servants, recruited from many of the member countries. Most of the Secretariat's employees work at the headquarters in New York, but others are in Geneva, Switzerland, or at one of the several field offices the United Nations maintains throughout the world.[5]

The present secretary general, Javier Pérez de Cuéllar (Peru), is the fifth person to hold this position. The job of the secretary general has an unavoidable problem—most of the time he has to "walk a tightrope." If in fulfillment of his duties he speaks out too loudly and forcefully, he may incur the wrath of one or several of the permanent members of the Security Council; yet if he does not speak out at all, he would doom his office to sterility. It takes a most talented person to play, under the strains of this dilemma, an effective role in the work of the United Nations.

The Economic and Social Council: The Promotion of Economic and Social Welfare

One of the main purposes of the United Nations, as stated in the charter, is "to achieve international cooperation in solving problems of an economic, social, cultural, or humanitarian character." **The Economic and Social Council** was established to serve as the key agency for coordinating the United Nation's activities in the economic and social realms. The functions of the council are spelled out in Chapter X of the charter and include the initiation of studies and reports on international economic, social, cultural, and educational

---

[5]For an examination of some of the complexities of international administration, see Robert S. Jordan, ed., *International Administration: Its Evolution and Contemporary Applications* (New York: Oxford University Press, 1971).

matters; preparation of recommendations for the General Assembly; and giving assistance to the Security Council on economic and social matters when so requested.

The founders of the United Nations had hoped that the organization's activities in the economic and social realms could be kept out of the arena of political conflict. Moreover, they hoped that the habit of peaceful collaboration in the economic and social realms could later be extended to the organization's political and military activities. In the composite perspective, the Economic and Social Council has become a very important organ of the United Nations and a stimulant of international cooperation.

The Trusteeship Council: Protecting the Rights of Non-self-governing Societies   This is the successor to the League of Nations Mandate System, which was established after World War I to render international control over former German colonies and the territories once held by the defunct Ottoman Empire. With the establishment of the United Nations, those former league mandates that had not yet achieved independence were turned into trusteeships of the United Nations and placed under the supervision of the Trusteeship Council.

Chapter XII of the charter declares that the basic objectives of the Trusteeship Council are "to promote the political, economic, social, and educational advancement of the inhabitants of the trust territories, and their progressive development toward self-government or independence." Since 1945, most of the former trust territories have become independent. As of 1990, only the Carolines, Marianas, and Marshall Islands in the Pacific (administered as a strategic trust territory by the United States) remain under the jurisdiction of the Trusteeship Council. Once these Pacific Islands become independent, the Trusteeship Council will have no further duties to perform and thus will cease to function.

A Brief Evaluation of the United Nations

The shortcomings of the United Nations mirror the problems of today's world. Its strength and productivity rest, in essence, on the support given by the member countries, especially by the great powers.

During the past decades, the United Nations has undergone a great deal of change, with its membership increasing from the original 51 to 159. While during the first decade the UN was basically a pro-Western, U.S.–dominated institution, over the years it has become a global organization with the General Assembly, the Secretariat, and most of the affiliated agencies now dominated by the voice of the more than 100 developing countries.

To cope with the changing fortunes of international politics, the United Nations has exercised flexibility in various ways. First, it has amended the charter to enlarge the membership of the Security Council and the Economic and Social Council in recognition of the organization's growing membership. Second, it has reinterpreted the charter on several occasions. For example, it has established the UNEF in such a way that the global powers are excluded from partaking in the actual peacekeeping operations. Third, it has shifted, depending upon the need, the initiation of action between the Security Council, the General Assembly, and the Secretariat. This has been made possible through the passage of the Uniting for Peace Resolution and initiatives taken by the secretary general, such as the actions taken by Dag Hammarskjöld during the Congo crisis. Finally, the secretary generals have succeeded in maintaining, at all times, enough political consensus within the United Nations to ensure the survival of the organization.

The globalization of the United Nations led to a decline in the support rendered by the United States and the Soviet Union during the 1970s and early 1980s because of their corresponding decrease of influence in the General Assembly and some of the UN-affiliated agencies. This, in turn, led to an overall decline of the comprehensive effectiveness of the United Nations. Both superpowers, along with some other countries, withheld some of the financial assessments. Furthermore, the United States withdrew from UNESCO (the United Nations Educational, Scientific and Cultural Organization) in 1984. According to U.S. spokespeople, UNESCO had atrocious management practices and was serving anti-American political ends.

A new spirit developed in the later 1980s. Mr. Gorbachev signaled an increased Soviet interest in the United Nations and pledged that his government would pay its full share in all United Nations operations. The Reagan administration in its final years, too, became more supportive of the United Nations, a trend followed by President Bush. Secretary General Javier Pérez de Cuéllar helped to increase U.S. support by making major changes in the staffing of the Secretariat as requested for years by the U.S. government. The improvement in U.S.–Soviet relations has had a healthy impact on the United Nations. In several instances joint U.S.–Soviet prodding has led to an increase in United Nations effectiveness and action.

Any evaluation of the United Nations will leave the observer with mixed reactions. It has not met the founders' hopes in some areas while meeting or surpassing them in others. The plain fact is that the United Nations cannot be much stronger than it is because of the limitations imposed by the present-day nation-state system. The member countries are neither ready nor willing at this stage to surrender their rights of national sovereignty to the United Nations.

The United Nations has helped to bring representatives of the various people of the world closer together. The General Assembly constitutes the only permanent worldwide forum where the representatives of the many member countries can meet, exchange opinions, and publicly voice their views on regional and worldwide problems. The importance of this forum should not be underestimated. In the area of economic and social development, the United Nations renders important help to many of the developing countries and has contributed, beyond original expectations, to the improvement of the general welfare. Finally, the United Nations helps to maintain peace throughout the world. Although its intended role as mediator and conciliator has not borne fruit at every occasion, its partial results have been of help to the world community. Any composite and realistic evaluation of the United Nations must lead to the conclusions that the international institution has made a positive contribution to international order and well-being. In the absence of a better alternative, the global community depends on the United Nations and will need its services in the future.

HARASSED NURSEMAID

Justus, the *Minneapolis Star.*

REGIONAL INTEGRATION

Since World War II, a number of regional organizations have been created. These systems may be defined as groupings of three or more countries that have formed distinct arrangements for the purpose of economic, military, and/or political integration at the regional level. Regional integration denotes the establishment of common goals by the member countries, increasing cooperation in joint endeavors, and the voluntary surrender of certain aspects of national decision making to the authoritative organs of the regional organization.

Regionalism, according to some theorists, can serve as a stepping-stone toward universalism. Advocates of this theory emphasize that the present world is too diverse culturally, economically, ideologically, and psychologically to develop global common loyalties. Integrating commonalities could be established more readily within regions. The building blocks created by regional integration can serve in the future for the creation of a greater degree of worldwide order. Some supporters of regionalism support the "federal approach" and others the "functional approach." The first calls for the establishment of supranational agencies within regional organizations. The members would surrender part of their sovereignty to the supranational bodies. The "functionalists," in contrast, have encouraged the development of broad-scale intergovernmental collaboration in lieu of supranational agencies. According to their view, economic, social, and cultural cooperation is a paramount prerequisite to political integration. The regionalism that has developed in recent decades appears to contain aspects of both theories.[6]

Some degree of "regionalism," in the sense of grouping a number of countries together for the pursuit of a common policy, existed prior to 1945. The defense alliances, formed before and after World War I, and the British Commonwealth serve as examples. Regional organization gained considerable momentum in the late 1940s and during the 1950s, leading to the establishment of a large number of military, economic, and political arrangements, which will be discussed later. The move toward regional association was spearheaded by arrangements in the Atlantic community area and in the Americas. They were countered in the 1950s by the establishment of similar systems among the Communist countries. Other regional organizations were established in the Middle East, Africa, and Southeast Asia.

The multitude of regional organizations developed after World War II can be divided into three categories:

1. Multipurpose organizations.
2. Security organizations.
3. Economic organizations.

Multipurpose Organizations

The major post–World War II regional organizations that fall into this category are the League of Arab States (commonly known as the Arab League, established in 1945), the Organization of American States (OAS, 1948), the Council of Europe (1949), and the Organization of African Unity (OAU, 1963).

Of these four, the Council of Europe has maintained perhaps the most limited profile. Over the years its activities have been overshadowed by questions and issues relating to NATO and European economic integration.

The Organization of American States was established as a follow-up to the Rio Pact (1947). Under the active leadership of the United States, OAS has been used to coordinate hemispheric American politics. OAS has occupied itself with a number of broad issues involving political, economic, and military matters. For example, the Alliance for Progress program was carried on, at least technically, under the auspices of OAS. The Alliance for Progress was based on the U.S. commitment to Latin American countries to help them raise their standard of living. The most notable military action of the OAS occurred in 1965 in conjunction with a governmental crisis in the Dominican Republic. Civil war and the threat of an apparent Communist takeover in late April and early May of that year led the U.S. government to send troops to the Dominican Republic. After a ceasefire had been achieved between the warring factions, an Inter-American Peace Force was established under

---

[6]For a theoretical discussion of regional integration, see Ernst B. Haas, "International Integration, the European and the Universal Process," and Amitai Etzioni, "The Dialects of Supranational Unification," in *International Political Communities, An Anthology* (Garden City, N.Y.: Doubleday, 1966), pp. 93–147.

OAS auspices, consisting of U.S. troops plus contingents from Brazil, Costa Rica, El Salvador, and Nicaragua. The force was directed by a Brazilian general and remained at the scene until the fighting was stopped and a new, viable government was established.

Perhaps the most successful role performed by the OAS has been that of a fact-finding and conciliation agency. It helped to settle a number of disputes among Latin American countries in the 1950s and 1960s.

The most serious outside threat against a member of OAS (the United States) occurred in 1962, when the Soviet government began to ship missiles and missile launchers to Cuba. In this case the United States carried out the necessary measures to get the Soviet missiles and missile launchers removed from Cuban soil. The U.S. actions had the full support of the other members of OAS.

In the 1980s, the OAS faded into semioblivion. A major reason has been the difference in views held by the governments of the United States and various Latin American countries regarding hemispheric issues. Efforts to solve the civil wars in El Salvador and Nicaragua have come largely from individuals such as President Arias of Costa Rica and the governments of a small number of Central American countries known collectively as the Contadora group.

The Arab League is the oldest of the four multipurpose regional organizations. Its espoused purpose has been to foster and increase cooperation among the Arab countries. Although its original aim was essentially to seek the liberation of all Arab countries from colonial rule, it soon became involved in military actions when it tried to prevent the establishment of the country of Israel. Since then, a shared hostility against Israel has been perhaps the strongest motivating force within the Arab League. Integrated economic pursuits were added to the Arab League's responsibilities in later years. Perennial divisions of interest among some of the Arab countries, however, have limited the effectiveness of the Arab League over the years.

The OAU is the newest of the multipurpose regional organizations. It is the only regional organization combining the black and Arab African countries. Established in 1963, it has sought to unite under its framework the divergent groupings of African countries. The charter of the OAU calls for achieving the aspirations of the African people through economic and political development. The members of OAU have pledged themselves to coordinate their policies, defend their sovereignty, and eradicate colonialism in Africa. Some of OAU's major accomplishments have been related to the prevention or settlement of disputes between members. One of its more successful achievements occurred in 1963, when OAU officials achieved a ceasefire in the border dispute between Algeria and Morocco. Subsequent OAU meetings helped in bringing about a settlement.

OAU has been subject to various internal strains; however, the organization has endured the crises and has succeeded in achieving international importance. Perhaps one of its greatest problems in recent years has been the growing division between the Arab member countries on the one hand and the black countries on the other. Requests for financial aid made by several of the sub-Saharan countries to counter the cost of oil have not yet been met with an adequate response by the newly rich oil-producing countries of the north. It appears that this problem and

President Nujoma, the leader of Africa's youngest country, Namibia, is greeted by Ethiopia's President Mengista on arrival in Addis Ababa for the 1990 meeting of the Organization of African Unity.

the rivalry over black or Arab leadership in OAU will continue for some time to come. Thus, although OAU has had some success as a regional arbitrator, it has done little to further "pan-African unity."

Security Organizations

Regional arrangements whose primary function is that of security include the **North Atlantic Treaty Organization** (NATO, established in 1949); the Australia, New Zealand, United States Security Treaty Organization (ANZUS, 1952); the **Warsaw Treaty Organization** (WTO, 1955); and the Rio Pact (1947), which led to the establishment of the OAS one year later.

Underlying all of these security-oriented regional arrangements is the principle of collective security; that is, the concept that an attack upon one member of an association should be considered as an attack on all members, and all shall rally to the defense of the attacked country. For example, Article 3 of the Rio Pact states

The High Contracting Parties agree that an armed attack by any State against an American State shall be considered as an attack against all American States, and, consequently, each one of the said Contracting Parties undertakes to assist in meeting the attack in the exercise of the inherent right of individual or collective self-defense recognized by Article 51 of the Charter of the United Nations.[7]

Similar provisions are found in the treaties that serve as the constitutional foundation for NATO, ANZUS, and WTO.

Let us look briefly at the specific purposes of some of these security arrangements. The Rio Pact was designed to provide an inter-American treaty of military assistance and to establish a system of collective security in the Americas. NATO was created to contain the perceived Communist threat to Western Europe. To counter the Western military alliance system, the Soviet government converted in 1955 its bilateral military treaties with other East European countries into a multilateral agreement, WTO, commonly referred to as the Warsaw Pact. The large-scale development of nuclear weaponry in the 1970s rendered questionable the basic premises upon which the two military alliances (and the others, too) were built. Increasingly, West Europeans had growing doubts as to whether or not the United States would come to their defense. In essence, how much credibility does the assumption of collective security carry in a time when warfare in the Northern Hemisphere carries the risk of nuclear annihilation?

NATO celebrated its 40th anniversary on April 4, 1989. This happened at a time when some of the European members raised new questions regarding the purpose of NATO in the light of President Gorbachev's far-reaching arms reduction proposals.

During its 40 years of existence, the NATO alliance has been helpful in maintaining the political status quo and peace in Europe. Although the Warsaw Pact has counterbalanced NATO, it has done so at a substantial cost. The Warsaw Pact seems to be the only military alliance in history whose forces have been used to invade member countries (Hungary, 1956; and Czechoslovakia, 1968).

The rapid changes in Central and Eastern Europe, which commenced with the opening of the Berlin Wall and the Iron Curtain in late 1989, raise substantial questions regarding the future of NATO and WTO. Will NATO be turned into a political organization? WTO, as it appears, will just wither away.

Economic Organizations

The largest number of regional organizations have developed in the economic realm. Some of them have achieved substantially more structure and organizational viability than others. They differ also in size, ranging from the macrosized Organization of Economic Cooperation and Development (OECD), which includes a

---

[7]The text of the Rio Pact is reprinted in M. Margaret Ball, *The OAS in Transition* (Durham, N.C.: Duke University Press, 1969). For the text of the North Atlantic Treaty, see, among others, A. H. Robertson, *European Institutions* (New York: Frederick A. Praeger, 1958). The English-language text of the Warsaw Treaty is published in Robin A. Remington, *The Warsaw Pact* (Cambridge, Mass.: The MIT Press, 1971).

number of developing countries, to such microsized organizations as the Nordic Council, which consists of the five Scandinavian countries. The basic effort underlying the economic regional groupings has been to decrease trade barriers between the member countries and to increase commerce between them. This pursuit has led to substantially increased economic cooperation in some parts of the world. The most important strides toward economic integration have taken place in Western Europe under the auspices of the **European Economic Community (EEC)** (the Common Market).

The EEC was established in 1957 for the purpose of integrating the economic policies of Belgium, the Netherlands, Luxembourg, France, the Federal Republic of Germany, and Italy. These were joined in 1973 by the United Kingdom, Denmark, and Ireland, by Greece in 1981, and by Portugal and Spain in 1986. In 1951, the original six countries, also known as the "Inner Six," had established the European Coal and Steel Community to provide a common market in coal and steel and its byproducts among the six members. The EEC provided a still broader scope and aimed to integrate the entire economies of the member countries. A European Atomic Energy Community (Euratom), with the purpose of establishing a basis for the joint exploitation of atomic energy, was created simultaneously with the EEC.

The ostensible purpose of the moves toward West European economic integration was to increase the economic well-being of all the member countries. In actuality, however, the major impetus came from French leaders, especially Robert Schuman, who sought integration as a means of eliminating the danger of any future armed conflict between France and Germany. It is in this aspect that one of the major rationales underlying West European integration differs from those of economic integration in other parts of the world.

Although there has been considerable economic integration among the Common Market countries, progress has been faster in some specific areas than in others. Accomplishments include the creation of a Customs Union, which became operative in 1968; the establishment of a common agricultural policy, which by 1974 encompassed most of the community's agricultural production; the creation of a communitywide Monetary Cooperation Fund; and endeavors toward common policies in environmental, scientific, and technological affairs.

West European economic integration showed its greatest momentum during the early and mid 1960s and leveled off in the 1970s. Among other problems, the oil crisis of late 1973 led to divisive tendencies among the Common Market countries and policies that were based on an "each for his own" attitude rather than constructive, joint endeavors.

The next step in the EEC integration process aims to establish by the end of 1992 a common economic environment among the 12 member countries. This involves the scrapping of all barriers to travel, trade, employment, and investment among the EEC members, thereby creating a full-fledged common market for capital, goods, labor, and services among the 330 million people of the EEC. This is the most far-reaching plan toward regional integration ever undertaken in the modern era.

By the end of 1989 approximately one-half of the 279 formal, legal directives of this plan had been approved by the member countries. However, a good deal of hard bargaining lies ahead on major issues. These involve, among others, problems that have to do with national sovereignty versus supranational integration, equity in financial assessments, the flow of labor among the member countries,[8] and the question of how to keep an effective check on political terrorists in a setting where people may move freely—without border checks—from one EEC country to another.

In sum, however, the integration of 330 million people in a single internal market seems to entail more opportunities than risks and promises a substantial impetus to economic growth. If the plan materializes, the EEC, which has achieved already more economic integration among its members than any other regional economic organization, would become the largest trading bloc in the 1990s.

The **Council for Mutual Economic Assistance** (COMECON or CMEA) is the regional economic organization of Communist countries. In 1989 the members were the Soviet Union, Poland, the former German Democratic Republic, Czechoslovakia, Hungary, Bulgaria, Romania, the Mongolian Republic, Vietnam, and Cuba. (Albania, one of its original members, left COMECON in 1961.) Its creation came as a reaction to the Marshall Plan and subsequent West European economic integration. Over the years a close system of economic interdependence was developed, under the auspices of COMECON, between the Soviet Union and the other members. During the 1950s and 1960s COMECON members conducted most of their foreign trade within the organization and a considerable portion thereof with the Soviet Union. A leveling-off tendency in this trade pattern occurred in the 1970s, however, with Hungary, Poland, and Romania, increasing their trade with the West.

Two unique COMECON projects are the construction of an oil pipeline linking the Soviet Union with Poland, Hungary, Czechoslovakia, and the former German Democratic Republic and an electric power grid system connecting the Soviet Union with these same countries plus Bulgaria and Romania, thereby making these polities more energy dependent on the Soviet Union.

One of the basic differences between the EEC and COMECON is that in the latter the Soviet Union, because of its power and influence, has played a dominant role. No such great predominance has been exercised by any country within the Common Market. The Soviet leadership has been able to utilize COMECON to increase, at least temporarily, its control over the member countries, despite occasional setbacks such as the departure of Albania and the defeat in 1963 of Khrushchev's plan to introduce a still greater degree of specialization among the industries of the COMECON countries. The major political changes that have occurred in Eastern Europe since the late 1980s are leading also to economic changes. The former German Democratic Republic has become part of the hard-currency, free-market Germany. Most of the other members of COMECON are moving toward a market orientated economy. As a consequence COMECON is disintegrating.

---

[8]According to U.S. Department of State data (Gist, July 1989), the 1987 per capita income among the EEC countries ranged from U.S. $3,368 in Portugal to $19,092 in Denmark, and the unemployment rate, from 1.6 percent in Luxembourg to 20.5 percent in Spain.

One more economic organization deserves our attention, namely, the Organization of Petroleum Exporting Countries (OPEC). OPEC was founded in 1960. It is not so much a regional organization, as it is a producer's cartel, having as its members a number of oil-producing and exporting countries in the Middle East, Africa, Asia, and Latin America.[9]

OPEC members produced more than 50 percent of the world's crude oil in 1973, but its share has fallen since then. OPEC exercised a substantial influence on the world economy in 1973 and 1979 when, in the face of a rapidly increasing worldwide demand for crude oil, the organization succeeded in increasing the price fourfold in 1973 and tripling it again in 1979. However, the high oil price enticed a number of non-OPEC countries to increase their oil production drastically, thereby breaking the stranglehold imposed by OPEC. For example, Canada and Mexico, countries that produced little oil prior to 1960, have become two important suppliers for the United States. In addition, most major oil-consuming countries have introduced various conservation methods, which have led to a slight decline of worldwide oil consumption. The increased oil production of non-OPEC countries and conservation has decreased OPEC's export share and its power in world affairs.

The rapid rise in crude oil prices in 1990 was not OPEC-caused, but resulted on account of Iraq's occupation of Kuwait and the developing consequences.

An Assessment of Regional Organizations

What has been the success of regional organizations in the post–World War II era? The composite picture shows a "mixed-bag" situation in that some regional organizations have been much more successful than others: Regional organizations dominated by one or the other superpower, such as NATO, OAS, the Warsaw Pact, or COMECON, have been used extensively and perhaps understandably to protect and perpetuate their spheres of influence. According to Nye:

> Regional organizations are not a major cause of spheres of influence, but to some extent they help to perpetuate them. One can argue that these spheres of influence have been useful no-trespassing signs that help to prevent miscalculation by the superpowers and thus help to avoid nuclear holocaust.[10]

An alternative argument, however, is that regional spheres are "likely in the long run only to provoke rather than prevent further conflict both within and without."[11]

In any case, regional organizations have made some constructive contribution

---

[9]The members of OPEC in 1990 were Algeria, Nigeria, Gabon, Libya, Venezuela, Ecuador, Saudi Arabia, Kuwait, Iraq, Iran, and Indonesia.

[10]J. S. Nye, *Peace in Parts: Integration and Conflict in Regional Organization* (Boston: Little, Brown, 1971), pp. 179–180.

[11]Evan Luard, *Conflict and Peace in the Modern International System* (Boston: Little, Brown, 1969), p. 167.

to world peace. They have helped in varying degrees to create a greater sense of commonality among the populations of the member countries. Good examples are the Council of Europe and the Common Market. Both organizations have contributed much toward overcoming the historic national rivalries between France and Germany. The regional consciousness in Western Europe—the feeling of belonging together—is greater today than ever before. Regional organizations have helped in curtailing conflict among member countries. Admittedly, the disputes settled by regional organizations were cases of low intensity in terms of their seriousness for the global community.[12]

INTERNATIONAL LAW

Our discussion of the international area concludes with a brief examination of law among the countries. We would like to explain its nature, sources, and role in contemporary international politics.

The Nature of International Law

International law is of a different nature than domestic law. The governments of countries, usually having a preponderance of power in their respective societies, enforce domestic law. On the international scene, however, there is no world government and therefore no agency that can consistently and effectively enforce international law. Definitions of international law usually recognize this important difference between the roles of domestic and international law. According to J. L. Brierly, "The Law of Nations, or International Law, may be defined as the body of rules and principles of action which are binding upon civilized states in their relations with one another."[13] A still more pointed definition comes from Charles Hyde, who states:

> The term international law may fairly be employed to designate the principles and rules of conduct declaratory thereof which states feel themselves bound to observe and, therefore, commonly observe in their relations with each other.[14]

Hyde's definition stresses the aspect of voluntarism in international law, the fact that countries "feel themselves bound to observe" the law for commonsense reasons and thus usually do so voluntarily.

Governments of countries will adhere to certain aspects of international law for various reasons. First, many countries follow international law simply because

---

[12]See Nye, *Peace in Parts*, for his analysis of the OAS, OAU, and Arab League and their performance in controlling conflicts.

[13]L. Brierly, *The Law of Nations*, 6th ed., rev. by Sir Humphrey Waldock (New York: Oxford University Press, 1963), p. 1.

[14]Charles Cheney Hyde, *International Law Chiefly As Interpreted and Applied by the United States*, vol. 1 (Boston: Little, Brown, 1945), p. 1.

it is customary to do so. This would apply, for example, to the field of diplomatic practices. Second, governments may adhere to some parts of international law out of a belief that it is morally right to do so. Third, some governments may obey international law out of expediency. They will refrain from violating international principles out of the consideration that otherwise other countries would do likewise. An example of this would be the general adherence of Western countries to the prisoner of war (POW) rules as stated in the Geneva Convention of 1929 and revised in 1949. In World War II, for example, the authorities of the United States, Britain, and Germany treated their respective prisoners more humanely as compared with the treatment of German POWs in the Soviet Union and Soviet POWs in Germany. The Soviet Union has not been a signatory of the Geneva Convention. Finally, governments may adhere to international law out of fear of sanctions, which may take the form of condemnation by other governments and outside public opinion or the threat of or initiation of retaliatory actions, such as severing diplomatic relations, instituting economic sanctions, or taking military actions. These economic or military actions may be pursued against the perpetrator by one or several countries, a regional organization, or the United Nations. Examples of the last would be the economic sanctions imposed by the United Nations against the country formerly known as Rhodesia (now Zimbabwe) and the application of military sanction to combat aggression in Korea.

International law deals with many aspects of international behavior and developments. It includes, for example, the principles and rules having to do with the establishment of nation-states and their recognition by other countries, as well as the privileges accorded to diplomats. International law deals with the rules that have been developed in regard to the conduct of military hostilities and the treatment of prisoners and enemy civilians. Contemporary international law places certain restrictions on countries concerning their resort to war. Such stipulations are found in the Kellogg–Briand Pact (1928) and the United Nations Charter. A substantial part of international law deals with commercial relations between countries.

The Development of International Law and International Legal Organizations

When the Dutch scholar Hugo Grotius, commonly known as "the father of international law," published his famous work, *De Jure Belli Ac Pacis (On the Law of War and Peace),* in 1625, he categorized and codified in his book all aspects of international law that had been developed in the previous centuries of Western civilization. He placed into a modern setting the interstate rules and principles that had been developed by the Greeks, the Romans, and subsequent Western cultures. His book was the first comprehensive treatment of the subject and has served as the basis for further study and growth.[15]

---

[15]For an English-language translation of Grotius's writings, see A. C. Campbell, *The Rights of War and Peace Including the Law of Nature and the Law of Nations Translated from the Original Latin of Grotius* (Washington, D.C. and London: M. Walter Dunne, 1901). A useful biographical discussion of Grotius is Hamilton Vreeland, *Hugo Grotius* (New York: Oxford University Press, 1917).

In the modern nation-states era, which began roughly with the Treaty of Westphalia (1648), international law has grown in a fashion similar to the growth of common law, and this process of growth is continuing steadily. New features were added in recent decades in the form of international forums and agencies rendering decisions on disputes between two or more nation-states.

The first permanent International Court of Arbitration was established by the first Hague Conference (1899). A second international judicial body was established in 1920 as part of the League of Nations. It became known as the Permanent Court of International Justice. In 1945 the founders of the United Nations established the **International Court of Justice** as successor to the Permanent Court of International Justice. The International Court of Justice is one of the six principal organs of the United Nations. Located, like its predecessors, in The Hague, it consists of 15 judges who are elected by the General Assembly and the Security Council of the United Nations. The members of the court are elected for nine-year terms on a staggered basis (five every three years) and may be reelected.[16] The court deals with legal cases (that is, questions having to do with what the law is in a particular case), rather than political cases (questions about what the law should be). Issues of the latter category cannot be adjudicated by the court. They have to be dealt with by methods producing peaceful change (diplomacy) or, if these fail, by means of violence (such as war or threat of war).

Only countries may be parties in cases before the International Court of Justice. The court can try only those cases that parties in dispute submit voluntarily. It does not have any enforcement powers enjoyed by domestic courts. Even if two countries agree to submit their dispute to the International Court, they do not have to adhere to its judgment. An exception to the foregoing statement is that, in conjunction with Paragraph 2 of Article 36 of the Statute of the International Court of Justice, a number of countries have pledged themselves to accept compulsory jurisdiction of the court. By 1989, 47 countries had pledged themselves to this "optional clause," some, however, with various kinds of reservations that limit their cooperation with the International Court of Justice.

All in all, the role of the International Court of Justice is different from and weaker than that of domestic courts.

The Sources of International Law

As domestic law has grown from the needs of people living within societies, international law has grown out of the needs of countries. The following are some of the major sources of international law.

International Conventions   This refers to treaties concluded on a multilateral basis. Bilateral treaties rarely create a new rule of international law. They usually are built upon and are declaratory of existing rules. Treaties constitute an important part of international law. As an international practice, they date back as far

---

[16]The United Nations has published an informative handbook on the court. See United Nations Office of Publications, *The International Court of Justice*, 9th ed. (New York: United Nations, 1984).

as written records have been found. In our century a number of multilateral treaties and agreements have come into existence. While none of them have obtained universal ratification, they have achieved the support of enough countries to be considered part of international law. The Covenant of the League of Nations of 1919, the Kellogg-Briand Pact of 1928, the United Nations Charter of 1945, the Nuclear Test Ban Treaty of 1963, and the Nuclear Non-Proliferation Treaty of 1968 are examples of multilateral treaties.

While bilateral and multilateral treaties are considered binding on the signatories, history shows a number of examples where governments of participant countries have broken their promises and have either partially or fully terminated their respective international obligations. This, obviously, decreases the force of international law. The Nazi German government, for example, unilaterally terminated several treaties with the questionable assertion that the other party had violated them.

Copies of some multilateral treaties have been deposited with the United Nations in order to give them a greater degree of international legal standing. This practice was followed by the United States and the Soviet Union after their ratification of the Nuclear Test Ban Treaty and the Nuclear Non-Proliferation Treaty. We may assume that this practice will be followed by these countries and others in the future.

International Customs Established customs among countries constitute an important part of international law. These are rules of behavior that were introduced decades or even centuries ago by some countries in dealing with each other and slowly were adopted by others because they found them useful. Once an adoption of this kind has become nearly universal, a new international law has been established. A great number of customs that now are accepted universally have developed over the centuries in the area of diplomacy and the rights and privileges of diplomats. A good example is the principle of diplomatic immunity enjoyed by accredited diplomats throughout the world. Violations of this principle, as, for example, that committed by Iranian militants with the approval of the Khomeini government against U.S. diplomats in Tehran in 1979, have been condemned by all civilized governments.

General Principles of Law A third source of international law is made up by generic principles of law, which are recognized by "the civilized nation-states" of this world. What are these general principles? Although there is some disagreement among students of international law on the exact nature of these principles, a number of them point out that Article 38 of the Statute of the International Court of Justice refers to the general principles of justice and reason as found in natural law as being rationally understood and applied to modern society. An example of such a general principle is the application of equity. How are these principles applied to present-day cases? According to Frederick H. Hartmann:

> The "general principles" of law, to be applied at all, must be applied in a particular case to specific facts that are the corollaries of those principles. The question asked

is: what does the principle mean in this case? The answer is the result of the use of reason and, where necessary, analogies from principles pervading the municipal law of nations in general.[17]

It appears from this that the "general principles" stated in Article 38 constitute an element of international law that is less defined and more difficult to apply than the principles originating from treaties and customs.

Judicial Decisions and Writings of Scholars   Both are indirect and subsidiary sources of international law. Decisions rendered in domestic courts may help international jurists here and there in forming their opinions. More important are the decisions rendered by international tribunals, such as the trials of war criminals at the end of World War II. The growing body of these decisions will serve as precedents for international jurists in years and decades to come.

The writings of experts were very important during the formative stage of modern international law; however, with the formation of a body of modern international law and the establishment of international tribunals, the publicist has become a commentator and interpreter, rather than a maker of international law.[18]

The Role of International Law in Contemporary Times

Because of the lack of universal executive enforcement powers, international law has not taken on the effectiveness of domestic law, nor has the International Court of Justice achieved the important role of national supreme courts. According to Stanley Hoffmann:

> The nature of the international system condemns international law to all the weaknesses and perversions that it is so easy to deride. International law is merely a magnifying mirror that reflects faithfully and cruelly the essence and the logic of international politics. In a fragmented world, there is no "global perspective" from which anyone can authoritatively assess, endorse, or reject the separate national efforts at making international law serve national interests above all.[19]

Modern international law has developed essentially within the framework of the Western countries. The rise of the Communist countries and the developing nation-states of the Third World has brought about a high degree of pluralism on the international scene, which in turn may call for the revision of some formerly accepted international principles in order to make them universally acceptable. One may assume that this adjustment will continue for years to come. All countries, whether postindustrial Western, Communist, or developing, engage in similar

---

[17]Frederick H. Hartmann, *The Relations of Nations*, p. 115.

[18]For more extensive discussions of the sources of international law, see Michael Akehurst, *A Modern Introduction to International Law*, 6th rev. ed. (London: Unwin Hyman, 1987), or Gerhard von Glahn, *Law among Nations: An Introduction to Public International Law*, 5th ed. (New York: Macmillan, 1986).

[19]Stanley Hoffmann, in Lawrence Scheinman and David Wilkinson, eds., *International Law and Political Crisis: An Analytic Casebook* (Boston: Little, Brown, 1968), p. xvii.

basic activities. They all have certain interests in common. It is in the area of commonality that universal principles can be achieved first. As stated by Oliver J. Lissitzyn:

> The conflicts of interest do not prevent mutually acceptable regulation of transnational activities in the areas of international relations where there is some community of interest, however limited. Since all states engage in such activities, there is a basis for the existence of "universal" international law in the sense of a number of concepts and norms understood, invoked, and honored by all states, as well as of "particular" international law-norms that apply to some but not all states. Both universal and particular international law may be expected to grow in scope and complexity as the volume and variety of transnational activities increase.[20]

The governments of all countries have common interests (although there may be a difference in degree) in internationally accepted rules pertaining to the exercise of diplomacy, the issue of maritime jurisdiction, traffic on the high seas, regulation of outer space, treatment of enemy nationals and their property during wartime, as well as the rights and obligations of neutrals. In this context, it is of interest to note that two adversary countries, Cuba and the United States, were able to conclude a reciprocally beneficial agreement against skyjacking.

The presence of international law exercises a moderating influence on the foreign policy activities of governments. It provides basic norms of conduct governments can use for their communication with each other. It furnishes means for channeling conflict so that issues can be decided by peaceful means instead of force. It serves as a moral force in that international condemnation can be directed against the violation of universally established norms.

The problematic nature of international law will continue for some time. Its plight, in the words of Stanley Hoffmann,

> is that, now as before, it shows on its body of rules all the scars inflicted by the international state of war. The tragedy of contemporary international law is that of a double divorce: first, between the old liberal dream of a world rule of law, and the realities of an international system of multiple minidramas that always threaten to become major catastrophes; second, between the old dream and the new requirements of moderation, which in the circumstances of the present system suggest a downplaying of formal law in the realm of peace-and-war issues, and an upgrading of more flexible techniques, until the system has become less fierce.[21]

In the complete absence of international law, this world of ours would be much worse off than it is now. One only can hope that the world community will make speedy headway in transforming traditional international law into the norms and principles that can be accepted universally by the multiple world we live in. Moreover, it is hoped that governments will use increasingly the existing body of

[20]Oliver J. Lissitzyn, "International Law in a Divided World," *International Conciliation* (March 1963), pp. 3–69.

[21]Stanley Hoffmann, *International Law and Political Crisis*, pp. xvii and xix.

international law to settle disputes by peaceful means, so that the world can become a more lawful community.

RECOMMENDED READINGS

Bennet, LeRoy A. *International Organizations: Principles and Issues,* 4th ed. Englewood Cliffs, N.J.: Prentice-Hall, 1988. This informative text covers all major aspects of international organizations and includes a chapter on regionalism.

Calleo, David P. *Beyond American Hegemony : The Future of the Western Alliance.* New York: Basic Books, 1987. The book focuses on the North Atlantic Treaty Organization, the basis of the Atlantic Alliance. The author examines the fundamental question whether the Atlantic Alliance can remain viable in its present form or, if not, whether there is an alternative form that can be substituted so that the alliance will retain its viability.

Diehl, Paul F., ed. *The Politics of International Organizations: Patterns and Insights.* Chicago: Dorsey Press, 1989. This is a comprehensive selection of articles dealing with important aspects of international organizations. Two of the articles focus specifically on the United States and the United Nations.

El-Ayouty, Yassin, and William I. Zartman, eds. *The OAU after 20 Years.* New York: Praeger, 1983. A collection of articles assesses the successes and failures of the Organization of African Unity during its first 20 years of existence.

Everyone's United Nations, 10th ed. New York: United Nations Office of Public Information, 1986. This is the basic source book on the United Nations.

Feld, Werner J. *The European Community in World Affairs: Economic Power and Political Influence.* Boulder, Colo.: Westview Press, 1983. The author examines and analyzes the effects and impact that the European Economic Community has had and is likely to have on the world's economic and political relations.

Fromuth, Peter J., ed. *A Successor Vision: The United Nations of Tomorrow.* Lanham, Md.: University Press of America, 1988. A thoughtful assessment of United Nations activities, together with a number of useful suggestions for substantive and institutional reforms of the organization. The contributors include prominent leaders from Africa, the Americas, and Europe.

Holden, Gerard. *The Warsaw Pact: Soviet Security and Bloc Politics.* London: Basil Blackwell, 1989. The author traces the development of the Warsaw Pact and examines its military and political functioning within the setting of European bloc politics prior to the opening of the Iron Curtain.

Mackinlay, John. *The Peacekeepers: An Assessment of Peacekeeping Operations at the Arab-Israel Interface.* London: Unwin Hyman, 1989. Since 1974 United Nations peacekeeping forces have been deployed in the Eastern Mediterranean. The author evaluates the success and failure of these forces.

Peterson, M. J. *The General Assembly in World Affairs.* London: Allen & Unwin, 1986. The book contains a comprehensive overview of the activities and procedures of the United Nations General Assembly.

Von Glahn, Gerhard. *Law among Nations: An Introduction to Public International Law,* 5th ed. New York: Macmillan, 1986. Written by one of this country's leading experts on international law, the text covers comprehensively all the major aspects of the subject.

Yoder, Amos. *The Evolution of the UN System.* New York: Taylor & Francis/Crane Russak, 1989. The author focuses on the conflicting pursuits of United Nations members to use the organization for their own purposes on one hand and efforts to achieve a greater degree of world order based on international law on the other.

Glossary

adaptation stage The third stage of revolutionary one-party systems. Technicians and managers have a greater role and less dependence on party bureaucracy. Sometimes characterized by a slowly evolving pluralism.

adversary system The practice in Anglo-American law whereby each side presents its case, with the judge or jury determining the truth of the facts and reaching a decision for one side or the other.

affirmative action A program or policy to correct past racial or sexual discrimination usually in reference to admittance to an institution such as school or trade union, hiring, promotion, and equal pay. A part of the American equal rights movement legislated under federal law.

aggregation Occurs when demands/claims are brought together into a smaller number of policy alternatives. A principal function of political parties.

antitrust policy A policy designed to foster competition and make capitalism work. This includes forbidding monopolies and price controls, and preventing competitors from acquiring each other's stock.

apathy Lack of interest in politics. It is a support when an individual is relatively satisfied. Sometimes based on a sense of hopelessness. As a reservoir of frustration, can be mobilized against a regime when there is a sudden, revolutionary turn of events.

appellate court A court that reviews decisions of a lower court; for example, the federal courts of appeals to which cases are brought from federal district courts.

arraignment A proceeding in Anglo-American law before a court whereby the criminal charge is read and the accused enters a plea of guilty or not guilty.

authoritarian Rule by a small elite with very limited popular input and few civil rights. Some authoritarian regimes are striving to become more pluralistic, such as Brazil, the Republic of Korea, and the Soviet Union.

authority A type of power generally regarded as rightful or legitimate. The more authority, the less the need to use force.

authority patterns The effective patterns of command, influence, and decision making that exist in an organization or political system. These patterns may be informal or formal.

avoidance politics Traditional political system in which the average individual had no political input. All one could do was avoid government rules or hope to modify them as they were enforced. Has characterized most political systems throughout history.

behavioralism Movement within political science that began in the 1920s. It intended to make the discipline more scientific by focusing on the individual and using new research techniques such as survey research. Initially emphasized quantitative methods almost exclusively.

bicameral Describing a two-house legislature such as the U.S. Congress, composed of the Senate and the House of Representatives, or the British Parliament, composed of the House of Commons and House of Lords.

Bill of Rights The first ten amendments to the U.S. Constitution that set limits to governmental actions and powers by putting basic civil rights beyond the powers of Congress. Protected are the basic rights of the First Amendment and many procedural rights. Today most of the Bill of Rights restricts the states through application of the Fourteenth Amendment. See **nationalizing civil rights.**

bipolarity An international condition that existed for several years after World War II. There were two overwhelming global powers, the United States and the Soviet Union, that dominated much of international politics.

Board of Regents v. Bakke **(1978)** The U.S. Supreme Court decision holding the quota system for minority groups at the University of California Medical School at Davis unconstitutional but approving the admissions policy of taking race into account as part of a plan to have a diverse student body.

Brown v. Board of Education **(1954)** The Supreme Court decision holding segregated schools to be a form of "invidious discrimination" violating the equal protection clause of the Fourteenth Amendment.

bureaucracy Civil servants and government agencies that are involved with day-to-day policy implementation. The bureaucracy is expected to be efficient and impartial, yet it has negative connotations of delay, red tape, pettiness, and ritualistic attachment to rules.

certiorari A writ issued by a higher court such as the U.S. Supreme Court calling up the record of a lower court for review.

chief executive The chief decision-making and administrative official of a government, such as the British and Japanese prime ministers, the German chancellor, and the American president. The American president also serves as chief of state.

chief of state The principal role is symbolic or ceremonial, holding limited power, such as the British monarch, or the German, Indian, and Singapore presidents.

***City of Akron v. The Akron Center for Reproductive Health* (1983)** A complex decision that states that the right to abortion includes the right of access to abortion services without state interference.

civil liberties Citizens and residents are free from government interference in basic areas protected by the constitution or a basic law. These liberties include such freedoms as speech, press, religion, and the right to own property. Most democracies consider these inalienable rights.

civil service Persons employed by a government in a civil, as opposed to military, capacity. It is synonymous with ''bureaucracy'' in many countries.

classical democratic theory Political theory of the eighteenth and nineteenth centuries that stressed individual responsibility and individual choice based on rational evaluation of all the factors involved. Did not stress group identifications or influences.

communism Followers of Marx and Lenin who believe that the aims of socialism as they interpret them—the common ownership of the means of production and exchange—can be achieved most effectively through a violent revolution. Communism is distinguished from democratic socialism, which favors attaining its objectives through democratic means.

community A group of people with a feeling of common identity and self-interest, possessing many characteristics in common, usually living in the same geographical area.

congressional committee Permanent or standing committees in the U.S. Congress—18 in the House of Representatives, 15 in the Senate, and 4 joint committees. They exercise a great deal of power.

conservative The movement originally associated with Edmund Burke against the French Revolution. It initially drew support from the European aristocracy and stressed support of established institutions such as churches and the monarchy. Conservatives are not opposed to all social change but with orderly change with due regard for what is good and beneficial in traditional practices and institutions.

consolidation stage Second stage of revolutionary one-party systems. The old order has been destroyed and the regime legitimizes itself on the basis of its new institutions and performance. A period of institutionalization.

constitutional monarchy A form of government where the authority of the ruler (usually a hereditary position) is shared with and often subordinated to other parts of the elected government, such as a parliament.

Council for Mutual Economic Assistance CMEA, or COMECON, was organized by the Soviet Union in 1949. It was designed to encourage economic cooperation between Eastern Europe and the Soviet Union. It has been dominated by Moscow. Most economic ties are between Moscow and the individual countries.

criminal procedure The steps involved in the law enforcement process beginning with the arrest of the law violator, followed by a preliminary hearing, preferring of charges, arraignment, trial, and concluding with punishment or acquittal.

democracy A political system where political leaders are chosen in competitive elections and the bulk of the adult population is enfranchised. Basic civil rights are protected, usually in a constitution.

democratic centralism Introduced by Lenin for the Bolshevik, later Communist,

Party of the Soviet Union to achieve a small, hierarchical party. Members vote, but once a decision is made there can be no objection. In practice, subordinate party levels are appointed from above so loyal followership can be assured.

dependent variable A characteristic or trait that is considered a consequence rather than a cause. For example, the more education one has, the more likely one is to vote. Voting is the dependent variable in this case.

developing countries Often used interchangeably with **Third World** countries to identify the countries of Africa, Asia, Latin America, and the Middle East, which are primarily agricultural and have a low per capita income. This term has less negative connotations than one frequently used in the past, "less developed country" (LDC).

dialectical materialism The doctrine based on a transformation of Hegel's dialectical philosophy, which asserts that all ultimate reality is matter in motion. Economic forces working themselves out in history determine the character of the state and its institutions, including the cultural and religious ideas of any given period.

diplomacy The formal relations that independent countries maintain with each other short of war. The basic diplomatic functions are to convey and gather information, conduct negotiations, and be the principal means of implementing foreign policies.

Economic and Social Council (of United Nations) Key agency to develop and coordinate UN activities in the economic and social areas. Twenty-seven members; nine elected each year for three-year terms.

electioneering Participating in elections, whether running as a candidate or supporting a candidate or party.

elections The chief institutional mechanism by which representatives are selected. In democracies this is done through the secret ballot with competitive candidates for the same office.

elitism A hierarchical social and political system. A small percentage of the population controls most of society's resources and receives most of the benefits.

entrepreneur (organizer) Individual(s) who offers potential members benefits if they join the organization. Often the moving force behind the creation of the organization.

equity A supplement to the English common law that provides judicial remedies not allowed by the common law, such as the injunction.

***Escobedo v. Illinois* (1964)** The U.S. Supreme Court decision holding that in criminal prosecutions the right to representation by counsel extends back to the time a suspect is subjected to questioning.

Eurocommunism Western European Communist parties sought to win votes by moderate policies; clean, efficient government; and a verbal commitment to pluralism. Such parties do not support revolutionary violence and avoid control by Moscow.

European Economic Community (EEC) A customs union, effective 1958, initially consisting of six European countries—France, the Federal Republic of Germany, Italy, Belgium, the Netherlands, and Luxembourg—to create free movement of goods, capital, and persons between member countries, and to harmonize their economic policies. Six additional countries—Denmark, Greece, Ireland, Portugal, Spain, and the United Kingdom—have joined. Often referred to as the Common Market.

executive agreement An agreement between the president of the United States and a foreign government that, unlike a treaty, does not require Senate approval. Sometimes these agreements are secret. The president can do this under his or her constitutional power as commander-in-chief or under his or her authority in foreign affairs under Article II. Congress may nullify such agreements.

executive branch One of three branches of government; the others are the legislative and judicial. Includes the head of government (prime minister, premier, president), the cabinet, and the bureaucracy. Implements laws; is also responsible for major policy input and decision making.

factions Groups within a party, usually organized around an individual rather than an issue. Numerous factions mean a party cannot be highly centralized.

fascism The philosophy of the dictatorships in Italy under Mussolini and Germany under Hitler. It is characterized by belief of the supremacy of the state over the individual, the leadership principle, and a totalitarian one-party state. The German version, known as national socialism, was more extreme than Italian fascism and stressed the doctrine of the supremacy of the "Aryan race" and inferiority of Jews and other races.

feedback Results from the changing opinions and actions of citizens in response to government output. May only affect attitudes or how a person will vote in the next election, or in some situations may lead to revolutionary action. All governments need some type of feedback to assess reaction to government actions.

fiscal policy Government using its financial powers of taxing and spending, including such policies as deficit budgets or tax cuts to influence the national economy's performance.

foreign policy A country's official relations with other countries involving economic, cultural, military, and political interaction. Efforts to protect and promote the national interest in the international arena.

future shock The idea that information and values acquired during childhood are inadequate to the new social, political, and economic realities of an altered world during adulthood.

General Assembly The largest unit of the United Nations; organized on the basis of equal representation and voting power for all member countries. It meets annually each fall and generates many resolutions, but has no real power to affect the behavior of sovereign countries.

general will The concept of the French philosopher Jean-Jacques Rousseau that the common good is expressed in the general will, which is more than the will of the majority. It is possible that the general will may be expressed by a minority or even one person, although usually it is an expression of the will of the majority.

gerrymandering Drawing electoral boundaries of a legislative district so as to favor one political group over another. Often the district is quite irregular in shape.

glasnost A term espoused by Mikhail Gorbachev after he came to power in 1985. Literally it means openness in terms of oral and written expression. New ideas and public expression were to motivate and critique a sluggish bureaucracy and ruling party.

government The institution that successfully upholds a claim to the exclusive use of physical force in enforcing its rules within a given territorial area. It is the most inclusive institution in society. Sometimes refers to the executive political leadership, that is, the president and the cabinet or the prime minister and cabinet. For example, "the government is proposing an additional gasoline tax."

grand jury A body of from 5 to 23 persons that is summoned by the prosecutor to determine whether the evidence against a person accused of a crime is sufficient to return an indictment. Originated in England.

gross national product The total value of goods and services produced in a single year in a given political system. The annual increase or decrease in gross national product is one important measure of economic viability.

habeas corpus A writ that permits a person who claims that he or she is unjustly imprisoned to apply to a federal court for a hearing. If a court finds that the imprisonment is contrary to some provision of the Constitution or laws of the United States, the person will be released.

hegemony When country *A* exercises hegemony over country *B,* it does not legally exercise control of that country but maintains preponderant influence in the domestic and foreign affairs of the subservient country.

indictment A formal written charge of a crime, prepared by a prosecutor and brought up by a grand jury. The accused is thus made aware of the specific charges against which he or she must prepare a defense.

individualism One of the characteristics of the modern age that began around A.D. 1500. The result was a new humanism centering on a person as the ''measure of all things.'' The new individualism was a revolt against existing restraints of the social order and religion and a movement toward personal autonomy. One result was the social contract theory of government that began with the individual who voluntarily created government.

influence Inputs or access that have some impact on the behavior of another person or a group. The outcome when using influence is less predictable than when using power. Most political decisions or actions are subject to influence from several sources.

inputs Functions of the political system that include claims or demands, supports, apathy. Democratic political systems allow for the greatest freedom of citizen inputs.

insurgency Violent, guerrilla actions against an established government. An insurgency does not involve the number of persons associated with a revolution. The objectives of an insurgency may range from minimal to far-reaching change.

interest groups A formally organized group of people seeking to promote particular causes or points of view. Often the members' own well-being is a major concern. Most interest groups engage in activities including self-help, education, discounted insurance, etc. as well as seeking to influence government.

intermediate groups Another term for interest groups. Used by William Kornhauser in discussing dangers of mass society.

International Court of Justice Established in 1945 and located in The Hague, a successor to the Permanent Court of International Justice created in 1920. Fifteen judges, elected by the UN General Assembly and the Security Council, hear only cases voluntarily submitted by the parties (nation-states). The court has no enforcement power.

international law The totality of treaties, customs, and agreements among countries. It includes the general principles and specific rules that most members of the international community consider binding upon them in their mutual relations.

international politics Politics among countries; the principal actors are spokesmen of nation-states, international and regional organizations, and often revolutionary organizations. In domestic politics government usually has the preponderant authority and power. There is no final or sovereign authority in the international setting.

intervention Direct interference by one country in the affairs of another. This type of interference is usually of broader scope than an act of reprisal and may occur without provocation by the other country.

Iron Curtain Term coined by Winston Churchill in a 1946 speech at Westminster College, Fulton, Missouri, to indicate the separation of Soviet-dominated Eastern Europe from Western Europe.

iron law of oligarchy Concept identified with Robert Michels. All groups eventually dominated by the leadership. The average member has little interest in, knowledge about, or influence on the group's policies.

iron triangle The close relations that develop between bureaucratic agencies, interest groups, and congressional committees or subcommittees concerned with a common problem such as tobacco, savings and loan associations, or public works. The close, constant interaction often limits outside awareness or influence on many issues.

irredentism The belief that smaller surrounding territories inhabited by peoples with similarities in religion, language, ethnic group, etc. should be joined to or annexed by an adjacent country.

judicial review The process by which courts determine whether the legislative or executive branches, especially the former, have exceeded their authority with the power to declare a law or act unconstitutional. The scope of judicial review is broadest in the United States.

justice The quality or determination of just, right, or fair action. It is a standard for judging the legal, social, and moral behavior in a political system. There are many philosophical debates over what is justice. Its definition varies among political systems.

justice of the peace A local officer who has authority to try petty cases. Originated in England and continues in some American states.

laissez-faire A hands-off style of government that emphasizes economic freedom for pure capitalism. It is associated with individualism.

League of Nations Created at the end of World War I, headquartered in Geneva, Switzerland. The moving force behind its creation was Woodrow Wilson, but the United States did not join. Through principles of collective security it was designed to prevent a second world war. It failed in this notable endeavor.

legislature Formal lawmaking institution in most political systems.

legitimacy That which is regarded as generally proper or acceptable. It varies between societies and emerges slowly in a political system.

liberal A liberal believes in democratic and constitutional government as opposed to dictatorship of any kind. Early liberals identified with John Locke, laissez-faire economics, and the social contract theory of government that put the individual before the state. In the late nineteenth century as a result of the evils of the industrial revolution and the philosophy of T. H. Green, liberals abandoned laissez-faire and adopted a policy that favored state intervention in the economy to remove social evils, such as poverty, that hindered the development of the individual.

lobbying Any individual or group activities that seek to influence legislative or bureaucratic action. Often sustained lobbying is by paid professionals. Originally the lobbies outside the legislature were the sites of contact with elected representatives, hence the name.

lower house In a bicameral legislature the elected house or the one most regularly responsible to the electorate. Examples: in Great Britain the popularly elected House of Commons that elects the prime minister; in the United States, all members of the House of Representatives are elected biennially.

Maoism Doctrine based on the practice and theory of Mao Zedong, the late Chinese Communist leader who died in 1976. Advocated revolution from the countryside, people's war, permanent revolutionary fervor over practical development, and rejection of post-Stalin communism.

***Marbury v. Madison* (1803)** The first decision of the U.S. Supreme Court holding an act of Congress unconstitutional.

martial law Law system initiated by the chief of state (civilian or military), applied generally through military tribunals. Civil liberties and individual freedom of action are restrained.

mass media Communication media capable of reaching large audiences nationwide. Includes newspapers, national magazines, radio, and television.

mass society This society leads to the loss of interest groups and other intermediate level affiliations. Large numbers of people engage in mass movements, usually during crises periods, outside of acceptable procedures and organizations. Mass society weakens democracies or the evolution of democratic political systems.

***Miranda v. Arizona* (1966)** The U.S. Supreme Court decision that held that for a conviction based on custodial interrogation to stand it is necessary to inform the suspect in advance of the question of his or her right to remain silent and to be represented by counsel.

mixed market economy An economic system that is somewhere between socialism and laissez-faire capitalism. This includes all industrialized countries in the free world. For example, the United States enforces antitrust laws in a basically capitalistic economy.

monetary policy Government policies that attempt to influence the amount of money in circulation and the amount and cost of credit available. Often directed against either inflation or recession.

Mother of Parliaments The British legislature whose institutional history goes back to the twelfth century. The first parliamentary legislature.

multinational corporation A corporation that duplicates or divides up essential parts of its productive operation in two or more countries.

nation-state Political entities with officially recognized boundaries. Sovereignty is within each political system and supposedly not subject to outside interference. "Country" and "nation-state" are terms popularly used interchangeably.

national interest A basic premise is that each nation-state is required to protect and promote certain basic interests if the country is to survive physically and its basic political, economic, and social values are to be maintained. Usually within each political system there are disagreements on the indispensable or national interests. A national interest supposedly benefits everyone and is more than the sum of individual or group interests.

nationalizing civil rights The incorporation by the U.S. Supreme Court of the First Amendment of the American Constitution and most of the remaining Bill of Rights into the due process clause of the Fourteenth Amendment. This makes most of the Bill of Rights binding upon the states through the Fourteenth Amendment.

natural law The concept originating with the Stoic philosophers of Greece and Rome that there is a law of reason in agreement with nature above and beyond human law. This doctrine was developed by Thomas Aquinas and carried into modern time by John Locke.

natural rights Rights derived from natural law. All people should possess them. These rights should not be taken away or transferred by government or any other group.

negotiation A diplomatic process for the peaceful settlement of disputes to include advancing or maintaining the countries' or groups' self-interests. Bargaining, adjustment, and accommodation are integral to this process.

newly industrializing countries (NICs) These Third World countries are characterized by self-sustained growth. An increasing percentage of the work force is engaged in manufacturing. A significant and generally growing percentage of their gross national product is based on the export of manufactured goods.

new right Post–World War II resurgence of groups in the West opposed to socialism; supportive of capitalism; and critical of leftist, costly, indecisive liberalism.

North Atlantic Treaty Organization (NATO) Major security organization, established in 1949. Based on collective security principle. Includes the United States, Canada, and 13 European countries.

north-south split The economic division some analysts identify between the industrialized, developed countries (generally located in the Northern Hemisphere) and the poor, developing countries (located mainly in the Southern Hemisphere).

nuclear club Countries with substantial quantities of nuclear weapons and extensive delivery systems: United States, Soviet Union, France, Great Britain, and the People's Republic of China.

oligarchy Rule by the few for the benefit of the few. It is a term used by Aristotle (384–322 B.C.) to describe one type of political system.

Organization of Petroleum Exporting Countries (OPEC) The 13 members are Saudi Arabia, Iran, Iraq, Kuwait, Nigeria, Algeria, Libya, Indonesia, Venezuela, Ecuador, United Arab Emirates, Gabon, and Qatar.

***Oregon v. Mitchell* (1970)** The U.S. Supreme Court decision holding that by statute Congress could reduce the voting age to 18 in federal elections but that Congress lacked the authority to reduce the voting age to 18 in state elections.

outputs Government decisions such as laws, executive-administrative orders, court decisions, or a conscious government decision not to take action.

parliamentary government Originally, power concentrated in the legislature with the prime minister or premier selected by and serving at the pleasure of the legislature. In some political systems with strongly disciplined parties, most decision making is in the hands of the prime minister and cabinet.

parliamentary supremacy The legislature is not subject to or controlled by a hereditary monarch. The premier or prime minister is in office only if he or she has a majority in the legislature or at least the popularly elected lower house.

participatory political system A type of system in which a significant number of the citizens have legal means, usually through elections, to influence or determine important political decisions.

patronage Appointments to government service or the distribution and assignment of favorable economic opportunities or benefits to faithful political supporters. Used to build a political organization or ensure that individuals in a government agency are strong supporters of the elected officials.

peer groups People with similar status and often similar interests, such as close friends, colleagues, neighbors, small clubs, and informal associations.

perestroika A doctrine promoted by Mikhail Gorbachev after coming to power in 1985. Literally it means restructuring. At first applied to the economy but more recently applied to the political system.

philosopher-king Advocated by Plato. A near-perfect ruler who would rule to achieve justice, harmony, and stability in a political system.

***Plessey v. Ferguson* (1896)** The U.S. Supreme Court decision that set forth the separate but equal doctrine allowing segregation in public facilities.

pluralism Extensive participation in the political process through competing and autonomous groups.

polis The ancient Greek term for the most sovereign and inclusive political association.

political analysis Studying a problem or question, organizing the data into categories or elements, and relating the parts to one another. Inductive, empirical research.

political culture A community's attitudes, beliefs, values, and information about or toward the quality and style of its political process and government operation. Political culture is not monolithic, and subcultures generally are present.

political development Innovative responses to challenge and change by political leaders with a bias toward nonrevolutionary, nonviolent, and orderly adjustments. Working toward optimum degree of social, economic, and political choice and freedom. Every country has unique features, and the end objective is not necessarily some form of the Anglo-American model.

political economy The study of the interrelationships of politics and economics and the influence each has on the other. Often discussed in terms of the relationship between government and economics. For example, mortgage rates increase as government policies reduce the amount of money available for loans.

political indoctrination The manipulation and control of public norms, attitudes, and behavior in a particular political system. The term has a negative connotation and should be distinguished from socialization.

political integration The population in a country develop relationships and a feeling of community. Social, economic, and psychological ties evolve that give a population feelings of identity, self-awareness, and exclusiveness. Political integration refers to the efforts of government to foster this cohesiveness.

political modernization Sometimes criticized because as a concept restricted to contemporary societies only. Some authors associate it with sudden increases in mass participation when the political system has no institutions into which to channel this participation.

political party In a democracy a group of voters organized to nominate and elect candidates to political office in order to influence and/or control personnel and policy.

political science A discipline within the social sciences. Deals with the political behavior and characteristics of individuals, groups, institutions, and societies, as well as the influences that affect this behavior.

political socialization The process, both conscious and unconscious, through which persons acquire political orientations, attitudes, values, and behavior.

political system The institution, individuals, and processes (including government) that interact in supporting or opposing public policy and other government activities. The more democratic the political system, the more inputs there will be.

politicized Politics increasingly touches on an individual's life with the expansion of government activities. More and more disagreements in which groups or individuals turn to government.

positive law The philosophy of law associated with the nineteenth-century Utilitarian philosopher John Austin. Law consists of well-defined rules of human conduct enforceable by appropriate sanctions of government.

postindustrial society Characterizes the democratic political systems of Western Europe, North America, Japan, Australia, and New Zealand. Society is highly complex, technologically advanced, and interdependent. This stage emerged after World War II. The service sector rather than industry dominates the economy, and white-collar jobs are more numerous than blue-collar jobs.

power The ability to make someone or some group behave or not behave in a given way. Power is not an easily transferable commodity, and it varies from situation to situation. The outcome when using power is more predictable than when using influence.

presidential government The chief executive (president) is chosen independently of the legislature and serves a full term subject to impeachment (rare) or physical or mental disabilities. Associated with separation of powers where the president has some powers largely independent of the legislature.

primary elections A largely American phenomenon that evolved in this century. An election in which party members or supporters select the party nominee who will run in the general election. Reduces the influence of party leaders and the party organization.

primary groups Those groups that are small and highly effective, perform several functions, and involve frequent and close interaction among their members. Family and friendship groups are two examples.

primordial sentiments Basic attachments and identifications with which one is born such as race, language, religion, kinship, or tribal group.

proportional representation An electoral system that seeks to ensure that each political party, minority group, and various interests will obtain the number of legislative seats in proportion to their electoral vote. This system requires complicated voting procedures and is not widely used in political systems based on the Anglo-American model.

public administration The process by which public resources and personnel are organized to carry out public policies and laws. It is often characterized by bureaucracies and large-scale activities.

public policy All the laws, decisions, rules, and regulations produced by the political processes of a country. It is a course of action for the purpose of dealing with a problem of public concern.

purposive benefits Suprapersonal benefits—such as saving the environment or opposing the spread of nuclear power plants—that motivate some members to join an organization.

regime The overall constitutional process including the major political institutions and the rules of the game that determine procedures with reference to demands, how policy is made and implemented, and the types of acceptable policies.

regionalism Intergovernmental collaboration at the regional level, recognized by Articles 52–54 of the UN Charter. These usually deal with economic, political, and security matters. Some believe these are stepping stones to universalism, but this has not been the case to date.

representation A process for making demands and translating them into policy. Representatives are people who act on behalf of other people in the decision-making process. In a democracy, these individuals are elected.

reprisal A deliberate, unfriendly, and illegal action taken in response to a prior violation of international law by another country.

retorsion A deliberate and unfriendly but legal act that has a retaliatory purpose; for example, one country's decision to sever diplomatic ties with another country.

***Roe v. Wade* (1973)** The Supreme Court in effect established a national abortion policy. Abortion is a private matter. States have a limited right to restrict abortion, although their right to intervene increases as the pregnancy progresses over time, especially in the last trimester.

runoff election A second election held in some states if no candidate for an office receives a majority of votes. Voters then choose between the two candidates who received the most votes in the first election.

secondary associations Those groups that are formally organized and often involve impersonal interaction and relationships. A business organization or trade union are two examples.

secretary general The best known secretary general is that of the United Nations. This office is filled by a career diplomat from a country perceived as relatively neutral by both the Western alliance and the Soviet bloc.

Security Council of the United Nations Composition and voting procedure emphasize big power (United States, Soviet Union, China, France, and Great Britain) cooperation and control, acting as "world sheriff." The preceding five are permanent members and each has the power of veto. There also are ten nonpermanent members elected biennially.

separatism   The belief that a community of people have a right to separate territorially from their existing country and establish an independent sovereign country.

separation of powers   Usually associated with presidential government. The three branches of government (legislative, executive, judicial) have different powers, generally assigned by a constitution. Often one branch has some powers belonging to another; the result in practice is overlapping and not complete separation of powers.

single-member district   An electoral district that elects one member. The winner is elected by a majority or a plurality to a legislature such as a city council, state assembly, or the U.S. House of Representatives.

socialism   The doctrine that there should be common ownership of the means of production and exchange in the economic system. Socialists do not agree on the extent to which the economic system should be nationalized. Socialism is a response to the problems and abuses of the industrial revolution. Some Socialists believe private property should be restricted, others believe it should be abolished. Although socialism is frequently associated with the doctrines of Karl Marx, all socialists are not followers of Marx. Socialism is distinguished from communism in that Socialists generally believe that the transition from capitalism to socialism can be attained by peaceful means.

socialization   The process of instilling in individuals how to behave in social groups. Socialization includes values, beliefs, orientations, information, and behavior patterns.

social mobilization   Concept developed by Karl Deutsch. A set of quantifiably measurable social changes in society such as growth in urbanization, literacy, newspaper circulation, and industrialization, affecting politics and to which government must respond in terms of a wider range and increased outputs.

society   Persons living in a geographic area who share at least some traditions, institutions, activities, and objectives.

standing committees   Permanent legislative committees to which a bill is first referred after it is introduced. For example, there are 43 in the U.S. Congress and 6 in the British House of Commons.

stare decisis   "Let the decision stand." A court follows previous decisions in similar cases unless it chooses to overrule the previous decision.

state of nature   State of persons outside organized political society. Often assumed to be a position or idealized condition of humankind before the establishment of organized government.

statutory law   The interpretation courts give to statutes that determines the meaning of the statutes.

stoicism   The philosophy originating in Greece and Rome that emphasized the basic equality of all people regardless of wealth or social position. The individual was a citizen both of the secular state in which he or she was born and of the community of all people. Natural law was another important Stoic doctrine. See **natural law.**

stratarchy   One type of democratic party organization opposite to the iron law of oligarchy. There are numerous leaders and areas of influence. Power is scattered; individuals higher in the organization often depend on support of those below them.

stratification   The creation of social classes (strata) of individuals, often with associated life-styles. The high strata have a disproportionate share of resources. Movement to a higher stratum may occur, but it is difficult.

strict constructionist A U.S. Supreme Court justice who interprets the powers of the court and the text of the Constitution narrowly so as to strike down as unconstitutional laws and interpretations of the Constitution not consistent with his or her judicial philosophy.

suffrage The right to vote. In the democratic political systems suffrage was extended from a small percentage of property-owning adult males in the late eighteenth century to nearly all adults in the twentieth century. People given the vote are described as being enfranchised.

summit meetings Meetings between the heads of several governments.

support-inputs Sometimes provided by foreign governments to maintain a regime in power and allowing for some influence on the supported government's policies.

supports Given to a political system or regime by individuals even if they oppose a specific policy or leader. Includes such things as loyalty, patriotism, identity, and paying taxes.

symbiosis The interaction and interdependence of dissimilar parts, often with different objectives, in the social, economic, and political systems. There are, however, benefits to be achieved by all groups or components through associating together. An orientation that facilitates the evolution of political pluralism.

system conflict Conflict over the basic nature of the political system and regime. Competition often is intense, uncompromising, and leads to political instability.

third parties A political party that is formed when the two major parties fail to meet a need or demand. These parties are sometimes temporary and usually fail to get their candidate elected, but they get their interests recognized by the major parties.

Third World Often used to refer to the developing countries. The First World consists of the democratic, industrialized countries. The Second World, the Communist countries. The Third World includes most of Africa, Asia, Latin America, and the Middle East.

Titoism The practice of national communism first espoused by the late Yugoslav leader Josip Broz Tito. This approach emerged in 1948; first to break away from Stalin's control and then to initiate pragmatic domestic policy and a nonaligned foreign policy based on the special and appropriate needs of the country.

totalitarian Political control by the elite permeates all of society. A single mass party, highly structured ideology, and a terroristic secret police characterize such regimes. They usually try to spread their ideology and influence to other countries. Examples are Nazi Germany, Fascist Italy, the Soviet Union under Stalin, the People's Republic of China under Mao, Cuba, and Vietnam.

transformation stage The most brutal stage of revolutionary one-party systems as the old system is destroyed. Much loss of life occurs.

unicameral A single-house legislature. One American state, Nebraska, has such a legislature. Several countries, including Israel, Egypt, New Zealand, Finland, Panama, and Hungary, also have one-house legislatures.

United Nations Established in 1945. In 1990 there were 159 members. Headquartered in New York City. Its objectives are to maintain international peace and security and to facilitate international cooperation in solving economic, social, and cultural problems.

upper house In a bicameral legislature, usually the oldest, smaller, and more senior of the two Houses. The elected U.S. Senate has slightly more power and prestige than the House of Representatives. In Britain, the hereditary and appointed House of Lords has little power today.

vote of no confidence A vote in a democratic parliamentary system of government. If the prime minister or premier loses the vote the government (prime minister and cabinet) must resign. A new government may be elected by the legislature or the defeated government may call for parliamentary elections in order that a new parliament will be able to form a working majority.

war Armed hostilities between two or more countries. Armed conflict within a country often is described as internal war.

Warsaw Treaty Organization (WTO) Major Communist collective security organization designed to counter NATO. Established in 1955. Members are the Soviet Union and its East European allies. Scheduled to be disbanded in 1992.

***Yates v. U.S.* (1957)** The Supreme Court decision that has made it more difficult to prosecute Communists. Urging people to act unlawfully is illegal, but only advocating that people believe in revolution or other aspects of Communist doctrine is not illegal.

Photo Credits

Index

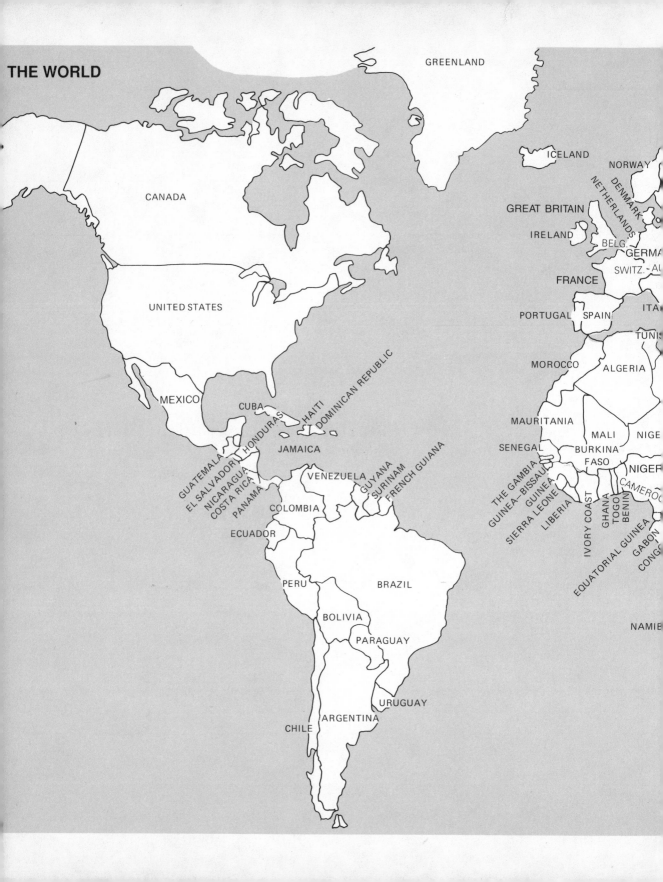